Fantastic Tales by Ji Xiaolan
纪晓岚志怪故事选

Edited and Translated by
Sun Haichen
孙海晨 编译

NEW WORLD PRESS
新世界出版社

First Edition 1998

Copyright by **New World Press**, Beijing, China.
All rights reserved. No part of this book may be reproduced in any form or by any means without permission in writing from the publisher.

ISBN 7-80005-357-1

Published by
NEW WORLD PRESS
24 Baiwanzhuang Road, Beijing 100037, China

Distributed by
CHINA INTERNATIONAL BOOK TRADING CORPORATION
35 Chegongzhuang Xilu, Beijing 100044, China
P.O. Box 399, Beijing, China

Printed in the People's Republic of China

Introduction

The 144 stories in this volume are adapted from *Notes of the Thatched Abode of Close Observations* by Ji Yun of the Qing dynasty (1644-1911). Though they appear more or less weird, as most feature ghosts, fox spirits, demons or deities, they are not horror stories. This point can be settled beyond a doubt if one compares the gluttonous, wily but still lovable house cat in the seventieth story "Revenge of a House Cat" with the demonic black cat portrayed by Edgar Allen Poe. The author would not even have agreed to call his work fiction, for his intention was to record experiences and hearsay rather than making up imaginary tales.

Ji Yun, whose polite name was Xiaolan, was born into an official's family in Cui village of Xian County, Hejian Prefecture (modern Hebei Province) in the second year of the Yongzheng reign (1724). Like many famous figures in China, his birth was said to have been accompanied by astounding phenomena, which caused him to be regarded as a fire god incarnate — he himself alleged to have the ability to see in the dark as a child. Legends aside, he was a true child prodigy who learned to read at four, showing an extraordinary retentive memory. He perused books of all schools of thought, so that his father often blamed him for being too wide in his interests, which was nevertheless beneficial to his writing facility. After passing the metropolitan examination at the age of thirty-one, he enjoyed a successful official career and was appointed to various high posts including Minister of Rites. The only setback he suffered was a three-year exile to Urumqi in Xinjiang due to his leakage of some court secret to an in-law. However, as a misfortune may turn out to be good luck in disguise, the exile to the northwest frontier enriched his life experience and provided him with source materials for his writing. As a scholar his greatest achievement was acting as chief compiler of the *Complete Collection of the Four Libraries*, but ordinary readers get to know him chiefly through *Notes of the Thatched Abode of Close Observations*, composed in his later years "to while away the time." Comprising over one thousand notes of what he had seen and heard in Beijing, Hebei, Fujian and Xinjiang, the book gives a social panorama covering life in the official circles and folk customs in addition to tales of the supernatural.

Stories about ghosts and deities originated from myths and legends in China's remote past, which were intermingled with ancient history as our ancestors seemed to lack the ability to tell reality from imagination. The propagation of Buddhist and Taoist doctrines in the Six Dynasties (222-589) induced quite a few scholars to write about marvels and extraordinary phenomena, but they took ghosts and gods seriously and believed they were making brief notes of actual occurrences. Chinese fiction, in the true sense of the word, emerged in the form of prose romances in the Tang dynasty. Apart from a marked increase in length, the prose romances were consciously made up as imaginary tales, but ghosts and spirits played only a minor part in them. The Qing dynasty saw the flourishing of supernatural tales, the representative works being Pu Songling's *Strange Tales from the Carefree Studio* and Ji Yun's *Notes of the Thatched Abode of Close Observations*. The former, modeled on Tang-dynasty prose romances, featured intricate plots and minute description, whereas the latter favored a pithy style and laconic account in the tradition of the writings from the Six Dynasties, with the addition of a few comments.

Demons and spirits depicted by the authors of the Six Dynasties, who were contented enough to make brief records of strange tales and anecdotes, often behaved in inexplicably bizarre manners. On the other hand, Ji Yun wanted his work to be "conducive to moral persuasion," hoping that people would gain some enlightenment from each story. Thus the apparitions in his work are much more humanlike. The Qing dynasty was governed by the Manchus, a minority people who enlisted the service of Han scholars but regarded them with deep suspicion; many authors were persecuted when the imperial court found their writings offensive. To speak through the mouths of gods and ghosts was therefore a self-protection strategy just like using the past to allude to the present. Social criticism took a prominent position in the many views Ji Yun expressed in his book. The Cheng-Zhu school of philosophy, the dominant Confucian doctrine at the time that advocated "annihilating human desires to uphold heavenly principles," was an invisible dagger that killed without spilling blood. Many of its theorists, in spite of their solemn airs, turned out to be hypocrites committing fraud in the name of safeguarding public morality. Thus the eighty-fourth story intimated that if a man had books on human nature and moral principles on his desk, he was very likely to be an insincere man with ill intentions. Lu Xun wrote that Ji Yun "was, among his contemporaries, a man of great courage who dared criticize ridiculous conventions and social customs during the harsh rule of Emperor Qianlong."

Ji Xiaolan's tales appeal to modern readers due to their intriguing story line, plain style, wry sense of humor, and witty comments. *Notes of the Thatched Abode of Close Observations* was written by a man of great erudition, vast experience, and a large mind, who had the benefit of narrators from all walks of life: servant women, maids, tenants, peddlers, as well as nobles and high officials; the result being this rich and fascinating book. In his opinion, since the world with its myriads of phenomena abounds in wonders and surprises, it is a pleasure to attain a deeper understanding of life while entertaining oneself by listening to strange tales — whether one believes them or not. The huge success of the book since its publication attracted quite a few imitators, who mistook its stories of ghosts and foxes for parables created for the sole purpose of preaching retributive justice. It comes as no surprise that their works, which were mostly drab sermons, have now sunk into oblivion.

引 言

　　本书所收一百四十四个故事都选编自清人纪昀的《阅微草堂笔记》,因大多涉及鬼魂、狐精、妖怪或神仙,读着多少有点古怪诡异之气。不过它们并非恐怖小说,为此我们只需把第七十则"家猫复仇"里那个贪嘴、狡猾却不失可爱的家猫与爱伦·坡笔下令人毛骨悚然的黑猫作个比较,就一目了然。纪昀甚至不会同意把它们称作小说,因为他是在记录见闻,并非只凭想象编造故事。

　　纪昀,字晓岚,清雍正二年(1724)生于河间府(今河北省)献县崔庄的一个官宦家庭。象中国的许多名人一样,据说他出生时也颇有异象,因而被认为是火精转世——他自称小时候有对夜光眼。撇开传说不谈,纪晓岚是位名副其实的神童,四岁开始读书,过目不忘。他喜欢博览百家之言,父亲常责备他爱好过于广泛,但这肯定对他的写作大有好处。他三十一岁中进士,随后仕途坦荡,历任礼部尚书等高官,只有一回因向一位姻亲透露朝廷机密而被谪戍新疆乌鲁木齐三年。塞翁失马,焉知非福;谪戍西域丰富了他的人生体验,也为他的作品提供了素材。主持编纂《钦定四库全书》是他最大的学术成就,普通读者对他的了解则主要来自其晚年"消遣岁月"的作品《阅微草堂笔记》。此书收入他在京师、河北、福建、新疆等地的见闻一千多则,除志怪故事之外还有关于官场世态、风土人情等社会生活的记述。

　　作为志怪故事的源头,中国远古的神话传说就与历史浑然一体,因为我们的祖先有点分不清现实和想象。六朝时佛道思想广泛传播,出现不少文人所著的志怪书,但那些作者都认为鬼神之事确实存在,自己仅仅是加以简要记录。中国真正意义上的小说始于唐代的传奇,它们篇幅明显变长,更关键的是作者开始有意编造故事了,但其中志怪成分并不多。清代志怪小说很兴盛,代表作是蒲松龄的《聊斋志异》和纪昀的《阅微草堂笔记》。前者模仿唐代传奇，情节曲折、描写细腻；后者则效法六朝传统，文风质朴、叙事简要，只不过多了几句议论。

六朝志怪书的作者只满足于把奇闻异事简录下来，故事中精魅的行为往往古里古怪，不合情理。纪昀则要求他的著作"有益于劝惩"，希望每个故事都能给读者一些启示，于是在他笔下，鬼怪的行为更近人情。清朝是异族入主中原，统治者对于汉族文人既利用，又严加防范，不少作者因文字触犯朝廷而获罪，所以借鬼怪之口抒发自己的见解，正如借古讽今，也是当时文人的一种自我保护手段。纪昀在书中表达了许多看法，对社会的批评尤其突出。当时流行的儒家学派——程朱理学提倡"存天理，灭人欲"，成为一把杀人不见血的刀子。而众多理学家道貌岸然，内心肮脏，沦为以维持风化为名招摇撞骗的伪君子。所以第八十四则故事里暗示，谁桌上摆满讲人性道德的书籍，他十有八九心术不正。鲁迅曾言，纪昀"生在乾隆间法纪最严的时代，竟敢借文章以攻击社会上不通的礼法，荒谬的习俗，以当时的眼光看去，真算得很有魄力的一个人。"

今天的读者喜爱纪晓岚的志怪故事主要因为其情节生动，风格质朴，文笔诙谐，议论隽妙。他写作《阅微草堂笔记》时已是饱学之士，见多识广，胸襟开阔，而且为他提供素材者来自社会各个阶层，既有达官贵人，也有仆妇婢女、佃户贩夫，书中表现的内容也就丰富多采，趣味盎然。在他看来，宇宙之大，无奇不有，对异闻怪谈"姑妄听之"，既得到了消遣，又能从中悟出一点人生哲理，何乐而不为。《阅微草堂笔记》一经刊印即大受欢迎，引来不少文人竞相模仿，但他们误以为那些狐鬼故事纯粹是为了宣扬因果报应而编写的寓言，依此效法，作品多成为枯燥无味的劝善书，自然就被今天的读者所遗忘了。

CONTENTS
目 录

1. The Old Scholar Meets a Dead Friend — 1
   老学究遇亡友 — 187

2. A Fox-Wife — 2
   狐妻 — 187

3. A Taoist Talks About Fate — 3
   道士谈天命 — 188

4. A Night-Long Chat on the Nonexistence of Ghosts — 4
   夜话无鬼论 — 189

5. An Apparition Put to Shame — 5
   见怪不怪，其怪自败 — 190

6. Lü, a Taoist Magician — 6
   吕道士 — 190

7. Two Magicians — 8
   两位术士 — 191

8. The Magic Tile — 9
   神奇的瓦片 — 191

9. Underworld Passports — 10
   冥司通行证 — 192

10. A Monk-Poet — 11
    诗僧 — 193

11. A Ghost Drinks Himself to Death 醉死鬼	12 194
12. The Wrong Number 糊涂鬼复仇	13 194
13. A Greedy Tutor 贪心的塾师	14 195
14. The Land-God Lends a Hand 土地神显灵	16 196
15. The Haunted House 老儒闹鬼	16 196
16. A Fiend Disguised as a Maiden 厉鬼扮少女	17 197
17. A Transient Incarnation 短暂轮回	18 197
18. A Merchant from Shanxi 山西商人	19 198
19. A Fake Fox 假狐仙	21 199
20. Encounter with a Ghost in Broad Daylight 老儒白日遇鬼	23 200
21. Careless Talk Costs a Donkey's Life 毛驴开口惹祸	24 201
22. Turtle Treasure 鳖宝	24 201
23. Ghost Versus Man 鬼控告人	26 202

24. Death of a Monk	27
异僧之死	202
25. Ghost-Chasing Strategy	29
驱鬼有术	203
26. A Ghost-Hermit	30
鬼隐士	204
27. The Capture of a Robber	31
大盗被擒	205
28. A Well-Earned Libation	32
善鬼求食	205
29. An Ox Saves Its Master	32
义牛救主	206
30. A Ghost Story Told by a Ghost	33
鬼讲鬼故事	206
31. Reap the Whirlwind	34
种瓜得瓜	207
32. The Wrong Woman	35
李代桃僵	208
33. The Broom-Fiend	37
扫帚精	209
34. A Ghost Beyond the Wheel of Reincarnation	37
跳出轮回的鬼	209
35. Taoist Magic	39
奇门遁甲	210
36. Jiang Sanmang Tries to Catch Ghosts	39
姜三莽捉鬼	211

III

37.	A Fatal Enchantress 求仙遇妖	40 211
38.	A Ghost Matchmaker 鬼为媒	41 212
39.	A Broken Mirror Joined Together 破镜重圆	42 213
40.	Pride Goes Before the Fall 骄者必败	43 214
41.	The Boat-Fiend 船怪	44 214
42.	A Dispute on Abortion 堕胎是非	45 215
43.	Near-Death Experience 濒死经历	46 215
44.	An Old Scholar's Savings 老儒的积蓄	48 216
45.	Abduction by an Old Woman 老妪劫女案	49 217
46.	A Rogue Disguised as a Ghost 恶少装鬼	50 218
47.	The Blood-Drop Test 滴血验亲	51 218
48.	Mr. Shen's Encounter with a Fox 申先生遇狐	53 219
49.	Drink the Wine While You Can 喝酒趁年华	54 220

50.	A Fox-Woman's Two Husbands	56
	狐女事二夫	220
51.	A Wily Ghost	57
	鬼的智谋	222
52.	The Old Tiger-Hunter	58
	打虎老翁	222
53.	A Boy Growing Old in Half a Day	60
	少年半日变老翁	223
54.	The Father Pays the Debt for His Son	60
	子债父还	224
55.	A Fox-Woman Pays Her Debt	62
	狐女还债	225
56.	A Fox Saves an Old Confucian's Life	63
	狐狸救老儒	226
57.	A Skilled Fortune-Teller	64
	神奇卦术	226
58.	Foxes Against Monks	65
	和尚遭暗算	227
59.	Fatal Predictions	67
	算卦肇祸	228
60.	Setting a Case by Leaving It Unsettled	68
	糊涂案	229
61.	The Bell-Demon	69
	钟怪	229
62.	The Importance of Etiquett	70
	礼不可缺	230

63.	Playing a Trick on Oneself	71
	自己戏弄自己	231
64.	The Price of Desecration	72
	渎神的报应	232
65.	A Fake Fox-Woman	74
	假冒的狐女	232
66.	A Female Ghost Seeks a Post for Her Husband	75
	女鬼为夫谋职	233
67.	The Spirit of a Broken Jar	76
	瓮片精	234
68.	A Small Gain at a Big Price	78
	占小便宜吃大亏	234
69.	Ghosts Obtain Food by Fraud	78
	黠鬼骗食	235
70.	The Revenge of a House Cat	80
	家猫复仇	236
71.	A Next-Life Couple	80
	今生好友，来世夫妻	237
72.	Unrequited Fancy	82
	失望的猎艳者	238
73.	Dream and Reality	83
	梦与真	238
74.	A Gift from the Fairies	84
	仙女的礼物	239
75.	A Dose of One's Own Medicine	85
	以彼之矛，攻彼之盾	240

76.	A Fox-Hunting Taoist	86
	捕狐道士	241
77.	Take the Tide at the Flood	89
	因势出奇谋	242
78.	A Ghost's Lie Is Laid Bare	90
	鬼扯谎，露马脚	242
79.	Wrong Message from a Rustic Ghost	90
	乡下鬼传错信	243
80.	Kindness Repaid by an Immortal	91
	仙人报恩	243
81.	Courtesans Visited by Foxes and Ghosts	94
	狐鬼嫖妓	245
82.	Journey of the Spirit	95
	婢女离魂	246
83.	A Ghost Cowers Before the Bully	96
	鬼怕横人	246
84.	A Gentleman Does not Connive with a Ghost	96
	君子不施鬼计	247
85.	A Past-Life Debt Crossed Out	97
	前世冤仇一笔销	248
86.	The Art of Augury	99
	占物术	249
87.	Justice Is Restored by a Fox	100
	狐狸打抱不平	249
88.	To Love or Die	101
	生死恋	250

89. Trial of a Ghost Case	103
巧断鬼案	252
90. How A Fox-Maid Wins Her Freedom	105
狐婢巧脱身	253
91. The Revenge of Condemned Prisoners	106
死囚的报复	254
92. Wife Comes Back to Life in Maid's Body	108
借尸还魂	255
93. A Hapless Loving Couple	109
患难夫妻	255
94. Black Magic	111
邪术	257
95. The Ghost of One Devoured by a Tiger	113
虎伥	258
96. The Interaction of Dream and Reality	114
半梦半真	259
97. Quest for the Stone Beasts	115
石兽的下落	260
98. A Luckless Dandy	117
阴差阳错	260
99. Unable to Tell Friend from Foe	118
敌友不分	261
100. A Moralist Shows His True Colors	119
道学先生现原形	262
101. An Official-Turned Servant Woman	120
官员变仆妇	263

102.	The Bizarre Capers of Foxes and Ghosts 狐鬼的戏侮	121 263
103.	Flight of a Fox-Wife 狐女逃婚	124 265
104.	A Young Man Runs an Errand for a Fox-Woman 狐狸抓差	125 266
105.	A Clandestine Affair Between a Married Couple 夫妻偷情案	126 267
106.	A Sly Robber Hurls Himself into the Net 黠盗自投罗网	128 268
107.	Ghosts Bet on a Poem 鬼打赌	129 269
108.	A Peasant Woman Saves a Fox 农妇救狐	131 269
109.	A Maid Is Molested by Foxes 婢女遭狐戏	132 270
110.	Two Fox-Hunters 两个捕狐人	133 271
111.	If Mountains and Rivers Could Speak 假如山川会说话	134 272
112.	Trickeries in the Imperial Capital 京城骗术	136 273
113.	Use the Enemy's Strategy Against Him 以贼攻贼	138 274
114.	Helper-Turned Harassers 求人帮忙，得不偿失	139 275

115.	A Valiant Courtesan	140
	侠妓	275
116.	Tricked by a Peasant Woman	141
	农妇的智谋	276
117.	Man-Eating Ghosts	144
	吃人鬼	278
118.	Messenger for a Ghost	145
	代鬼传信	278
119.	A Taoist Tames a Shrew	147
	道士驯悍妻	279
120.	An Old Fox Speaks up for Justice	148
	老狐仗义执言	281
121.	Offend Two Ghosts by Saving One Person	149
	救人遭鬼怨	281
122.	Punished by a Fox for Making a Pass at His Wife	150
	调戏狐妻的后果	282
123.	A Demon Invoked by a Prayer	151
	祈祷招妖	283
124.	Underworld Runners Take Food on the Sly	152
	鬼卒偷食	283
125.	Authentic and Fake Immortals	153
	真假仙人	284
126.	A Man Falls Victim to a Fake Fox-Woman	156
	假狐女媚死人	285
127.	A Girl Who'd Rather Be a Concubine than a Wife	157
	妻作妾	286

128. Yang the "Savage Tiger" 杨横虎	159 287
129. A Ghost Avenges the Loss of His Wife 鬼报夺妻之仇	160 288
130. A Talking New-Born Baby 能说会道的婴儿	162 289
131. A Hero Is No Match for a Beauty 英雄难过美人关	163 290
132. A Courtesan Identifies Her Lover 妓女巧认情郎	164 291
133. Reincarnated as a Pig 转世为猪	166 292
134. Marking a Ghost 给鬼作记号	169 293
135. The End of a Family of Robbers 土匪杀强盗	170 294
136. Help from One Fox Provokes Ill Will from Another 以狐召狐	172 295
137. The Fateful End of an Evil Taoist 邪道士受天诛	173 296
138. A Case of Robbery and Adultery 奸盗奇案	175 297
139. The Slaying of a Picture-Demon 诛灭画妖	176 298
140. Taught a Lesson by a Heavenly Fox 天狐的惩诫	178 299

141.	A Folly Repaid by Good Fortune	180
	做蠢事，得好报	300
142.	A Fox Painter	182
	狐狸画家	301
143.	A Prophetic Poem	184
	预言诗	303
144.	A Ghost Who Has Read the Wrong Books	185
	笨鬼读错书	304

1. The Old Scholar Meets a Dead Friend

A pedantic old scholar made his living as a private tutor. Out walking late one evening he ran into the ghost of a dead friend. "Where are you going?" asked the old scholar, who as a stern and upright man had nothing to fear from a ghost. "I am a runner in the underworld," the ghost replied. "I am on my way to the southern village to seize a man's spirit. We happen to be going in the same direction." So they went along side by side.

As they passed a dilapidated house, the ghost remarked, "This is the residence of a scholar." When asked how he knew the ghost explained, "A man's rational spirit is concealed in the daytime when he has to attend to mundane affairs. During sleep the spirit becomes free of perplexing thoughts and regains its purity, so that the man's learning emanates from his body to suffuse the surrounding air, with each word from the books he has read turning into a spark of light. If this is a man of truly great learning and elegant writing style, the light will pierce the clouds to compete with the moon and the stars. There are people whose light shines for a dozen meters, a few meters, and so on down the scale. The light from a man with a smattering of learning appears like a flickering lamp, barely enough to brighten the door and the window of his house. This light is visible only to ghosts and deities. As the light from the house we just passed rose to some seven or eight feet, I could tell it was the dwelling place of a scholar."

At this the old scholar asked, "I've devoted my entire life to studying. I wonder how much light I give off during sleep?" The ghost stumbled over his words, unable to speak his mind. After a long pause he finally said, "I happened to pass your class yesterday and find you nodding off. I saw nothing in your chest but a few Confucian classics and high-score strategies for taking the imperial examination. The words had turned into black smoke hanging over the entire house, and the recitation of your pupils shrouded in the smog was barely audible. I really did not see any light at all." As the old scholar began to swear at him angrily, the ghost let out a fit of laughter and instantly vanished.

2. A Fox-Wife

Zhou Hu, a servant in the Zhou household of Xian County, lived with a fox-woman like a happily married couple for over twenty years. The fox-woman once told him, "I have practiced the art of immortality for more than four hundred years. I was indebted to you in my past life and must pay you back during this lifetime. Unless the debt is completely cleared, I won't be able to go to heaven. Once the time allotted to us is used up, I will have to leave." One day she looked unusually happy, then shed tears sadly. "The nineteenth of this month will be our parting day," she told Zhou. "I have found you a wife. You can settle the marriage by sending her family some money." She gave him a few pieces of silver to buy a betrothal gift. After that she became unusually amorous toward him and spent every minute of the day and night in his company.

On the morning of the fifteenth the fox-woman got up to bid Zhou Hu good-bye. Surprised, he asked her why she should leave before schedule. Tearfully, she explained, "The number of days we can spend together is fixed, impossible for me to add or detract, but when they shall be spent is somewhat flexible. By saving three days I make the chance for us to meet again."

A few years later she actually returned to spend three days with him in a happy reunion. When she took leave this time, her voice was choked with tears, "So long forever!"

"This fox-woman conducted herself with room to spare," someone commented. "Such appreciation of one's good fortune is to be emulated," another disagreed. "After the three-day reunion the fox woman still had to leave, so what was the point of delaying the inevitable? After four hundred years' practice for immortality, she still found it hard to cut her tie with the mundane world. It won't do one any good to follow her example."

It seems neither of these comments are incorrect, as each of them has made a good point.

3. A Taoist Talks About Fate

Ming Cheng, the Magistrate of Xian County, was a native of Yingshan. On one occasion he could not made up his mind to redress a wrong case for fear of his superior's disapproval. Wang, a servant at the county's Confucian School by the nickname "demi-immortal," was acquainted with a fox who could predict future occurrences in people's daily lives. Ming Cheng sent Wang to consult the fox on the matter. Assuming a serious expression, the fox replied, "The Magistrate Mr. Ming should look after the people in this county with the solicitudes of a parent. Thus he should ask himself whether the case is wrong, regardless of whether his superior will approve of him. Doesn't he remember the words of Governor-General Li Wei?"

When Wang brought him the fox's reply, Ming Cheng was deeply affected, knowing the fox was referring to an incident that had happened to Li Wei before he became a high official. Li was once ferrying across a river when he found a Taoist priest on board. As a quarrel broke out between a passenger and a boatman, the Taoist sighed, "Why squabble over a few cents when your life will end in a minute?" A short moment later the passenger, accidentally swept by the sail, fell into the river and was drowned. Li Wei was astonished. In mid-stream a gust rose, threatening to overturn the boat. The Taoist began to walk in circles while chanting incantations, and the wind soon stopped. When the boat moored safely, Li Wei bowed to the Taoist to thank him for saving his life. The Taoist replied, "I could not save the man falling into the river a moment ago because that was decreed by his fate. I could not help saving you because, as a worthy man, you are destined to turn ill luck into good. What do you thank me for then?" Li Wei bowed again, saying, "I will bear your instruction in mind and resign myself to fate for the rest of my life."

"You are only partially correct," said the Taoist. "Whether a man will attain wealth and honor is decreed by fate, so he should accept what comes by without question. Otherwise he would commit various misdeeds for personal gains, pushing other people aside or even trampling over them. As for matters concerning national welfare and people's livelihood, one must not depend on fate. It is precisely to complement the deficiency of fate that talents are created by heaven and officials appointed by the imperial court. If someone in a position to give orders simply folds his hands, leaving everything to the dictates of destiny, why should heaven have endowed him with his ability or the imperial court appointed him an official?"

Li Wei respectfully received the instruction from the Taoist, then asked to know his name. "I might scare you by disclosing my name," said the Taoist. He left the ferry boat and, after a few dozen steps, suddenly vanished into thin air. Later Li Wei recounted his experience to some friends, and somehow the fox learned of the story too.

4. A Night-Long Chat on the Nonexistence of Ghosts

Ji Ru'ai, a native of Jiaohe, and Zhang Wenfu, a native of Qing, were old Confucian scholars teaching in the same school in Xian County. One moonlit night they took a walk from the northern to the southern villages. Far away from their house, they found themselves in a silent wasteland. Zhang grew fearful and wanted to return, saying, "The graveyard abounds in ghosts. This is no place to linger at!" Just then an old man with a walking stick emerged and bowed to them. "How can there be any ghosts? Haven't you read about the argument of Ruan Zhan of the Jin dynasty? As Confucians, you must not believe in Buddhist heresy!" He sat down for a long chat with them, expounding the nonexistence of ghosts by quoting great Confucian scholars from the Song dynasty. Both Ji and Zhang were deeply impressed and acknowledged that the old man had grasped the truth of the matter. In the warm conversation it never occurred to either of them to ask the old man's name.

Just then they heard in the distance the jingling of bells from a few ox-drawn carts heading toward them. The old man got up abruptly. "I have been alone in the underworld for such a long time," he said. "You would not have stayed to chat with me tonight if I had not chosen to argue against the existence of ghosts. I tell you the truth before I leave and hope you won't regard it as a hoax." In the blink of an eye he vanished. Very few scholars were buried in that area, but a Mr. Dong Kongru's tomb happened to be nearby. Possibly he was that ghost.

5. An Apparition Put to Shame

On a hot summer day a man named Cao stopped by at a friend's house on his way from Xi County to Yangzhou, and he was ushered into a spacious studio for a chat. When he asked to sleep in the studio, his friend said, "No one can stay the night here, for the room is haunted." However, Cao insisted on sleeping there. At midnight something as thin as a piece of paper squeezed its way through the crack of the door. Once inside the room, it gradually spread out to take the shape of a woman. Cao was not in the least afraid. Suddenly she loosened her hair and stuck out her tongue like the ghost of a hanged woman. Cao merely smiled, "It's still hair, only a bit tangled; it's still a tongue, only a bit too long. What's scary about this?" The ghost suddenly took off her head and put it on the desk. Cao laughed, "I did not fear you with your head on, so why should I fear you when you become headless?" At her wits end, the ghost disappeared instantly.

On his way back from Yangzhou Cao again stayed the night in the studio at his friend's house. At midnight something again tried to crawl in through the crack of the door. Cao spat at it, saying, "Is this the same dreary thing again?" Then the ghost went away without troubling him. Apparently, fear leads to confusion of the heart, which causes a man to lose his presence of mind and be vulnerable to the attack of specters. Fearlessness leads to tranquility of the heart, which causes a man to remain clear in mind and be able to ward off evil influences, so specters or demons can only leave in shame.

6. Lü, a Taoist Magician

A Taoist priest named Lü was skillful in magic. He once stayed in the house of an official named Tian. With wistarias in full bloom in his courtyard Tian invited many guests to a feast to appreciate the flowers. At the table there was a vulgar scholar who kept rattling away to the irritation of other guests. When a quick-tempered young lad told him hotly to shut up, the two nearly got into a fight. An old Confucian scholar tried to mediate, but when neither paid him any attention he looked greatly offended. This dampened the spirits of all the other guests.

Lü asked for a writing brush and some paper, then he drew three magic figures and burnt them on the spot. Suddenly the three men stood up and began walking back and forth in the courtyard. The vulgar scholar made his way to the southeast corner, where he sat down and began muttering. Listening closely, the other guests realized he was discussing household affairs with his wife and concubine. First he looked left and right as if trying to mediate between the two women. Then he seemed to be defending himself with a complacent air. Afterward he appeared to be pleading guilty, first falling on one knee, then on both knees, finally kowtowing nonstop. In the meantime the lad had seated himself at the southwest corner beside the flower fence. He cast amorous glances around and spoke in a low, gentle voice, now laughing merrily, now declining by way of modesty. Then he started to sing a popular song, beating rhythm with his hands, looking quite crude and unseemly. The old scholar, seated on a stone stool, seemed to be lecturing on a piece of classic prose to four or five pupils. Sometimes he shook his head and said "incorrect"; sometimes he scowled at someone for failing to understand him. Every now and then he paused to cough and clear his throat. Astonished at first, the other guests started to giggle with amuse-

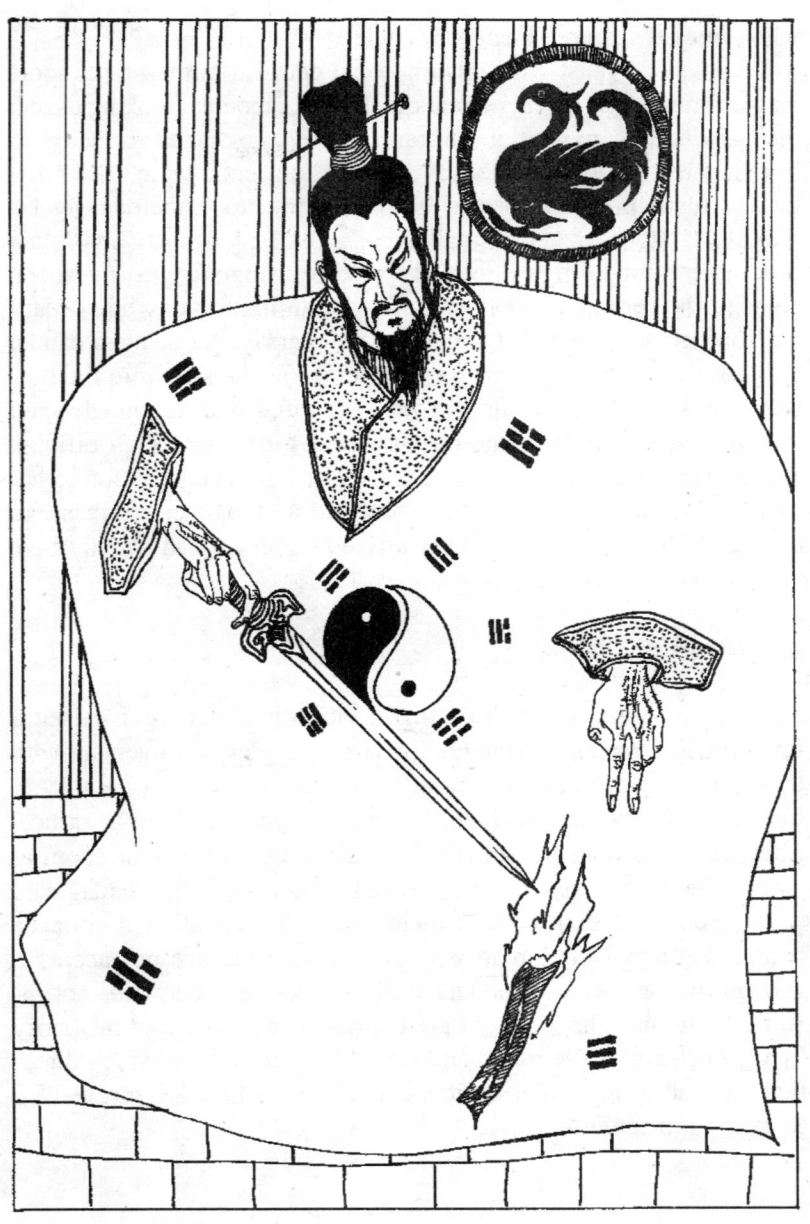

ment, but Lü gestured them to be quiet.

When the feast was drawing to an end, Lü burned three more magic figures. The three men sat quietly for a moment looking dazed, then gradually came out of the trance. They apologized for being so ill-mannered as dozing off after drinking too much wine. The other guests, restraining themselves from laughing, took their leave. Lü remarked, "It was merely a small antic. In the Tang dynasty Ye Fashan used such a magic figure to lead Emperor Minghuang to the moon palace. The common people took him for an immortal, while pedantic Confucians dismissed the incident as hearsay. All of them can be compared to the proverbial frog who looks at the sky from the bottom of a well." Later, while staying at an inn, Lü used a magic spell to summon the spirit of the concubine of a traveling high official. When she came out of the trance, she got on a carriage, found her way back to the inn and told her husband to send men posthaste to seize the Taoist. By the time they arrived there, Lü had already fled.

7. Two Magicians

As the story goes, when Wu Sangui, the Prince of Pingxi, raised a revolt in Yunnan against the Qing court, a magician conversant with the art of augury decided to offer his service to Wu. On his way to Yunnan he met a man who said he was also going to join the prince. They traveled along for some time and put up in the same room at night. When the second man lay down by the west wall, the magician said, "You'd better not sleep there because the wall will collapse before midnight." The man was unmoved. "You are not accurate enough in your prediction. The wall will collapse outward, not inward." Late into the night his prediction came true. I find this story hard to believe. If the man had been able to foretell in which direction the wall would collapse, how could he have failed to foresee Wu Sangui's inevitable defeat?

8. The Magic Tile

A vagabond monk who was well-versed in magic once stayed in the house of an official named Su in Jiaohe County. He claimed to have been a fellow disciple of Lü, the Taoist magician. One day he kneaded mud into the shape of a pig. After he chanted a few magic words, the pig started to stir. As he went on chanting, the pig grunted, then jumped to its feet. He had the pig slaughtered by the cook and made into dishes, which were then served to the guests, but the meat did not taste good. After the meal all the guests vomited mud.

Because of rain a guest was put up for the night in Su's house to share the room with the monk. In a hushed voice he asked, "I remember reading somewhere in a book about a magician. After he chanted a few magic words to a tile, the man using it was able to cut through walls and sneak into a woman's boudoir. Is your skill equal to that?" "That's not so difficult," replied the monk. He picked up a tile and chanted incantations for a moment, then handed it to the guest. "You can go and have a try. On no account should you speak, otherwise the spell will be broken." The man used the tile to slash the wall, which fell apart instantly. He walked into a room to find an attractive woman undressing for bed. Bearing in mind the monk's warning, he dared not say anything but bolted the door and got in bed to make love to her. The woman looked happy and pleased. Afterward he felt sleepy and drifted into a nap. When he woke up, he opened his eyes to find himself in his own bed with his wife.

While the perplexed couple were questioning each other, the monk called at the door to rebuke the husband. "Because of a single mistake, Lü was struck dead by thunder. And you tried to induce me to do wrong! I played a small trick on you, so that your virtue has not been seriously blemished. Never bear such an improper thought again." Then he sighed, "As soon as the wrong thought emerged in your mind, the god overlooking your destiny would record it in the book. I'm afraid your future will be unfavorably affected." Sure enough, the man turned out to be unlucky in his official career. In his old age he finally got appointed to assistant instructor at the local Confucian school, which helped little to alleviate his poverty.

9. Underworld Passports

When I was in Urumqi, a clerk in the army once brought a few dozen printed documents for me to sign. "When a non-native soldier dies," he explained, "his remains will be moved back to his hometown, and a passport will be issued for his soul. Without it the soul will not be permitted to enter the pass." The passports, he said, were meant for the underworld. I glanced at them and found the words crude and ludicrous: "This passport is to certify that so-and-so died here on the day of —. His family members will be carrying his remains back to his hometown, and underworld guards at the passes along the way should allow the soul to enter without delaying him or extorting money from him." "This," I said to the clerk, "is obviously a money-making scheme devised by some petty officials." Thereupon I wrote a report to the general and had the practice abolished.

Ten days later I was told that ghosts in the graveyard west of the city were crying because they could not go home for lack of passports. I dismissed it as nonsense. When ten more days went by I was informed that the ghostly howling could be heard near the city wall, and again I denounced it as baloney. After another ten days I heard ghostly wailing just outside the wall of my residence, and thought it was a trick of the petty officials concerned. One evening a few days later the noise was heard outside my house window. With the moon shining as bright as day, I got up and searched around, but there was no one to be found. A colleague of mine said to me, "Your opinion on the matter was correct in principle, so the general was unable to turn you down, yet all of us have heard the weeping ghosts. If by any chance the dead really need these passports you refused to sign, they would bear a grudge against you. Why don't you simply sign the passports to give the petty crooks no excuse to slander you? If the ghostly noise doesn't stop, you will be able to prove your point." Reluctantly I accepted his advice, and that very night all became quiet. Well, strange things of every description exist in this world of ours, but many Confucian scholars tend to take commonplace phenomena as the only truth.

10. A Monk-Poet

Fan Hengzhou was about to cross the Qiantang River when a monk asked to be carried in the same boat. He put down his stool and leaned his back on the mast, not bothering to exchange greetings with Fan. When Fan tried to talk with him, he answered absentmindedly while looking elsewhere. Annoyed by his arrogance, Fan stopped speaking to him. A strong west wind was blowing, and Fan composed on the spot two lines of poetry:

With white waves tossing the bow,
The traveler cowers in contrary wind.

He repeated the two lines several times, unable to come up with two more lines to complete the poem. Suddenly the monk, his eyes closed, intoned,

Why is the red-sleeved girl
Leaning on the highest tower?

Fan, not knowing what the monk meant, tried again to speak to him but got no answer. When the ferry boat was being moored, Fan spotted a young girl in red sleeves standing on a high tower. Astonished, he pressed the monk for an explanation. "I happened to catch a glimpse of her," the monk replied. But there was a dense mist over the river and the tower had been blocked from the view by other houses, so that it would not have been possible to see the girl from the boat. Thinking the monk was able to foretell the future, Fan intended to bow and show his respect, but the monk had walked away on his staff. Unable to tell what the monk was, Fan felt both perplexed and disappointed.

11. A Ghost Drinks Himself to Death

A butcher by the name of Xu Fang walked alone one night carrying two jugs of wine on a shoulder pole. Feeling tired, he stopped for a rest under a big tree. The moon was very bright. Suddenly, he heard a hooting noise in the distance, then saw a horrifying ghost leap out from the graveyard. He hid himself behind the tree and made ready to fight for his life with the bamboo pole. Running to the spot, the ghost danced in joy at the sight of the wine and started to drink at once. After emptying one jug he moved on to the other, but only managed to get the lid half open when he dropped flat on the ground intoxicated. By this time Xu was gnashing his teeth with rage. As the ghost didn't seem to have any trick up his sleeve, Xu suddenly attacked with the pole, but it went right through the ghost. He kept hacking furiously until the ghost gradually melted down into a ball of dense smoke. To prevent the ghost from taking another form, Xu gave it over a hundred strokes. The smoke slowly dispersed over the ground, growing thinner and thinner until it faded completely.

In my opinion a ghost, being the remnant of vital energy from a dead person, will gradually diminish and disappear. Therefore some ancient books recorded that new ghosts are big while old ones small. Some people can see ghosts, but no one has seen any ancient ghosts because these have already died out. Doctors often use liquor, which has the function of dispersing the vital energy, to concoct drugs for promoting blood circulation and inducing perspiration. It was therefore all too natural for the ghost in the above story, consisting merely of a vestige of vital energy, to vanish after downing a whole jug of wine. He was not beaten to death; instead, he drank himself to nonexistence. A man who never touched liquor commented, "The ghost should have been able to change forms, but being drunk he lay helpless on the ground to receive the beating. The ghost should have been able to frighten the man, but being drunk he was beaten to death. Those in love with the wine bottle must draw a lesson from the story!" A man who had a weakness for wine retorted, "A ghost has no physical body but is nevertheless chained down by all kinds of emotions such as joy, happiness, sorrow or anger. However, he will have attained total freedom when lying in a drunken sleep or even sinking into nonexistence. That is the essence of wine-drinking! Like nirvana sought after by Buddhists, it is way beyond the comprehension of mere mortal beings busily engaged in having their stomachs filled."

12. The Wrong Number

My late father told the following story. When he took the imperial examination in the capital in the eighth year of the Yongzheng reign, he was assigned to share a room with Tang, a candidate from Xiong County. At midnight the door curtain was abruptly lifted, and the ghost of a woman with disheveled hair burst into the room and began to tear up Tang's exam paper. A resolute and upright man, Tang felt no fear and sat up to address the ghost, "I know nothing about my past life, but in this life I have harmed no one. What do you want to do?" The ghost, stepping back in dismay, asked, "Aren't you number forty-seven?" Tang replied, "No, I am number forty-nine." It seemed that in counting the houses the ghost had failed to include two vacant ones. She stared at Tang for a long time, then made off with a bow of apology. A moment later they heard a clamor of noises from room forty-seven about someone being seized by an evil spirit. That was indeed a muddle-headed ghost who inflicted undeserved calamity upon Tang. Fortunately he was a man of clear conscience and had the presence of mind to argue with her, so that only one piece of his paper was torn. Otherwise his loss would have been much greater.

13. A Greedy Tutor

In Suning County there was a private tutor who lectured on the Cheng-Zhu School of Confucian philosophy.* One day a roving monk came to beg for alms outside the school. He knocked on a wooden clapper nonstop from morning till noon. Disgusted, the tutor went out to drive the monk away. "A heretic like you can only fool ignorant people," he said, "but here in this school we are all disciples of sages and saints. Why try in vain to move us?" The monk made a bow and replied, "A follower of the Buddha begging for food and clothing is no different from a disciple of Confucius seeking after fame and wealth — both have gone astray. Why should you make things difficult for me then?" Incensed, the tutor picked up a birch to hit the monk, who ducked the blow and muttered, "How intolerable you are!"

The monk went away, leaving behind a cloth bag. The tutor expected him to come back for it, but he did not. When dusk fell, the tutor felt the bag and found it filled with unstringed coins. His pupils wanted to take money from the bag, but he stopped them, saying, "We should wait and see if the monk really won't come back. And we must count the coins first to avoid quarrels." As soon as the bag was opened, a host of wasps darted out toward the tutor and his pupils, whose faces soon became swollen with stings. Hearing their cries and screams, the neighbors all came to find out what was the matter. Just then the monk burst in. "Are the disciples of sages and saints trying to pilfer another man's money?" he asked. He picked up the bag and turned to leave. At the gate he saluted the tutor with clasped hands. "Forgive a heretic for offending the disciples of sages and saints by accident," he said. The onlookers roared with laughter. Someone said the monk had used magic. Another one said, "The tutor likes to denounce Buddhism. That's why the monk hid wasps

---

*Known as the philosophy of principle, it was founded by Cheng Hao, Cheng Yi and Zhu Xi of the Song Dynasty and endorsed by subsequent rulers of imperial China.

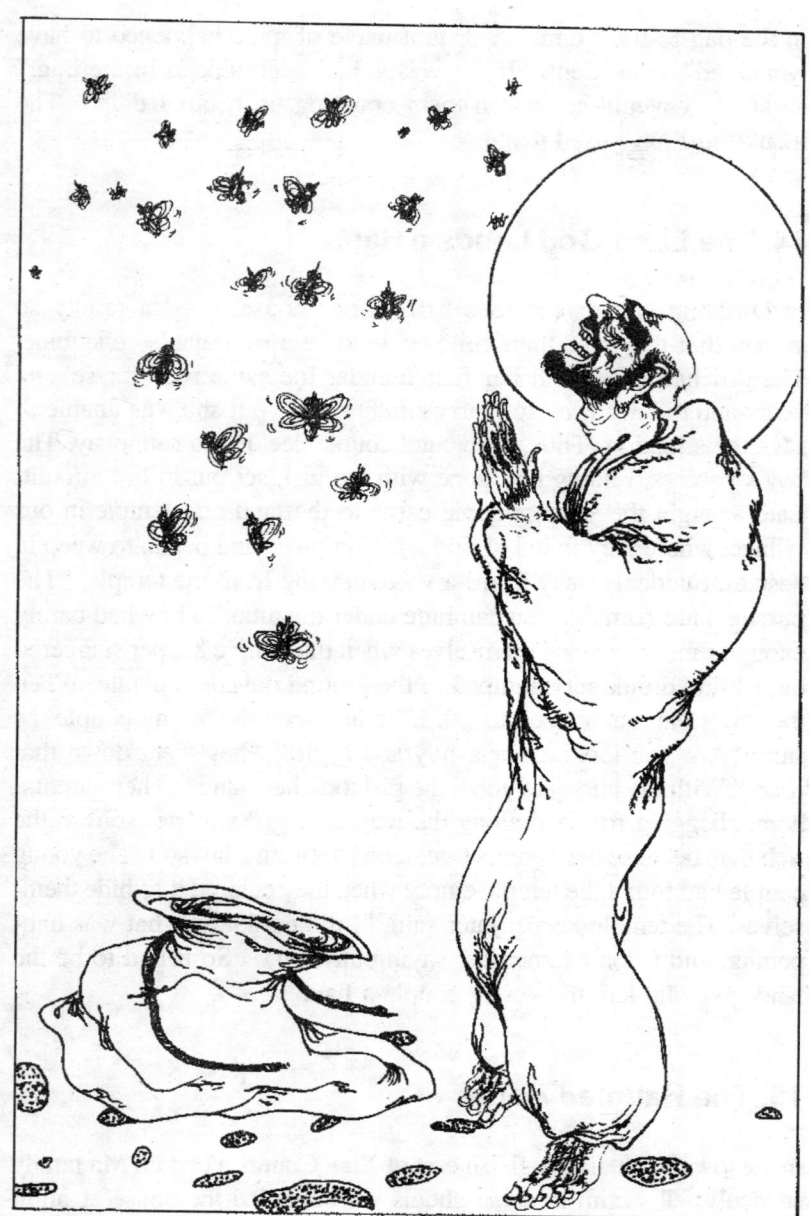

in the bag to trick him." A distant uncle of mine happened to have witnessed the incident. "If the wasps had been hidden in the bag," he said, "I would have seen them crawling in it, but I didn't. The monk must have used magic."

14. The Land-God Lends a Hand

In Dusheng village, eighteen li from our house, lived a family so greedy that they sold their child-bride to be a rich man's concubine. The girl had lived with her fiancé under the same roof for several years and did not want to marry another man, but she was unable to save the situation. Thus, the young couple decided to run away. The boy's parents, finding him gone with the girl, set out in hot pursuit. Late at night the young couple came to the land-god temple in our village, where they failed to find a hiding place and began to weep in despair. Suddenly, they heard a voice coming from the temple, "The pursuers are coming. You can hide under the altar." They had barely enough time to conceal themselves when the temple keeper staggered back blind drunk and slumped to the ground outside the gate. When the boy's parents arrived to ask if he had seen the young couple, he said, "Are you looking for a boy and a girl? They went down that road." With the pursuers gone, the girl took her fiancé to her parents' home, begging for food along the way. The girl was not sold to the rich man because her parents threatened to bring a lawsuit. The young couple had found the temple empty when they entered it to hide themselves. The temple keeper later said, "I did not know what was happening, and I don't remember saying anything." So it had to be the land-god who lent the young couple a hand.

15. The Haunted House

In the town of Huai fifty-five li east of Xian County a certain Ma family suddenly fell victim to some ghouls who prowled the house at night throwing stones around, hooting and howling, and setting things on fire in abandoned corners. This lasted for over a year. The Ma family tried sacrifice and prayer, then invited a magician to exorcise the spirits, but to no avail. Finally they moved to a newly purchased residence and rented out the old house. But the tenants, also molested by the spirits, moved away after a short time, and no one else would rent the house after that. Then there came an old Confucian scholar who was not at all bothered by the evil reputation of the house. He bought it for a good price and moved in on an auspicious day. When nothing unusual happened to him, word got around that the fiends were afraid to confront the old scholar because of his true integrity. Later a robber called at the house and quarreled with the old scholar, whose scheme was thus exposed. For there had been no evil spirits in the house; the old scholar had actually hired the robber to make troubles there at night. My father commented, "The defining trait of a fiend is its ability to play various tricks. That old scholar was so deceitful that it would be quite appropriate to call him a fiend."

16. A Fiend Disguised as a Maiden

My family had a servant named Wei Zhao, a flighty person who enjoyed ogling women. One day he ran into a young girl outside the village. He seemed to know her by sight, though he did not know her name or address. When he approached her to strike up a conversation, she merely gave him a meaningful glance and walked on toward the west. As he watched, she turned as if to beckon him over, so he followed her down the road. When he came close to her, her cheeks flaming, whispered, "There are too many people on the road. They may grow suspicious to see us together. Please keep half a li's distance from me. When I get home, I will wait for you in the cart shed outside the courtyard. Before the house you will find a date tree with an ox tethered to it and a stone roller nearby."

Following the girl, Wei Zhao walked a long way. At dusk he came to Lijiawa village thirty li from home. As it had rained the day before, the mud was nearly knee deep on the road, and he had sore toes from the walk. From a distance he saw the girl entering the cart shed. Overjoyed, he hastened to join her. The girl, with her back to him, suddenly turned around. She had changed into a ghastly fiend with ragged teeth, claw-like hands, and a deep blue face with eyes glittering like two lamps. Terrified, Wei Zhao turned and ran, with the fiend close at his heels. Running wildly for twenty li, he reached Xiangguo village late at night. He recognized the house of his parents-in-law and banged madly on the door. The moment it was opened, he rushed in, knocking down a girl and falling over himself. With cries of indignation several women started to beat him on the legs with clubs they used for washing clothes. Gasping for breath, he was unable to speak coherently but could only cry "It's me, me." After a while an old woman came out with a lamp. Only then did they recognize him, to their surprise and amusement, as the son-in-law of the family. The following day he was carried home in an ox cart, and it took him two months to get up from bed again.

When Wei Zhao followed the girl and fled from the fiend, people on the road had found him alone, without any girl or fiend. Was it possible that a fox or a demon played the trick on him because of his improper intention? My elder brother Qinghu remarked, "After the incident Wei Zhao has mended his ways. He always lowers his head when he comes across a woman on the road. It might be said that the gods have taught him a lesson."

17. A Transient Incarnation

Mr. Sun Eshan once fell ill in Gaoyou County, and he lay in a boat to recuperate. In his dream he took a delightful walk along the bank. Then someone came to lead his way. In a trance Sun followed the man without questioning him. They got to a decent-looking house, and the road at the front was clean and tidy. Entering the inner room, Sun saw a woman ready to give birth. He was about to step back when the guide smacked him heavily on the back, sending him into a coma. When he gradually came to, he found that he had dwindled into a newborn baby wrapped in swaddling clothes made of brocade. He realized he had been reborn, and there was nothing he could do about it. When he opened his mouth to speak, a cold shiver ran down from the top of his head, making him unable to utter a word. Looking around, he saw a desk, a bed, various antiques, and works of painting and calligraphy.

Three days later a maid giving him a bath accidentally dropped him to the ground. He went into a coma again and woke up in his boat. His family told him he had stopped breathing for three days. They had not buried him because his limbs felt soft and his bosom warm. Sun sent for paper and brush, wrote down what he had seen and heard, and had the letter delivered to the family he had visited in his dream, along with a request for the host not to punish the maid who had dropped the baby. Then he recounted his experience in detail. That day he had a full recovery and went to call on that family. The servant women in the house looked quite familiar to him. After listening to Sun's incredible tale the host, an old man without a son, sighed in deep regret.

Most Confucians do not believe in reincarnation, but incidents of rebirth are not uncommon in everyday life. Looking closely, one will find a causal relationship in each case. But it is hard to explain why Mr. Sun Eshan, after a three-day rebirth, returned to his own body. It will remain an unsolved case.

18. A Merchant from Shanxi

A merchant from Shanxi was staying at Xingcheng Hotel in the imperial capital. Splendidly dressed, he had a servant and a carriage. He was planning, he said, to secure an office by making a donation to the government. One day a poor old man came to look for him, but the servant would not let him in, so he stood at the door for a long time until the merchant finally came out. The merchant received him rather coolly, offering him a cup of tea, and did not ask him what he needed. When the old man timidly asked him for a loan, the merchant was quite displeased. "I don't have enough money to buy myself an office. How can I have anything left to give to you?" Indignant, the old man told the other guests how he had helped the merchant in dire circumstances. For ten years the merchant had been kept from starvation by his help, then he had lent the merchant a hundred taels of silver to start a business and gradually build up a fortune. Just relieved from his post in the capital, he had been delighted to learn of the merchant's arrival. He just wanted to get back the money so that he could pay his debts and return to his hometown. With this the old man began to weep, but the merchant turned a deaf ear to him.

One of the guests, a man from Jiangxi whose family name was Yang, bowed to the merchant with clasped hands and asked, "Is the old gentleman telling the truth?" The merchant reddened, "Yes, he is. I want to help, but it is really beyond my means." "You will soon become an official and get loans with no difficulty," said Yang. "If someone were willing to lend you a hundred taels of silver for a year interest-free, would you use it to pay back the old man?" Reluctantly, the merchant said he would. "In that case, please sign an IOU," Yang told him. "I have the silver ready." Feeling the pressure from the other guests, the merchant gave in. Yang tucked away the paper, opened his worn chest, and took out a hundred taels of silver, which he handed to the merchant. Glumly the merchant gave the silver to the old man. Then Yang invited the old man and the merchant to a feast. At the table the old man was in high spirits, but the merchant, who looked rather out of humor, drank a few cups of wine joylessly. After the meal the old man thanked Yang and left. A few days later Yang checked out of the hotel and did not show up again. Then the merchant found a hundred taels of silver missing from his chest, but there was nothing he could do as the lock remained intact. A foxskin vest had also disappeared, replaced by a tick from a pawnshop with the face value of two thousand coins — roughly the amount Yang spent on the feast. Only then did the merchant realize he had been fooled by Yang, who must be a magician. In shame and anger he moved out of the hotel, and no one knew where he went.

19. A Fake Fox

When I was a child I once stayed with an aunt named Lü in Cangzhou. There I saw a witch named Hao, who was a very wily village woman. She claimed to be the medium of a fox spirit who could tell fortunes, and a lot of people believed her because she seemed to know in detail what was happening in their daily lives. Actually she had sent her cohorts to court the friendship of servant women in the village and have them spy on their hosts. Thus she was able to fool villagers with her knowledge of their family secrets. A pregnant woman who consulted the witch about the sex of her unborn baby was told that it was a boy. When, having given birth to a girl, she came to demand why the fox spirit had made a mistake, the witch regarded her with a glare. "You were at first blessed with a son. Then on a certain day you were given twenty pancakes by your parents, but you gave only six to your parents-in-law and ate the rest yourself. The god of the underworld had your son substituted by a daughter to punish you for such unfilial behavior. Why not repent now?" In consternation the woman pleaded guilty, with no idea how the witch had spied out her behavior. By such ingenuity the witch managed to deceive many people.

One day the witch was invoking the fox spirit before the incense burner when she suddenly straightened up and spoke in a clear voice, "I am a real fox spirit. Though foxes like me share a living space with humans, we are too busy in our daily practice to collaborate with an old hag and meddle with trivial affairs in the village households. This crooked old woman has amassed an ill-gotten fortune in my name. By speaking through her own mouth today, I want to make all of you see through her scheme." The fox went on to relate the various misconducts of the witch and name all her accomplices. Then the witch came out of the trance with a start and took to her heels, never to show up in the village again.

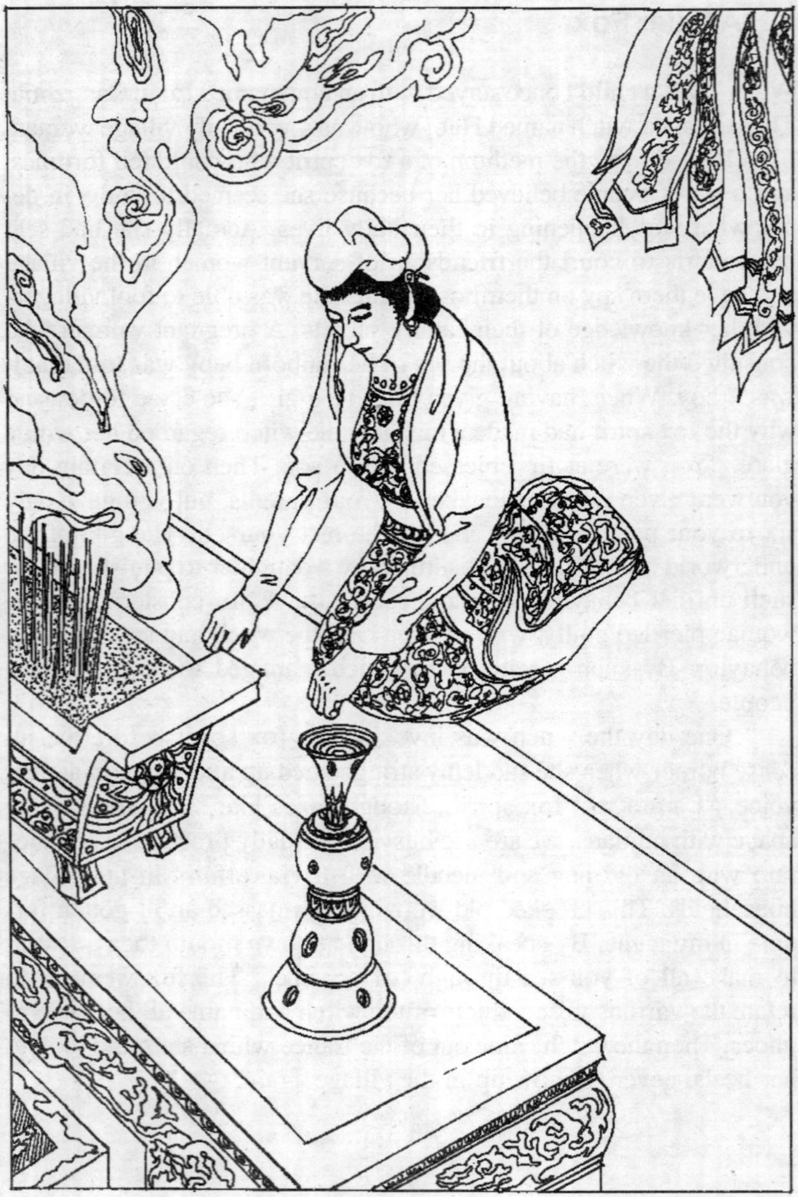

20. Encounter with a Ghost in Broad Daylight

My father's ex-tutor, Wang De'an, was an old Confucian scholar of Suning County who passed the metropolitan examination in the forty-fifth year of the Guangxu reign. Calling on a friend on a summer day, he found the pavilion in the garden spacious and pleasant, so he wanted to stay the night there. When his friend objected, saying the place was haunted, Wang told the following story.

A scholar named Cen came to Cangzhou from the south and was put up by Zhang Diezhuang. On the wall of his room was a life-size picture of Zhong Kui, the legendary ghost-catcher, with a chime clock at the front. Cen was too drunk to notice them when be entered the room to sleep. At midnight he woke up, puzzled by the noise of gear wheels from the clock, then caught sight of the picture on the wall lit up by the moon shining in through the window. Taking Zhong Kui for a devil, he picked up the Duanzhou-made inkstone from the table and flung it upward. At the crushing noise the servants rushed into the room to find Cen dripping with ink from his face and hair. The chime clock in front of the picture, along with a jade vase and a porcelain tripod, was broken. Everyone who heard of the incident had a good laugh.

At the end of the story Wang remarked, "There are people who often claim to have seen ghosts, but that is no more than a reflection of their inner fear. Where on earth do ghosts exist?" As soon as he said this, a voice came from a corner of the room, "Here is a ghost who will pay you a visit tonight. Please don't fling an inkstone at me." Speechlessly, Wang stood up and left the room. Later he recounted the incident to a few disciples with the comment, "How could a ghost have spoken to people in broad daylight? That must have been a fox. As I didn't consider myself a man of great virtue capable of subduing a fox, I made myself scarce." In other words, he still believed in the nonexistence of ghosts.

21. Careless Talk Costs a Donkey's Life

A scholar from Jimo by the name of Yu was on his way to the capital, riding a donkey. Climbing up a hillock, he tethered the donkey to a tree and sat down for a nap with his back leaning against a rock. Suddenly, the donkey raised its head, looked all around, and said with a deep sigh, "After dozens of years the hills look the same, but the village has changed a lot." A very curious man, Yu leapt to his feet. "An ancient, Song Chuzong, was said to have raised a talking rooster. Now that I have this donkey, I can chat with it every day and never feel lonely again on my journey." He bowed to the donkey and spoke to it, but it kept grazing on the grass. Yu tried his best to persuade the donkey, promising to treat it as a friend instead of an animal, but it was in vain. Enraged, Yu began to whip it fiercely, but the poor beast could only kick the ground and bray. Yu broke one of its legs and sold it to a butcher, then returned home on foot. This incident seems farcical. Could Yu have had a hallucination? Or perhaps the donkey had offended a demon in its past life, and the demon got its own back by speaking through the donkey to enrage its master.

22. Turtle Treasure

Zhang Baonan, my grandmother's younger cousin on the paternal line, once served as Provincial Administration Commissioner of Sichuan. His wife's favorite dish was turtle soup. One day the family cook bought a giant turtle. The moment its head was cut off, a tiny figure a few inches tall jumped out of the turtle's neck and started running around it. The cook swooned out of fright, and the tiny figure disappeared. When the turtle was cut open, the figure was found dead in its belly. It had distinctive facial features and four limbs, and was wearing a yellow hat, a blue jacket, a red sash, and a pair of black boots. At the sight of this a family tutor named Cen said, "It is a turtle treasure. If you catch one, you can cut your arm open to raise it, for it feeds on human blood. With the turtle treasure in your arm,

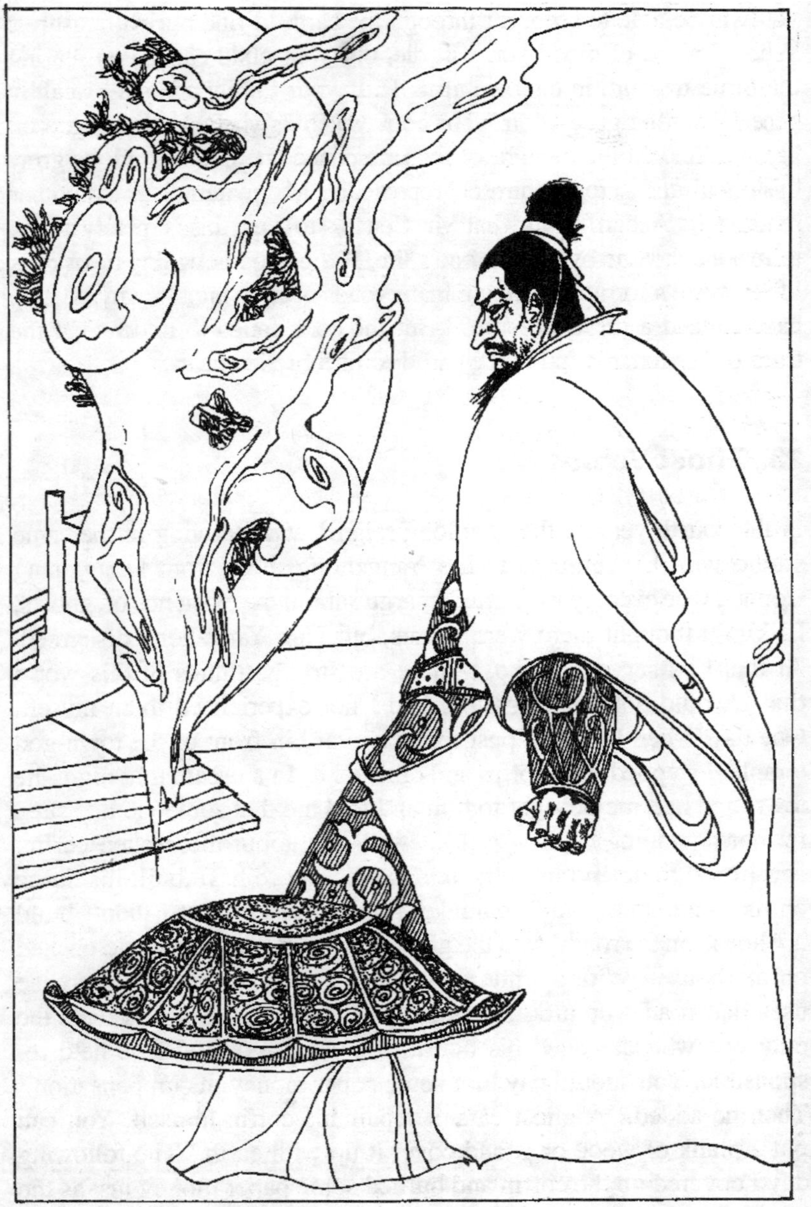

you will be able to see right through the earth to find buried treasures. When drained of blood you will die, but your child can go on rearing the turtle treasure in his own arm. Thus your family can stay wealthy generation after generation." The cook was overwhelmed with regret on hearing this. At the thought of the rare chance he had missed, he grew hysterical and slapped himself repeatedly. My maternal grandmother remarked, "According to what Mr. Cen has told us, this is merely a way to make a fortune by risking one's life. If a person is willing to risk his life to make a fortune, there are many roads open to him — why does he have to feed a turtle treasure?" But the cook failed to understand the truth of her remark and in the end died of a broken heart.

23. Ghost Versus Man

In the fourth year of the Qianlong reign I was studying in the same studio with Li Yunju and Huo Yangzhong, both from Dongguang County. One evening we started to argue about the existence of ghosts. Li Yunju thought there were ghosts, but Huo Yangzhong disagreed. At this Li's servant spoke, "There are strange things in this world that I would not think possible had I not experienced them myself. One day, when I walked past the graveyard in front of the town-god temple, I stepped on a coffin and crushed it. In a dream that night the town-god had me brought to him and told me that someone had sued me for damaging his house. I knew it was about the broken coffin, and I tried to defend myself, 'It was his fault to have built his house on the road, and I didn't damage it on purpose.' 'But I didn't build my house on the road,' said the ghost. 'It was the road that encroached on my house.' With a smile the town-god said to me, 'As everyone uses that road, you are not to blame for taking it. But you were the only one who damaged his house, for which you must be held responsible. You should pay him some paper money in compensation.' Then he added, 'A ghost cannot repair his coffin himself. You can put a plank of wood on it and cover it up with earth.' The following day I covered up the coffin and burned some paper money just as the town-god had told me. I saw a whirlwind carrying the ashes away. Then one evening I again walked past the spot, when someone called me to go over and rest for a while. I recognized the voice of the ghost and took to my heels. He roared with laughter, like an owl hooting. It still gives me goosebumps to remember it."

After listening to the story Huo Yangzhong said to Li Yunju, "You have a servant to speak up for you, and two voices are certainly louder than one, but I simply cannot believe in other people's experience as if it were my own." To this Li retorted, "Suppose you were to try a case. Would you believe nothing but what you saw with your own eyes? Or would you have to get information from other people? It would be impossible for you to see everything with your own eyes, but by getting information from others, you would be treating their experience as if it were your own. What would you do then?" Looking at each other, both men chuckled and dropped the debate.

24. Death of a Monk

A monk left Guangdong for Taiwan to offer his service to Zheng Chenggong, who was then ruling the island in defiance of the central government. Skilled in martial arts, the monk could sit down and have a man armed with a broadsword hack away on his bare arms, which would remain unharmed as if they were made of stone. He also knew a lot about military strategies and could talk very eloquently on the topic. As Zheng was eagerly enlisting men of talents, he treated the monk with great courtesy and deference. As time went by the monk grew increasingly arrogant, something Zheng found hard to bear. He also suspected the monk was a spy. This made him want to eliminate the monk, but he did not know if it could be done. At this Zheng's chief general Liu Guoxuan said, "If you really want to be rid of him, count on me to handle it."

Liu called on the monk and, after chatting amiably for a while, asked abruptly, "You are a highly accomplished monk, but do you still feel stirred by the sight of beautiful women?" The monk replied,

27

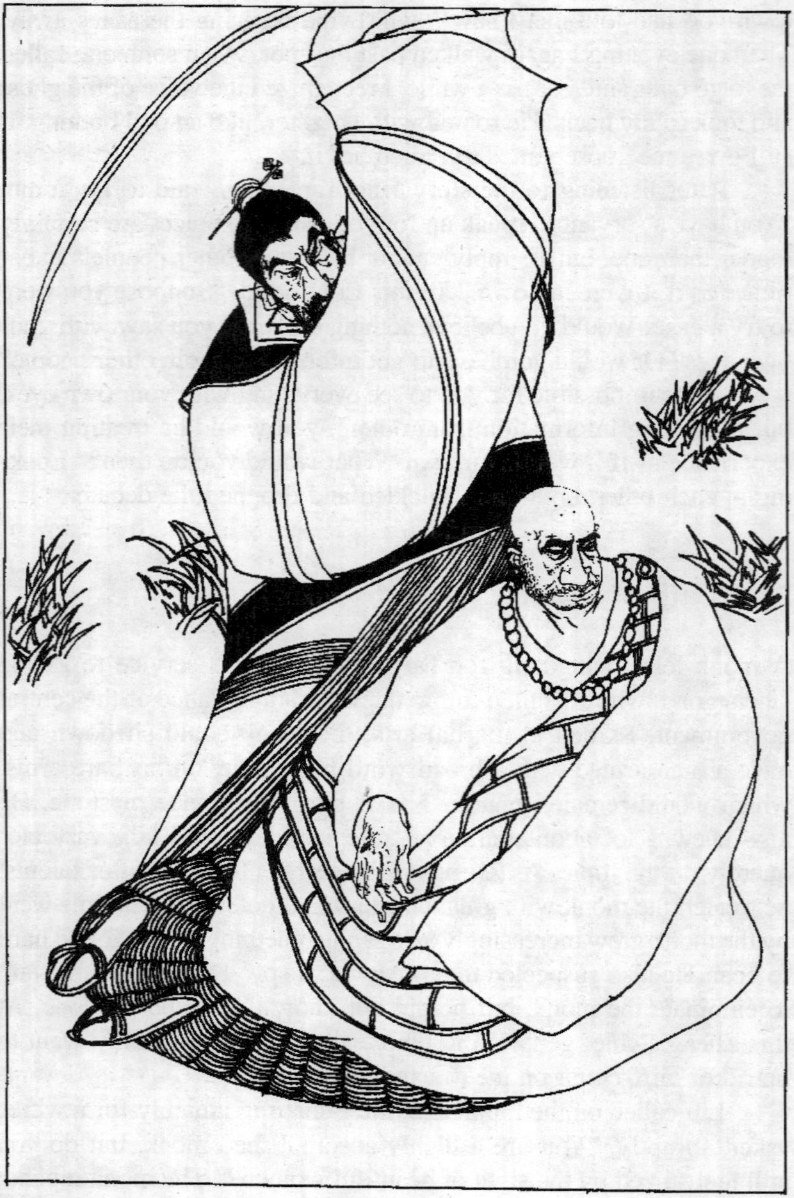

"I have long lost interest in such things." In a joking tone Liu suggested, "Let me test your attainments in this respect and make the others admire you even more." He sent for a dozen young lads and beautiful girls, who put beddings and pillows on the floor, then proceeded to undress and make love with wild abandon, their lascivious air utterly bewitching. For quite a long time the monk went on chatting away oblivious to the scene, then suddenly closed his eyes. Liu Guoxuan quickly drew his sword and with a sweep cut off the monk's head. He explained afterward, "The monk did not have supernatural powers but was merely good at strengthening himself by manipulating his vital force. When the mind is calm, the vital force will become concentrated; when the mind is disturbed, the vital force will disperse. At first the monk kept his eyes open because his mind remained unperturbed. When he shut his eyes, I knew he was trying to regain his lost composure and would be unable to resist my sword." His analysis was sound and brilliant. It is not surprising that the rebel troops commanded by such a man were able to overrun Taiwan for over a dozen years.

25. Ghost-Chasing Strategy

Mr. Xu Nanjin of Nanpi County, a fearless man, was once studying in a temple where he shared a room with a friend. At midnight the north wall was suddenly lit up with two lamps. Looking closely, he found the lamps to be the eyes on a man's face as large as a dustpan. While his friend trembled in fear, Xu threw a coat over his shoulders and slowly sat up. "I wanted to read, but my candle burned out a moment ago. It's so nice for you to come." Sitting with his back to the wall, he picked up a book to read aloud. He finished but a few pages when the light from the eyes gradually faded. He knocked on the wall and called out, but the ghost did not come back.

Another evening Xu went to the toilet followed by a servant boy carrying a lamp. All of a sudden the same face emerged from the ground to grin at them. The boy was so scared that he fell on the ground and dropped the lamp, which Xu picked up and put on the ghost's head. "I was looking for a stand for the lamp," he said. "How nice for you to come!" When the ghost looked up at him without moving, he said, "You can go anywhere you want, but you have chosen to come to the toilet. This could not have been accidental. I must not disappoint you." He picked up a filthy paper to smear on its mouth. The ghost vomited, blew out the lamp with a few wild roars, then vanished, never to emerge again. Mr. Xu once remarked, "Ghosts and goblins do exist, and I have met them on rare occasions. But they never frighten me, for when I look back I find nothing on my conscience."

26. A Ghost-Hermit

In the Ming dynasty a man named Song went deep into the mountains in Xi County in search of a well-located burial ground. A storm was rising at nightfall when he saw a cave and went over there to take shelter. "There is a ghost inside," a voice came out of the cave. "Please do not enter." "But why are you in the cave?" asked Song. "The ghost is me," came the reply. When Song asked to see the ghost, it said, "If we should meet face to face, my *yin*-energy would encroach upon your *yang*-energy, and you would shiver with cold. Let's speak to each other from a distance. Keep yourself warm by building a fire at the opening of the cave."

Song did as he was told, then asked, "You must have a tomb, so why are you staying here?" The ghost replied, "I used to be a county magistrate in Emperor Shenzong's reign. When I grew tired of the endless deception, scheming, and rivalry among the officials, I quit and returned to my home village. After death I got permission from the god of the nether regions never to be reborn again into the human world. With what wealth and rank I deserved in my next incarnation transferred to the underworld, I was made an official there. But I failed to foresee that the official circles in the underworld abounded likewise in contentions, intrigues and pitfalls. Finally I resigned from my post and returned to my tomb. But many ghosts lived nearby; they kept coming and going and raising no end of a racket, so I left my tomb in disgust and moved into this cave. Though it is a forlorn place assailed by wind and rain all the year round, life is blissful compared with the hardships and frustrations I suffered in my official career. So I go on living utterly alone in this uninhabited mountain, oblivious to the passage of time. I can't remember the last time I saw a ghost, much less the last time I saw a man. I was happy at last to be rid of all worries and enjoy a carefree existence. Unfortunately this is no longer an untraversed area. Tomorrow morning I will move away, and you need not call on me again." The ghost stopped talking and would not disclose his name. Song happened to have some ink and a writing brush with him, so he wrote two huge characters, "Ghost-Hermit," at the opening of the cave before making off.

27. The Capture of a Robber

Qi Shunting was a fierce robber who could cut down his opponent from a distance by throwing a dagger tied to a rope by the handle. In order to expand his stable, he forced a neighbor named Zhang Qi to sell his house. A servant was sent to threaten Zhang, saying, "Get out without delay, or something terrible will happen to you!" Zhang had no choice but to flee home with his wife and daughter. Not knowing where to go, he went into a temple to pray, "I have become homeless because of a robber's persecution. I will plant this wooden stick before the altar and let go. Whichever direction it points to, I will make my way there." As the fallen stick pointed to the northeast, the family begged their way to the port city of Tianjin, where Zhang married his daughter to a so-called "salt-man" who made salt by boiling sea-water. She became his assistant in salt-making, and in this way managed to support the family.

Some three to four years later someone reported Qi Shunting to the government about his robbery of military supplies. When some soldiers came to arrest him, Qi fled at night under the cover of wind and rain. As a fellow robber was then working on a commercial ship in Tianjin, Qi decided to join him and escape by sea. On his way there he took cover in the daytime and traveled at night, feeding on stolen fruits and melons. One night he was feeling hungry and thirsty when he saw in the distance a house with the light on. He went over and knocked on the door. A young woman came out, stared at him for a long time, then shouted at the top of her voice, "Here is Qi Shunting!" It turned out that the official notice offering a reward for his capture was already put out in Tianjin. At the shout many salt-men rushed over, and Qi, who was bare-handed, was caught without a fight. The young woman was none other than Zhang Qi's daughter. If Qi Shunting had not driven Zhang Qi from his hometown a few years before, no one in Tianjin would have recognized him in his disguise, and he would have been able to sail safely away, the place where he got caught being only a few li from the coast.

28. A Well-Earned Libation

Qin Eryan, a hired hand, was driving a cart from Lijiawa village to the town of Huai when he came across a man shooting birds with a musket. The gunshots stampeded the horses. In his panic Qin fell out of the cart and landed right before the wheels. "This is the end," he told himself, but the horses halted abruptly. On his return in the evening, he bought wine for a celebration and told others the story of his narrow escape. Just then a voice said outside the window, "Do you think the horses stopped all by themselves? It was the two of us who stopped them by seizing their muzzles." When Qin rushed out, there was no one in sight. The next day he went to the spot where he had fallen from the cart and offered wine to the two ghosts. My father commented on the incident, "Should all ghosts try to earn an offering in this way, there would be no reason for us to detest them!"

29. An Ox Saves Its Master

The story took place at the beginning of the Yongzheng reign. A peasant of Lijiawa village by the family name of Dong lost his father, who left behind a lame ox. Dong wanted to sell the ox to a butcher, but it ran away and lay down in front of Dong's father's grave. Dong pulled at its muzzle and whipped it, but the beast dug its heels in, lowing and wagging its tail. Gradually a crowd gathered there to watch. An old man named Liu suddenly beat the ox with his staff, looking angry. "His father fell into the river — so what? It would have been nice to let him sink under the waves and end up in some fish's stomachs! But you were so meddlesome you rescued him and made him live another dozen years. He needed to be fed when alive and treated when sick, and at death he left behind this grave which needs a sweeping and sacrifice every year. You have created endless troubles for his offsprings, and the butcher's knife is exactly what you deserve for your crime. What's the use of bellowing like this?" Apparently Dong's father had once fallen into the river and would have been drowned had not the ox leapt in after him. Then he seized the ox's tail and struggled his way onto the bank. It was the first time that Dong was told of the incident. Filled with shame and regret, he led the ox home at once. When the ox died of illness a few months later, Dong wept and buried it.

30. A Ghost Story Told by a Ghost

A scholar sailing on the Poyang Lake had the boat moored at the end of the day to take a walk under the moonlight and relish the coolness of the night. At a wineshop several men introduced themselves to him and claimed to be his fellow townsmen. He sat down for a drink, and they chatted and told ghost stories, all of which were rather strange and exotic. Then one of them said, "You all told fantastic tales, but none can compare with my experience. I once went to the capital and stayed at a flower grower's house in Fengtai district to avoid the bustling noise of that big city. One day I met a man dressed like a scholar, and struck up a conversation with him. When I told him I enjoyed the luxuriant trees and blooming flowers there but detested the ghosts haunting the graveyard, he said, 'Not all ghosts are loathsome; though some are coarse, others are refined. On a trip to the West Hills I met a man who talked about poetry with me. He quoted quite a few exquisite lines from his poems. For example: The remote hills have a late sunrise, /And the ancient temple in early autumn. Another example: As the bell's ringing spreads across the village, / The houses are lit with candles. I was about to ask where he was staying when we heard the jingling bells from some caravans in the distance, and the man vanished before my eyes. Would you find that ghost detestable?' Impressed by the scholar's pleasing address, I invited him to sit down for a cup of wine. 'I am honored enough to have caused you no aversion,' he said. 'How dare I bring myself to drink your wine?' With a chuckle he vanished. Only then did I realize the man who had just told me a ghost story was himself a ghost."

"This is the weirdest thing I've ever heard," the scholar said. Then he went on jokingly, "Come to think of it, it is not unlikely to find one weird thing hiding behind another. Who knows if those telling ghost stories here are not themselves ghosts?" At his words all the others changed countenance. With a breeze sweeping across the room, the lights dimmed, and the men turned into thin smoke that quickly scattered and drifted away.

31. Reap the Whirlwind

A few tumbledown houses on Yuhuangmiao road outside Fengyi Gate, locked and kept vacant for a long time, were said to have a fox living inside. A scholar from Jiangxi who had passed the provincial examination arrived in the capital with a few friends to take the metropolitan examination. After they failed, they decided to stay in the capital to review their lessons until the examination opened again. They took lodgings near the haunted houses because the place was very quiet. One day the scholar saw a lovely young woman standing in the porch. An intrepid young man, he was not at all afraid though he knew this must be the fox-woman. At dusk he went to bow before the ill-reputed houses and made a few lascivious remarks. That night he heard rustling in the dark. Knowing it was the fox-woman, he put out his arm and pulled her onto his bed. The woman threw herself into his arms, and they made love passionately until he was utterly exhausted. When the rising moon shone in through the window, the scholar found himself holding a gray-haired, dark-faced old hag. "Who are you?" he asked in dismay. Looking unashamed, she replied, "I am an old fox who used to live in the gate tower. My mistress disliked me for being hoggish and lazy, so she drove me to the broken house on this street. I lived alone for many years and no one ever took notice of me. Then you come along and take a fancy in me, so I have put my coyness aside and dedicated myself to you." Enraged, the scholar slapped her face hard and looked around for a rope, intending to tie her up and give her a severe beating. Awakened by the grappling noise, his friends rushed over to his assistance. The old fox freed herself from his grip and escaped by breaking through a window.

The next evening the old woman sat under the eaves and called to the scholar in a gentle voice. As he began to swear, a flying tile struck him on the head. Another night he was going to bed when he found her stark naked inside the mosquito net, waving and smiling at him. He drew his sword to stab her, and she went away weeping. For fear that the fox would hassle him nonstop, the scholar quickly found another residence for himself. When he was taking leave in his carriage, the charming young woman he had seen several days before walked out of the house. He immediately sent a servant to find out about her. She turned out to be the landlord's niece. A few days before she had come out of the house to buy rouge and powder.

32. The Wrong Woman

An official-in-waiting staying at an inn in the capital to await appointment once saw a young woman through a gap in the back wall. Her clothes were worn but quite clean and neat, and her fair visage stirred his heart. The innkeeper's mother was a refined woman in her fifties who had once worked as a maid for a big family. She often assisted her son in receiving and attending to guests. Thinking she might be able to help, the official-in-waiting gave her some money and asked her to arrange a rendezvous with the young woman. "She must have moved in only recently, for I do not remember seeing her before," said the old lady. "Let me test the water for you, and don't count on my success." More than ten days later she had news for him at last. "I have settled it for you. This is a woman from a good family, but poverty has forced her to accept your offer. For fear of being discovered, she will come only late at night when the moon is not bright. You must not have any lit candle in the room, chat with her, or do anything that might attract the attention of your servants or other guests. Allow her to leave as soon as the bell rings in the morning. Two taels of silver will be enough for each night you spend with her." He agreed to all this and began meeting the woman every night.

This went on for nearly a month until one night a neighbor's house caught fire. As he scrambled out of bed, his servants swarmed into the room to remove his chests. In the frenzy someone pulled forcefully at the mattress on the bed, and a naked woman thudded to the floor. To everyone's dismay and amusement, it was the innkeeper's mother. Matchmakers in the capital were known to be very crooked. When an official-in-waiting wanted to buy a concubine, the matchmaker would often show him a pretty girl but replace her with a plain one at the wedding ceremony. If the bridegroom discovered the fraud in time, he might bring a suit against the matchmaker. In some cases, the bride entered the room with her head covered by red cloth, then turned her back to the lamp and put a fan before her face. The bridegroom who did not discover the deception until after the wedding night often chose to accept his ill luck. The innkeeper's mother was therefore following an established tradition when she substituted herself for a young woman. However, after further inquiry among the neighbors, the official-in-waiting learned that the pretty young woman he had seen was not among the local residents. "He must have met a demon," someone suggested. Another one said, "That was a prostitute hired by the old woman to trap him."

33. The Broom-Fiend

On New Year's Eve a man selling flowers made of ricepaper pith knocked on the gate of a village house in Qing County, shouting, "Why do you keep me waiting so long? Where's the money for the flowers?" The head of the family asked around, but no one had bought any. The pedlar insisted that a little girl had walked into the house after taking some flowers. The argument was interrupted by an old woman's cry, "How queer! There are some flowers planted on the old broom in the toilet!" When the broom was brought to him, the pedlar found the flowers planted on it were exactly those taken by the little girl. The broom was thrown into the fire at once. It made some moaning noises as a stream of blood oozed out. Since it had learned to assume human form, this broom fiend might as well go on cultivating its energy, yet it chose to make trouble and destroy itself. Many people act likewise. They are eager to show off before they accomplish anything, and throw caution and modesty to the wind if they have a little success. These people rival the broom-fiend in stupidity!

34. A Ghost Beyond the Wheel of Reincarnation

Wang Kunxia, a Taoist priest, once took a pleasure trip to Jiahe County in early autumn, when the weather was very pleasant. Strolling by the lake, he got to a deserted garden with a thick growth of trees but no trace of human presence. After a walk around he grew sleepy and dozed off. In his dream a man dressed in ancient robes bowed to him with clasped hands. "It is rare to have a distinguished visitor in this remote jungle. I am so delighted to see you. Please don't shun me just because I belong to a different realm." Knowing the other was a ghost, Wang asked where he had come from. "My family name is Zhang, and I am a native of Leiyang," replied the ghost. "I drifted to this place in the Yuan dynasty and was later buried here. The place suits me well, so I have no intention to return to my homeland. During my stay here the garden has had over a dozen different owners."

"Why do you prefer to be a ghost when most people cling to life and fear death?" Wang asked. "Whether dead or alive, one remains the same in his heart," said the ghost, "so does the world we live in. A living person can see mountains, rivers, the moon and other sights; so can a ghost. A living person can get to a hilltop to compose a poem; so can a ghost. Why should ghosts be considered inferior to men? Moreover, there are places too remote or perilous for men to go, but not so for ghosts. There are awe-inspiring sights in secluded places which men have no chance to see, but ghosts can feast their eyes on them in the dead of the night. Therefore ghosts are actually superior to men in some respects. A man clings to life because he cannot eschew temporal desires and finds it hard to part with his wife and children. On entering the nether world he will feel unbearably lonely like a high official sent back to his home village after losing his office. But there are people who have always lived in the countryside. They are content to dig their own well and till their own land, and find nothing to feel sad about."

"The cycle of death and rebirth is dictated by nature," said Wang. "How did you free yourself from it?" The ghost replied, "A ghost chooses to be reborn, just as a man chooses to take office — it is an act of one's own volition. A ghost can avoid rebirth just as a man can decline to take office, and the gods will not intervene." "Since you are so fond of sightseeing, you must have composed a lot of poems," Wang remarked. "I chant a line or two when in the mood," the ghost said, "but I seldom complete a poem. Afterward I often forget the lines and do not bother to cast my mind back. There are only four or five poems that I can remember and submit to your criticism and advice." Then he intoned, "The sun sets behind the vacant hill, / Shrouding the world in the shades of dusk." Wang uttered an involuntary cry of admiration. At this moment a loud noise awakened him. He looked to the lake and saw some fishermen yelling greetings to one another. He closed his eyes again and leaned back on a tree, but was unable to return to his dream.

35. Taoist Magic

None of the many books on Taoist magic give the true formula, which consists of a few pithy sentences. Mr. Song Qingyuan of Dezhou once visited a friend who put him up for the night. "Let me invite you to watch a show on this fine moonlit night," offered the friend. He took a dozen stools and put them in the courtyard in alternate directions. Then they sat down in the front hall to drink wine by candlelight. In the dead of night a man climbed over the wall into the yard and began circling in front of the steps. Whenever he came to a stool, he paused and climbed over with great difficulty. He kept moving back and forth among the stools until he dropped on the ground totally exhausted. By this time it was already daybreak.

Song's friend led the man into the hall and asked where he had come from. Kowtowing, the man answered, "I am a thief. After I jumped into the courtyard, I saw short walls all around me. I climbed over one wall after another but could not get to the end of them. I turned to leave, but again there were endless walls ahead. I was too exhausted to fight when you came to catch me, and now I place myself at your mercy." The friend laughed and sent the thief away. Turning to Song he said, "Yesterday I divined that a thief would pay me a visit tonight, so I prepared this trick for him." "What magic was that?" asked Song. "It was Taoist magic," replied his friend. "An ordinary man will usually harm himself after learning it. Since you are upright and prudent, I can teach you if you are interested." When Song declined the offer, his friend sighed deeply, "Those willing to learn cannot be taught, and those suitable to be taught are unwilling to learn. Will this become a lost art someday?"

36. Jiang Sanmang Tries to Catch Ghosts

Jiang Sanmang, who lived in Jingcheng, was a headstrong, dauntless man. When someone told him the story of Song Dingbo, a native of Nanyang who had sold a ghost, he could hardly contain his excitement. "Now I know you can catch a ghost and sell it! If I catch a ghost every night, make it change into a goat, then sell it to some butcher the next morning, there will be enough money for meat and wine for the day!" From then on he prowled the graveyard every night like a hare hunter carrying a stick on his shoulder and a rope in his hand, but no ghost ever appeared. Even when he went to places reputed to be haunted and feigned a drunken sleep to lure the ghosts, none fell for the bait. One night he saw some will-o'-the-wisps in the woods and rushed over in high delight, but they scattered in all directions before he got there. Again he returned home in disappointment. Still empty-handed at the end of a month, Jiang gave up. Generally speaking, a ghost bullies a man by taking advantage of the latter's fear. Since Jiang Sanmang was convinced that he could catch ghosts, his opinion of them must very low and his courage was great enough to triumph over the ghosts. As a result, ghosts shunned him in fear.

37. A Fatal Enchantress

Shen Tiechan, a native of Yangqu County, was made a magistrate after passing the provincial examination in the twenty-fifth year of the Qianlong reign. While serving an office in Shaanxi on probation in the autumn of the fifty-fifth year of the Qianlong reign, he wrote me a sad farewell letter. I found its meaning difficult to decipher, for his words were confused and equivocal. Since he was not a man of thwarted ambitions, I could not think of an explanation. Soon afterward I was informed of his death. Later I managed to find out what had happened to him. He had been taken ill for several months in Xian. After recovery he took a hunting trip in the mountain. On his return he kept seeing, even with his eyes closed, two round objects rotating like windmills in front of him. This went on for a few days until the two balls suddenly broke apart and out came two maids who claimed to have brought him an invitation from a fairy. Shen followed them in spite of himself. They got to a splendid jade palace, where a matchless beauty offered herself to him, but he declined, saying he was not used to living in a place like that. Looking offended, the woman sent him away with a sweep of her hand, and he woke up with a start. More than a month later he again saw the two balls breaking up in front of him. The two maids came out and led him to a newly built residence, which he found to be quiet, peaceful and very pleasant. When the same beauty proposed to him once more, he succumbed to temptation and made love with her. He began to meet her frequently in his dream, and then she visited him even during the day and forbade him to meet with his friends. His health went from bad to worse. After taking some red pills prescribed by a magician named Li, he vomited and died. His farewell letter to me had been written during his illness.

Shen Tiechan was a man of rare intelligence. A good poet and calligrapher with charming manners, he had many friends and his fame spread far and wide. In middle-age he became obsessed with the quest for immortality; consequently something bizarre took place and brought about his inexplicable death. Specters are engendered by human behavior, and phantoms emerge from man's heart. It is a great pity that such a man of outstanding talents and lofty ambitions should have lost his life in the pursuit of immortality.

38. A Ghost Matchmaker

On the Qingming Festival an old woman named Meng went to sacrifice before her ancestral grave. On her way back she felt thirsty and went to a nearby house to find water. Standing under a tree was a young girl with an alluring figure and graceful carriage. The girl fetched water for Meng to drink and asked her to sit down for a rest, her attitude quite warm and affectionate. Meng then inquired after her parents and siblings. Impressed by the girl's fluent answer, she said jokingly, "Are you engaged? If you don't have a fiancé yet, let me be your matchmaker." The girl blushed and ran back into the house. Though Meng called after her, she would not come out again.

It was already getting dark, so Meng left without saying good-bye.

Half a year later someone visited the old woman with a proposal of marriage for her son. She was overjoyed to discover the would-be bride was the girl she had met on the Qingming Festival, and did her best to bring about the marriage. After the wedding Meng patted the girl on the shoulder and said, "You have grown quite a bit since we met a few months ago." Surprised, the girl did not know how to reply. After further inquiry Meng learned that the girl had lost her mother at ten and stayed for the next six years with her paternal grandfather, returning to her own family only after her engagement. That means she had spent the previous Qingming Festival in her grandfather's house. This girl came from a poor, small family. If Meng had not been impressed with her brightness and modesty, she might not have agreed to the match. Apparently a ghost had helped bring about the match in the girl's disguise. It is not known who the ghost was or why it wanted to bring about a happy marriage. This is one of the cases which defy the analysis of everyday logic.

39. A Broken Mirror Joined Together

In the fourth or fifth year of the Yongzheng reign a family of roving beggars came to Cui village. The couple, both terminally ill, waved a paper to passers-by saying they wanted to sell their small daughter as a maid and buy two coffins with the money. My grandmother paid for the couple's burial, let the girl stay and named her Liangui. According to the paper her father was named Zhang Li and her mother Huang, but their hometown was not mentioned. When asked, the couple had been too weak to speak. Liangui said their home was somewhere in Shandong, close to an official thoroughfare frequented by carriages of high officials. They had walked for over a month to get here. She had no idea in which county their home was located, but she remembered that the previous year she had been betrothed to the son of the Hu family living across the street. Later the Hu family had left home to become vagrant beggars, but she did not know where they had gone.

More than ten years went by with no visitor ever coming from Liangui's hometown, and she was married to our horse keeper, Liu Deng. Liu told us he had been born in the Hu family of Xintai County in Shandong. Upon the death of his parents he was adopted by the Liu family, and Liu became his new family name. When small he had heard his parents talking about his engagement, but he did not know the name of his fiancée. Liu Deng had Hu as his original family name, the official thoroughfare passed through Xintai County, and it would take about a month for roving beggars to travel from Xintai to our village — all of this coincided with Liangui's story. We suspected it to be a case of a broken mirror joined together, though there was no more than circumstantial evidence. Someone commented, "With a few embellishments the story could make a poetic drama. Unfortunately the heroine, who is gluttonous, lazy and thick-headed, does not lend herself to any embellishment at all." Another one retorted, "Even history records are full of exaggerations that stretch the truth, not to mention poetic dramas. *Romance in the Western Tower* depicts Mu Suhui as a surpassing beauty, but a friend of mine's grandfather actually saw her when he was a child. He described her as plump and short — just an ordinary woman. Therefore most of the so-called matchless beauties in those poetic dramas had to be fictitious. Though that maid is coarse and slow, would it be difficult for her to transform into an enchantress on stage if someone should write poetry and music for her? Judging by your viewpoint, you simply take books too seriously."

40. Pride Goes Before the Fall

When I was a boy of seven or eight my family had a servant named Zhao Ping, who prided himself on his audacity. Shi Yang, an old servant, waved his hand at Zhao disapprovingly. "Don't behave willfully just because you are bold. I made the same mistake and paid for it. When I was a hotheaded youth I once went to spend the night alone in an abandoned house said to be haunted. Close to midnight the ceiling cracked open, and a man's arm dropped on the floor and began bouncing about. A moment later there came another arm, two legs, a torso, and finally the head. They were bouncing all over the room as nimbly as a monkey, and I was too dismayed to do anything. Soon afterward these got together to merge into a man, his body a bloody mess of sword cuts and club wounds, and his hand reaching straight for my throat. Luckily it was a summer night, so the window was left open. I jumped out of the room through the window and ran away for dear life. That incident gave me such a fright that I have never dared to sleep alone again. If you go on parading your boldness like this, you will meet a rival someday." Zhao Ping was not convinced. "The mistake was yours. Why didn't you grab one of these body parts to prevent them from merging into a man?" Later Zhao Ping was walking home at night, drunk, when a host of specters accosted him and threw him into a cesspool. He was nearly drowned.

41. The Boat-Fiend

This happened in my maternal grandfather's mansion. Something was often seen by the family to dance in front of the house. If anyone went close to it, the thing would take to its heels. One moonlit night they watched it through a crack in the window and found it dressed in green and shaped like a big clumsy turtle, with four limbs but no head. Several hefty servants were dispatched one day to lie in ambush by the gate carrying knives and clubs. The moment the demon made its appearance in the evening, they rushed out to catch it. The demon staggered to the end of the staircase and came to a halt. When a lamp was brought over, they saw a silver boat leaning on the wall. It was wrapped in a piece of green brocade and had four wheels. The boat used to be a toy for the children during the family's better days. Apparently the fiend had the brocade for its green dress and the wheels for its limbs. It was then melted into more than thirty taels of silver. An old servant woman said, "When I was young, it was suddenly found missing, and all the servants about my age received a flogging. I don't know who stole it and put it here. After a long time it somehow turned into a demon."

42. A Dispute on Abortion

One evening a doctor, a very cautious man, was called on by an old woman wanting to buy aborticide with a pair of gold bracelets. The startled doctor flatly refused. The next evening the old woman came back offering two pearl hairpins in addition to the bracelets. The doctor, astounded, told her to go away in a stern voice. Over half a year later he dreamed that a guard from the nether world came to seize him, saying someone had accused him of homicide. In the underworld he saw a woman with loosened hair and a red towel tightened around her neck. Tearfully she described how the doctor had refused to help her induce abortion, so that she had been forced to hang herself. "Drugs are used to save people's lives," the doctor said. "How can I use them to kill for a profit? Moreover, you died because you had committed adultery. What did that have to do with me?" The young woman answered, "When I sent someone to buy drug from you, the baby had not yet taken shape in my womb. An abortion would have saved my life by removing a senseless lump of blood. Because I did not get the drug, I was compelled to give birth. As a result, my baby son was strangled to death and endured great pain for nothing, and I was forced to hang myself. You wanted to save one life but ended up killing two. You are the last person in the world I would call innocent!"

After hearing them out, the official sighed and said to the woman, "In your argument you stressed expediency while the doctor maintained the correct principle. Since the Song dynasty many people have chosen to stick to principle with no regard to expediency; why should the doctor alone be held responsible for it? Let's leave the matter at that." With this he banged the desk with a wooden slab, and the doctor woke up with a start.

43. Near-Death Experience

Yi Shi, a clerk in the Hanlin Academy, had taken part in the expedition to Yili. In a fierce battle to break out an encirclement he passed out after suffering seven wounds from the spear. Two days later he regained consciousness, then galloped for a whole day, finally catching up with the troops. When Bo Xizhai and I worked together in the Hanlin Academy, we noticed Yi Shi's wounds and asked where he had got them. Thus he told us about his extraordinary experience.

After being seriously injured, he had felt no pain but very sleepy instead. Waking up a moment later, he found his spirit had left his body. He looked around to see nothing but sand and dust blown by the wind and could not tell the direction. It suddenly occurred to him that he had left his family in dire circumstances and his son was not yet grown up. Overcome with sadness, he felt like a fallen leaf drifting in the wind, soon to be blown away. Then he thought how unworthy it was to die like that and vowed to turn into a demon to go on fighting the enemy. The moment the thought came into his mind, he felt like a towering iron pillar firm and unshakable in the wind. After lingering for a while, he decided to rush to a hilltop to find out the enemy's whereabouts. Suddenly, as if awakened from a dream, he found himself back in his injured body lying in blood. Bo Xizhai sighed deeply after hearing the story. "According to what you have told us, I think there is nothing fearful in dying on the battlefield. It is quite easy to be a loyal subject and die a martyr. Why don't we all act in that way?"

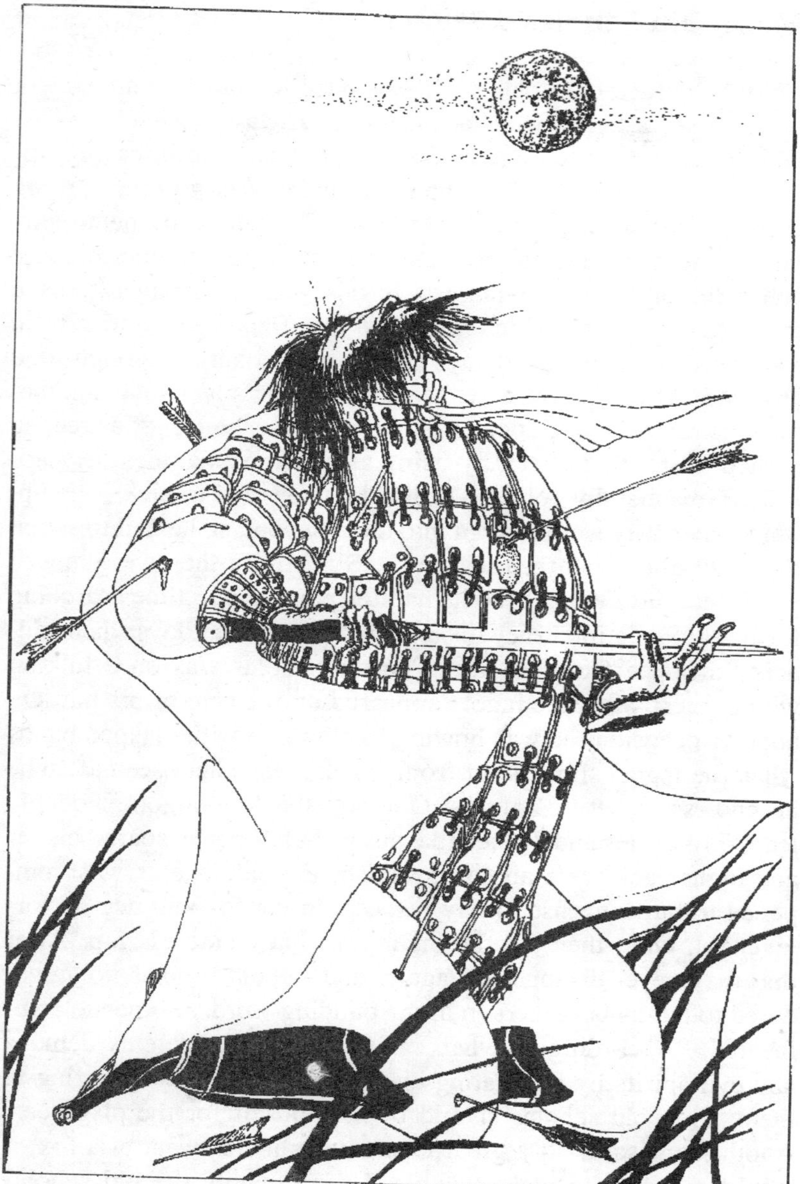

44. An Old Scholar's Savings

An old Confucian scholar in Shanxi once walked past an ancient tomb. When a fellow traveler mentioned it was dwelled by a fox, he blurted out some words of abuse, but nothing unusual happened to him at the time. The old scholar was good at cutting corners. He had neither a fur coat in winter nor any hemp garment in summer. He ate no meat and drank no tea, and his wife and children often went hungry. In this way he managed to save forty taels of silver, which he melted into four ingots and kept in a secret place. He was always saying he had barely enough food at home. After he swore at the fox, his four silver ingots sometimes emerged on the roof of the house or at the top of a tree, so he had to get them back by using a ladder. Sometimes they appeared in a marshy pond, so he had to wade over to pick them up. Sometimes they were thrown into the cesspool, so he had to scoop them out and wash them carefully. Sometimes they were moved to another hiding place, so he had to spend a long time searching for them. Sometimes they disappeared for several days, then suddenly dropped from the sky. The old scholar was once talking with a guest when the ingots appeared on the hem of his hat. On another occasion, he was bowing to someone with clasped hands when the ingots slipped out from his sleeves. There seemed to be an endless variety of antics. One day the four ingots suddenly leapt into the air and danced like butterflies. As they soared higher and higher and were about to vanish, the old scholar was compelled to burn incense to pay respects to the fox and beg its forgiveness. Only then did the ingots fall back onto his lap. After that they never disappeared again, and the old scholar no longer dared to admonish others in high-sounding words. Someone commented, "According to what I have heard, one defeats demons and evil spirits by cultivating his own virtue, not by swearing at them. That old scholar should blame himself for the disgrace." Another one said, "If a great Confucian should swear at a fox, it would not dare to make trouble. Unfortunately the old scholar did not possess high morals in spite of his solemn airs." "A truly great Confucian would never swear at anyone unprovoked," commented a third man. "It was precisely because he lacked in moral cultivation that the old scholar put on such a belligerent front." I think his words hit the bull's-eye.

45. Abduction by an Old Woman

A person forced into an impasse may hit upon a most unusual solution. When something seems to defy rational explanation, there must be a reason behind it. To deal with such a case one should rise to the occasion and break away from old rules and conventions. In my hometown a few dozen women headed by an old woman stormed into a house in the neighboring village and abducted the daughter of that family. The old woman could not be seeking a quarrel, for the two families were not even acquainted. She could not be abducting the girl for a daughter-in-law, for she did not have a son. People in the area were all astonished, unable to think of an explanation. The girl's family reported the case to the county office, but when runners came to seize the old woman, she had fled with the girl to an unknown destination. Even her accomplices in the abduction were all gone.

Many people were taken to the yamen for interrogation until someone revealed the truth of the matter. The old woman used to have a son. When he was dying of illness, she put her hands over him and wept bitterly. "Maybe heaven wants you to die, but you have left me no grandson. Your late father will go hungry in the underworld because there's no one to offer him sacrifices." Moaning, her son told her, "I can't say it for sure, but you may yet have a grandson. I've had an affair with a girl in the neighboring village. She is now eight months pregnant. I am worried that her family may kill the baby when it is born." After her son's death the old woman kept muttering to herself for a dozen days, then suddenly abducted the girl. It was reasonable to suppose that she just wanted to save the baby.

49

On learning this, the county magistrate remarked, "In that case, there is no need to issue a wanted-notice. She will come back of her own accord in two or three months." The old woman did return in time with her grandson to give herself up at the county office. The magistrate, who did not consider her act a serious offense, sentenced her to a beating of the birch, which could be exempted if she paid a fine. The case had broken out without warning, the old woman acting with the swiftness of a thunderbolt. After abducting the girl, she had split up with the other women in four carriages, so that no one could find out which way she had taken. By keeping away from main roads and taking byways she had made it impossible for anyone to trail her. She set out in early morning and put up in the evening, never staying in the same place for over a day. Only after the girl had given birth did she rent a place to stay for a few days. In this way she had been able to prevent anyone from locating her hide-out. It was obvious that she had made her plan with great circumspection. On her return the girl was rejected by her parents, so she went on living with the old woman to bring up her son. She never got married. Because she was united with the old woman's son by an illicit affair instead of a legal marriage, she received no official recommendation for preserving her chastity after his death.

46. A Rogue Disguised as a Ghost

One moonlit night a young village woman and her husband's younger sister, who were both very pretty, slept under the eaves in the courtyard to enjoy the cool. Suddenly a red-haired, black-faced demon leapt out from the cattle pen and began dancing in a terrifying way, as if he wanted to swallow the women alive. The men in the house were all out keeping watch on crop fields and vegetable gardens, so the two young women were too frightened to utter a sound. The demon came up and raped them one by one. When he leapt up the short wall to get away, he suddenly screamed in horror and fell flat on the ground back in the yard. The two women waited, but the demon did not stir. Only then did they pluck up their courage to cry for help. When the neighbors hurried to the scene, the demon in the yard was found to be a young local bully in disguise, who still remained unconscious. There was another demon-like figure standing outside the wall, a pottery devil from the land-god temple. The onlookers all agreed that the land-god had manifested its power and decided to offer sacrifices before the altar the following day.

Just then a young man in the crowd burst out laughing. "Early every morning Zhang San walks down this road carrying manure on his shoulder pole, so I hauled a little devil from the land-god temple and put it here, just to give him a fright and get a good laugh. And this scoundrel pretending to be a ghost took this statue for a real ghost and dropped to the ground in terror. How can you interpret this as an intervention of the land-god?" An old man spoke up to refute him. "Since Zhang San carries manure down this road every day, why did it occur to you to play a trick on him today instead of on another day? Since there are many tricks you can play, why did you happen to carry this pottery figure here? Since it could be placed anywhere along this road, why did you happen to place it outside this house? There must have been divine guidance even though you were not aware of it yourself." Finding the old man's words reasonable, the onlookers pooled some money to offer sacrifices to the land-god. The young ruffian was carried home by his parents and died after lying in a coma for several days.

47. The Blood-Drop Test

A merchant in Shanxi, before leaving home to do business, had entrusted his household property to his younger brother. While away from his hometown he got married and had a son. Over a dozen years later his wife died, and he took his son home. Unwilling to give back the property entrusted to him, his younger brother claimed that his son was adopted and therefore not entitled to family inheritance. A dispute broke out between the two

51

brothers, who brought a suit to the county yamen. The magistrate was so muddle-headed that he did not order an investigation into the case. Instead, he adopted the ancient "blood-drop test" to determine the father-son relationship. Fortunately the blood-drop of the father merged with that of the son. The younger brother was give some strokes of the birch and driven out.

Refusing to accept the validity of the test, the younger brother used his own blood and that of his son's for a test, and indeed they did not merge. Using this as evidence, he declared that the county magistrate had made an unjust verdict. Disgusted with his greed and barbarity, the other villagers submitted a joint letter to the county office testifying that as his wife had committed adultery, the child was not his natural son, therefore their blood had not merged. They were unanimous in their claim, and the facts given were clear and unequivocal. When the alleged lover was brought in for an interrogation, he pleaded guilty. Overwhelmed with shame, the merchant's younger brother divorced his wife, drove away his son, and fled his hometown, so that all the family property came into the possession of the merchant. Everyone who heard the story clapped and cheered.

The blood-drop test began to be used to determine blood lineage as early as the Han dynasty. An old clerk once told me, "Under normal circumstances a man's blood-drop will indeed merge with that of his blood relations. But if on a winter day you put the utensil out in the snow to make it very cold, or if you rub the utensil with salt and vinegar in summer, the blood-drops will condense instantly in it, and even those from blood relations will not merge. Therefore the blood-drop test should not be relied on to judge a case." Nevertheless, if the county magistrate had not ordered a blood-drop test, the merchant's younger brother would not have appealed, and his wife's illicit affair would not have been uncovered. As there might have been divine intervention behind all this, we should make allowances for the county magistrate for adhering to an ancient method.

48. Mr. Shen's Encounter with a Fox

Mr. Shen Qianju, a native of Jingzhou, passed the provincial examination in the fifty-second year of the Kangxi reign just as my father did. He was mild in temperament and never flared up in anger, but he was also a forthright, proud gentleman. He always wore clothes made of coarse hemp and ate coarse meals. Occasionally, when a disciple gave him some meat, he would take it to the market to trade for beancurd. "It isn't that I want to seek fame by acting differently," he said. "I simply do not like to eat this." After taking the examination in Hejian, he rode a donkey on his way back and hired a young boy to hold the halter. When the boy got tired from walking, he would change places with him. Caught in a rain at dusk, they had to take shelter in a deserted temple, which had only one room. It was stripped of everything, and the floor was too dirty even to step on. Shen took down a door plank and lay down on it in front of the gate. At midnight he was awakened by a whisper in the temple. "I want to leave the temple to avoid you, but I can't get out with you blocking the gate." "With you in the room and me out at the gate, we won't disturb each other," Shen replied. "Why do you need to avoid me?" After a while the voice whispered again, "There should be a prudent reserve between a male and a female. You'd better let me get out." Shen said, "The reserve between the sexes is well maintained by keeping one inside and the other outside. It would not be convenient to let you out." With this he rolled over and went back to sleep. The next morning a villager was astonished to find him there. "In this temple lives a fox who occasionally comes out to seduce young men," he said. "Those who follow her inside will be attacked by bricks and tiles. Why were you able to pass the night here in safety?" When Shen told my father of the incident, he raised his head and chuckled, "Fancy that! A fox trying to seduce Shen Qianju! What a joke!" "You must be the last person in the world the fox-woman wanted to seduce," said my father in jest. "At the sight of your monstrous visage, she took you for an

53

unknown demon and ran as fast as her legs could carry her." From this incident one can get an idea of Mr. Shen's character.

49. Drink the Wine While You Can

Mr. Sun Duanren, who had a graceful, delicate writing style, was excessively fond of his wine glass. When intoxicated he could still write articles as usual. He was therefore compared to the great Tang poet Li Bai, who always enjoyed an overflow of poetic genius after a drinking bout. While in Yunnan Sun sat alone on a moonlit night to drink beside a bamboo grove. He saw a dim figure staring at the wine pot and wine cup with an avid look. Knowing it must be a ghost, Sun did not feel afraid. He covered the cup with his hand, saying, "I don't have much wine left today, so I can't invite you for a drink." At this the ghost drew back and vanished. After sobering up Sun regretted over what he had done. "No ordinary ghost would go around looking for wine," he said to himself. "And that ghost showed high regard for me when he came to drink with me. Why should I have disappointed him like that!" Then he bought three bowls of good wine and put them in the bamboo grove on a small table. When he went there the following day, the wine had not been touched. With a sigh he said, "That ghost is not only well-bred but also very proud. Because I treated him unkindly last time, he would not taste a single drop of my wine." A house adviser said to him, "Ghosts and deities can smell the fragrance of wine but cannot drink any." Sun sighed with deep feeling on hearing this, "In that case, I will drink wine to my heart's content while I am still alive rather than merely smell it when I become a ghost."

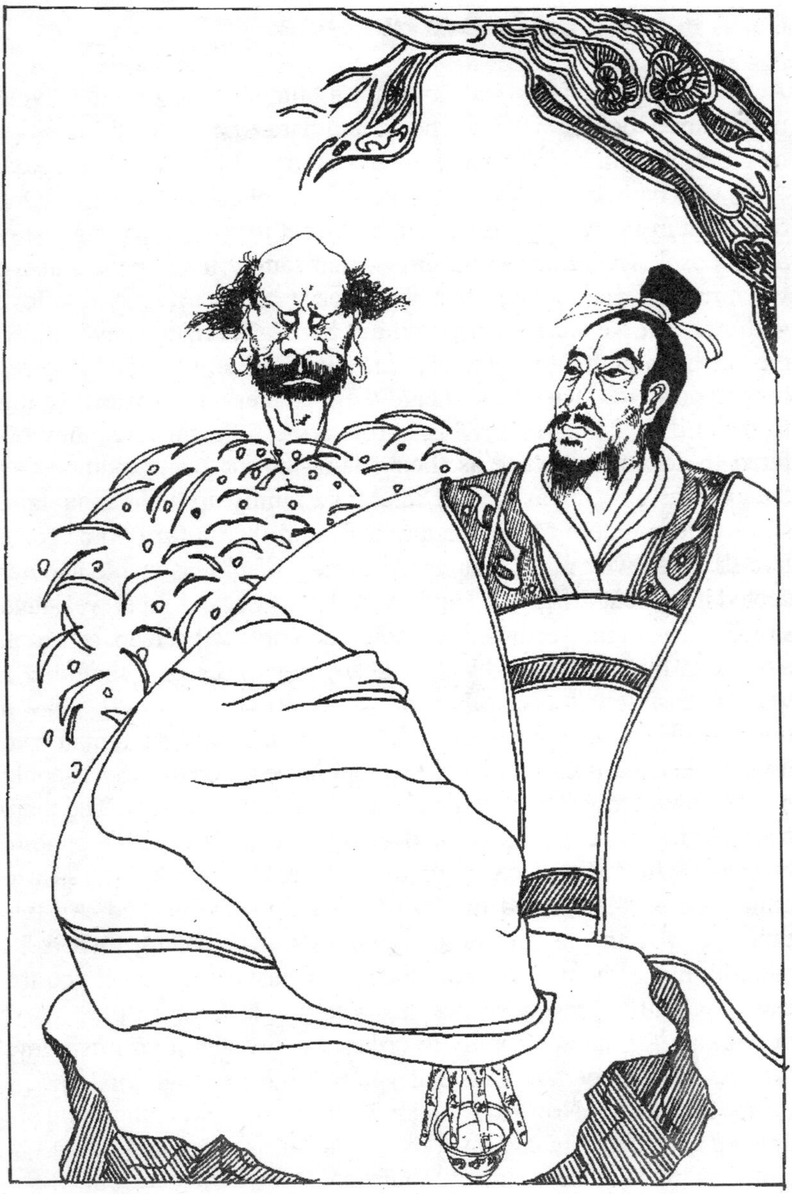

50. A Fox-Woman's Two Husbands

At the foot of the Shaohua Mountain a hunter found two men lying under a tree looking listless. They could barely get to their feet when he greeted them. "Why have you wandered to this place?" he asked. "We were both seduced by a fox-woman," replied one of them. "One day I lost my way in the mountain and went to request a night's stay at a house. A very attractive girl of that family made passes at me when no one was looking. Unable to resist her charms, I made love with her, but we were soon found out by her parents. They scolded me harshly and threatened to give me a beating, so I fell on my knees to beg for mercy. Then I overheard them chattering away as if trying to make a decision. To my big surprise the following day they offered to acknowledge me as their son-in-law on one condition: As the girl was working as a hired hand for a family up in the mountain, she would go there for a five-day shift and then return home for a five-day stay with me. I thought the arrangement reasonable and accepted it without difficulty. Half a year later I began to feel weak and sapped. One night I coughed so badly I couldn't fall asleep, so I took a walk in the woods. Suddenly I heard the voices of a man and a woman teasing with each other and went over to take a look. I saw a house with a rock in front of its gate, and on that rock sat a man with my wife in his arms — they were watching the moon together. I could hardly contain my rage and rushed over to pick up a fight. The man, also looking very angry, shouted at me, 'How dare you scoundrel covet my wife!' He came straight toward me. Fortunately he was also quite sick. In the tangled fight we both fell on the ground. All this time the woman just sat there watching and chuckling to herself. 'Stop fighting, the two of you!' she said at last. 'Let me tell you the truth. Actually I have been sleeping with you in turns on the pretext of working for another family in order to give each of you five days for rest and recuperation, so that you will have enough vital energy for me to soak up. Now that you know the secret, and both of you are drained and therefore useless to me, let's call it a day and part company.' With this she suddenly vanished. We tried to get out of the mountain but lost our way. Then we crumbled to the ground, too hungry and tired to go on. Fortunately you have come to save us." The other man's story was roughly the same.

After hearing them out, the hunter offered them some of his field rations. Somewhat recovered, they took him to the dwelling place of the fox-woman to take a look. When they got there, both cried out in surprise, "There used to be an earthen wall, wooden beams and pillars, and windows and doors that could open and close — all of those were not phantoms but a physical reality. How did it turn into an earthen cave? The ground in the courtyard used to be flat and tidy; why is the ground outside the cave so rugged? What's more, such a small cave could only hold the fox-woman herself; how did we manage to live inside? Were we also turned into phantoms?" Then one of them caught sight of some broken pieces of porcelain scattered on the cliff facing the cave. "I broke it when I was climbing the stairs," he said. "There is only a cliff without a path. How was I able to go up and down there?" The two men walked around looking dazed and feeling as if they were in a dream. The more they thought about what they had gone through the more they hated the fox-woman, so they asked the hunter to go deep into the mountain to hunt and kill her. "A chance meeting followed by a happy marriage is too much of a bargain," said the hunter. "In such cases one will surely get more than one bargains for, just as a fish will swallow the hook along with the bait. Think about your own mistake. What's the use of venting your hatred on the fox?" Rendered speechless, the two men gave up the thought of seeking revenge.

51. A Wily Ghost

There was once a ghost-defying man who was ready to move into any haunted house. He was preparing to take the provincial examination one year when someone told him about a haunted garret behind a temple in the Western Hills, so he took up lodgings there to go on with his study. Every night his bed was surrounded by grotesque shadows, but he remained calm and unperturbed. On a bright moonlit night he opened the window to peer out and saw a beautiful woman standing under a tree. "So you are trying to seduce me after you failed to scare me away?" he scoffed. "I am not surprised that you don't recognize me," said the woman with a smile. "I am your grand-aunt buried in this mountain. I was told that you are fighting with ghosts here every day. For over ten years you have pored over the classics. Are you seeking an official career to bring honor to your family and ancestors, or merely a reputation of not being afraid of ghosts? You measure your strength with ghosts at night and sleep soundly during the day. With the date of the examination drawing near, you have all but stopped studying. Is this what your parents expected when they sent you here with money and provisions? Though I am now living in the underworld, I cannot ignore our kinship. That's why I have come to advise you. Think about it carefully." With this the ghost vanished. Finding her words rather reasonable, the man packed his belongings and left the temple. On his return he learned from his parents that he did not have any grand-aunt buried there. He stamped his feet in anger and shame, saying, "I was duped by that wily ghost!" In his rage he wanted to set out again for the temple, but a friend stopped him, "Since the ghost did not dare to match you in strength but chose to disguise itself and speak to you in polite terms, it must be afraid of you. Why should you pursue an enemy who has already acknowledged defeat?" The friend's advice was accepted. This friend was skillful at resolving a dispute, but the words of the ghost pointed to the correct principle. The man refused to accept an argument based on the correct principle, but was persuaded by the expedient words of his friend. From this we can learn something about the best strategy to counter and reduce an intrepid force.

52. The Old Tiger-Hunter

When my distant brother Ji Zhonghan served as magistrate of Jingde County, several hunters were injured by a fierce tiger near the city district. The local people submitted him a petition, saying, "The tiger cannot be killed unless we hire someone from the Tang family in Huizhou to help us." As the story goes, in the Ming dynasty a newly wedded young man in the Tang family was killed by a tiger. After giving birth to a son, his wife offered a prayer, saying, "I won't acknowledge him as my son, if he does not become a hunter of tigers. And I will disown any of my offsprings who cannot hunt tigers." From then on the Tangs remained adept tiger-hunters all through the generations. Ji Zhonghan granted this request and sent an envoy with some gifts to visit the Tang family. The envoy returned with a gray-haired old man who coughed incessantly and a boy some sixteen to seventeen years old. Though disappointed, Ji ordered a feast to be prepared to welcome them. Sensing the magistrate's dissatisfaction, the old man bowed and said, "I was told the haunt of that tiger is less than five li from the city. Let's go and kill it before the meal." A runner from the county office was dispatched to lead the way for the Tangs. When they got to the opening of a valley, the runner was afraid to go further. "Why should you be afraid when I am here?" said the old man with a smile. Nearly halfway into the valley the old man turned to the boy, "The beast seems to be asleep. Wake it up." The boy started to whistle like a roaring tiger. Suddenly a tiger rushed out of the woods and headed straight for the old man, who raised his arm holding a sharp hatchet. When the tiger lunged, the old man dodged to the side and let it leap overhead. The tiger dropped on the ground, bleeding profusely. A closer look showed that it had been sliced open from chin to tail. Ji Zhonghan gave the hunters a handsome reward. According to the old man, he had spent ten years strengthening his arms and another ten years sharpening his eyesight. His eyes would not bat even if someone brushed them with a broom, and his straightened arm would remain still even if a hefty man threw his weight on it.

53. A Boy Growing Old in Half a Day

When it rains in the capital, the forty-li road from Huangchun village to Fengyi Gate will become muddy and difficult to walk on. A man named Li Xiu was driving an empty carriage from Gu'an County back to the city when he saw a young boy about fifteen or sixteen trudging along the muddy road, his face as fresh and pretty as a young maiden. The sun was already going down. When Li Xiu passed him in the carriage, the boy looked as if he wanted to ask for a ride but was too shy to speak. A lascivious man, Li Xiu took a fancy to the young boy and invited him to ride in the carriage. The boy got in, looking timid and bashful. When Li stopped to buy nibbles for the boy, he did not decline all too vigorously. Li began to speak to him softly, throwing in a seductive remark now and then, but the boy merely responded with a blush and a smile, not saying anything. After going on for a few li, Li noticed that the boy looked a bit older than before, but he did not pay much attention. A dozen li onward it began to get dark, and the boy's face again seemed to have changed a little. By the time they reached the West Gate of Nanyuan, the boy had turned into a middle-aged man with a broad forehead, high cheekbones, and prodigious facial hair. When they finally got to the inn, he had become a gray-haired, gray-bearded old man. Shaking hands with Li Xiu to bid him farewell, he said, "I am infinitely grateful for your amorous attention. Sorry to disappoint you, but I am too old and ravaged to share the bed with you tonight." Then he laughed and made off. It was not known what a kind of demon that was. Li Xiu told his experience to a younger cousin who worked in our family kitchen, saying he regretted having courted humiliation by a fox or a fiend because of his frivolous behavior.

54. The Father Pays the Debt for His Son

There was a young lad who had no one to discipline him because his father was away from home for years doing business. Lured by a banker to the gambling table, he lost several hundred taels of silver in the game. The banker offered to pay the debts for him on condition that he wrote an agreement to sell his house. The lad did so as there was no other choice. Too ashamed to face his mother and wife, he did not return home in the evening but went into the woods to hang himself. He had just tied a knot with the rope when he heard the sound of horse hoofs beating the ground. Turning, he saw his father. "What made you want to do this?" his father asked in dismay. Knowing it would be futile to conceal the truth, the lad confessed to what he had done, but his father did not look angry. "This is a nothing serious," he said. "There is no need for you to act like that! What I have earned during my absence from home should be enough to pay your debts. Now go back home, and I will visit the banker, pay him the money and get back the agreement." A gambling game was still going on when the lad's father stormed into the banker's house. One by one he called out the names of the gamblers, who were all his acquaintances, and blamed them for leading his son astray and pressing him to pay his gambling debts. Caught in surprise, they were at a loss what to say. Then he said to the banker, "Since my unfilial son has written an agreement to sell the house, I cannot sue you at the county office. If I pay you the money, will you divide them among my son's creditors tomorrow and give me back the agreement now?" The banker, somewhat struck by a guilty conscience, agreed. The father then opened his waist bag, took out the right amount of money in silver and paid the banker. When he was given the agreement, he burnt it on the lamp and stormed out of the house.

Back home the lad prepared a meal and waited in vain for his father's return. Early the next morning he went to inquire at the banker's house, and was told his father had left after burning the agreement. The lad then realized that something strange had happened. After daybreak the bank opened his chest to find the silver ingots given to him the night before were actually made of paper. However, as many people had seen him taking the money, it was impossible for him to explain to them what had happened. Therefore he had no choice but to pay the lad's debts out of his own pocket.

And he suspected that he had met a ghost. Over ten days later news arrived that the lad's father had died in a strange land several months before.

55. A Fox-Woman Pays Her Debt

The Zhu family had a maid who was at first coarse and dumb in appearance. On coming of age she grew clever, and her features also became attractive. Thereupon Zhu made her a concubine. A resourceful woman, she knew the affairs in the house like the back of her palm. The servants did not dare to play any tricks, because the few times they tried to cheat her they were invariably found out. In addition, she had such business acumen that whatever goods she decided to purchase always underwent a price rise the following year. Zhu came to be quite well off and treated her with increasing favor.

One day she abruptly asked Zhu, "Do you know who I am?" "Are you crazy?" Zhu said with a smile and called her by her pet name. "You are mistaken," the girl replied. "I am not that maid. She ran away long time ago and is now married with a seven or eight-year-old son. I am in fact a fox-woman. Nine lifetimes ago, you were a rich merchant, and I kept the accounts for you. You treated me very kindly, but I embezzled over three thousand taels of silver. In the underworld I was punished by being reincarnated as a fox. After several hundred years of practice I succeeded at last, but I could not become an immortal yet due to what I owed you. So when the maid ran away, I roughly took her form to serve you. In the past ten years or so I have helped you make enough money to pay for my debt. Now I will discard my earthly body and leave for heaven. After my departure my body will change back into a fox. I will tell you which servant you should send to bury me. He will cut open my body and skin it, but you must not blame him for that. Four lifetimes ago he starved to death by the road. At that time I was unaccomplished in my practice, and I made a meal of his corpse. It will give him a chance to get even to let him dispose of my remains." She dropped on the ground, turning into a fox, and from its head floated out a beautiful woman a few inches tall. The woman, who did not look like Zhu's concubine, slowly flew away. Zhu could not bring himself to carry out her will and buried the body of the fox himself. But then the servant dug it out in secret, skinned it and sold the fur. Zhu could only sigh deeply, knowing it was a past-life debt that must be repaid in kind.

56. A Fox Saves an Old Confucian's Life

In Bazhou lived an old Confucian scholar who was a true gentleman enjoying high prestige. One day a fox spirit broke into his house to make trouble. When the scholar was there all would be quiet, but the moment he left the fox would start shaking the doors and windows, smashing utensils, throwing rubbish around, and doing other sorts of mischief. Thus kept from going out, the old scholar stayed home all day reading. Just then a group of scholars in Bazhou met in the local school to sign a joint petition against the prefect about a river control project. They wanted to elect the old scholar as their leader, but as he was unable to attend the gathering because of the fox in his house, they elected a Mr. Wang instead. Wang, charged with gathering a crowd to defy authority, was subsequently tried and executed, and the old scholar had a narrow escape. As soon as the case broke out, the old scholar's house ceased to be disturbed by the fox. Only then did he realize that the fox had tied him down in the house in order to prevent him from getting involved in the case. Therefore nothing auspicious will ever happen to a petty man; if any such thing should happen to him, it must have been generated by heaven to make him aggravate his sin. Likewise, a gentleman will not meet any demon; if he should meet one, it must have been sent by heaven to help him avoid a catastrophe.

57. A Skilled Fortune-Teller

In the late years of the Kangxi reign Li Luting made a living by dealing in curios and antiques. A good diviner, he was in the habit of making a prediction for himself every morning, but declined to tell fortunes for others. "Frequent disclosure of future occurrences will offend the gods," he once explained. When someone compared him to Shao Kangjie, the Song dynasty scholar famous for his expertise in divining by *The Book of Changes*, Li was modest in his reply, "I have acquired only sixty or seventy percent of his skill. Once I predicted that on a certain day an immortal would come on a bamboo walking stick, drink wine and compose a poem before taking leave. When the time came, I burned some incense and waited. Finally a man came to sell a bamboo carving of the immortal Lü Dongbin, by whose side was placed a wine gourd inscribed with a poem. Did Shao Kangjie ever make such a mistake in his divination?"

In his fifties Li Luting, who remained childless, had a young concubine. One day an old friend called at his house to hear his concubine complaining tearfully, "Why did you say these things to make fun of me? Are you trying to test my loyalty?" "I was not joking," said Li Luting. "I simply told you the outcome of my divination." When the friend asked why they were arguing, Li said, "This is really strange. When I consulted the oracle this morning I found out that two customers would come to buy curios today. One was her past-life husband and still had a night to spend with her in this life. The other was her future husband who would marry her in half a year. When I told her the result of my divination, she was annoyed and began to weep. A person cannot change his fate, which is determined in heaven. I didn't weep for my fate, but she did. I didn't resent my fate, but she did. What a foolishly sentimental girl!" Half a year later Li Luting passed away. His young concubine, sold to an official of the Hanlin Academy, was driven out after a night's stay because the official's principal wife could not tolerate her. Then another official took her to be his concubine, and this time she settled down in his family in peace.

58. Foxes Against Monks

Fei Changfang, a man in the Han dynasty capable of commanding ghosts and spirits, finally died in their hands after he lost his book of magic figures. Ming Chongyan of the Tang dynasty died with a sharp knife planted on his chest, believed to be a victim of some ghosts whom he had been subjugating to backbreaking labor. It is therefore not uncommon for a person with magic powers to fall victim to his own magic. A monk skilled at chanting magic words was once lured to the open country where hundreds of howling foxes leapt at him. Wielding an iron club, he struck down an old fox in the form of a man and broke out of the encirclement. Afterward he met the old fox on the road. The fox knelt and kowtowed, saying, "Since you spared my life last time, I have repented. I am willing to follow the laws of Buddha and become a monk." The monk put out his hand to touch the fox on the head, a gesture of initiating it into monkhood, but the fox suddenly threw something over the monk's face and fled by turning itself invisible. The covering, neither cloth nor leather, was colored like amber and as sticky as paint. The monk, who nearly died of suffocation, had the covering peeled off his face forcefully. His facial skin was torn off, and he passed out because of the terrible pain. After the wound healed, his face remained terribly disfigured.

The other story was about a roving monk who rented a house and styled himself a "Fox-Exorciser" with a notice pasted on his door. When a fox in human form came to entice him, the monk recognized it to be a fox and began chanting a Buddhist spell and shaking his bell. The fox fled in fright. About ten days later an old woman knocked on the door and told the monk that her house, which bordered on a graveyard, was disturbed by foxes every day. She asked him to subdue the foxes with his magic power. The monk took out a demon-detecting mirror, in which the old woman's reflection remained in human form, so he left with her. Having led him to an embankment, the old woman suddenly seized his bag and threw it into the river, then fled into a tract of sorghum field. The monk was staring in dismay at the book of magic figures and ceremonial instruments in

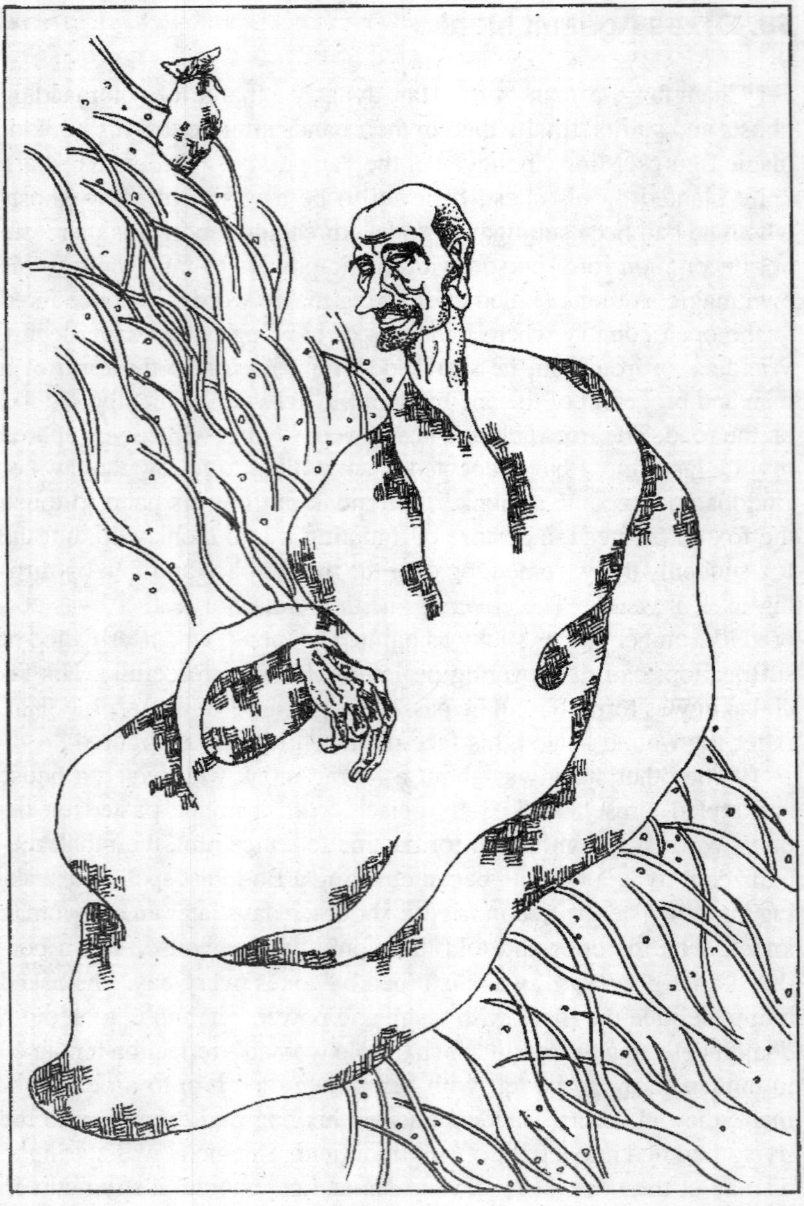

his bag floating down the river when a sudden attack of bricks and tiles gave him a bloody nose and swollen face. Hastily he began to chant Buddhist incantations to keep the fox at a distance, and took to his heels. The following day he left the place shamefacedly. Later it became known that the old woman was a local inhabitant. She had been bribed by the fox, who was her daughter's lover, and asked to steal the monk's book of magic figures. The monks in the above two stories, both endowed with the power to vanquish foxes, ended up in defeat because they did not take ample precautions against the foxes' cunning schemes and fought single-handedly while the foxes had recruited cohorts. If a man without much magic power should rush into a confrontation with demons and evil spirits, he would surely have less chance of gaining a victory.

59. Fatal Predictions

A carpenter in Liufu village of Xian County once consulted a fortune-teller about his marriage prospects. The fortunate-teller decided to play a prank on him. "There is a Mr. A living a hundred li to the southwest. He will die today, and his wife is destined to marry you. If you go there in a hurry, you will get what you want." Taking the fortune-teller at his words, the carpenter went to that place and checked into an inn. Then he went out to ask the first local inhabitant he met, "Do you know where Mr. A lives?" "Why do you want to see him?" asked the man, who happened to be A himself. When the carpenter told his story, Mr. A flew into a rage and drew his sword. The carpenter ran back to his room at the inn, then got away by climbing over the wall. Mr. A suspected the innkeeper of trying to hide the carpenter and wanted to search the inn. When the innkeeper refused, they got into a fight. After killing the innkeeper, Mr.A was arrested and executed. It was impossible to look for the carpenter as no one had bothered to ask his name or address.

After a year or so an old woman with her son and a widowed daughter-in-law came to Xian County. When the old woman died abruptly of an illness, the son asked his sister-in-law to remarry so that they could use the wedding gift to pay for his mother's funeral. Reluctantly the woman agreed. As the carpenter was still single, he was persuaded to marry the young widow. Only later did he find out that her late husband was none other than Mr.A. This incident was bizarre indeed. If the fortune-teller had not made the joke, the carpenter would not have met Mr.A, Mr. A would not have fought with the innkeeper, the innkeeper would not have been killed, Mr.A would not have been decapitated for homicide, and his wife would not have become the carpenter's wife by her second marriage. The series of cause and effect seems to indicate that the outcome had been predetermined.

A somewhat similar incident happened to a man living at Xisi Archway. Every day he set up a stand in the street to tell fortunes. He suddenly predicted one day that he would die in a disaster two days later. Though this outcome was clearly indicated by the hexagram, he could not imagine where the disaster would come from. When the day came he locked himself up at home, intending to find out how he would meet his death. Unfortunately an earthquake took place. The house collapsed, and he was crushed to death in the rubble. If he had not divined his future, he would have gone out to the street to tell fortunes and would not have died in the earthquake. This incident also appeared to be predetermined, for it was the man's divining skill that had led to his death.

60. Settling a Case by Leaving It Unsettled

When my father served as director of the Jiangsu section in the Ministry of Justice, a case of a young girl's rape by a boy was submitted by the Xicheng district. The boy was sixteen and the girl only fourteen. He went out playing one day and on his way home saw the girl picking vegetables in the garden. He went up to intimidate her and tried to rape her. At the girl's cry for help some patrolling soldiers arrived and caught the boy in the act. While the case was on trial, the parents from the two families came to petition at the *yamen*, saying their children were engaged and the boy had offended the girl without knowing who she was. According to law a man could not be convicted of rape against his fiancée. Before a decision could be reached, the girl suddenly retracted her former testimony by claiming that the boy had only teased with her. Thus the boy was given a severe reprimand, then set free. Someone said, "The girl's parents received a handsome bribe from the boy's family, and the girl also took a fancy to the boy. Therefore she lied to cover up for him." "That was quite possible," agreed my father. "However, this case involves nothing but a marriage. If a murder case were to be resolved because of bribery, the victim would suffer a deep wrong in the underworld. But the young boy was merely guilty of attempted rape, for which there could be no factual evidence; the girl's family might have been bribed, but there was no evidence to justify further inquiry into the matter. Both the girl and her parents accepted the engagement, a matchmaker and a guarantor testified for them, the neighbors did not offer any countering evidence, and there was no contradiction between the testimonials of the two families. Under such circumstances a gentleman would rather resign himself to being cheated than get to the bottom of the case and exile the teenage boy to a remote area."

61. The Bell-Demon

According to Li Huating of Wenshui County, there was a deserted Buddhist temple about a hundred li from his home. No one dared to stay in the temple, which was reputedly haunted by a demon. Caught in the rain, over a dozen sheep dealers once took shelter there. At night they heard a whooping sound, then saw a creature clumsily making its way toward them in the dark. Its body was bulky and cumbersome and its face blurred. The sheep dealers, all of them flighty young men, did not feel scared, but picked up some broken bricks to attack the creature. Whenever a piece of brick hit the target, there would be a clear, metallic sound. The creature faltered and turned to make off. Aware that it was at its wits end, the sheep dealers shouted and gave chase. The creature stopped at a broken wall by the gate of the temple, and remained there motionless. When the men came close, they saw a broken bell containing many pieces of bone, which it must have swallowed for food. The following day they told the story to the local people, who had the bell melted and made into other utensils. From then on the temple ceased to be haunted. That creature had brought on its own destruction by molesting people despite its clumsiness. Perhaps it was merely modeling itself on some other creatures with changeable forms who went around creating troubles for people. Incidentally I am reminded of a story told by a maid in my family who came from Shanguo village in Cangzhou. Many people in the village were robbers. When a man who had no ability whatsoever found out that some people had got rich by being robbers, he went to join them. In a subsequent siege by government troops, all the other robbers fought their way out; the talentless man alone was captured and sent to the execution ground. This man's behavior resembled that of the broken bell.

62. The Importance of Etiquette

An official-in-waiting who had just rented a house on Hufangqiao Road in the capital was informed, "A fox lives in this house. You will not be disturbed if you offer it a sacrifice before you move in." Being a tightfisted man, he refused, but nothing unusual happened when he moved in. Shortly afterward he married a concubine. Received into his house on the wedding day, she was sitting alone in the room when she heard dozens of whispering voices outside the window commenting on her looks. Bashfully she kept her head lowered. When they went to bed that night after blowing out the candle, the whole room was suddenly filled with giggles. The moment he made a move, it was described by a loud voice. Several nights passed like this. Unable to bear it any longer, he went to a Taoist priest asking him to exorcise the fox. After hearing him out the priest said, "Only when a demon has harmed people can I invoke the heavenly gods to seize it and punish it. If the demon has merely been playing a prank without causing much harm, there is no need for divine intervention. Likewise, the government does not take any action against someone for playing a prank without causing real trouble. How can you bother the gods with such a trivial matter?" At the end of his rope, the official-in-waiting offered a sacrifice and libation to the fox. That very night his room became quiet. He said with a deep sigh, "Now I understand the importance of social etiquette!"

63. Playing a Trick on Oneself

Dong Qiuyuan told the following story. A scholar of Dongcang Prefecture was traveling one night in the open country when he caught sight of a magnificent mansion. "This should be the site of a family grave," Dong wondered. "Where did this house come from? Maybe it has been conjured up by foxes." As he had read many stories about a young scholar meeting and marrying a lovely fox-woman, he expected the same to happen to himself and slowed his pace. After a while a team of carriages came from the west, the people all resplendently clad. A middle-aged woman lifted the window curtain and pointed at the scholar, "That is a nice young man. We can invite him in." Stealing a glance into the carriage, the scholar was overjoyed to see a maiden as beautiful as a fairy seated at the back. The carriages drove into the house, then out came two maids to the scholar with the host's invitation. Convinced that he was meeting a host of foxes, the scholar entered without bothering to ask the host's name. A sumptuous feast was laid out, but the host did not appear at once. His heart pounding with anticipation, the scholar waited anxiously for the moment to enter the bridal room with the fox-maiden. In the evening the air was filled with the sound of gongs and drums as well as wind instruments. Lifting the door curtain, an old man came in and bowed to the scholar with clasped hands. "The bridegroom has finally arrived. As a scholar you must be familiar with the procedures of a wedding ceremony. My family is honored to have you as the best man." The scholar was sorely disappointed on hearing this. Since no one had promised to marry the maiden to him, he could find no excuse to refuse to be the best man, especially after his carousing at the feast. After going through the wedding procedures as fast as he could, he took his leave in low spirits. His family was looking for him all over the place since he had failed to return for the night. When he described what had happened to him indignantly, the listeners all burst out laughing. One of them said, "You cannot blame the foxes for playing a trick on you, for it was you who played the trick on yourself!"

When Dong Qiuyuan finished his story, I told mine. A man named Li Erhun, who could not make ends meet, left for the capital to make a living. When he met a young woman riding a donkey along the way, he went up to her and tried to make her talk by teasing and joking. The young woman did not look offended but simply ignored him. The following day they met again on the road. Throwing a bundle wrapped with a handkerchief, she called back, "I will stop in Gu'an County tonight." Li opened the bundle to find a few pieces of jewelry inside. He had just run out of money to pay for his trip, so he took the jewelry to a nearby pawnshop. It turned out that these had just been stolen from the shop. Tied up and flogged, Li had no choice but to plead guilty to the theft. At the end of the story, I remarked that Li Erhun was indeed the victim of a hoax played by the fox. Dong Qiuyuan disagreed. "If he had not made passes at the young woman, would he have suffered such consequences? I would still say he played the trick on himself."

64. The Price of Desecration

Zhu Shenghuan, a native of Sichuan, came out second in the provincial examination in Shuntian; it was I who nominated him a successful candidate after going over his examination paper. One day I got together with him and a few others in my Thatched Abode of Close Observations. At the dinner table our conversation turned to strange tales and hearsays, and Zhu told us the following story. While traveling in a boat, he noticed a helmsman with a plaster on his forehead. When asked, the helmsman said he had a sore which must not be exposed to wind. After they had sailed for a few days, a boatman told some passengers in a whisper, "He was lying when he said he had a sore. Actually something incredible happened to him. He used to be the head of the boatmen's guild, so he had to light joss-sticks and pray at the sacrificial ceremony in honor of the river god. The night before the ceremony he did something unclean, thus breaking the rule of abstinence. When he was praying on his knees, a gust of wind suddenly blew the incense dust on his face. He was so scared that he could hardly finish his prayer. When he came down and wiped off the dust, we saw an erotic painting in black ink on his forehead — it was a very vivid and lifelike portrait of him and his wife. The more he washed it with water the more visible it became, so he had to cover it up with a plaster." Though they did not quite believe the story, the passengers could not help glancing at the helmsman's forehead when they walked past him. When he noticed this, the helmsman said, "That rascal must be wagging his tongue again!" Then he heaved long sighs. It seemed that the boatman had told the truth. The passengers felt it a pity that they could not have the plaster peeled off to take a look at the picture.

The above story reminded me of what Granny Li, my wet nurse, witnessed on a trip she took to Mount Tai. A prostitute and her lover ran into each other at an inn on their way to burn incense at a temple on the mountain. After they stole a kiss, their lips became glued together, and any attempt to separate them would result in piercing pain. Some people went to the altar to offer a prayer of repentance on their behalf, and their lips finally came apart. One of the onlookers said, "The keeper of the temple must have bribed the woman to put on a show in order to convince people of the temple's magic power." There was no way to find out if that was the case.

65. A Fake Fox-Woman

There was a certain scholar who bought a young girl in Guangling to be his concubine. His infatuation with her was enhanced by her literary talents, and they often amused themselves by composing poems and antithetical couplets at their bridal home. One day the scholar went out to drink wine and returned late to find all his servants and maids asleep. When he entered his unlit room, his concubine was nowhere to be found. There was a written message left on the desk. "I am a fox-woman who used to live in a remote mountain. Because of my indebtedness to you in my past life, I came to keep your company for half a year by way of compensation. After spending all the days assigned to us by heaven, I dared not stay any longer. It was my initial intention to tell you all about this in person, but I feared I would not be able to bear the pain of parting with you. So I went away without saying good-bye. I was heartbroken when I took my leave, overwhelmed in sorrow and regret. Perhaps such strong feelings of mine will plant the seed of our future encounter in the next life. I hope you will take good care of yourself and refrain from excessive grief over my departure. This will be a great comfort to me."

    The scholar felt devastated. On reading the farewell letter, his friends also expressed both wonder and sympathy. As incidents like this could be found in ancient records, no one raised any doubt. After a month or so the woman, sailing north with a lover, was pilfered. They reported the case to the local *yamen* and had to wait for the thieves to be caught so as to get back their stolen goods. They ended up waiting for several months in vain until someone recognized her. It turned out that her mother had resold her to this man, and she had made an easy escape from the scholar's home by pretending to be a fox. Someone commented, "The woman was indeed a fox — how else to describe her? This might be the truth behind many of the amazing tales about some scholar's chance encounter with a fairy who later left him without saying good-bye."

66. A Female Ghost Seeks a Post for Her Husband

After a few cups at a wineshop an official-in-waiting walked home under the moonlight, a servant boy leading the way with a lantern. When the lantern suddenly went out, he went to a house by the road with the lights on to ask for help. The young woman who answered the door invited him to have some tea. Taking her for a prostitute, he decided to go ahead and enjoy himself. After he entered the room, the woman lowered her head, looking sad and ashamed. He stood up to leave, but she stopped him by pulling at the hem of his dress. So he walked up to tease her and found her willing and submissive. Hand in hand they got into bed to enjoy some intimate moments.

Afterward he handed her a few taels of silver, which he happened to have brought with him, but she declined and said, "Please do me a favor if tonight means anything to you. There is a man living somewhere who is a widower with small children. His long-time unemployment has driven the family to the verge of starvation. If you can hire him as a servant when you receive your appointment, I will be forever grateful to you." "Are you coming too?" he asked jokingly. "I am not a living person," the woman said tearfully, "but the man's deceased wife. Because he is unable to feed our children, I have swallowed my sense of shame and come to seek your help." The official-in-waiting shuddered in fear and hastily took his leave. When he turned to look, the house had transformed into a new grave. When he finally got his appointment, he recalled the ghost's request and hired her husband, taking him along with his children to his new office. To help her husband obtain the profitable position as an official's attendant, the female ghost was willing to offer herself in return. It is therefore easy to imagine how lucrative such a position could be. And how can an attendant make huge profits except by cheating his superiors and extorting the common people?

75

67. The Spirit of a Broken Jar

For a period of time Liu, a native of Mengyin County, stayed in the house of a relative. Someone accidentally mentioned to him that the place was frequented by a spirit, whose hide-out was unknown. Anyone running into it in the dark would fall on the ground, as if hit by a hard rock. Liu enjoyed hunting and brought a fowling piece with him wherever he went. "I'll use this to defend myself then," he said.

There were three studios in the house, and Liu was put up in the eastern one. While sitting alone before the lamp one night, he saw a creature standing at the door of the western studio. With its limbs and face it looked like a man, but its eyes and eyebrows were wide apart, and its nose and mouth almost stuck together. As soon as Liu took aim with his fowling piece, the creature shrank back into the room. Then it peeped out showing only half of its face, with one hand placed on the door, as if it were about to run out. The moment Liu raised his fowling piece, it again drew back into the room. Apparently it was afraid of being attacked from the rear on leaving the room. For fear that the creature had some dirty tricks up its sleeve, Liu dared not venture out to attack it. After peeping out several times, the creature suddenly showed its entire face, shaking its head at Liu and putting out its tongue. Liu hastily pulled the trigger, but the lead bullet hit the door and the creature fled. This seemed to have illustrated a military law stating that when two armies confront each other, the party that moves first will be defeated. If Liu had refrained from firing until daybreak, the creature, which apparently was unable to fly through the window, would have been shot on leaving the room by the door. Or it would have shrunk to its original form should it choose to stay in the room. But from this encounter Liu found out that the creature was afraid of the gun. He hid himself behind the window one night until the creature emerged, then fired. The creature dropped to the ground with a cracking sound. On a closer look, he found it to be a piece from a broken jar. On the part near the opening uncovered with enamel was drawn a human face in a child's scrawl, its facial features grossly misplaced just as Liu had seen on a previous night.

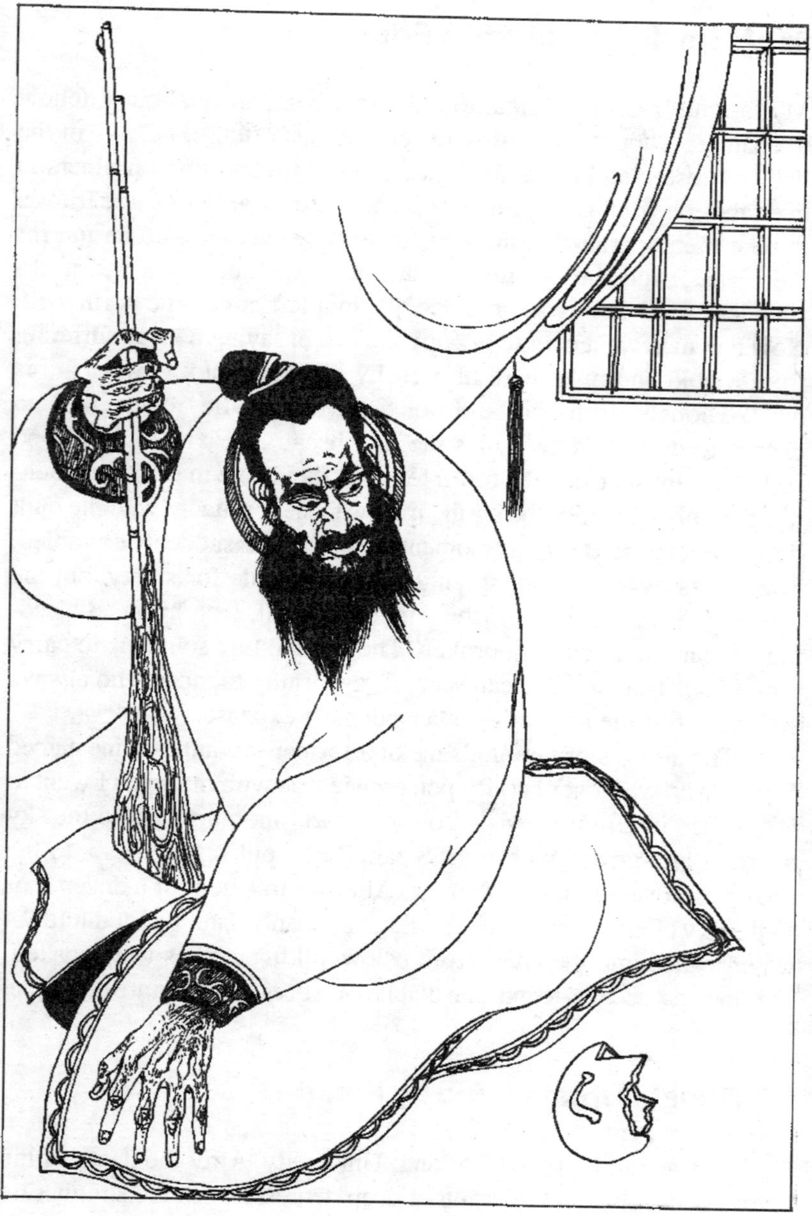

68. A Small Gain at a Big Price

My late tutor Chen Wenqin told the following story about a fellow townsman. Though not guilty of any serious offense, he was in the habit of reserving profits for himself and inflicting loss on others in everything he did. One year he went to the capital with some friends to take the imperial examination. After they checked into an inn for the night, it suddenly started to rain heavily. Their room had a terrible leak until there was only one dry spot left beside the north wall. Now this man went over to occupy the place, saying he was suffering from a cold and must cure himself by breaking into a sweat in his quilt. Though his friends did not believe him, they could find no excuse to drive him away. As the rain became heavier, it leaked so badly that those inside the room felt as if they were in the open country, the only exception being the man who slept soundly with the quilt drawn over his head. At this moment the north wall suddenly crumbled. The others, who were all staying up, ran outside for safety, but the sleeping man alone was crushed under the wall, with his head bleeding and an arm and a foot broken. They had to hire someone to carry him home. This incident can serve as a warning to those who always seek to profit themselves at other people's expense.

The above story reminds me of a former servant of mine named Yu Lu, who was a very crafty person. He was with me when I went to take office in Urumqi. We set out one early morning to find the sky overcast and gravid with rain. Stealthily he put his clothes into the chest and covered them with mine. After we traveled for a dozen li or so the sky cleared up, but the carriage suddenly sank into a ditch. As water leaked into the chest from below, all his clothes were soaked. This incident seemed to indicate that heaven does not favor artful people.

69. Ghosts Obtain Food by Fraud

Liao was a student at the National University. After the death of his favorite concubine he sank into a deep depression. In the summer he went to live in his cottage, where the window of his room overlooked a clear stream. He always kept the window open in the evening to let in the moonlight. One evening he heard the sound of someone being beaten and begging for mercy on the hill across the stream. Gazing into the distance he saw a woman squatting on the ground to receive a beating of the birch. He was staring at her when she called out, "How come you are here? Why do you look on without giving me a hand?" Looking closely, Liao realized this was his deceased concubine. He was surprised and filled with pity, but the deep stream and precipitous cliff made it impossible for him to approach her. "You were buried somewhere else," he said. "Why have you come here?" The woman began to sob. "Because you treated me with great favor, I grew unscrupulous and did many bad deeds. After death I was exiled to this place, like a living person sentenced to a term of banishment. The land-god here is very harsh and cruel and has me flogged frequently. I hope you can invite some monks to conduct a sacrificial ceremony to feed the ghosts here, otherwise my sufferings will never end." After she said this, some horrible ghosts swarmed up and dragged her away. Deeply attached to his beloved concubine, Liao did not have the heart to turn down her request. He hired some monks to conduct a ghost-feeding service, hoping thereby to save her from misery.

    A month or so afterward he heard the sound of flogging again. Looking into the distance by the window, he saw the young woman stripped naked, her arms tied up behind her back, to receive another flogging, with a crowd of ghosts looking on. At the sight of him she pleaded piteously, "The heavenly god refused to set me free because the Buddhist ceremony had not been properly conducted, and since then the land-god has treated me even more harshly than before. Only a grand ceremony lasting for seven whole days can gain me my release." Liao suddenly grew suspicious. "If the land-god is not present, who is there to supervise the flogging? If the land-god is present, how dare she speak ill of him face to face? Could this be a trick played by some wily ghosts to obtain food?" He was turning these thoughts in his mind when the woman said, "I am really your late concubine. Please don't be so mistrustful." Fully aware of what was happening, Liao asked, "There is a mole on your body. Tell me where it is, and I will believe you." The woman could not answer him. Gradually the ghosts scattered away, never to show up again. In conclusion, deception and subterfuge not only plague the world of man but the nether regions as well. Liao said afterward that a maid of his family was buried under that hill. Aware of her master's longing for his late concubine, she might have worked in collusion with other ghosts to swindle sacrificial offerings from him.

70. The Revenge of a House Cat

A cat kept in the house of my grand-uncle Chen Deyin was often beaten by a maid for stealing food. A slight cough from her was enough to send the cat on its heels. When the family went out one day the maid was told to keep the door. With nothing better to do, she bolted the door and went to sleep. She woke up to find several pears missing from the plate. As there was no one else around, and the cat never ate pears, she was unable to prove her innocence and received a flogging. In the evening the pears were discovered in the stove, much to everyone's surprise. A closer look showed that each pear had the imprints of the cat's teeth and paws. Apparently the cat had done it on purpose to implicate the maid. In her rage the maid wanted to grab the cat and give it another beating, but my grand-aunt stopped her. "Of course I won't allow you to beat the cat to death. Even if I would, its spirit would surely return to seek revenge, and who knows what consequences would follow?" Thus admonished, the maid ceased to beat the cat, and the cat no longer fled from her presence.

71. A Next-Life Couple

A scholar was touring Mount Song to copy ancient inscriptions from stone tablets. Night fell before he realized it. As it was in mid-summer, he lay down on the grass to sleep under a pine tree. At midnight he woke up with a cold shudder, his sleeves soaked with dew. Unable to fall back to sleep, he lay on his back to watch the moon. Suddenly he saw a few men walking up a narrow path to the top of the hill, where they laid out a mat and sat down to drink wine. Knowing they must be ghosts, he was too scared to make a sound and listened quietly to their conversation. One of them said to the two men seated in the place of honor, "The two of you have finished your terms in the nether world and will soon live under the sun again. Do you know where you will be born?" "Not yet," the two men replied.

Just then they all stood up, saying, "Here comes the land-god!" A moment later an old man on a walking stick came up and greeted the two men with clasped hands. "I just received an official document and have come to tell you the good news. As good friends in your previous lives, you will be a loving couple in your next." Pointing to the man on the right, he said, "You will be the husband." Then he turned to the man on the left. "You will be his wife." The man on the right chuckled. As the other man remained silent, the land-god said, "Why are you so unhappy? You don't suppose the god of the nether world has made a mistake, do you? In his past life your friend was a stern, upright man who failed to understand the ways of the world or adapt to the changing trend of his times. Though his achievements were many, he also committed quite a few mistakes, for which he was detained in the underworld for two hundred years. Nevertheless, his mistakes were those of a gentleman, therefore he will again become a high official in his next life. As for you, your worldly wisdom made you unwilling to affect other people's fortunes with your action. But in many cases a minor mistake, if not corrected in time, will lead to a great disaster. As punishment you were detained in the underworld for two hundred years and will become a woman in your next life. Since you concealed your feelings without being deceitful and conducted yourself with mildness and civility without being sycophantic, you will still enjoy wealth and honor. Furthermore, as your friend was liable to give offense in dealing with people, but you always remained on good terms with him, the two of you will be joined in marriage. Since the god's decision is obviously wise and just, what makes you so unhappy?" Amid a roar of laughter the other ghosts said, "He is not unhappy, just a bit shy to be a bride for the first time! Since we have meat and wine here, let them celebrate their wedding in advance with the land-god as witness!" Their voices rose to a hubbub until it became impossible to make out what they were saying. At cock-crow the ghosts all scattered in haste. And the scholar did not find out who the two men had been in their past lives.

72. Unrequited Fancy

Yao Biefeng, a native of Tongcheng, was a good poet and calligrapher. Invited to produce calligraphical works, he was once put up by his host in a small garden on the west side of the mansion. On a clear, moonlit night he caught a glimpse of a woman's figure outside the window, but no one was in sight when he went out to take a look. Glancing around, he seemed to spot a woman in a green skirt and red dress hidden behind the rocks, trees, bamboos and flowers. The moment he got there, the woman had moved to the other side of the garden. He tried to approach her, but again she shunned him. Half the night went by and he failed to catch a glimpse of the woman's fair visage. In disappointment he went back to his room to rest. Just then he heard a woman's voice outside the window, "If you can take the trouble to copy the Diamond Sutra for me, I will salute you on my knees to offer my thanks. The sutra consists of no more than seven thousand words. Will you do me the favor?" "Who are you?" Yao asked eagerly, but got no answer. He happened to have a stack of rice paper at hand. The following day he put other matters aside and devoted himself to copying the Diamond Sutra. After completing the work, he put it on the table and lit a joss-stick. The next morning the sutra was gone. He waited impatiently until nightfall, when a woman emerged from behind the flowers, walked briskly toward him, and prostrated herself. Before he could reach out to help her to her feet, she suddenly got up and raised her face. Her eyes staring upward, her chest soaked in blood, she turned out to be the ghost of a woman who had committed suicide. With a shrill cry of terror Yao fell on the ground. At the noise some servants arrived with lit candles, but the ghost had already gone. Stamping his feet angrily, Yao swore at the ghost for cheating him. After listening to the story, his host said to him, "The ghost promised to offer her thanks, and she kept her word. Therefore she did not cheat you. How can you blame her for failing to gratify your own improper wish?"

73. Dream and Reality

During my stay at the Western frontier I once accompanied Mr. Ba, the Superintendent of Qinghai, to inspect a military post station. After he left the station, I had to stay there with an officer named Liang to deal with some unfinished work. That night an urgent dispatch was brought to the station. As all the soldiers had been sent out, I woke Liang from his dream and sent him off on horseback with the dispatch. I told him he could delegate the task to any soldier from the station he came across along the way. After riding swiftly for a dozen li or so, Liang ran into some soldiers from the station and returned to go back to sleep. The next morning he told me, "In a dream last night you sent me to pass on an urgent document. For fear of losing time I sped my horse into a wild gallop. When I got up this morning my legs actually felt very sore. How puzzling it is!" Apparently he had taken what had happened to him for a dream, and all the attendants burst out laughing. Later I wrote a poem about this incident.

  In contrast to what happened in the story above, people can also mistake a dream for reality. A distant brother of mine told the following story that took place in Jinghai County. One evening a man went to bed when his wife was still weaving cloth in another room. In his dream his wife was abducted by several men. Waking up with a start, he did not know he had been dreaming and rushed out of the house club in hand. After running for over ten li he saw in the open field ahead of him several men pushing a young woman around. They were trying to rape her, and she was crying for help. Burning with rage, he rushed forward and attacked the men furiously. They all got wounded and scattered in every direction. He went up to the woman and found her to be an acquaintance from a neighboring village. After escorting her back home, he returned in a daze to his own house to find his wife still weaving cloth under the lamp. Perhaps it was not an ordinary dream but an instrument of divine guidance.

74. A Gift from the Fairies

A scholar living at the foot of the Wuyi Mountain learned from some tea-gatherers that on moonlit nights there was the sound of singing and a flute being played near a certain rock in the mountain. From a distance it appeared to be a group of fairies. A giddy and frivolous man, the scholar found a lodging in a mountain house and went out at moonrise to wait by the rock. He did this for several nights without seeing anything. Then his landlord told him that the story about music-playing fairies was true, but one could hear the music only a few times every year, and only under a full moon. Restraining his impatience, the scholar waited for over ten days until one night a faintly audible sound caught his attention. He sneaked his way there and concealed himself in a grove. Peeping out, he saw a few ravishing beauties. With a flute placed on her lips, one of the girls was about to play when she caught sight of the man's shadow in the grove and pointed at him with the flute. Instantly paralyzed, the scholar could not stir anymore, though he remained clear-minded. Then the girl started to play, the soul-stirring music resounding to the skies. The scholar could not help expressing his admiration. "Though I am unable to move," he said, "I have feasted my eyes and ears on the sweet sounds and charming postures of the fairies." He had barely finished these words when a handkerchief darted toward him and landed squarely on his face. He could no longer hear or see anything as a drowsy, hypnotic feeling crept over him.

After some time he gradually came out of the trance. At the order of the fairies, several maids dragged him out of the grove and rebuked him, "What an impudent scoundrel! How dare you peep at heavenly flowers?" They picked some bamboo twigs to beat him, but he begged for mercy in a pitiful voice, saying he was a music lover who had come to overhear some heavenly tunes without any improper thoughts. One of the girls smiled. "We rather appreciate your sincerity, so we will make you the gift of a maid who can also play the flute." The scholar kneeled in haste to kowtow his gratitude. When he got up on his feet, all the fairies were nowhere to be seen, and he turned to find a maid left behind. Puffing and blowing, she had a very broad forehead, big eyes, short hair and a thick waist. Startled and irritated, he turned back to leave, but the maid rushed over to grab him and make indecent moves. Unable to fend her off, the scholar was so enraged that he raised his hand and sent her sprawling with a smack. As soon as she touched ground the maid turned into a pig and ran away bellowing. From then on music was never heard again at that mountain rock. Judging by the transformation of the maid into a pig, the young girls might be demons instead of fairies. Some people presumed that the fairies had turned a pig into a maid in advance in order to play a trick on the scholar.

75. A Dose of One's Own Medicine

A Confucian scholar, who posed as a man of high principles and conducted himself with caution, was fond of finding faults with and passing harsh judgements on others. In the fifth month a friend of his completed the mourning period for a lost parent and planned to take a concubine in the seventh month. This prompted the scholar to write him a letter, saying, "You want to take a concubine less than three months after the mourning period ended. Obviously you have harbored that intention for a long time, thereby breaking the code of ethics in spirit. As friends ought to advise one another to follow the right path, I cannot refrain from calling this to your attention. What do you have to say about this?" Such an act was typical of the scholar.

When the scholar's wife left for a visit to her parental home, she agreed with him on the date of her return. But she returned the day before the appointed date, much to the surprise of her husband. "I made a mistake in counting the days," she explained, and he did not doubt her word. The following day saw the return of another wife. In consternation the scholar searched the house for the first woman, who was nowhere to be found. From then on he grew weaker day by day until he was taken down by consumption. It turned out that a fox-woman had disguised herself as his wife in order to soak up his vital energy. During that night he had given way to his carnal desires and become drained of his vitality. At the news the friend who had received his chastise for taking a concubine wrote him a letter, saying, "What a couple do in their bedroom is part of human nature, and the visit from a fox in human disguise cannot be foreseen. Yet the depletion of one's vitality in a single night could only have resulted from overindulgence in the desires of the flesh. Is a couple supposed to act without restraint in their bedroom? Moreover, evil spirits have never dared to harm men of virtue. Since ancient times, people of outstanding virtue and merits have never been known to encounter demons and spirits. Since a fox has taken liberties with you, can't we conclude there is something lacking in your moral integrity? As friends ought to advise one another to follow the right path, I cannot refrain from calling this to your attention. What do you have to say about this?" The scholar, on reading the letter, adamantly denied his encounter with the fox-woman, claiming it to be a rumor spread by the villagers. That friend of his had truly given him a dose of his own medicine.

76. A Fox-Hunting Taoist

A young scholar had a fox-woman for his lover. When they first got acquainted, she gave him a small gourd to fasten to his belt, then crawled into it. To meet her he only had to pull off the cork on the

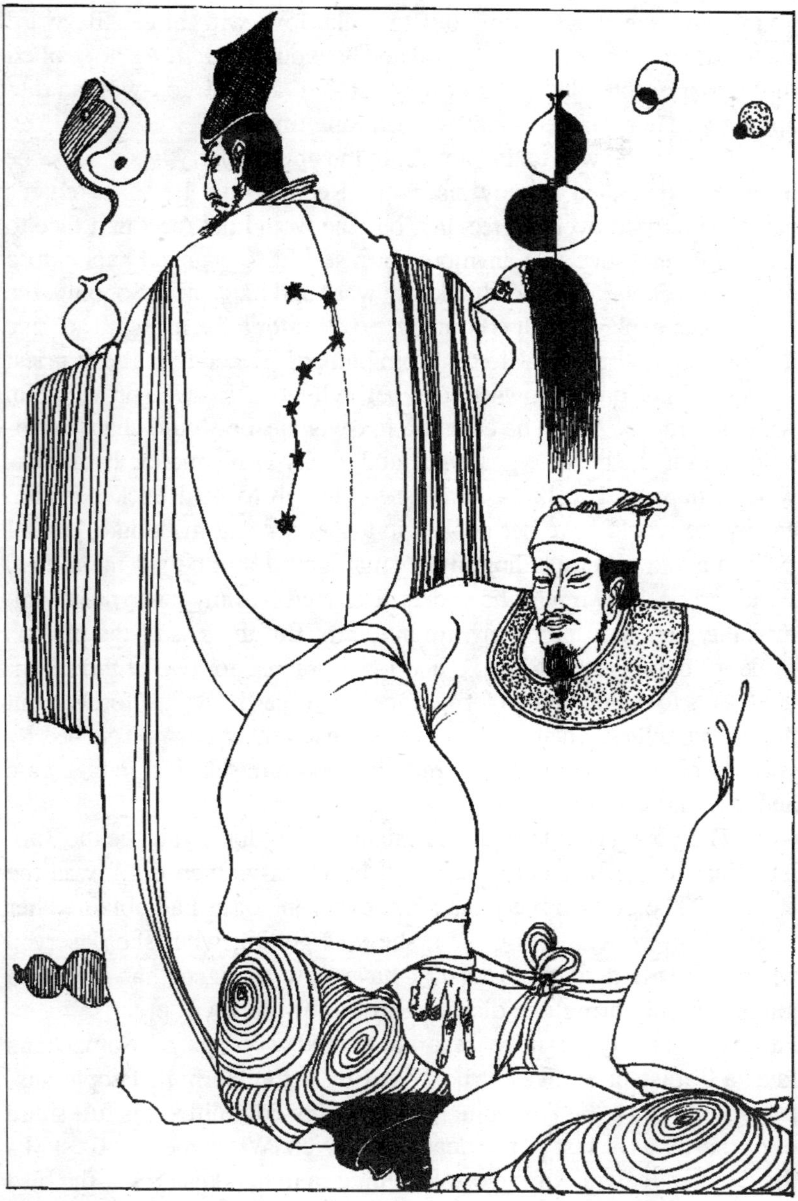

gourd, and she would come out to make love with him. Afterward she would slip back into the gourd and he would cork it. As he strolled in the market one day the gourd got stolen, and the fox-woman disappeared. He remained gloomy for a long time.

One day he was taking a walk in the open country when someone in the woods called him by his name. Recognizing the fox-woman's voice, he hurried over to greet her, but she would not meet him face to face. "I cannot face you anymore because I have changed back into a fox." The scholar demanded to know what had happened. Sobbing, the fox-woman explained, "It is common practice for a fox trying to achieve immortality to draw vital forces from humans. Recently a Taoist priest suddenly came out of nowhere and began hunting foxes to provide him with vital forces. When he caught a fox-woman, he would chant incantations until she became paralyzed and totally at his mercy. If the fox-woman happened to be accomplished enough to hold back her vital energy, he would have her cooked in a steamer and made into jerky. I tried to avoid him by hiding in the small gourd, but he got me at last. Afraid to be thrown into the cooker, I offered him my inner pill of immortality and was spared my life in return. But the loss of the pill has made me degenerate into a fox, and I will practise for two or three hundred years to regain human form. The sky and earth will last forever, but there is no telling when we will ever see each other again. Touched by your devotion, I have waited here to bid you farewell. Please take care and stop missing me."

The young scholar was indignant. "Why don't you sue the Taoist priest to the heavenly gods?" "Many fox-women did," was the answer. "The gods argued that since everyone of us had obtained her vital energy by exploiting men, she was getting what she deserved when she lost it to the Taoist. I have now realized that ill-gotten gains can only bring one disaster. From now on I will practise meditation exclusively and never resort to my old ways again." Some years later a Taoist priest was struck dead by a thunderbolt. People suspected him to be the fox-hunter who, having committed his full share of crimes, was at last put to death by heaven. While the mantis stalks the cicada, unaware of the oriole behind, a man takes aim at the bird with his catapult — the story above is a perfect exemplification of this well-known fable.

77. Take the Tide at the Flood

Crafty and evil people have a whole bag of tricks which they will put to use whenever there is a chance. The following story was told to me as a child. One night a family in our village heard footsteps in the courtyard. With lit torches they gave the place a thorough search for a thief or robber. Failing to find anyone, they dismissed it as antics played by a ghost or spirit. When a thief learned of the incident, he slipped into the house in the dead of night. Though they heard some noise, the family took it for a specter and went on sleeping. The thief ravaged the place to his heart's content and went away loaded with spoils.

There was a county magistrate who upheld Confucianism and denounced Buddhism, showing a strong aversion to monks. One day the head monk of a local Buddhist temple called on the magistrate to report a theft. The magistrate rebuked him, "If Buddha is not powerful, why should he enjoy any sacrifice? If Buddha is powerful, why doesn't he punish the thief rather than trouble the government?" Having sent the monk away with these words, he declared smugly, "If every official under heaven adopts my method, the monks will disperse of their own accord." The head monk turned out to be a very crafty man. He made a repentant prayer before the shrine with his disciples, and in the meantime arranged for a beggar to come and kneel at the temple gate, holding some clothing and articles of daily use in his arms. Thereupon the local people were made to believe that the Buddha in the temple had manifested his power by making the thief give himself up, and they became more generous than before in their donations. Thus the monk managed to exploit an adverse situation to his own advantage. Since deception is rampant in this world of ours, how could the county magistrate expect to triumph over such crafty people just by stubbornly adhering to his own opinion?

78. A Ghost's Lie Is Laid Bare

Outside the county seat of Xian there were some mounds reputed to be a burial ground in the Han dynasty. While tilling his crop field a peasant blundered over one of the graves. Back home, he was taken down with a fever alternating with chills. A spirit began to speak through his mouth, accusing the man of damaging his grave. A scholar who happened to be present asked the ghost, "Who are you?" "A man from the Han dynasty," was the reply. "Where did you live in the Han dynasty?" the scholar asked. "I was a native of Xian County in the Han dynasty," the ghost said. "Therefore I was buried here. Why should you ask?" "This strikes me as very strange," observed the scholar. "In the Han dynasty this place was under the jurisdiction of the Hejian State and named Lecheng County. It was called Xian Prefecture in the Jin dynasty and was not renamed Xian County until the Ming dynasty. How could it have been known as Xian County in the Han dynasty?" The ghost gave no answer. When urged to speak, the peasant came out of the trance, his illness gone. It seemed that the ghost, aware of the popular belief that the graveyard was buried with people from the Han dynasty, had attached itself to the peasant and tried to obtain an offering by pretending to be a Han-dynasty ghost. However, its lie was laid bare by the scholar.

79. Wrong Message from a Rustic Ghost

During the summer a scholar named Han lodged in a mountain hut to read books. The window opened to a cliff overlooking a deep ravine. As the ravine was rather steep, it was impossible to cross over to the other side. Under the moonlight a phantom was often visible across the ravine. Knowing it must be a specter, the scholar felt no fear as it could not approach him. By and by he got used to its presence and tried to speak to it. In their conversation the ghost disclosed that he met his death by falling into the ravine and was waiting to be reborn. Half in jest the scholar reached out of the window and poured the residue in his wine cup into the stream. The ghost went down to take a drink, looking grateful. After that they became friends. Han found it delightful to have a chat with the ghost during the intervals between his rigorous study sessions.

Han once asked the ghost, "It is said that ghosts can foretell the future. I will take the imperial examination this year. Do you know whether I will succeed?" The ghost said, "Even a deity will know nothing about the future without referring to his documents, let alone a ghost. A ghost can tell a man's lease of life by the amount of positive energy in his body, and judge his moral character by the amount of light he gives off. As for what fortunes await a man, ghost underlings in the underworld may be able to overhear something, and ghosts in the city can exchange hearsays, but rustic ghosts will have no way to find out. Moreover, ghosts in the city may be either smart or slow; the stupid ones won't get any news. By the same token, when you come into the mountain to pursue your studies, you will know nothing about what happens in the local government, let alone the secret undertakings of the imperial court." A few days later the ghost called out to Han across the ravine in the evening, "Congratulations! The town god toured the mountain just now, and in his conversation with the land-god I seemed to hear him mention that you would be the number one candidate in the next provincial examination." Han rejoiced inwardly at the news. When the outcome of the examination was announced, it was another scholar with the family name of Han who came out first. Thereupon Han sighed, "It is indeed useless to seek official information from a peasant!"

80. Kindness Repaid by an Immortal

A man named Cui was banished to Guangdong after a brush with the law. For fear that his wife and concubine would come to harm if they should travel with him, he bade them good-bye and left for his exile all by himself. In Guangdong he sank into a gloomy mood with nothing to comfort him. The thought of his wife and concubine missing him in return only added to his melancholy. Then he made the acquaintance of an old man named Dong, with whom he had a most agreeable chat. Dong took pity on him and hired him to tutor his son. At Dong's invitation, Cui sat down to some wine one evening in the old man's house. His feelings stirred by the bright moon, he leaned against the balustrade, cup in hand, totally lost in thought. "You must be missing your family," the old man said with a smile. "The matter has been on my mind for a long time, and I am already seeing to it on your behalf. I did not tell you earlier because I was not sure if your wife and concubine could be fetched here. We'll have to wait and see."

Half a year later Dong suddenly ordered his servants and maids to clean out a room for an urgent arrival. In a short time three sedan chairs arrived at the house, and Cui's wife and concubine and a maid walked out. Both surprised and delighted, Cui asked his wife and concubine to explain. "Some days ago we got your letter telling us to come and to travel with an official's family," they said. "In a hurry we packed up and left. We entrusted our household affairs to an elder brother, who promised to collect our annual land rent in grains, then sell them and send us the money." "Where did you get the maid?" asked Cui. His wife replied, "She was the official's concubine. Since she did not get along with the principal wife, I got her for a good price." Moved to tears, Cui bowed to the old man in gratitude. Reunited with his family, he no longer felt homesick. A few months later the old man suggested, "Maybe the maid was destined to meet your family on the way. You might as well let her share your bed rather than leave her totally alone." Cui agreed.

Some years later the emperor proclaimed a general amnesty, which meant Cui was allowed to return home. At the news he was too excited to sleep at night, but his wife, concubine and maid all looked joyless. Cui tried to comfort them. "Are you missing the old man for his kindness? As long as I am alive, I will repay him someday." They made no reply but began to help him with the packing up. At the farewell dinner given by the old man, he called the three women over and said to Cui, "It's time now to tell you the whole story. I am in fact an earthly immortal. In a previous life I was an official and you my colleague. After my death you spared no efforts in taking care of and giving financial assistance to my wife and children, for which I shall always feel grateful. When you took leave of your family and came alone to this strange land a few years ago, I thought it my duty to arrange for the reunion of your family, but the journey here would be too arduous for two mortal women. Therefore I sent three nymphs to spend half a year in your house to get familiar with your wife and concubine's voices and appearances and listen in to family anecdotes, so that you would not have any doubts. As they were three sisters, one of them disguised herself as a maid. You need not miss them, for what you regard as their looks is merely an illusion. When you return home to join your family, you will scarcely see any difference."

Unwilling to part with the three nymphs, Cui asked Dong to let him take them home. "Spirits and deities have their own domain," Dong explained. "They are allowed only temporary stay beyond the boundary." In tears the three women bade Cui good-bye, then vanished. When he got on the boat, he found them standing on the bank gazing after him from a distance. On his return his wife told him that the financial situation in the family had been going from bad to worse, and she would not have been able to make ends meet but for the money sent by him every year. Obviously this had also been arranged by the old man. If everyone separated from his family had the luck to meet this old man, there would be no lovesickness in the world. The above story was told by a compiler in the Hanlin Academy named Wang Shi, who concluded, "Since earthly immortals can be found in Guangdong, they must also exist in other places. Since Dong is capable of such magic feats, other earthly immortals must be equally accomplished. Others do not share Cui's good fortune simply because they did no immortal any favor in their past lives and naturally will not get generous help in return."

81. Courtesans Visited by Foxes and Ghosts

In the town of Bo a traveling merchant stayed the night with a prostitute. When he paid her, she examined the piece of silver in her hand carefully and heated it over the lamp. "It's not made of paper, I hope!" she said with a smile. The surprised businessman asked what she meant by that. A few days before, she said, she had gone to watch a sacrificial performance put on by a ship carrying a cargo of grains. Returning late at night, she ran into a young man who handed her a piece of silver, and they consummated the arrangement in a shed by the river. Back home, she took out the silver from her bosom. It felt very light in her hand, and on a close look she found it made of paper. Only then did she realize she had met a ghost. Then she told the merchant what had happened to another prostitute living nearby. She had met a patron who was very generous with gifts of clothing and jewelry. After he left, she discovered that all those clothing and jewelry had been taken from her own chest, which had always remained locked. Thus she suspected herself to have been the victim of a wily fox. On hearing this, the merchant joked, "Perhaps it is the way of heaven for one to get what one deserves!"

The following story was told by a blind man named Liu Junduan. A man in Qing county was friendly with a fox. They often drank wine together like good chums. But then the fox failed to show up for a long time. One day the man was walking across a wasteland when he heard someone moaning in the grass. Hurrying over, he found his fox friend. "How did you get yourself into such a mess?" he asked. Despondent and shamefaced, the fox said after a long pause, "A few days ago I saw a young prostitute who looked strong and vigorous, so I assumed human form to sleep with her, hoping to absorb some of her vital energy. Unfortunately she had been carrying a vile disease. The poison of her disease flowed into my body along with her vital forces and merged with all the energy I had ever gathered. Like oil mixed into flour, they became totally inseparable. Gradually the poison permeated my whole body and spread to my face. Too embarrassed to meet anyone, I have shunned my friends for a long time."

82. Journey of the Spirit

A wealthy man was very fond of a maid and showered favors on her. The maid, infatuated with her master, vowed to marry no one but him. The man's principal wife burned with jealousy, but there was nothing she could do. Then the man left on a business trip. Seizing the chance, his wife secretly sold the maid to a middlewoman. On her husband's return she would tell him the maid had run away of her own accord. Aware that the matter would be reversed on the master's return, a house servant bought the maid back from the middlewoman and consigned her to a convent. On her arrival at the middlewoman's house the maid stared blankly, not saying anything, and allowed herself to be pulled to her feet, led to a seat or bed. If left alone, she remained motionless all day like a wooden figure. She ate and drank when given food and water, but never asked for them. Her conditions did not change after her entry into the convent. The physician summoned to treat her diagnosed heart blockage by phlegm caused by excessive anger, but the medicine he prescribed had no effect on her. Thus she stayed on in the convent, more dead than alive.

A month or so later the man returned home to find his beloved woman gone. He flew into such a rage that he pulled a dagger at his wife. The servant, knowing the secret could not be kept from his master, divulged to him what had happened. The man immediately went to the convent and brought back the maid, who remained in a trance. When he called her name into her ear, she came to with a start. She told her master that when led away by the middlewoman, she told herself that it was the mistress's idea to sell her, but the master would never give her up. Therefore she let her spirit run back home and her body stayed in the convent. To avoid being discovered by the mistress, she went into hiding to wait for the master's return. When he called out her name a moment before, she was overjoyed and ran out at once.

83. A Ghost Cowers Before the Bully

Tian Buman, a hired hand, lost his way one night. He stumbled into a graveyard and stepped on a skull. "Don't crush my face!" growled the skull, "Or I'll do you harm!" Tian, a rash and bold fellow, responded harshly, "Why did you get in my way?" "I didn't want to get in your way," answered the skull, "Someone moved me here." Tian shouted again, "Then why don't you go and do harm to that man?" "I can't do anything to him," said the skull, "because he is in good luck." Both offended and amused, Tian said, "So you think I'm in bad luck? Why do you bully the weak and fear the strong?" The skull started to sob. "You are also in good luck, so I dare do nothing against you. I was only making empty threats. It is common for a man to bully the weak and fear the strong, so why blame a ghost for doing the same? If you take pity on me and move me into a pit, I'll be most grateful." Tian ignored the ghost's plea and walked away in strides. He heard the skull weeping piteously behind him, but nothing unusual happened to him after that. In my opinion, Tian could have shown a bit benevolence and sympathy, but the ghost itself was to blame for enraging an intrepid man with big talk.

84. A Gentleman Does not Connive with a Ghost

My late teacher Chen Baiya told the following story about his tutor (whose family name was Zhou, as far as I can remember). A firm believer in the Cheng-Zhu school of Confucianism, he did not court fame by posing as a man of high principles and therefore remained obscure and neglected all his life. He was nevertheless a true gentleman with a heart of gold. Once he took lodgings in a few empty rooms. In the evening a voice said outside the window, "I have to tell you something, but do not want to cause any alarm. What shall I do?" "Just come in," Zhou said. The man walked into the room, holding his head with both hands. He was wearing no headcloth, and half of his gown was soaked in blood. Bowing with clasped hands Zhou invited him to take a seat, and the man returned the salute politely. "What do you want to tell me?" Zhou asked. "I was killed by robbers at the end of the Ming dynasty," the man began, "and my spirit has lingered in this house ever since. There were people who came before you. Though I did not go out of my way to disturb them, it was unavoidable for their positive energy to clash with my negative energy. As a result they raised alarms, and neither did I enjoy any peace. Now I have come up with a solution: The neighbor has a mansion big enough for your whole family. I will go and haunt the place until they move out. If others come to stay, I will go and make troubles again. Finally the house will be abandoned. Then you can buy it for a good price and move in, and I will be able to live here in peace. Don't you think it a marvelous plan for killing two birds with one stone?"

"I have no use for schemes and intrigues," said the old gentleman. "To help a ghost harm people is out of the question. I won't do anything like that. I use this room as my studio because I enjoy peace and quiet. Since you are staying here, I will use it as a storeroom and keep it locked all day. What do you say to that?" Looking shamefaced, the ghost bowed by way of apology. "I made the offer because I saw some books on the cultivation of human nature on your desk. I did not know that you are a true gentleman. Please forgive me for speaking nonsense. Since you are kind enough to let me stay, I will avail myself of your hospitality." Zhou lived in the house for four years without encountering anything unusual again. Maybe it was his righteous attitude that kept the ghost at bay.

85. A Past-Life Debt Crossed Out

Jiang Ting, a cloth peddler, had a spotted dog who followed him everywhere. One day he happened to be walking alone when an old man accosted him. "I don't know you," Jiang said. "Why do you stop me?" The old man knelt and kowtowed, then replied, "I am a fox. In my past life I killed you, and three days later you will send your dog to break my throat with its teeth. I cannot escape, for this has been predetermined in the underworld. But it occurs to me that it has been over a hundred years since I killed you. I have degenerated into a fox, and you have been reborn as a man. You can get no benefits by chasing and killing a fox. In addition, you do not remember how you were killed in your past life, so you will not get any pleasure out of killing a fox. I am willing to give my daughter to you if you spare my life. Will you accept my offer?"

"I dare not let a fox into my house," Jiang responded, "nor will I take a girl against her will. I am willing to spare you, but who can guarantee that my dog will never attack you?" The old man replied, "You only have to write a note saying you agree to overlook the past-life debt owed to you by so-and-so. After I show the note to the god of the underworld, the dog will not bite me anymore. As long as a victim agrees to forget past grievances, the gods will not raise any objection." Jiang happened to have some paper and a writing brush with him to keep accounts, so he wrote a note there and then. The old man took the note and went away in jubilation.

Seven or eight years afterward Jiang, out on a trading trip, was crossing a big river when a storm rose. In the crucial moment the sail could not be lowered, so that the boat was about to be overturned in the violent wind. Just then a man was seen climbing swiftly up the mast, broke the rope and leapt onto the sail, riding it down to the deck. From a distance Jiang seemed to recognize the old fox he had met before, but in the twinkling of an eye the man was gone. On hearing the story, everyone praises the fox for returning the favor he had received, but I have a different opinion. How could the fox, who was unable to save its own life, have gone a thousand li to rescue someone else? The gods must have increased Jiang Ting's lease on life to reward him for sparing the old fox, who was then dispatched to come to his rescue.

86. The Art of Augury

Li Xuan, an assistant regional commander in the army stationed in Gansu, could make accurate predictions by observing various signs. He once joined an expedition to the western frontier as a member of Grand Academician Wen's staff. After a soldier accidentally set fire to the dry grass in front of the commander's tent, leaving a burnt area, Wen asked Li Xuan to make out what the incident signified. "It indicates that in a few days you will submit a secret memorial to the emperor," Li replied. "The fire burning swiftly over dry grass points to an urgent dispatch. The smoke going up to the sky points to presentation to a higher level. Therefore there will be a secret memorial." "But I have nothing to write a secret memorial about," Wen said. To this Li replied, "It was also by accident that the grass caught fire, not by prearrangement." A few days later his prediction was borne out.

To tell a man's fortune Li Xuan would ask him to pick up something at random. Sometimes two men who picked up the same object were given different prognoses. During a stay in the imperial capital Li was asked by an official from the Hanlin Academy, who picked up a bronze pipe, to tell his fortune. "The pipe is lit, with smoke circulating inside. This means you are not holding an indifferent post. Neither do you have a high-profile position, though, for the pipe need someone to breathe air through it." "How long will my term of office last?" "Forgive me for being blunt," Li said. "There isn't a big fire to begin with. Once it goes out, only debris will be left, so that the heat will not last very long." "How old will I live to?" "Though a bronze object is quite durable," Li replied, "no one would expect a pipe to last a hundred years." At this the official left in a huff, but what happened to him afterward proved the accuracy of Li's prediction. After the Hanlin official left, a director seated in the same room picked up the pipe again, asking Li for a reading. "The fire in the pipe has died down, which means you are in a much neglected position. It was left on the bed a moment ago, which means you were dismissed from your office. Now that it is picked up, you must have resumed office with someone's help. The pipe will be lit again, but then what I said about the other man will apply to you as well." His prophesy came true afterward.

87. Justice Is Restored by a Fox

Cheng, a pedantic old man in the village, had a very pretty daughter. One day, when she went out to buy rouge and powder, a young man in the neighborhood acted lewdly toward her. Back home, she gave her parents a tearful account of the incident. Cheng was indignant, but he dared not go and reason with the young man, who was a local bully wont to throwing his weight around. The old man sank into a very gloomy mood. He was friendly with a fox, whom he often invited home to drink wine. One day the fox noticed the old man's dejected look and asked what was troubling him. After Cheng told the story, the fox took his leave without making any comment.

Some days later the young man came again to Cheng's house to find the girl leaning on the door and smiling at him. They got into a conversation, then made love in an empty room in the vegetable garden. When they parted, the girl was reluctant to let him go. Tearfully she asked him to elope with her. That night the young man returned to Cheng's house and took the girl back home. To prevent the old man from finding out where his daughter had gone, he pulled a dagger at his wife, saying, "I'll kill you if you tell anyone!" When several days went by without incident, the young man realized that Cheng, considering his daughter's elopement as a family disgrace, would not breathe a word about it. Well pleased, he gave himself up to unbridled licence with the girl.

Gradually the girl began to behave in a weird and secretive way. By the time the young man realized that she was actually a fox-woman, he had become too infatuated with her to drive her away. After a year or so his health broke down because of overindulgence in sex. With his life hanging by a thread, the fox-woman took her leave. He survived after spending all the wealth of his family on his treatment. He and his wife became homeless and had to sleep out on the street. As he was too weak to work, his wife had to earn their daily bread by prostitution. The bully in him was nowhere to be found. One day Cheng, who did not know the story behind all this, mentioned it to the fox. "I dispatched a cunning maid to wreck him," the fox explained. "She disguised herself as your daughter in order to lead him into the trap. Then she revealed herself to be a fox in order to protect your daughter's reputation. When he was on the point of dying she took her leave, for he had not committed a capital offense. Now that he has received the punishment he deserves, you no longer need to feel depressed." It is extraordinary and commendable for the fox to exercise restraint in his gallant act to aid the old man.

88. To Love or Die

Ding Jing, a tenant in Dongjia village, had a son named Erniu and a son-in-law named Cao Ning, who had married into the family to help out with the work in the field. When Erniu had a son, he named the baby Sanbao—"Third Treasure". A few days later Cao Ning's wife gave birth to a daughter, whom he named Sibao, or "Fourth Treasure", as they belonged to the same family living under one roof. As the two babies were born only a few days apart in the same month of the same year, their mothers took turns carrying and milking them. Thus Sanbao and Sibao grew to be intimate companions. When a bit older, they always kept each other company. In a small family like theirs no prudent reserve was maintained between the sexes. While playing together, the two children was often told by the elders, "This is your husband, and that is your wife." Though the meaning of husband and wife was beyond them, they were used to such terms. On reaching seven or eight years of age they began to understand a few things, but they continued to sleep in the same room with their grandmother.

    Then the area suffered crop failure for several successive years. Both Ding Jing and his wife died of illness. Cao Ning left for the capital, where he was forced by poverty to sell Sibao as a maid to a family named Chen. Somewhat later Erniu also came to the capital. As the Chens happened to need a servant boy, Sanbao was also sold into their house after being warned against mentioning his engagement with Sibao. Under a harsh discipline, servants of the Chen family received frequent flogging. Whenever Sibao got flogged, Sanbao would weep silently; whenever Sanbao got flogged, Sibao would also shed tears for him. Growing suspicious, Chen sold Sibao to a Zheng family and drove Sanbao out of the house. Sanbao went to work as a servant boy for another family. After some time he found out Sibao's whereabouts and left to work for the Zheng family. At their reunion the two children embraced and burst in tears. They were then both thirteen to fourteen years old. Upon Zheng's curious inquiry, they told him they were brother and sister, and Zheng believed them because of the connection in their names. As they were assigned to separate quarters of the house, all they could do was exchanging amorous glances when passing each other at the gate.

After the village enjoyed a good harvest, both Erniu and Cao Ning arrived in the capital again to fetch their children. With some difficulty they found their way to the Zheng family. Only then did Zheng learn that Sanbao and Sibao were engaged. Moved by pity, he expressed his willingness to arrange for their wedding and continue to hire them, but was stopped from doing so by Yan, the family tutor who regarded himself as a man of firm principles. "Marriage between cousins," Yan declared, "will be punished by heaven as it goes against the rites and violates the law. Though my host's offer is well-intended, a scholar like me has the duty to safeguard public morality. Failure to stop incest would amount to abetment of such wrongdoing and would be unworthy of a true gentleman." Zheng was timid and weak in character, while Erniu and Cao Ning were both illiterate peasants. Informed that it would be a felony to marry Sanbao and Sibao, they gave up the idea in trepidation. Afterward Sibao, sold to an official-in-waiting as a concubine, died of illness a few months later. Crazed with grief, Sanbao ran away, never to show up again. Someone who claimed to be in the know said, "Though she was coerced into marriage, Sibao disfigured herself, wept bitterly all day, and never spent a single night with her husband." In that case her death did not spell an end to the romance between this couple, who will surely enjoy a reunion someday, be it on earth or in heaven. Yet it is difficult to understand Yan's motive for doing something so outrageous. No doubt he will get the punishment he deserves when justice is carried out by heaven. Someone else said, "Actually Yan was not motivated by bigotry, nor was he trying to earn a reputation for upholding moral principles. He simply took a fancy to Sibao because of her good looks and wanted to make her his own." If that is the case, Yan will surely end up in hell, established specially for the likes of him.

89. Trial of a Ghost Case

Two men, A and B, came to accuse each other before the magistrate of Zhangye County in Gan Prefecture. A called B a liar, but B claimed to be telling the truth. Under interrogation it was found that they were cousins. A and his wife had been traveling to the western frontier accompanied by B. One night they lost their way a few dozen li east of Gan Prefecture, when they saw someone dressed like a servant from a wealthy family. This man told them his master's mansion was nearby and offered to put them up for the night and direct them back to the main road the following day. Walking for three or four li after him, they got to a small castle. The man went in and, after what seemed a long time, returned to beckon them in. "The master invites you to enter," he said. They were led through several doors and brought before a man seated in a hall. After an inquiry of their names and places of birth, the man said, "It is getting too late to invite you to a meal, so I will just let you stay the night here. The small room by the gate can hold two people. As for this lady, she can sleep with the servant women." After A and B went to bed, they seemed to hear a woman shouting. When they got up in the dark, they could not find the door. Then the shouting stopped. They thought they were mistaken and went back to sleep.

The following day they woke up to find themselves lying in the open country. They got up in a hurry to look for A's wife. She was lying under a tree half a li away, her arms tied behind her back, her hair tousled, her clothes stripped and hanging from a branch high above the ground. The night before, she told them, she had been brought here by a maid. She saw several splendid rooms and a few maids and serving women. After a while the host came in and told her to sit by his side. When she resisted, the maids and serving women grabbed hold of her, stripped her naked and tied her to the bed. She cried for help at the top of her voice, but none came to her rescue, so the host raped her. Just before dawn the host placed two objects by her neck. In an instant the entire house vanished, and she found herself lying on the ground in the open air. They looked beside her neck to see two fifty-tael silver ingots. According to the inscriptions, they were minted in the Chongzhen reign of the Ming dynasty. The surface of the ingots had turned black after long-time underground burial, which seemed to indicate that they were really over a hundred years old. A asked B to hush up the matter, offering to pay him half the silver in return. When A went back on his word later, B kicked up a big row, and the story became known.

When questioned by the magistrate, A and his wife flatly denied the story. Asked about the ingots, they claimed to have picked them up somewhere. As to the wounds of bondage on the woman, she said they were scratches. Judging by their equivocation, the magistrate knew there must be some truth in B's account. Thereupon he said to A with a smile, "The law requires you to turn in to the government whatever valuables you have picked up. In consideration of your family's financial difficulty, I will allow you to keep the silver." Then he turned to B with a glare. "If you were lying, the silver ingots were picked up and should be turned in to the government, and you will get nothing. If you told the truth, the silver was the ghost's payment to A's wife, so there will be still less reason to give you a share. Importunate no more, or you will be birched!" With this he sent the two men away. By dealing with an unusual case in an unusual way, the magistrate proved himself good at adapting to circumstances.

90. How a Fox-Maid Wins Her Freedom

My wet nurse, Granny Li, was a native of Cangzhou. Her son, Zhu'er, was told the following tale about a fox while he worked as a herdsman along the coast. A salt-man had gone to bed one night when he heard rustling sounds in the room. By the moonlight coming in through the window, he could see no one and concluded the noise had been made by a mouse. A moment later a noisy crowd approached the house from the distance. "She has slipped into this room," said a man's voice. The salt-man was puzzling over these words when the man outside knocked on the window and asked, "Are you in there?" "Yes, I am," replied a voice in the room. "Did the host let you stay?" "Yes, he did," came the reply. "Are you in the same bed with him or put up in a separate room?" the man asked again. "Who would have let me stay without making me share his bed?" the voice in the room shot back. The man outside the window stamped his feet, crying, "How terrible! How terrible!" This was followed by a woman's laughing voice. "I told you whatever place she ran to, no one would let her stay for nothing, and you did not believe me. Now what? Aren't you too ashamed to take her back home?" Then there came the noise of people walking to and fro. A moment later the woman laughed again. "You can't make up your mind on such a small matter—and you call yourself a man!" Knocking on the window, she called into the room, "Since the maid who ran away from our family has consigned herself to you, and you have kept her for the night, it would be impossible for us to take her back. The old fool has no excuse to vent his anger on you, for you did nothing to seduce or coerce the girl. Even if he bears a grudge against you, I can assure you that he dare do nothing. We will take our leave, and the two of you can go back to sleep."

The salt-man peeped out through a crack in the window and found the crowd gone. Turning back, he saw a beautiful girl lying by his side. Both surprised and delighted, he asked where she had come from. "I am a fox-woman," the girl replied. "I was bought by the fox who spoke to you just now to be his concubine. His wife was so jealous that she found an excuse to give me a beating every day.

Unable to bear it any longer, I ran away to save myself. I did not ask your permission for fear that you would not dare let me stay and I would be taken back by force. So I hid myself on a corner of your bed until they came, then told them I had already slept with you, hoping to send them away. Now that I am free at last, I am willing to stay with you through thick and thin." The salt-man expressed his worry that the sudden appearance of a beautiful wife by his side would rouse suspicion and jealousy and bring him harm. "I can make myself invisible," the girl said. "Have you forgotten how I hid on your bed a moment ago?" So she stayed. Thanks to her diligence and hard work in running the house, they gradually became fairly well-off. Zhu'er, being a distant relative of the salt-man, was able to learn about the story in great detail. In afterthought, the fox-maid was taking a great risk when she told a self-deprecating lie to save herself from suffering. It was precisely because of her self-claimed loss of chastity that her husband was unable to take her back home and her mistress was able to drive her away. Thus the risky move turned out to be a master stroke that achieved her purpose. As for her husband, by failing to anticipate the consequences when he took her for his concubine or resolve the conflicts that ensued, he should take the blame for driving her into desperation and flight. A little bit of self-knowledge on his part would have saved him all this trouble and disgrace.

91. The Revenge of Condemned Prisoners

It is said that Confucius never overdid anything. Apart from the intention to stay within proper limits in rectifying improper deeds, the sage was forestalling undesirable consequences in the future. Lao Zi wrote, "When people do not fear death, what is the use of threatening them with death?" Actually it is not so much that the common people are not afraid to die as that they will no longer fear death when death becomes inevitable. Once a man does not fear death, he will be capable of doing anything. In my childhood I was told the following story. After suffering a robbery, a wealthy family offered rewards for the capture of the robbers. In half a year or so all the robbers were caught and pleaded guilty to the charge. However, the head of the robbed family was so consumed with hatred that he offered handsome bribes to the prison guards in order to have the robbers tortured. Thus the robbers were unable to stand straight or lie down. They could not get untied even to relieve themselves, until they had maggots crawling in their pants. In the meantime they were given enough food, so that they could live on in misery. Filled with hatred against the family, the robbers had a talk among themselves. For armed robbery, the main culprit and his accomplices would all be beheaded. For raping women, the punishment was exactly the same. According to the penal code, if someone committed both offences, he would still be beheaded rather than receive an aggravated sentence such as having his body hacked into pieces and displayed in public. Therefore the robbers, when interrogated again, claimed in unison to have raped every female member in that family. Though the official in charge did not have this entered in the record of the robbers' confession, what they said was heard clearly by everyone present, and the story soon became known. Some people begrudging the wealthy family eagerly chimed in, arguing that since the robbers were about to be punished for the robbery, the only reason why the head of the family spared no expense to have them tortured in various ways was that he hated them bitterly for having raped every woman in his family. The story spread quickly, and no one could tell if it was true. With his family name suffering a terrible blot, the head of the wealthy family sank into deep remorse.

The robbers would not have blamed the head of the wealthy family for their death sentence. Neither would they have blamed him for their arrest and interrogation under torment. However, it would have been impossible for them to resign to the various tortures inflicted on them illegally. If one tosses a stone against a rock too forcefully, it will bounce back to harm oneself. The man certainly overreached himself when he, in return for a momentary sense of triumph, brought disgrace to his family for countless generations to come.

92. Wife Comes Back to Life in Maid's Body

An official-in-waiting named Zhang arrived in the capital with his wife and a maid and took lodgings on Haifengsi Road. A year later his wife died from illness. After another year or so the maid also died of a sudden illness. As he was about to have her put into the coffin, she was heard to be breathing again. A moment later she rolled her eyes and regained consciousness. Taking him by the hand, she said tearfully, "I did not expect to see you again after over a year's separation!" He stared at her in dismay, not knowing what she was talking about. "I am not delirious," said the woman. "I am your wife and come back to life in the maid's body. Though you let her wait on you in bed, she was not content to be below me, so she plotted with a vicious nun to harm me by sorcery. After I died of illness, they had my spirit locked up in a vase, sealed it with a magic spell and buried it under a wall of the convent. I spent a terrible time in the dark and muggy vase. Then the wall collapsed. When the ground was dug up to rebuild the wall, a digger broke the vase, and I was set free. I looked around in a daze, not knowing where to go. Fortunately I met a temple deity who told me to petition to the town-god. I did not know then that wicked sorcerers always had some evil gods to back them up; thus my petition was rejected. Finally I sent a direct appeal to the God of Eastern Mountain. After the nun was summoned and made to confess, the maid was seized and thrown into hell. As there were some years left of my lease on life, and my own body had already decayed, I was allowed to reincarnate in the maid's body."

After listening to her story all the family were delighted and treated her as the mistress of the house. However, the accused nun declared that the official-in-waiting had arranged for the maid to fake death because he wanted to make her his principal wife. She threatened to bring him to court on a charge of slander. For lack of concrete evidence of his wife's revival, he decided to stop talking about it; otherwise the local authorities might suspect him of spreading a rumor to mislead people. But according to his house servants, their mistress could recall with perfect accuracy what had happened before and her speech and conduct remained unchanged after her rebirth. Moreover, the maid was sloppy at needlework, while the mistress was very skilled at embroidery. After coming back to life she went on to embroider a shoe left unfinished at her death, and when completed it seemed to be the work of the same person. Judging by this, the wife had really been restored to life. The incident took place in the late years of the Yongzheng reign.

93. A Hapless Loving Couple

In the following story a couple, after an initial separation, met frequently yet remained out of each other's reach. It was hard to understand why such a fate should have befallen them. In Zhongzhou a scholar named Li was married only ten days when his mother fell seriously ill. In the next seven to eight months the newly wedded couple took turns caring for the sick, too busy to undress for the night. After the old woman's death they practiced abstinence for three years in observance of an ancient rule. Then they were forced by poverty to take refuge in her grandfather's house. Her grandfather's family was barely able to make ends meet, and there was scarcely any spare space left. Nevertheless a room was cleaned out to put them up. In less than a month Li's mother-in-law received her own mother into the house, for her younger brother, who had been taking care of the old woman, had found himself a post far away from home. To make room for the old woman, Li's wife had to share a room with her mother, while Li himself began to sleep on a couch in the studio. From then on the couple met only at mealtime. Two years later Li went alone to make a living in the imperial capital, while his father-in-law took his entire family to Jiangxi, where he had found a post as an official's in-house advisor. Soon afterward Li got news of his wife's death. Overcome with grief, he was too disheartened to strife for self-advancement and went south to find his father-in-law. On his arrival in Jiangxi, his father-in-law had already left for an unknown destination to work for another official.

With no place to go, Li was compelled to earn a living by selling his works of calligraphy on the roadside. One day a hefty man, after looking at his works, said to him, "Your handwriting is excellent. Do you want to work as a scribe on thirty or forty taels of silver a year?" Overjoyed, Li followed the man onto a boat. As they sailed on the river amid a dense mist, Li had no idea where they were going. On his arrival Li was given a courteous reception. After leafing through the mail, he realized that the host was a robber, but there was no alternative for him but to stay. To prevent future trouble he concealed his true name and place of birth. The robber, who enjoyed luxury and merry-making, kept a host of singing girls. When he gave a feast, he never failed to invite Li. On such an occasion Li noticed that one of the robber's concubines looked exactly like his late wife. This might be a ghost, he told himself. The woman also eyed him frequently as if she knew him, but neither dared exchange a word. Li's father-in-law, in fact, had been held up by this robber while crossing the river. Attracted by the good looks of Li's wife, the robber took her away. Her father regarded this as a family disgrace, so he spread the news of her death and had a sheet-plank coffin transported back to their hometown and buried in haste. In the meantime Li's wife, coerced by the robber, became his concubine. Not knowing his wife was still alive, Li took her for a look-alike. Not knowing he was using a false name, she thought the same about him. Thus they failed to recognize each other. After that they met once every few days. By and by they got used to it and stopped gazing at each other. This went on for six or seven years.

One day the robber called Li over and told him, "A disaster will soon happen to me. As a scholar you need not get involved. Here is fifty taels of gold. Tuck it away and hide yourself among the reeds. As soon as the government troops are gone, find a fishing boat to get out of here. The local people know who you are and will help you." With a sweep of his hand he sent Li away. A moment later Li heard shouting and fighting noises. Then someone called out, "The robbers have sailed away. Let's count the valuables and women they left behind." It was already dark, but Li could see by the light of the torches the singing girls escorted by whip-snapping soldiers. They were scantily clad, hair dishevelled and arms tied behind their back. That concubine was also among them; she was trembling with fear, appearing so miserable that Li could hardly bear to look at her. The following day the island became totally abandoned. Li was standing on the bank in a stupor when someone called out, "Is that you, Mister? Our chief is safe. He has sent me to get you out." After sailing for a whole day the boat pulled in to shore. Afraid to be recognized by the locals, he set out northward at once, taking the gold with him.

    Li returned home to find his father-in-law already back. After selling the gold, he settled down to a comfortable life. It occurred to him that he and his beloved wife had shared the same bed for less than a month altogether during the years of their marriage. Now that he was a little better off, he could not bear to leave her buried in a sheet-plank coffin, and decided to buy a better one to replace it. He also wanted to take a look at her remains as a reminder of the love they had shared. Unable to dissuade him, his father-in-law told him the truth. Li left for the south at once and traveled day and night, hoping for a reunion with his wife. By the time he got there, the singing girls and concubines seized by the government troops had all been given away as rewards; there was no way to find out where they had gone. Whenever Li thought of the time spent on the island, when he had been so close to his wife yet failed to reach out for her, he was filled with remorse. Whenever he thought of the sufferings she had gone through, tied up and whipped together with the singing girls, and the sufferings that would surely befall her afterward, his grief knew no bounds. He never remarried and finally left home to be a monk.

94. Black Magic

A man on a sojourn away from his hometown was once invited to tour the lake on board a gaily painted boat. The guests were entertained with music from vertical flutes and drums and waited on by a young woman in a red skirt. On a closer look the man recognized her to be his wife, who should be at home two thousand li away. Afraid to be ridiculed by his companions, he dared not go up to address her. The woman did not seem to know him, for she was neither afraid nor ashamed. She drank a toast to the guests, then played a piece of music, looking perfectly at ease. He noticed that her voice sounded different from his wife's. In addition, unlike his wife, she did not cover her mouth with her hand to hide a smile. But then he discovered that, exactly like his wife, she had a red mole on her right wrist. Confused and perplexed, he was in no mood to drink wine, and took his leave as soon as the feast was over. Packing up his belongings, he was about to leave for home when a family letter brought him the news of his wife's death half a year before. This made him believe he had seen a ghost. His companions, who noticed his uneasy air, harried him for an explanation. When he told them the story, they all agreed that the young woman was simply someone bearing a striking resemblance to his wife.

Afterward something unusual happened to a man who frequently travelled between the Wu and Yue regions. He did not go out visiting friends, nor did he do any business. Instead, he stayed indoors all day with his team of concubines. Now and then he would send for a middleman and sell a woman or two. People suspected that he was a trader of women, but no one was concerned enough to look into the matter. One day the man suddenly bought a boat to take him to Tianmu Mountain. Before his departure he called on a revered monk in a temple and asked him to hold a sacrifice, saying, "I have acquired my skills from Buddha and should ask for Buddha's blessing." When pressed, he began to talk in vague terms, unwilling to give a clear explanation. The monk, doubtful of his motive, returned his donation and sent him away. Half along the way the man was struck dead by a thunderbolt. Later, a former attendant of his divulged the secret. This man had learned black magic from a red-robed Tibetan monk. By chanting incantations he could summon the newly interned body of a young woman, then instill it with a fox-spirit or a lustful female ghost mustered from somewhere else. This revived woman was made to wait on him as a concubine. After a period of time he would find another woman to replace her, who would then be sold for a good price. One day a god warned him in a dream that heaven had passed a death sentence on him as he had committed his full share of crimes. He hastened to the temple to express penitence and pray for mercy, but was unable to escape his doom. After this story became known, it occurred to some people that the traveling man's wife must have fallen victim to the black magician.

95. The Ghost of One Devoured by a Tiger

My disciple Ge Zhenghua, a native of Jizhou, told the following story. Several merchants from his hometown were driving some mules along in the mountain when they saw a Taoist priest standing on a narrow path used by firewood gatherers. Wearing a black robe and a bamboo hat, he waved at one of the travellers and asked, "What's your name?" After the man gave the answer, the Taoist wanted to know his place of birth, then told him, "You are the one I'm looking for. You are a heavenly immortal exiled to the human world. Now that your term is over, you can return to heaven. As your master I have come especially to lead the way for you. Come with me." The man thought to himself that a slow, thickheaded and totally illiterate man like himself was unlikely to be an immortal incarnate. Moreover, it would be unthinkable for him to leave his aged parents behind and go away to enjoy himself in heaven. Therefore he declined the offer adamantly. Heaving a deep sigh, the Taoist turned to the others. "Since he has given up on himself, I need someone to take his place. Our encounter today could be destined. Does any of you want to follow me? Such a chance only appears once in a thousand years." Surprised and doubtful, they did not answer him, and he left angrily. Stopping at an inn, the merchants told the story to the other guests. Some thought it a pity for them to turn down the offer of an immortal; others thought it dangerous to follow the Taoist, who must be a demon in disguise. The next day several inquisitive men traced back to the narrow path and climbed

113

up to a mountain ridge, where they saw carcasses in the grass of people newly devoured by tigers. Terribly frightened, they ran back as fast as their legs could carry them. Perhaps the Taoist was the ghost of a man devoured by a tiger, who must help the beast to devour others in order to be reborn. A gratuitous piece of good luck makes a greedy, brash person jubilant but a wise man alarmed. The merchant who had refused to follow the Taoist, though he considered himself slow and thickheaded, was in fact very smart.

96. The Interaction of Dream and Reality

The nature of dreams remains a mystery. History books contain an account of King Huai of Chu's journey in his dream to Gaotang to have a tryst with a fairy. This romantic episode has become fairly well-known. My elder brother Qinghu refuted the story in a poem, arguing that since one's dream concerns only oneself, the fairy of Gaotang had had nothing whatsoever to do with King Huai. However, there are people who have witnessed someone else's dream. A servant named Li Xing was strolling outside the village on a moonlit night to enjoy the cool when he spotted in a grove of date trees a young woman from a neighbor's family. As she might be keeping a night watch on the field and was probably accompanied by her husband or parents-in-law, he thought it inconvenient for him to greet her. Then she walked west along a ridged plot for half a li and vanished into a sorghum field. Suspecting that she was meeting a lover, Li stood gazing from a distance, not daring to pursue her. After a while she walked out of the sorghum field, paused before a ditch that blocked her way, then headed north along the ditch for a hundred steps or so. As the road ahead got muddy, she turned northeast into a bean plot, trudging along with difficulty, and tripped and fell over twice. Aware that she had lost her way, Li shouted, "Where are you going so late at night? Don't go further north or you'll fall into a mud pool!" The woman turned and recognized him. "I can't get out of here," she said. "Please come and lead me home." Just as Li was hurrying toward her, she suddenly disappeared. Knowing that he had seen a ghost, he felt a cold shiver down his spine and ran back home for dear life. On his return he saw the woman sitting with her mother under the wall outside their house. Because of fatigue she had nodded off while spinning cotton. In her dream she walked into a forest, lost her way, and finally woke up with a start when Li Xing called out behind her. Her description of the dream matched what Li Xing had seen. Apparently the woman's spirit had taken leave of her body temporarily due to exhaustion. Such a spirit, not completely severed from the body as in the case of a ghost, is sometimes visible to the living.

97. Quest for the Stone Beasts

In southern Cangzhou there was a temple built on the river bank. In a flood its gate had been destroyed, and the two stone beasts guarding the gate sunk into the river. When about a dozen years later the monks collected enough funds to refurbish the temple, they could not find the two stone beasts in the water. This made them believe that the beasts had drifted downstream, so they sailed down the river in small boats poking everywhere with iron rakes, but stopped after a fruitless search for over ten li. In the temple there was a Confucian scholar teaching a few students in a rented room. Informed of what was going on, he laughed. "People like you are unable to penetrate into the nature of something," he said. "How can stone beasts be carried downstream like a piece of wood? Stone is solid and heavy by nature, whereas sand is loose and light. Therefore a stone on sand will only sink deeper and deeper. How ignorant of you to think it would move downstream!"

The scholar's remark won the admiration of his listeners, but an old soldier in the river-control squad disagreed. "To retrieve a stone object from the river, one must go upstream," he declared. "Stone is solid and heavy by nature, whereas sand is loose and light. Unable to move the stone, the river water will bounce back to wash away the

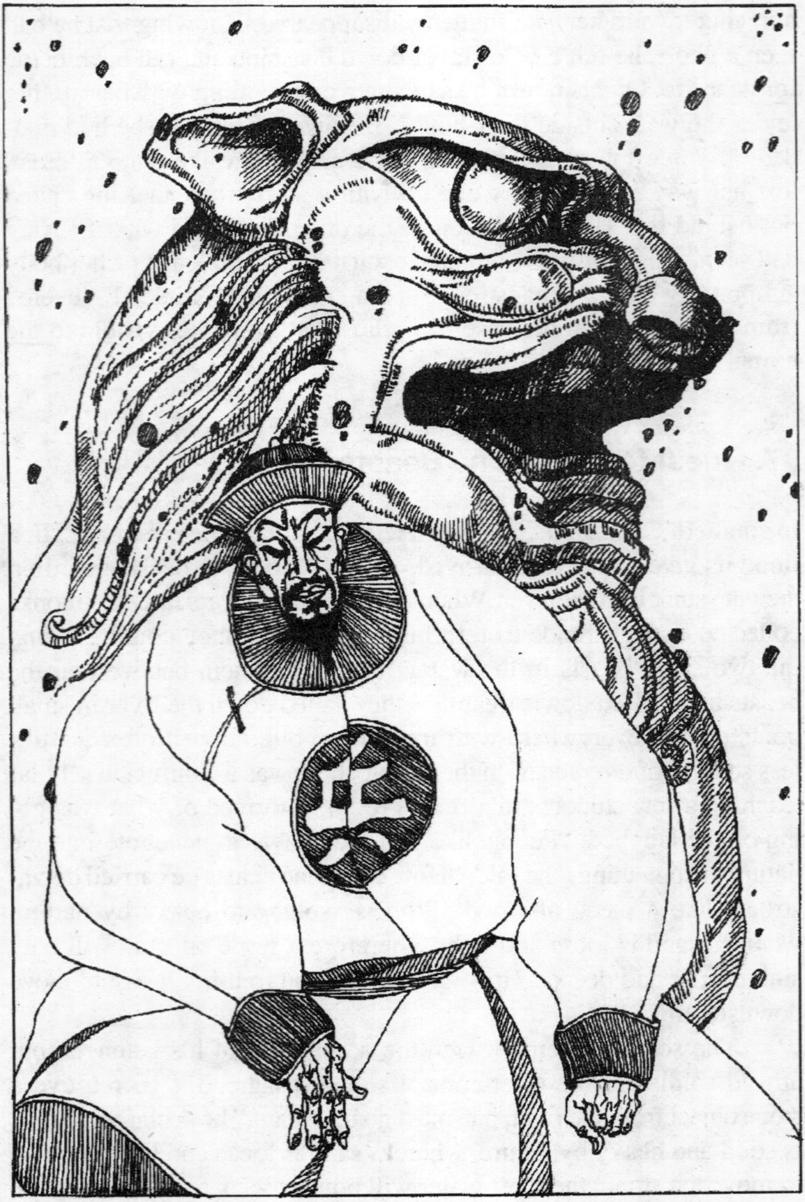

sand underneath. With half the sand below the stone object washed away, it will fall backwards. The water will go on washing away the sand underneath, and again the stone will roll over backwards. By and by it will move upstream. It is wrong to look for the stone beasts downstream, but to search for them upstream would be even more ludicrous." Following his advice, the monks located the stone beasts a few li up the river. This incident indicates that faced with the myriad of phenomena in this world, one is liable to a one-sided view and should therefore refrain from making a hasty conclusion by simple reasoning.

98. A Luckless Dandy

On the evening of the Lantern Festival in the first lunar month a young man in Tianjin, on his way home from a lantern display, saw a pretty young woman lingering at a crossroads as if she were waiting for someone. She must have come out with a few companions to watch the lanterns, he told himself, but lost them in the crowd. When he went up to speak to her, she made no reply. Nor would she disclose her name or address. This made him think that she might be waiting for her lover and therefore subject to his blackmail. He invited her to take a rest in his house, but she flatly refused. Ignoring her protest, he took her by the hand and dragged her all the way home. The family feast was not yet over, so he made the woman sit at the table in between his wife and younger sister.

Timid at first, the young woman gradually began to chat and laugh with the man's wife and younger sister, teasing with them and urging them to drink in a most charming and seductive manner. Overjoyed, the man asked her in a faltering voice to stay the night. Smiling, she replied, "With your gracious consent, I'll seize this chance to take off my costume. Forgive me for leaving in such a hurry, but my mates are waiting for me anxiously." She took off her outer garment, rolled it into a bundle, and made for the door after a bow to the young man. This was actually a man who had played a woman's role in the dance show. Maddened, the young man ran out after him to pick a fight. Among the neighbors who came to find out what was going on, some had seen the young man drag the dancer home by force, so that he could not accuse the dancer of unlawful entry into his house at night; some had seen the dancer perform in the show, therefore he could not be charged with molesting the young man's wife and sister by disguising himself as a woman. In the end, the young man looked on helplessly as the dancer walked away, and the crowd dispersed in an uproar. The disgrace suffered by the young man was unequivocally self-inflicted.

99. Unable to Tell Friend from Foe

In Haidian District of the imperial capital there was a man who made a living by tending the graveyard for a rich family. One day he saw a fox running before his house pursued by a host of dogs, its body already covered in bloody wounds. Moved by pity, he drove the dogs away with a club and carried the fox into his room. He waited a long time till the fox recovered a bit, then took it to the open field and sent it away. One evening a few days later his door was pushed open without warning, and in walked a matchless beauty. Startled, he asked who she was and where she came from. The girl made a bow, then said, "I am a fox-woman. You saved me last time when I was in deadly danger, so I have come to wait on you in bed." He reasoned that there should not be any ill-will on her part, so he let her stay. The next two months flashed by in a ceaseless spree of unbridled love-making. Though increasingly weak and emaciated, he was too infatuated with the fox-woman to put the blame on her. They were lying in bed one day when a woman's voice called out at the window, "Ahliu, you little whore! How dare you harm him like that in my name, before I can recover from my wounds and pay him my debt of gratitude? If anything untoward should happen to him, the whole clan would blame me for returning evil for good—how would I be able to clear myself then? Even if you could be proven guilty in the end, how can I let you murder the man who saved my life? I am here today with my sisters to dispatch you!" The fox-woman got up hastily to escape, but several women broke into the room and beat her to death on the spot. The grave watcher, by this time deeply attached to the fox-woman, was filled with grief and cursed the women roundly for killing his beloved. The fox-woman tried repeatedly to explain the truth of the matter, but in vain. When he finally drew his sword at her, she leapt over the wall and went away weeping bitterly. The grave watcher still felt a lingering anger when he told others about the incident afterward.

100. A Moralist Shows His True Colors

There was a rather cranky and ill-tempered Confucian scholar who subjected his students to rigid discipline. Though the students found this unbearable, they could find no fault with him since he conducted himself with perfect decorum in his daily life. One moonlit night he was strolling in the small back garden of the school when he glimpsed a shadow among the flowers. As a lingering rain had caused several damages in the cob wall, he suspected that a neighbor had got in to steal vegetables, so he went over to rebuke the thief, only to find a beautiful woman hiding behind a tree. She knelt in salute and admitted she was a fox-woman. "Because you are a true gentleman," she said, "I dare not disturb you. That's why I have come to pick flowers only after dark, yet you have found me after all. Please don't take offense." She spoke in a gentle, sweet voice and kept stealing amorous glances at him. When the enchanted scholar teased her with a lewd suggestion, she responded by throwing herself into his arms. She could make herself invisible, she said, coming and going without anyone's knowledge, so that his students would find nothing. Thus they went to bed hand in hand to enjoy a torrid night.

At the break of dawn the scholar urged the fox-woman to leave in haste. "I hear the sound of people walking outside," she said, "but don't worry. In a moment I'll leave through a crack in the window."

She was still lying in bed when late in the morning all the students had arrived at the school. The scholar, filled with trepidation, hoped that she was indeed invisible to others. Just then an old woman called at the school saying she had come to fetch someone. At this the fox-woman put a coat over her shoulders, walked out leisurely, and sat down in the scholar's seat in the classroom to arrange her hair casually with her hand. "I don't have my make-up kit with me," she said, "so I have to go home to make my toilet. I'll visit you again when I have the time and get my pay for last night." This woman turned out to be a courtesan newly arrived in the area, hired by a few students to trap their tutor. The scholar was plunged into the most sorry plight, looking thoroughly crestfallen. After the morning lesson the students returned home for breakfast. Seizing this chance, the scholar packed up and absconded. As the saying goes, a fierce appearance always hides a faint heart. How precise!

101. An Official-Turned Servant Woman

The story took place in the early Qianlong reign in the house of Chang Tai, a vice director of the Ministry of Revenue. A servant's wife, in her early twenties, went unconscious after a seizure and breathed her last that very night. The following day they were about to put her into a coffin when she stirred. Gradually she could bend and stretch her arms and legs, and after a while she sat up. "Where am I?" she asked. This made the family think she was still delirious. As she looked around the room reality seemed to dawn upon her, and she heaved long sighs without saying anything. Though her illness was gone, she moved and talked like a man, was unable to do her make-up, and even failed to recognize her husband. Aware that something was amiss, the family pressed her for an explanation. It turned out that she used to be a man who had died a few days before. His spirit was escorted to the underworld, where the official in charge found out on consulting the records that he still had some years to live but should be turned into a woman as a punishment. Thus he was ordered to reincarnate in the servant woman's body. Drifting into sleep, he woke up with a start to find himself a servant woman in Chang Tai's house. This revived woman adamantly refused to disclose her original name and address, saying there was no need to bring further disgrace to her ancestors. At first she would not sleep with the servant, but finally gave in reluctantly as her rejection could not be justified. However, each time they had sex she would weep afterward until the next morning. She was once overheard muttering to herself, "Why should I end up being humiliated by a servant after studying the classics for twenty years and serving office for thirty?" One night her husband heard her talk in her dream, "Why should I amass a fortune only to be enjoyed by my children and grandchildren?" He woke her up to ask her about it, but she denied having said anything. As Chang Tai was aversive to talks about ghosts and spirits, he ordered the servants in his house to keep quiet about the incident. About three years later the woman died of anguish, her true identity still unknown.

102. The Bizarre Capers of Foxes and Ghosts

Guo, a scholar, was tough and eager to excel others. At a party on the Mid-Autumn Festival the conversation turned to deities and specters, whereupon he claimed he was not afraid of ghosts. When his friends urged him to prove his courage by going to a haunted house, he readily agreed and set out with his sword. The house consisted of a few dozen rooms kept vacant all the year round, and the courtyard, overgrown with weeds, looked quite gruesome. Guo closed the gate behind him and sat down amid the dead silence. At the fourth watch a man suddenly emerged at the gate. Guo quickly drew his sword, but before he could get to his feet the man brushed him with his sleeve, making him unable to move or speak, though his mind remained sober. The man bowed to him and said, "You are a brave man goaded into coming here. Since eagerness to win fame is part of human nature, you need not bear too much blame for it. As your host I should receive you with hospitality, but unfortunately it is the Mid-Autumn Festival tonight, and the female members of my family will come out to watch the moon. To maintain a proper reserve between the sexes, they have to be kept out of your sight. Since you have nowhere else to go so late at night, I'll solve the problem by inviting you to get into a jar; please don't feel offended. There will be wine and dishes inside, which I hope you will enjoy."

Several men came to seize Guo and put him into a huge jar, which was then covered with a square table and held down by a huge rock. After a while Guo heard talking and laughter outside. There must be a few dozen men and women having a jolly good time, eating, drinking and toasting. Suddenly he smelled the fragrance of wine. Able to move by this time, he fumbled in the dark to find a pot of wine, a cup, four dishes, and a pair of ivory chopsticks. Hungry and thirsty, he began to have a feast himself. Then he heard several young boys walking around the jar while singing a love song. Someone knocked on the jar and called out, "The master orders this performance to entertain the guest." The song sounded melodious and quite pleasing to the ears. After a long time Guo again heard a knock on the jar. "Don't be angry with us, Mr. Guo," a voice said. "We are too drunk to move the stone. Please bear it for a little longer; your friends will come soon." After that all became quiet. The next morning Guo's friends got to the house to find the gate bolted. Afraid that something terrible had happened, they got in by climbing over the wall. At the noise Guo shouted aloud for help. It took his friends a tremendous lot of work to move away the huge rock to let Guo crawl out of the jar. After Guo finished his story, they all clapped and roared with laughter. When he turned to look at the utensils left in the jar, they seemed to have been taken from his own house. As it happened, his family were about to enjoy a feast the night before when all the wine and dishes on the table vanished into thin air, so he returned to find his family members swearing angrily and searching up and down for the lost dishes. Those ghosts were indeed mischievous, but their trick made one feel amused rather than offended. Guo himself had burst out laughing the moment he was rescued from the jar.

But the following incident cannot be called a light-hearted antic. A young man staying in a temple in the mountain to study with his tutor was told that a fox-woman living in the tower often came out to seduce men. "The fox-woman must be a rare beauty," he told himself, so he went to the tower every night to make a silent prayer for an amorous encounter. When he was walking under a tree one evening, a young maid waved at him. Jubilant, he went up to her, knowing she must have brought him a message from the fox-woman. "A sensible man like you should have known better," the maid said. "My mistress is very fond of you, but how could you pray openly for something like that? The master was furious. As you were a worthy man, he dared not harm you, but he began to keep a watchful eye on the mistress. Luckily he is out tonight, so the mistress has sent me to fetch you. Come with me." Following the maid, the young man walked for a long time, making twists and turns down a road that did not seem to belong to the temple. Finally they got to a room with the door unbolted. Though there were no lights, a bed with a mosquito tent was dimly visible. "The mistress is a bit shy at this first meeting, and has lied down in the tent. Undress yourself and slip into the bed quietly. Don't speak, or the other maids may hear you." Having said this, she turned and left. The elated young man went up to the bed, lifted the quilt, and took the woman into his arms to kiss her. As she screamed in alarm, the young man stepped back in dismay. The next moment the room with its bed and tent was all gone, and the young man found himself facing his tutor, who had been enjoying the evening cool under the eaves. Shocked and furious, the tutor gave the young man a sound flogging. After the young man was compelled to make a confession, the tutor drove him away. That was really a wicked trick. My late teacher Qiu Wenda remarked, "Guo was merely trying to show off his courage, therefore the ghosts played a joke on him. The young student, however, was motivated by an evil intention, so the fox set him up in return. The severity of the retaliation they got depended on the nature of their offense, not on whether the ghosts and demons were benign or malicious."

103. Flight of a Fox-Wife

One day an official-in-waiting took a tour around Diaoyutai in the capital. As a temple fair was being held nearby, he saw many women coming and going in the street. At nightfall the bustling noise died down, with only a few carriages on the road. Just then a woman walked by swaying her hips voluptuously. She was holding a baby in her left arm and a rattle-drum in her right hand. At the sight of him she shook her rattle, and they exchanged a smile. An observant man, he thought to himself, "This woman is dressed like a lady from a wealthy family, but she walks alone carrying a baby in her arms like a peasant. Judging by her peculiar behavior, she must be a fox-spirit." When he went up to talk to her, she said her husband had died a few years before and she was living alone with her little son. "You need not waste your breath," he said with a smile. "I know who you are, and I am not afraid. I am rather poor, and people like you are reputedly good at making money. If you can support me, I will go with you." The woman smiled. "In that case, let's go home together!" On his arrival he found her house quite nice and clean though not very spacious. She was living with her parents, mother-in-law and sisters. By a tacit agreement they did not bother to exchange names or birth places at the dinner table. After partaking of enough wine and food, he went to bed with the fox-woman to enjoy a joyful night.

He went back to the city the following day to fetch a servant boy and his bed roll, then settled down in the woman's house. She turned out to be so insatiable in bed that he was hardly her match. His health began to go downhill. In the meantime she grew more and more peremptory, telling him to make the bed, attend to her washing and making up, tidy her clothes, and even serve her tea and the smoking pipe. After a while her mother-in-law and sisters also began to order him about like a servant. Greedy after her wealth and her person, he forced himself to swallow the humiliation. Then came one day when she told him to sweep the toilet, and he refused. "I have been satisfying your every wish," she said angrily. "Why don't you give in on such a trivial matter?" The other women also chimed in to blame and scoff at him. After that their relationship grew more and more strained. She began to stay out at night, claiming to have been put up by some relatives. Visitors said to be her relatives also called at the house frequently. She always treated them to a feast and flirted with them at the table, while the official-in-waiting was not allowed to join the company. When he protested angrily, she glared at him, then relaxed into a snicker. "How do you expect me to earn money otherwise? I can stop receiving guests anytime if you agree to support the over thirty members of my family. Can you do it?" Aware that he was unable to stay on, he went back to the city with the servant boy to rent a house. On his return the following day the fox-woman's house had disappeared; not a single utensil or piece of clothing was left. In its place was a wasteland overgrown with weeds. The official-in-waiting had come to the capital with several hundred taels of silver, but had been dressed rather shabbily for economy's sake. Afterward people had been surprised to find him in splendid clothes, but he removed their doubts by telling them he had moved in with his parents-in-law. Then he was again shabbily dressed and would not give any explanation. The servant boy, however, disclosed the secret. Someone commented, "By human standard it was not unreasonable for the fox-woman to run away. I have seen people doing much more outrageous things."

104. A Young Man Runs an Errand for a Fox-Woman

While a dike was under construction in Mozhou, a young woman was seen one day walking on the embankment with a bundle. Looking tired, she sat down for a rest under a willow tree, where a few dozen laborers happened to be enjoying their break. She told them she was on her way back from her parents' house. She had been riding a donkey with her younger brother holding the halter, but the donkey galloped halfway, throwing her to the ground. Running after the donkey, her brother disappeared into a sorghum field. She waited from morning till noon, but he failed to come back. Her house was just four or five li to the northwest, and she offered to pay a hundred copper coins to anyone for carrying the bundle for her and walking her home. One of the young laborers thought to himself, "I can take the chance to make advances at her. Even if she rejects me, I will still earn some money." So he set off with her.

On their way the young laborer kept teasing the young woman, who neither answered nor rebuked him. They had walked three or four li when over half a dozen men accosted them, shouting, "How dare you take liberties with a woman from our family, you scoundrel?" Swarming over, they tied up the laborer and gave him a sound beating. "Let's bury him alive here rather than take him to the *yamen*!" they said. The young woman then described how he had provoked her with lewd remarks. Unable to defend himself, he could only beg for mercy repeatedly. At this one of the men said, "We'll spare you if you dig up this ridge to drain off the water." They handed him a spade, then sat down urging him to quicken his work. At midnight, when he finally drained away the water, the woman and the men all disappeared, and he found himself surrounded by reeds, without any village in sight. Some people guessed the young laborer had been trapped by some foxes to drain water from their flooded lair.

105. A Clandestine Affair Between a Married Couple

A physician named Gu Demao was said to be one of those people who serve office in the underworld while still alive. He took immense pride in having redressed a wrong case. The following was his story, though he dared not disclose the names of the people involved. A young woman was driven out by her mother-in-law because her younger sister-in-law had spoken ill of her. It was impossible for her mother-in-law, a very obstinate woman, to change her mind in a short time, and both her parents had passed away. With nowhere to go, she took the veil at a local convent. As her husband visited her frequently, they found it hard to restrain their passions. She told him to wait for her at night in a tumbled-down house in a deserted garden nearby, and she would leave the convent by climbing over a gap in the wall to meet him. They had been carrying on like that for over a year when the head nun found it out. A woman of firm principles, she regarded their act as a sacrilege against Buddha. The young woman was told to stop meeting her husband or leave the convent. From then on her husband ceased to visit her. She was so brokenhearted that she died soon afterwards.

When she arrived in the underworld, the official in charge told her that as a nun she must abide strictly by monastic rules. Because of her transgression caused by indulgence in carnal desires, she would be sent to hell like other monks and nuns found guilty of sins of the flesh. At this Gu Demao demurred, saying, "The law has explicitly stipulated what punishment to mete out against a nun who has broken her covenant by sexual trespasses. However, the rule applies only to someone who took the veil of her own free volition; in that case she cannot excuse herself when punished for breaking her own promise. However, this woman was driven away from home on a groundless charge, so she still hoped to be reunited with her husband someday. She took refuge in the convent only out of helplessness. When she received her tonsure, it was not so much an initiation into the sacred order as a disfiguring operation, and when she moved into the convent she wanted to make a temporary stay rather than meditate on the law of Buddha. As for her attachment to and secret meetings with her husband, though their acts bordered on the licentious, there was no loss of chastity on her part as they were after all a married couple. By the law of the human world an engaged couple guilty of a sexual transgression are merely birched or fined. By comparison this couple violated rites and ethics to an even less degree, and her death in anguish should be enough to pay for whatever small mistake she had committed. Therefore she should be declared not guilty and sent straight into the next cycle of rebirth. That seems to me a reasonable and rightful decision." His advice was passed on and adopted by the King of the Underworld. Though it is hard to determine the authenticity of the story, Gu's argument sounds fair-minded and appropriate. On his deathbed, Gu said he had been demoted to a land-god for giving away too many secrets about the underworld.

106. A Sly Robber Hurls Himself into the Net

Li Yin, a soldier at a military post station, was traveling with an official in the mountain one day when they saw an arrow planted on an old pine tree on top of a cliff. This made the official puzzled. When they stopped at a post house for the night, Li Yin told the official that he had seen a mounted figure coming swiftly toward him the last time he passed that spot. Taking it for a robber, he lay down in the grass. When it came near, Li found it to be a human-like creature riding an unsaddled wild horse. Aware that it was a demon, he shot an arrow at it. With a metallic sound the arrow hit the target, and the creature escaped by transforming itself into black smoke. The arrow on the pine tree had made him realize the demon was actually the spirit of that old tree. "Why didn't you tell me there and then?" asked the official. "It did not see me shooting the arrow," Li replied. "As a demon it might be able to overhear me and run after me to avenge itself." This incident showed Li Yin to be a cautious and vigilant man.

But there was one time when Li Yin was duped himself while escorting a criminal named Man Daer, who was handcuffed, his feet linked with an iron chain going under the horse's abdomen. Man appeared to be on his last breath, for he could hardly eat anything, and he wobbled so badly on horseback that he would have fallen off if his feet had not been chained together. Li Yin kept worrying that he would die on the way and never expected him to try to escape. As they rode side by side into the Gobi desert, Man looked as if he were about to fall off, so Li put out a hand to steady him. Suddenly Man raised both hands, sent Li to the ground with a blow of the handcuffs, then turned and galloped away. Obviously he had been feigning illness all along. Li Yin later received a severe punishment. But it took a very short time for Man Daer to be caught again, and this time he actually flung himself into the net. As every bandit would get a handsome reward by giving himself up, Man Daer showed up for the money. When asked why he had thought it safe for him to come, he said, "I reasoned that as I had committed a felony, no one would expect me to come. And I mingled myself in a crowd so that no one would recognize me." His words made sense, but he had forgotten about an arrow wound on his forehead, which eventually gave him out. Cautious as he was, Li Yin could not avoid being deceived, and a crafty criminal like Man Daer ended up falling into a trap. Therefore the wisest men are not always wise. Those who are wont to employ cunning schemes will surely meet their downfall someday.

107. Ghosts Bet on a Poem

There was an old Confucian scholar who taught students in a rented room in a Buddhist temple. The temple bordered on a deserted graveyard where apparitions often stalked after nightfall, and ghostly voices were often heard. A man of courage, the old scholar was unperturbed, and gradually even his servants ceased to feel uncomfortable about it. One night he heard a voice outside the wall, "As your long-time neighbor, I know you feel no aversion to us. I once heard you reciting Wen Tingyun's poems, so you must have a copy of his works at hand. Please copy his 'Dharma Tune' onto a piece of paper and burn it." In a hushed voice the ghost went on, "As for the last line, 'The storm in the city of Ye connects the grass with the sky,' please substitute the word 'glue' for 'connect'. I have just wagered someone a meal over the word, and I shall be most grateful if you can help me win the bet." The old scholar did have a collection of Wen's poems, which he picked up and threw out of the window. After about a meal's time a gust of whirlwind rose outside. Fallen leaves swirled in the sky, while sand and mud pattered on the window like rain. The old scholar sneered, "Stop your silly antics—what I have done is fully justified. After the two of you laid a bet, one would be the loser and bear a

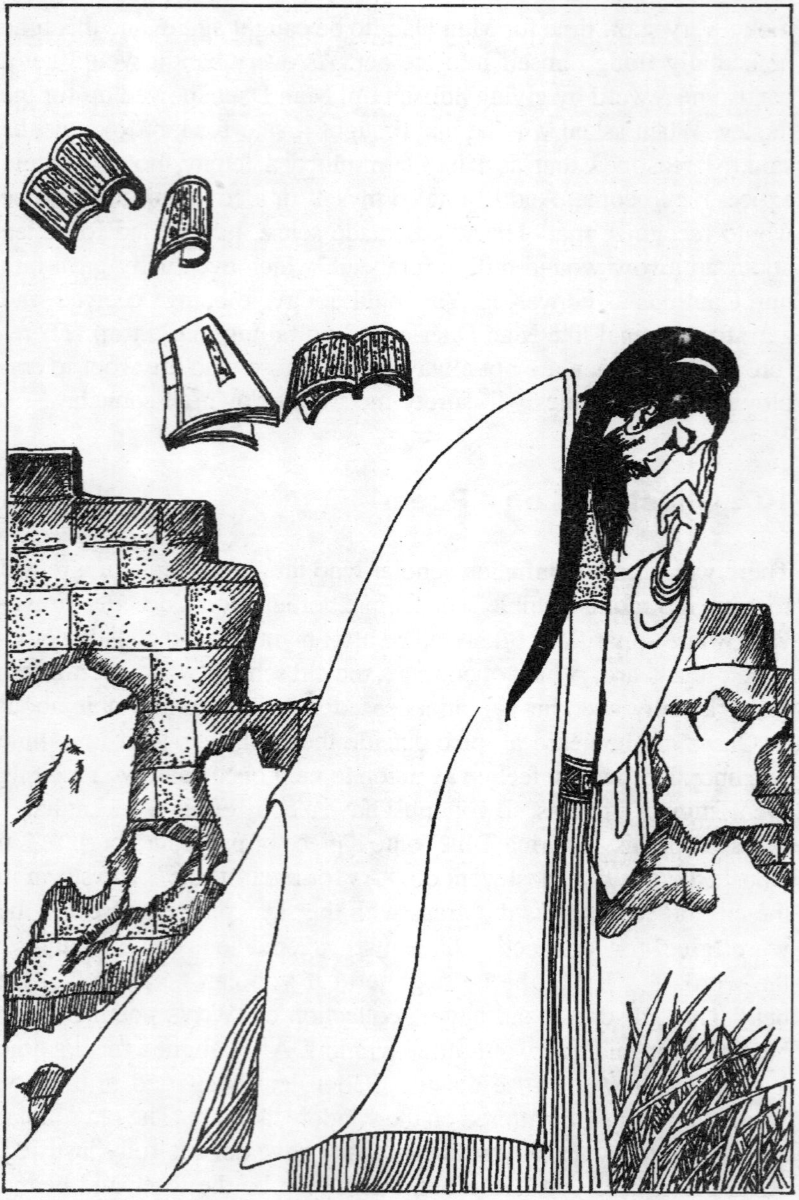

grudge against me. If I offended you by changing the word, I would be in the wrong; if I offended you by giving the correction version, I would be in the right. Whatever troubles you make, I have nothing on my conscience." As soon as he said this, the wind stopped. Someone commented, "There's something to be said for the ghost of a scholar. Though he tried to win the bet by cheating, he proved amenable to reason. But if the old Confucian scholar had not thrown out the poetry collection, he would have been able to avoid any confrontation, wouldn't he?" "You are talking about common sense," said another. "An old Confucian scholar who has enough common sense would cease to be known as an old Confucian scholar."

108. A Peasant Woman Saves a Fox

One evening the two dogs kept at a peasant's house suddenly started barking fiercely, but there was no one in sight when the peasant's wife went out to take a look. Then she heard a voice coming from the roof, "I can't go down because of your ferocious dogs. A run-away maid has hid herself in your stove. Please take the trouble to drive her out by smoke." When the startled woman went back into the room, she heard sobbing in the stove and asked who it was and why it had come. "My name is Lüyun," came the answer in a whisper. "I was a house maid of that fox. As I could not bear his flogging, I've run away so that I can live a few more days. Please take pity on me." The peasant woman happened to be a Buddhist believer who often practised abstinence from meat. Moved by pity, she went out and shouted to the rooftop, "She is too afraid to come out, and I can't bring myself to smoke her. Please have mercy and let her go if her offense is not too serious." The voice on the roof shot back, "I just bought her for two thousand coins. How can I let her go for nothing?" "Can I buy her out for two thousand coins then?" asked the peasant woman. "All right," the fox on the roof said after a pause. The peasant woman took the money and threw it to the rooftop, then went inside to knock on the stove. "Come out, Lüyun. I have paid your master for your freedom." "Thank you for saving my life," said the voice in the stove. "From now on I will put myself at your service." "How can humans employ a fox-maid?" responded the peasant woman. "You'd better leave. Take care to conceal yourself, or the children would be scared." Then she saw a black creature dash out of the stove and vanish in the twinkling of the eye. After that, the peasant woman never spent a New Year's Day without hearing a voice outside the window, "Lüyun has come to kowtow to you!"

109. A Maid Is Molested by Foxes

When a maid in Zhang Xuaner's house was suddenly found missing one evening, the family thought she had run away. The following day she was found lying in drunken stupor in the firewood storeroom behind the house. She did not sober up until noon to tell her story. The night before, she had heard laughing voices in the storeroom. As the place was known to be inhabited by foxes, she did not feel scared but went up to peep through a crack in the door. Several young men were carousing at the table laid out with wine and meat. Catching sight of her, they jumped up and dragged her into the room. She felt as if she were drifting into a trance, paralyzed and unable to speak. They made her sit down at the table and kept urging her to drink until she became totally intoxicated. She had no idea when she had fallen asleep or when the young men had left.

A stern man of firm principles, Zhang went in person to the storeroom to rebuke the foxes. "In the many years we've shared this place, my family never created any trouble for you apart from fetching firewood now and then. How could you do something so indecent, forcing the maid to sit with you at the wine table? Why didn't the elders of your family check the young men from behaving so rudely? Don't you feel any sense of shame for what you have done?" At midnight Zhang heard a voice outside the window. "The young ones have received a sound beating for their improper behavior, but there is an explanation I have to make. It was the maid who stretched out her hand to beg for some meat in the first place; she was not taken into the room against her will. Moreover, this girl has several secret lovers and lost her virginity a long time ago. That's why the young ones dared flirt with her. If it were not so, why didn't they dare take liberties with some other maids in your house who are just as pretty? It seems that you and I should share the blame for failing to maintain strict discipline." "Since you have punished your children," Zhang said, "I will also give the maid a thrashing." The old fox chuckled. "You haven't found a husband for her when she is well over the marriageable age; as a result she did things that went against public morality. Can you blame everything on her?" To this Zhang had nothing to say. The next day he sent for a matchmaker and had marriages arranged for several older maids in his house.

110. Two Fox-Hunters

Wang and Zhang, both fox-hunters, lived about ten li apart. One day they located a grave frequented by foxes and decided to get together after sunset to hunt them. When Zhang got to the appointed place, Wang was already waiting there. They arrived at the grave and found the vault big enough to hold a man. Wang told Zhang to stay in the vault while he hid himself in a grove of trees outside. On the foxes' return Wang would block their way of escape so that Zhang could catch them in the vault. Zhang waited until late into the night without hearing a sound. He decided to go out to discuss the situation with Wang, only to find the opening of the vault blocked by two tombstones leaving only a narrow crack. The stones proved too heavy for him to move. The next day he heard a cowherd passing outside and shouted for help. Informed by the cowherd, his family arrived at the scene and, with the assistance from some other people, managed to remove the tombstones. Convinced that this was an attempt on his life, Zhang went with his family members in search of Wang, intending to take him to the *yamen*.

Halfway to Wang's home they found him stripped naked and

tied to a willow tree, with a crowd whipping and swearing at him. As it happened, on his way to meet Zhang, Wang had run into a village woman carrying food to her family laboring in the field. She made passes at him, and they slipped into a sorghum field to get undressed. The moment Wang had taken off all his clothes the woman, leaping to her feet, grabbed them and ran away. Luckily no one was around, so Wang headed home in haste, only to run head-on into a crowd carrying torches and weapons. "We've found the ruffian!" they shouted at the sight of him. It turned out that several young women in the house of Wang's neighbor, sleeping in the courtyard that night, had waken up with a start to see Wang burst in, strip himself, and lie down beside them. At their scream the family got up to take a look, and Wang ran away by climbing over the wall, leaving his clothes behind. Caught by these pursuers, Wang was rebuked and beat up. He was unable to prove his innocence and could only look to heaven and cry. When Zhang and Wang finally met to describe their respective experiences, it finally dawned on them that they had both fallen victim to foxes. Come to think of it, they went to the grave in order to hunt and kill the foxes there, who chose to strike back merely by playing a trick. Zhang was shut up in the grave for a whole night, but a crack was left to save him from suffocation. Wang was stripped and got a sound beating without being able to defend himself, but as the fox did not rape any of the young women, the family had no intention to beat Wang to death. The foxes had therefore shown restrain in their conduct.

111. If Mountains and Rivers Could Speak

An official walking into his studio one night was terrified to find a man's head on the desk, which he considered to be an ill omen. There happened to be a Taoist priest living nearby who was good at drawing magic figures and chanting incantations, and who often took part in funeral proceedings. The official hastily sent for the Taoist and asked him to make divination by *The Book of Changes*. "Utmost disaster is shown in the hexagram!" gasped the priest. "But there is a way to get around this. You only need to spend a hundred taels or so on a prayer session." Their talk was interrupted by a voice outside the window, "I was unfortunate enough to be sentenced to death and beheaded. As a soul would be unable to be reborn if the head is missing, I have to take the trouble to carry it with me everywhere. Just now I found your desk very clean, so I happened to put my head on it. When you entered without warning, I made off in a hurry and forgot to take it with me, and as a result you were startled. It was a rude act on my part, with nothing to do with your good or ill fortune. Please don't be deceived by the glib-tongued Taoist." At this the Taoist priest slinked away shamefacedly.

There was an official whose house was haunted by foxes. A magician invited to exorcise the foxes was so inept that the beasts made a fool of him, so he went to seek help from his master, who gave him a magic figure. On his return he stepped onto the platform, making ready to invoke the heavenly gods again. Just then the family heard people moving heavy objects and calling at one another upstairs. As the hubbub died down, all the foxes were gone. Thereupon the magician glanced around the room with a smug look on his face, and the official's family felt very grateful to him. At this moment a note pasted on the wall caught their attention. The trace of ink still fresh, the note read, "We dared disturb you because your good fortune had run out. But yesterday you donated nine hundred taels of silver for the construction of an orphanage. Moved by your generous act, the gods increased your share of happiness in the mundane world. That's why we have to move away now. The magician just happens to be practicing his magic at the right moment, yet he crows over what he regards as his own success. You can give him something to eat before sending him away; if you should give him any reward, that would be too good a bargain for that bumbling fool." The magician, on reading the note, was struck speechless with shame. So goes a popular saying: "If mountains and rivers could speak, the diviner would starve; if internal organs could speak, the doctor would not earn a single cent." From the above two stories we may conclude that the magician has to watch out if ghosts and demons should choose to speak up.

112. Trickeries in the Imperial Capital

No place can match the imperial capital in deception and imposture. I once bought sixteen ink slabs reputedly made by Luo Xiaohua, a renowned manufacturer in the Ming dynasty. Placed in a faded lacquer box, they appeared like things from the remote past. When I tested them on my return, they turned out to be clay bars painted black. On another occasion I bought some candles which could not be lit, for they were made of clay with a coat of mutton tallow. One evening a man was selling roast ducks under the lamplight, and my cousin bought one. He returned to find the duck already eaten; the skeleton had been refilled with clay and pasted with a piece of paper colored like a roast duck and smeared with oil. Only the feet and head of the duck were not faked. Then there was our family servant Zhao Ping who bought a pair of leather boots for two thousand coins, a good bargain in his opinion. He changed into the boots on going out one rainy day but came back barefooted. Each boot, it turned out, was covered by oiled paper, crumpled to create the leather-like creases, and the sole was made of a cluster of cotton wrapped up in cloth.

The above are merely petty frauds. There was once an official-in-waiting who took a fancy to a pretty young woman living across the street. From a neighbor he found out that she lived with her mother while her husband was an assistant to an official in another city. A few months later the gate of her house was suddenly covered with white paper, and the family was heard weeping and wailing, for news of her husband's death had just arrived. A memorial tablet was erected in the hall, a ceremony was conducted by some monks to pray for blessing on the dead, and quite a few people came to offer condolences. Gradually the family, reputedly driven to the verge of starvation, began to sell clothes, then sent for matchmakers to find the young widow a second husband. This seemed to answer a dream wish of the official-in-waiting, who flung himself at the chance. He moved into her house after their wedding, but several months later her first husband suddenly returned. Apparently the news of his death had been a rumor. Flying into fury, he insisted on taking the official-in-waiting to court. After repeated entreaties by his wife and mother-in-law, he finally relented and allowed the culprit to go after leaving all his possessions behind. Half a year later the official-in-waiting happened to see the young woman questioned by a ward-inspecting censor. The so-called husband who had driven him out was actually her lover, who had schemed with her to cheat him of his money. The imposture was not exposed until the return of her real husband.

In the Western District there was a house to let consisting of forty to fifty rooms. At over twenty taels of silver per month a man rented the place for over half a year. As he always paid the monthly rent in advance, the landlord did not bother to pay any attention to what he was doing. One day the tenant suddenly left without saying good-bye. Hastening to the house, the landlord found it reduced to ruins, with only two street-facing rooms still standing. This house had both front and rear gates. Running a timber shop at the rear gate, the tenant had dismantled the entire house and sold the wood at the shop. The landlord, who lived on the front road, had failed to detect anything. It was really a stunning feat to pull down dozens of rooms and sell all that timber without anyone's knowledge. In all the instances quoted above, the victim was either anxious to get things on the cheap or to suit his own convenience, and therefore should not pin the blame entirely on others. Mr. Qian Wenmin commented, "One has to be extremely careful when dealing with people in the capital, and should consider himself lucky if he has not been tricked. Anything that looks like a good bargain must be a trap. With so many greedy tricksters in the world, how can any advantage befall people like us?" I find his words very reasonable.

113. Use the Enemy's Strategy Against Him

One night a group of robbers stormed into the house of a wealthy family in southern Cangzhou. The head of the family and his wife were both taken hostage, so that the others dared not do anything. A concubine living in the east room, having disguised herself as a servant, sneaked into the kitchen and told the maid tending the fire, "As our master is seized by the robbers, none of us dare fight back. The robbers have planted sentries on the roof to watch out for rescuers, but they cannot see anyone moving under the eaves. You can jump out of the rear window, walk under the eaves to find the other servants, and tell them to take some weapons and ride off to lie in ambush three or five li away. The robbers will leave after the fourth watch, for they have to return to their den before dawn. Our master will be taken along as hostage, but after a li or two they will let him go to prevent him from finding out where they are heading for. When the master is released, some of you can carry him back home while the rest continue to follow the robbers at half a li's distance. If the robbers turn back to fight you, run from them; if they go on their way, follow closely at their heels. If they fight back again, run from them as before. Thus you can follow them all the way to their den. As the robbers can neither fight you nor get rid of you, all of them will get caught by daybreak." At the risk of her life, the kitchen maid ran out of the house to inform the other servants, who thought it a good plan and carried it out accordingly. As a result, all the robbers were captured, and the maid got a big reward. Thereupon the principal wife, who had been at odds with the concubine, decided to forget her past resentment, and a harmonious relationship developed between them. Later she asked the concubine how she had been able to devise such a plan. "My late father was a head robber," the concubine replied, sobbing. "He once said he feared nothing more than that the robbed family should employ such a method, but none ever did. I tried it out when our family was in deadly danger, and fortunately it worked." Therefore a military commander must know his enemy. In other words, he can make use of the enemy's strategy to subdue it.

114. Helper-Turned Harassers

There was a man who put up a fox in a vacant room of his house. They often chatted, exchanged gifts and lent each other daily utensils, getting along peacefully like good neighbors. One day the fox said to him, "For many years the ghost of a hanged man had lived in the empty room of your other house. As you had the room pulled down not long ago, the ghost is now homeless, and he has the effrontery to try to occupy this room of mine by force. He often makes faces to terrify my children, and even uses his evil influence to inflict spells of fever and chills on them. This is really more than I can bear. In the Taoist temple nearby there is a priest good at exorcising evil spirits. Could you invite him to come and get rid of this scourge for me?" The man called on the priest at the temple and returned with a magic figure drawn on a piece of paper, which he burnt in the courtyard. A moment later a violent wind rose, accompanied by thunder-like rumbling noises. Astonished, he heard the tiles on the roof rattling furiously as if dozens of people were trampling on them. Then the fox called out from the roof, "What a mistake I've made! It's too late to repent! Just now some divine troops came down. They tied up the ghost and took him away, but I am also forced to leave. Farewell now!" Some people, unable to bear an insult, hanker after the sweet taste of revenge, but in the end their victory costs them so much as to be hardly worth winning.

There was once a man whose house was frequented by a fox, so he invited a magician to subdue it. With the fox driven away the magician, who turned out to be a very greedy man, kept sending wooden figurines and paper-cut tigers to make trouble for the family. By giving the magician some money they were able to enjoy peace for some time, but about a dozen days later he came up with some new tricks to extort money, creating more disturbances than the fox. Forced into an impasse, the man finally freed himself from the grip of the magician by moving to the imperial capital with his whole family. This incident clearly indicates that if one is so eager to win as to seek help from a petty man, he will eventually come to grief.

115. A Valiant Courtesan

There was a rich man who hoarded grain instead of gold and silver as a way to forestall robbery. In the late Kangxi and early Yongzheng reigns the area suffered crop failures for a few successive years. As a result rice price was very high. However, this rich man locked up his granary to await further price rises. The local people were indignant but helpless. At this a courtesan by the nickname Jade Faced Fox remarked, "That's easy to deal with. Just get your rice money ready." She called on the rich man, saying, "Though I've made a lot of money for the procuress, she treats me very severely. When we got into a quarrel yesterday, she told me I could leave by paying a ransom of a thousand taels. I've long been tired of this profession of mine and wanted to find an honest, dependable man to be my lifelong companion. After careful consideration, I've made up my mind that no one is more suitable than you. If you can pay the thousand-tael ransom, I will wait on you for the rest of my life. I know you are not in the habit of storing silver, so you can pay the equivalent sum of two thousand strings of cash. A timber merchant left for Tianjin yesterday to fetch the money and will be back in about half a month, but I really don't want to marry that crude fellow. If you can lay down enough cash in ten days to settle the matter, I shall be most grateful." The rich man, a long-time admirer of the courtesan, was overjoyed. To get the two thousand strings of cash needed, he immediately started selling his stored grain. Once his granary was opened, however, buyers swarmed in from everywhere, so that he was forced to sell his entire grain hoard. The day the granary became empty, the courtesan had someone bring a message to him, saying, "The procuress has cared for me for many years. In a flash of anger she told me to pay my ransom that day, but then she regretted it and asked me to stay. I don't have the heart to let her down, so our plan has to be put off." The rich man had made nothing but an oral agreement with her. There had been no matchmaker, no written statement, and no betrothal gift. Thus he could do nothing about her breach of faith. Aged only sixteen or seventeen, the courtesan proved herself a heroine by her valiant act.

116. Tricked by a Peasant Woman

A peasant in Jiaohe County, implicated by a robber, was thrown into prison. Unable to prove his innocence, he had someone bribe a functionary in the county office and ask for his help. Looking into the case, the functionary discovered the robber had made the false charge because the peasant had beaten him up for making passes at his wife. It occurred to him that the peasant must have a very pretty wife, so he refused to take the money by telling the caller, "I can't be of any help in such a secret matter unless his wife pays me a quiet visit." When told this the peasant, too scared of death to keep up his dignity, had his mother-in-law brought to the prison and told her everything. On her return she explained the situation to her daughter, who indignantly refused to commit herself to such an act.

Several days later someone called at the functionary's house. He opened the door to see a woman beggar wearing rags and a head cloth. Paying no attention to his questioning, she walked right in, undoing her headcloth and taking off her ragged outer garment to reveal the splendid inner clothing. Pressed by the astonished functionary for an explanation, she blushed and lowered her head. Without saying a word, she took a note out of her sleeve and handed it to him. Under the lamplight he read the following words: "So-and-so's wife." Delighted, he took her into his room and asked deliberately why she had come. Wiping off her tears, she replied, "Would I have come if I did not know what you want? Since I am here, please ask no more questions. I only hope that you will keep your promise." He readily swore an oath to keep his word, and they went to bed together. She stayed for a few days, making him so infatuated that he was ready to give in to her every whim. Then she said she had to leave him for a while. She also told him she was often bullied in the village. If he could rent a place for her in the county seat, the two of them would be able to go on with their relationship. This sounded to him almost too good to be true, so he spared no efforts in proving the peasant's innocence. After his release the peasant had a cold look on his face when he met the functionary, who thought to himself that the peasant must be feeling ashamed for having had sacrificed his wife's chastity. Some days later, when business took him to the village, the functionary called on the peasant and had the door slammed on his face. Only then did he realize to his indignation that the peasant had decided to break ties with him.

Just then a man reported to have employed a courtesan to induce others to gamble was brought on trial. The courtesan was sentenced to be flogged and sent back to her native town. On a closer look the functionary recognized her to be the peasant's wife and went up to speak with her. She expressed her regret for failing to come and meet him, for her husband had kept a close eye on her. Now that she had the good luck to see him again, she asked him to help her, if only for the sake of the few nights they had shared, get an exemption from the flogging and banishment. This gave him an idea. He went at once to see the county magistrate, saying, "That woman confessed to the residence of her parents, but she is the wife of a peasant in this area. We must call him to account." What he really wanted was making the magistrate have the young woman auctioned in the name of the county office, so that he could take the chance to buy her. But when the peasant was brought in for interrogation, he had a woman with him claiming to be his wife. A few of his fellow villagers were sent for, and they all bore out her claim. Thereupon the courtesan was compelled to tell the truth. Formerly, the peasant woman had found herself in a quagmire when her mother told her she had to sleep with the functionary to save her husband's life. She did not want to lose her chastity, nor could she bring herself to let her husband die in prison on a trumped-up charge. Finally she went to ask this courtesan, who had just arrived in the area, to come in her name, offering her clothes and adornments in return. On seeing the functionary when she was about to receive her flogging, the courtesan had attempted to make him get a remission for her by keeping on her false identity. But he was working at cross-purposes with her, so that both their lies were laid bare in the end. The magistrate took another look into the charge against the peasant and found him wronged, so he sent him away with his wife and punished the functionary severely. Func-

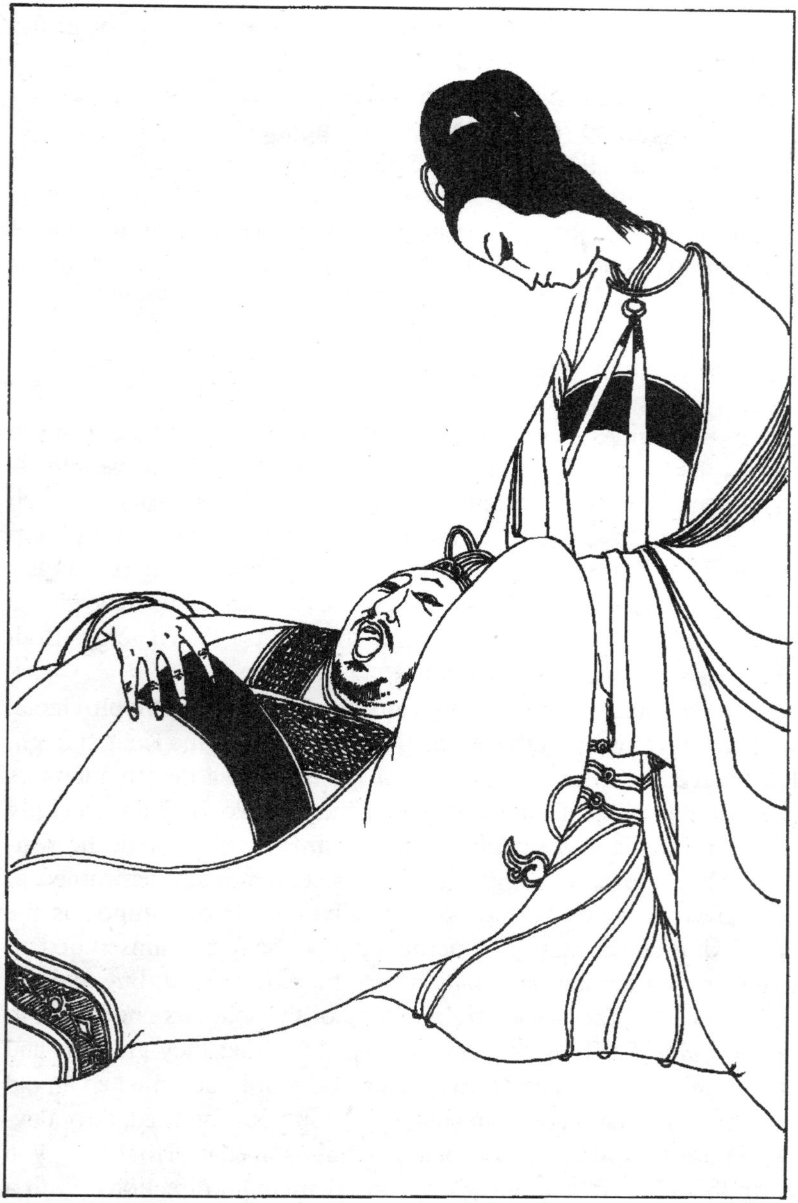

tionaries and petty officials belong to the most cunning lot in the world, but this one was twisted around the finger by a peasant woman. Generally speaking, a stupid man is no match for a wise man. But as things will develop in the opposite direction when they become extreme, so a so-called wise man will eventually meet his rival and make a fool of himself in trying to be smart. It is the way of heaven to take from the overabundant to supplement the inadequate. If the wise never stumbled, they would be the only people left on earth today.

117. Man-Eating Ghosts

Ghosts sometimes slay people for no apparent reason. According to one explanation, ghosts need to eat the souls of living people. A ghost consists of the remnants of a living person's vital energy, which will gradually dwindle and vanish. By absorbing vital forces from the living it can prolong its existence. Therefore female ghosts habitually seduce men to imbibe their primal essence, while male ghosts have to resort to killing people and soaking up their energy. Both practices serve the same purpose.

 I remember a story told by Liu Tingsheng about five provincial scholars travelling together in the fifty-ninth year of the Kangxi reign. Rain forced them to take shelter for the night in a deserted temple. Four of them fell asleep, but one remained awake. Suddenly a chilly wind rose as he saw several phantoms drifting in through the window. They started puffing at the four sleeping men, then turned to him. Clear-minded at first, he gradually sank into a stupor as the ghosts dragged him away. Sobering up a bit, he found himself tied up together with his four companions. He tried to call out, but couldn't find his voice. The ghosts grabbed one of the scholars and began to feed on him, finishing him off quickly. After that they grabbed and ate up another two. They turned to eat the fourth victim when an old man burst in to rebuke them sharply, "Stop your misdeed, dirty devils! These two men will become officials someday. How dare you harm them?" Terrified, the ghosts ran away in all directions. With a start the two scholars came out of their trance. Their memories of what had happened in their dreams were exactly the same. Afterwards one became the head of the local Confucian school and the other an instructor in the school. After listening to this story Mr. Bao Jingting laughed, saying, "I used to look down on positions like that. Who would expect them to mean so much to gods and ghosts?"

118. Messenger for a Ghost

In the sixth year of the Qianlong reign a scholar named Zhu Liyuan traveled north to take the provincial examination at Shuntian. Coming to the north of Yangliudian in the evening, he took an alternative route in order to avoid a muddy area, and lost his way. He was unable to find an inn but fortunately saw a house in the distance, so he decided to go there to request a night's stay. He arrived at the house to find six or seven rooms with mud walls and tiled roofs. To the young boy who answered the door he explained his intention to stay the night there. Shortly afterward an old man plainly yet gracefully dressed came out to meet him. He took Zhu to a wing-room and sent for a lamp, which gave off only a dim light. "We've had a bad harvest," he said, "and even the oil is poor in quality. It's a shame, but what can we do? As it's too late to prepare a meal for you, please honor me by drinking some wine." His manners were quite gracious. When Zhu asked if there were other people in his family, the old man replied, "I am all but alone, living with my wife and some servants and maids." After Zhu mentioned he was going to the capital, the old man said, "I need to send a letter and a packet to the capital, but this is such an out-of-the-way place that we don't even have postal service here. It is lucky for me to meet you today." Zhu asked, "Your family live here alone, with no neighbors around. Don't you feel afraid?" "I have a few *mu* of land to be tended by my servants, so I choose to live here. We don't worry about robbery as we have no valuables in this house." "According to what I've heard," Zhu remarked, "an open field like this abounds in ghosts." "I've never seen any," the old man responded, "but if you are afraid, let me sit up with you till daybreak." He borrowed Zhu's paper and writing brush and returned to his room to write a letter. He sealed the letter in an envelope and wrapped it up in a piece of used cloth, which he sewed carefully in neat stitches. Handing the packet to Zhu, he said, "You can open the packet on your arrival in the capital to find the address on the envelope." At dawn the next day Zhu rose to take leave. After urging him not to lose the letter, the old man bade him an affectionate farewell.

Arriving in the capital Zhu Liyuan opened the packet to find a pair of gold hairpins and a pair of silver bracelets. Addressed to "Mr. Zhu Liyuan," the letter read, "As I had no son at an old age, I made my son-in-law my heir at my wife's ill advice. My grandsons-in-law offered sacrifice to me occasionally, but the next generations have stopped treating me as their ancestor. I haven't received any paper money or cooked wheat for a long time, and this lonely grave of mine is almost in ruins. I am overcome with grief in the underworld, but the situation is already beyond remedy. Please sell the few worthless funerary objects I presented to you and use the money to refurbish the grave on your way back. Please dredge the ditch in the south to prevent the grave from being flooded. If you can fulfill my requests, I shall repay your kindness in my next life. Knowing that you are afraid of ghosts, I will bow to you in the dark without presenting myself to you again, so don't feel apprehensive on that account." The letter was signed "Yang Ning, Deceased." Aware that he had met a ghost, Zhu Liyuan broke into a cold sweat. From the words "on your way back" in the letter Zhu guessed that he would probably fail the examination, and this indeed was the outcome. Passing Yangliudian on his way back, he sent a servant to repair the old man's grave with the money from selling the hairpins and bracelets, for he did not dare visit the place again.

119. A Taoist Tames a Shrew

There once was a man who in his forties still had no son. His wife was a shrewish woman who forbade him to take any concubine, and this made him quite depressed. When he visited a Taoist temple nearby, a priest said to him, "Judging by your grave countenance, something must be on your mind. As a Taoist I have the duty to help people in distress. Why don't you tell me the cause of your worry to see if I can lend a hand?" At first a bit surprised, the man told the priest his true story. "Actually I already knew but I wanted you to tell me the story," the priest said. "If you can get someone to make you a dozen ghost guards' costumes, I will be able to help you. Or you can borrow these from some performers." The man was even more puzzled. He thought the Taoist could not be trying to trick him as there would be no practical use for the costumes, so he agreed to do as he was told. That night his wife was heard moaning and crying painfully in a nightmare, from which she could not be awakened. The next day her legs looked blue, but she just sighed and would not say what had happened to her. The same thing happened again three days later. After that she had a nightmare once every three days. This went on for half a month when she suddenly ordered the servants to find a matchmaker, saying she would buy a concubine for her husband. The servants could hardly believe their own ears, and her husband also felt doubtful, thinking she would soon renege on her words. Delirious for the next few days, she became more than ever anxious to find concubines for her husband when she came to. Summoning the servants, she placed the silver needed on the table and threatened to punish them severely if they failed to find concubines for her husband in three days or if the girls they bought were not good-looking. This time she looked dead serious. When two girls were thus procured, she let both of them stay. That very night she had a room decorated as the bridal chamber and urged her husband to sleep there. The whole family was amazed, and her husband felt as if he were dreaming.

The man met with the Taoist priest again, who disclosed he had the power to summon the spirits of the living. One evening he had

147

dressed up as an underworld official and let his disciples put on the costumes of ghost guards. Then he summoned the spirit of the man's shrew of a wife and told her that her husband's ancestors had brought a suit against her in the underworld for depriving him of his offspring. Then she was given a hundred strokes of the birch and a deadline for finding a concubine for her husband. At first she thought it just a nightmare, but it kept coming back to her every three days. In the few days that she remained delirious, her spirit had again been seized by the priest, who suspended her from a rope and had vinegar poured into her nostrils, threatening to throw her into hell unless she could find a beautiful girl for her husband in three days. The power of summoning spirits is not supposed to be a rightful one. But in the final analysis there is no distinction of good or evil in the magic itself but in how one chooses to make use of it. In the case of the shrew, she could be neither brought to reason nor punished by law, yet the priest was able to make her repent by means of magic. Thus a popular saying goes: "There is always one thing to overcome another."

120. An Old Fox Speaks up for Justice

One day a pair of gold bracelets were found missing in Liu Nishan's house. Under torture a young maid confessed to stealing and selling them to a scrap collector. They went out to hunt for the collector, but failed to find any who matched her description. As the maid was being given another beating they heard a light cough from the ceiling. "I have lived in your house for forty years without revealing myself," the voice said, "therefore you were not aware of my existence. But today I can no longer remain silent. Didn't the madam put the gold bracelets in a lacquer box when she was tidying up the house?" When they opened the box hurriedly, the bracelets were found inside, but by that time the little maid had been beaten black and blue. This incident was a lifelong remorse for Liu Nishan, who often admonishes himself, "We are liable to make such a mistake from time to time, but how can we expect to have such a fox everywhere?" Afterward, in over twenty years when he served as an official, he never used torture in case trials.

121. Offend Two Ghosts by Saving One Person

One evening a servant named Wang Fa, on his way back from a hunting trip, saw under the moonlight a woman caught between two people pulling at her arms, but there was no sound to be heard. Thinking the woman was under attack from two robbers, he fired a shot to the sky. The two attackers fled in different directions. and the woman in the middle ran back to the village. In an instant, all of them disappeared. Only then did Wang realize they were ghosts. On his return to the village he saw a house with the light on, where many people were talking excitedly about a bride who had hanged herself and just been revived. "I made pancakes for supper as my mother-in-law told me," she said, "but two or three of them were stolen by the dog. My mother-in-law thought I had eaten them on the sly and slapped me hard in the face. I was standing under the tree, with no one to talk with about my grievances, when a woman came up and said, 'It is better to die than to swallow such a humiliation.' When I hesitated, there came another woman who also urged me to commit suicide. In a daze, I took off my belt to hang myself. At first I felt suffocated, and the pain was awful, but then I seemed to fall asleep while my body drifted out of the door. One of the women said, 'I came first to persuade her, so she should be my substitute.' The other retorted, 'If I had not come, she would not have made up her mind. Therefore she should be mine.' They were quarrelling like that when a thunderclap struck and the sky was lit up by fire. The two women scurried away, and I came back home."

Later Wang Fa often heard women's sobbing and cursing voices when he walked home at night. They accused him of ruining their plan and threatened to kill him, but he was not afraid in the least. One night, on hearing the voices again, he shot back, "You tried to kill a woman, and I saved her. Even if the case is taken to the gods, I will be in the right. Try to kill me if you dare, and save your empty threats!" After that he never heard the voices again. As one may offend the murderer by saving his victim, no wonder most people are unwilling to lift a finger to help those in danger. That servant can be counted as exceptional.

122. Punished by a Fox for Making a Pass at His Wife

There was a merchant who was on good terms with a fox and often visited his house on invitation. The house looked nothing out of the ordinary, but if the man turned to look after walking out the gate, it would no longer be there. One evening the fox invited him home to drink wine and had his wife fill the cups for them. She was exceedingly beautiful. A bit drunk, the merchant lost his head and put out his hand to pinch her on the wrist. The fox-woman threw a glance at her husband, who smiled and went on chatting as if he were not in the least offended.

After that the merchant returned to his inn. One early morning his wife suddenly arrived on a donkey, with a house servant holding the halter. She had traveled overnight on this borrowed donkey after getting an urgent message about him suffering a stroke. The astonished merchant concluded an acquaintance of his must be playing a prank on him. As there was no room at the inn to put up his wife, he wanted to have the servant take her back, but found out the servant had already left. There was less than a day's trip to his home, so he decided to take his wife home on the donkey himself. On their way a young man passing them on the road stroked the woman on her foot. When she swore at him angrily, he apologized with a lascivious leer and went on to make some lewd remarks. Incensed, the merchant engaged him in a fist fight. As the startled donkey ran down a side road and disappeared into a sorghum field, the merchant let go of the young man to run in pursuit of his wife. After going for a distance he found the donkey caught in a mud pool, but his wife was out of sight. He searched up and down the place until daybreak, when he rode the donkey home, intending to think up a way to find his wife on his return. He had gone only a few li when someone at the roadside called out, "The thief is here!" This was a crowd from a nearby village hunting for a donkey stolen the night before. The merchant was caught, tied up and given a sound beating. Thanks to an acquaintance who pleaded on his behalf, the merchant was set free at last. Crestfallen, he returned home to find his wife spinning threads. When asked about what had happened the night before, she stared at him blankly, not knowing what he was talking about. It dawned upon him that the woman, the house servant and the young man on the road had all been the fox in disguise; only the donkey had appeared to him in its true identity. Though the fox was rather vindictive in his retaliation, the merchant could blame no one but himself.

123. A Demon Invoked by a Prayer

A member of the vanguard brigade in the city of Cangzhou had a daughter named Pingjie, who at eighteen remained unbetrothed. When she went out one day to buy rouge and powder, a young man made passes at her. She rebuked him harshly, then returned home. When her parents hastened out to look for the young man, he was nowhere to be found, and the neighbors denied having seen a young man matching her description. That night Pingjie, having bolted the door, was about to go to bed when the young man emerged before the lamp without warning. Though she knew this was a demon, she neither screamed nor spoke to him, but lay down in feigned sleep, holding a pair of sharp-edged scissors in her hand. Not daring to come close, the young man stood by her bed and used flowery words to seduce her, but she turned a deaf ear to him. He abruptly went away and in a short moment returned to put on her bed a few dozen pieces of jewelry made of gold and silver, but she did not even look at them. Leaving the jewelry behind, the young man went away. Just before daybreak he reappeared and said to the girl, "I have watched you closely all night, but you did not give so much as a glance at them. When someone is unmoved by profits, even the gods cannot force him to do anything against his will, let alone a demon like myself. I misinterpreted your secret prayer, thinking you were using your parents as a pretext, therefore I came to find you. Please don't take offense." With this he picked up the jewelry and went away. As it happened, Pingjie's family was very poor. Her mother was a sickly old woman, while her father's salary could barely pay for their daily expenses. Thus in a secret prayer made before a Buddha's shrine she had expressed the wish to find a husband soon so as to support her parents. Apparently her prayer had been overheard by the demon. This story indicates that a single remark and a passing thought will be detected by ghosts and spirits. What's the use of putting up a false front in public?

124. Underworld Runners Take Food on the Sly

Before passing the metropolitan examination Sun Xuchuan had worked as a private tutor for a family. One day the host's mother was dying. Sun was busy with his work when a servant boy brought supper, so he had it put in an adjoining room. Suddenly he caught a glimpse of a man in white darting into that room. He was puzzling over the matter when a short man in black also went in there. He walked over to find the two men sitting at the table helping themselves to his supper, and reproached them severely. The man in white scurried away, but Sun had by this time planted himself at the door, blocking the path of the man in black, who hid himself at a corner of the room. Sun pulled over a chair and sat down, intending to find out what the man would do next. Just then the host came running in a fluster. "A ghost spoke through my mother just now," he told Sun. "He said two ghost guards have been dispatched here to fetch her spirit, but one of them can't get out of a room where you are blocking the door. If they should fail to return on time, he said, the spirit of the dead would be punished in the underworld. I don't know if the ghost was telling the truth, so I have come to take a look." Hearing this,

Sun drew back a few steps, and saw the man in black run out helter-skelter. The next moment they heard loud wails in the inner room, for the host's mother had breathed her last. Though the underworld is famous for the stringency of its law, and the officials there are unusually observant, the runners sent to fetch the spirits of the dead still dare eat food on the sly in the bereaved family. Evidently it is necessary to put officials and runners in the human world under close surveillance!

125. Authentic and Fake Immortals

It would be difficult to deny the existence of immortals, for there are people who have seen them. It would be equally difficult to prove the existence of immortals, for sightings are very rare. Since the Han dynasty no less than a hundred books have been written on gods and immortals, who number over a thousand. But the immortals mentioned by the ancients failed to appear to subsequent generations, who only met other immortals if they met any at all. Is it possible that the so-called immortals only managed to somewhat prolong their lives by preserving their vital energy and succumbed to death in the end? Moreover, gods and immortals differ from magicians in that they enjoy peace and quiet while the latter are fond of playing tricks, but the books fail to discriminate between them, calling everyone endowed with magic power an immortal. My mother once heard a story from an old woman named Wang who lived in the remote mountainous area of Fangshan. In a small temple in the mountain there lived a Taoist priest about sixty to seventy years old, who picked up fallen fruits for food and drank from the spring when thirsty. He spent all day chanting scriptures and beating a wooden clapper, and never socialized with others. If someone went to the temple to talk to him, he seldom said anything in reply and would not accept any gifts. The old woman had a nephew who worked as a hired hand away from home. One night he came back to visit his mother, passing the temple on his way. At the sight of him the Taoist gasped, "The tiger has come out in the late night. How dangerous for you to travel at this hour! I have to escort you for a while." Beating the clapper, he led the way for the lad. They had barely walked half a li when a tiger leapt out from the darkness. As the Taoist stepped up to shield the young man behind him, the tiger turned and ran away. Then the priest walked off without a word. Later he suddenly left and no one knew where he went. Could this have been an immortal?

According to my father's younger cousin Zhang Mei'an, he had once seen someone make a boy climb up a three-storey house, then with a wave of his hand let the boy land lightly on the ground without suffering any injury. The man was also able to sink a copper jar into a stream and, with a loud shout, make it slowly float to the surface. But these were merely the feats of a magician, bearing no resemblance to the behavior of true immortals. Another story was told by my mother's brother Zhang Jianting. A peasant was herding cattle in the open field when all his oxen dropped dead on the ground. A Taoist priest who happened to pass by told him, "The oxen are not really dead; their spirits have been abducted by a fiend. Pour this medicine down their throats to protect their internal organs, and I'll try to bring back their spirits." He was invited to the peasant's house, where he walked in circles to exert his magic influence. After a while all the oxen were revived, and the priest went away, declining the peasant's invitation to a meal. Someone claiming to know the truth said, "That priest put poisonous herbs in the field in advance, then revived the oxen with anti-toxins. By not accepting any reward he was trying to make people believe he was not interested in profits, so that he could extort large sums in the future. I've seen him practicing such frauds somewhere else." After these words became known, the Taoist priest did not show up again. So even among so-called magicians there are humbugs with no magic power at all. How can one be so indiscriminate as to regard the whole motley crew as immortals?

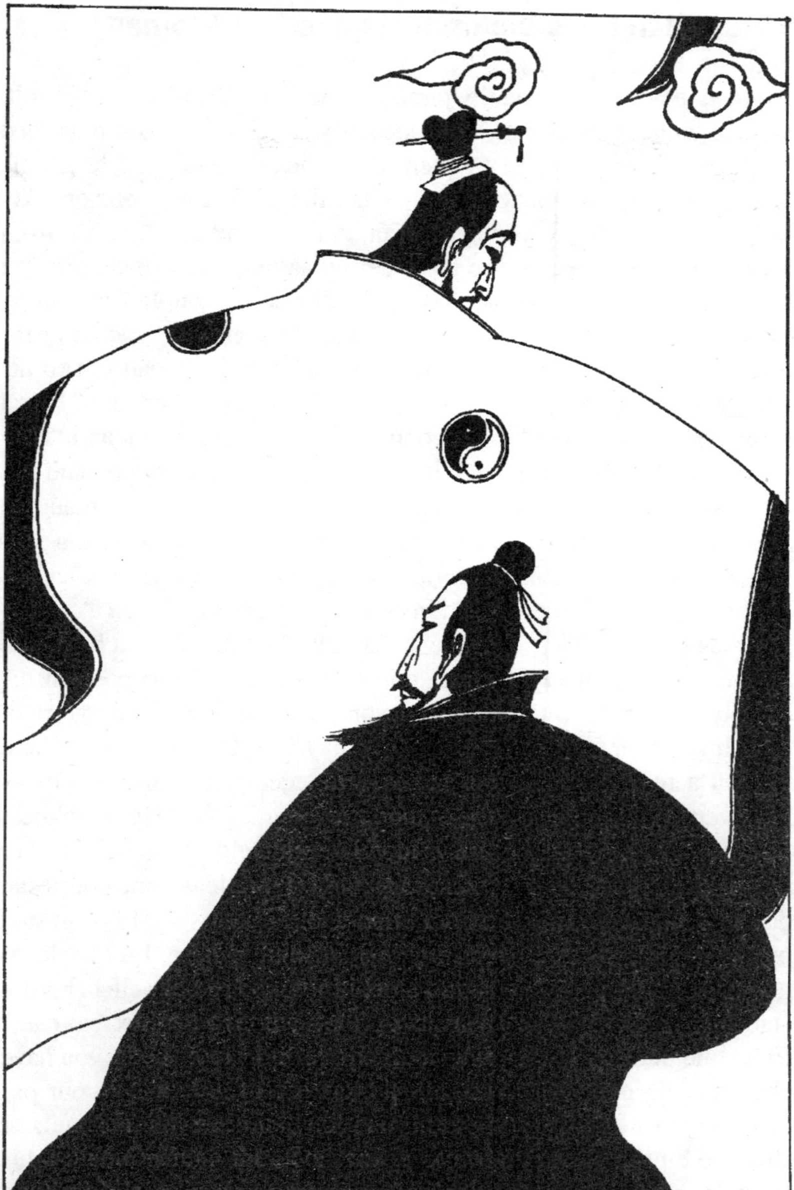

126. A Man Falls Victim to a Fake Fox-Woman

A young man from a wealthy family in the capital was clumsily built, walked with a gawky gait, wore slovenly clothes and seldom washed his face. Nevertheless he frequented brothels and stopped to goggle at every young woman he passed on the road. Walking alone one day he saw a very lovely young woman. As the road was muddy from recent rain, he walked up to tease her by saying, "It's so slippery on the road. Shall I lend you a hand?" "Don't ask for trouble," the young woman said harshly. "I am a fox-woman dedicated to practicing for immortality under the moon. I have never seduced a man to sap his energy. Look at yourself—how dare you take liberties with me? Don't bring harm to yourself!" She scooped up a handful of sand and threw it in his face. Staggering back in fear, the young man tripped and fell into a ditch. By the time he climbed laboriously out, the woman had already disappeared. In terror and uncertainty he waited for the fox-woman to make trouble for him, but nothing of the sort happened.

A few days later a friend invited him to a feast. When a courtesan was called in to pour wine at the table, he recognized her to be the young woman he had met on the road. Unable to contain his anxiety, he finally asked her, "Did you go to the eastern village right after it rained a few days ago?" "That day my elder sister went there to visit a relative," she replied absent-mindedly. "As the two of us look very much alike, maybe you saw her that day." Her equivocal answer further confused the young man, who could not decide whether she was a fox or not. After he found an excuse to leave, the courtesan described their encounter to the other guests. "I was really disgusted by his appearance. For fear that he would assault me, I told a lie to get away. Luckily he fell on the ground, so I hid myself behind a stack of firewood. That made him take me for a real fox-woman." Everyone burst out laughing. One of the guests said, "Since you have chosen such an occupation, you can't be particular about your patrons. He's one of those rich lads who can spend a thousand taels of silver to buy the smile of a woman. Why don't you go and make his acquaintance?" So he took the courtesan to the young man's house, telling him the names of her husband and parents-in-law, and explained the episode that had taken place a few days before. Then she began to coax him with sugary words, claiming to have known him from childhood. When he accosted her that day, she said, she had made a joke in a merry mood, and she deeply regretted having caused him such alarm. Then she offered to atone for her mistake by sharing his bed that night. Her style of conversation was quite refined, and her manners charming and graceful.

At her words the young man was beyond himself with joy. He kept her with him for several nights, then sent for her husband, who agreed to let him be her exclusive patron at a monthly payment. Thereafter the young man indulged himself in unbridled sex with the courtesan, until he was taken down by diabetes and died in a year or so. My elder brother Qinghu commented, "The young man was afraid to meet a fox in human form, who would make him worry for his life. Faced with a woman with a foxy nature, he not only felt no fear but no longer cared for his own life, though she had warned him not to bring harm to himself. Though he died of involvement with a prostitute, it was not much different from falling victim to a fox-woman."

127. A Girl Who'd Rather Be a Concubine than a Wife

A and B both had well-to-do families in Cangzhou, and A's daughter was betrothed to marry B's son in a year or two. One day a fortune-teller was caught in the rain and put up by A, who asked to have his daughter's future told. After a long pause the fortune-teller said, "I don't have my divination book with me, so it's difficult to make any prediction." A sensed something was wrong and urged him to speak the truth. At last the fortune-teller said, "Judging by the exact hour of her birth, she is destined to be a concubine, but this doesn't seem likely in view of the conditions in your family. Moreover, as you have told me, the time of her wedding has been fixed, and according to her birth chart she won't have a second marriage because of the early death of her husband. Thus I find it hard to tell her fortune."

When a crafty man in the village learned about this, he decided he could profit from the situation. Paying A a visit, he said, "Your family is not that wealthy, and you will be expected to prepare a large dowry to marry your daughter. This will make things more difficult for you. Since your daughter is destined to be a concubine, you might as well tell everyone she is ill, then spread the news of her death and buy a coffin for a fake burial. After that, leave home at night and take your daughter to the capital, where she can adopt a false name and be sold as a concubine into a very wealthy family. In that way you will be able to make a large sum of money." A thought this was an ingenious idea. A high official happened to be looking for a pretty maiden to wait on his daughter as the concubine of her future son-in-law. Seizing the chance, A sold his daughter for two hundred taels of silver. After a month or so the official's family sailed south. At Tianfei Floodgate the entire family died in a shipwreck, and A's daughter was the only survivor. No one in the area dared adopt an unmarried girl, so the matter was reported to the local *yamen*. In the short time she had stayed with the official's family, she learned about his family name but not his position and place of birth. When questioned about her family, therefore, she had to disclose the names and address of her own parents. An official letter soon arrived in Cangzhou, bringing to light the feigned death of A's daughter.

By that time B's son had married a younger cousin; to divorce her would be out of the question. Enraged that A had sold his daughter for a good price, B threatened to sue him. Finding himself in a predicament, A said he was still willing to marry his daughter to B's son. But the cousin's family found this unacceptable and also threatened to go to court. At this, relatives and friends of the two families got together to mediate and resolve the crisis. A was made to agree to pay the cost of fetching his daughter back, then marry her to B's son as a concubine. On the girl's return B's son arrived at once to fetch her, with B driving the ox-cart. On meeting her mother-in-law, the girl explained it had not been her idea to feign death. "If you had been unwilling to be sold into that family," retorted the old woman, "why didn't you just tell them you already had a husband?" The girl did not know what to say. When told to salute the principal wife, she hesitated for an instant. This caused her mother-in-law to remark, "When you were sold as a concubine, didn't you have to salute the principal wife?" Wordlessly the girl fell on her knees in a formal salute. For as long as she lived the old woman treated A's daughter like a slave. My grandmother was well acquainted with this incident, which took place in the late years of the Yongzheng reign. She once said to the maids, "That girl's father was merely trying to get extra money when he carried out his scheme, and she wanted no more than to live in wealth and comfort. But they ended up making a fool of themselves, with her deprived of the fortune that had been allotted to her at first. If you understand the reason behind this, you will stop all your wishful thinking."

128. Yang the "Savage Tiger"

A surgeon by the name of Yin Zang'an once went to Shenzhou to treat a patient. On his way home the family sent a servant named Yang to escort him. Brutal and ferocious, Yang was nicknamed "Savage Tiger." Wherever he went he provoked arguments so that not a day went by in peace. One day at dusk they arrived in a village to find the inn full, and they sought lodging at a temple. The monk explained to them, "There are three vacant rooms behind the Buddha's Hall but I have to warn you the place is haunted by a demon." Yang angrily replied, "What demon dare disturb Yang the Savage Tiger? I long to meet him!" And he preceded to order the monk to have one of the rooms cleaned out. That night he and Yin slept in the room. Yin was a timid man and chose to sleep by the wall, and Yang lay down on the outer part of the bed, with a lit candle by his side to await the demon. In the dead of the night they heard a whistling noise in the distance, then a moment later a beautiful young woman floated into the room. As soon as she came close to the bed, Yang jumped to his feet, took her into his arms and began feeling her up. Suddenly she took on the horrible appearance of the ghost of a hanged woman. At this sight

Yin shuddered in fear and his teeth clattered. Totally unperturbed, Yang said with a smile, "Though your face looks repulsive, you should be no different from any other woman in your lower body. Come and give me a good time!" Grabbing her by the back with his left hand, he pulled down her trousers with his right hand and went on to push her onto the bed. With a scream the ghost darted out of the room. Yang ran after her, calling her to come back, but she never showed up again. Thus the two men slept peacefully until the next morning. On leaving the temple Yang told the monk, "That room is really nice. I'll be back in a few days and I want the same room again. Please don't put up anyone else there." After he told the story to some friends, Yin said, "How incredible that anyone should attempt to rape the ghost of a hanged woman! The man really deserved to be called Savage Tiger."

129. A Ghost Avenges the Loss of His Wife

The crafty man with a whole bag of tricks at his disposal will eventually lose his game, and the moneybags who relies on his wealth to bully others will meet his downfall someday. However, if a man is both rich and cunning, and spares no cost in carrying out his scheme, it would be hard to pin him down for his wrongdoings. Li Luyuan, a native of Jingzhou, told the following story about a rich man who lived on the border of Hebei and Shandong. After his wife passed away, he took a fancy to a young woman in the village who was a newly wed. He enlisted the help of an old woman, who rent a house near the bride's home and tried various means, including a handsome bribe, to persuade her parents-in-law to find an excuse to drive her away, while their son was kept totally in the dark. Next he dispatched another old woman, a long-time acquaintance of the young woman's family, to bribe her parents and make them take her back to her parents-in-law's house. Her parents-in-law, feigning to be appeased, invited them to dinner and agreed to let the young woman stay. Then a quarrel broke out at the table, so that the young woman had to go back with her parents. All this plotting was done without the young woman's knowledge. Because the two families fell out in this way, no one would ever suspect them of conspiracy. After that, two old women offered to be matchmakers for the young woman and the rich man. He turned down the offer, expressing doubts that she might be an unfilial woman; her family also declined on account of the great disparity in wealth between them. This served to cover all traces of the rich man's scheme. When a few relatives and friends took up the matter again after an interval, the marriage was settled.

The young woman's former husband, though poor, came from a descent of scholars. Forced by his parents to divorce his wife, he became so downhearted as to fall seriously ill, but still he hoped to get her back someday. When he learned that a day had been chosen for her to remarry, he died in grief and indignation, and his ghost stayed to haunt the rich man's house. On the wedding night he emerged before the lamp to make disturbances, so that the couple could not sleep together. After this went on for several days, the rich man asked his bride to share his bed during the day. She felt so insulted that she broke into tears and flatly refused. Left with no alternative, the rich man sent for a magician to exorcise the ghost. The magician walked up to the altar, burned a magic figure, and was gesticulating forcefully as if in command of a heavenly army when something seemed to catch his attention. He immediately bade the host good-bye, saying, "I can dispel demons and evil spirits, but I can't drive away the ghost of a wronged man." The rich man then hired some monks to hold a sacrificial ceremony for releasing the soul from misery, but to no avail. It suddenly occurred to him that the man had been a very filial son, which was why he had not disobeyed his parents' order to divorce his wife. Therefore he bribed the man's parents again and asked them to come and chase him away. Their pity for the dead son outweighed by greed, the old couple came to the rich man's house to abuse him. Sobbing, the ghost said, "I dare no longer stay here now that my parents want me away. I will make a complaint in the underworld." After that the ghost did not appear again. In less than half a year the rich man died, perhaps because the ghost had won his suit in the underworld. Even if Lord Bao, the Song dynasty official famous for his ability to solve complicated cases, were to come back to life, he might not have been able to see through the artifices employed by the rich man, whose willingness to spend money had enabled him to expel the ghost. However, he could not escape the judgement of the underworld. In return for a transient period of gratification he was said to have spent several thousand taels of silver, and finally had to pay with his own life. This seems to be an epitome of foolishness rather than ingenuity.

130. A Talking New-Born Baby

There is actually such a thing as reincarnation. The uncle of a man named Heng Lantai, when a small child, alleged to have spent his previous life as a monk of Wanshou Monastery in western Beijing. Though he had never been there, he was able to draw a rough picture of the layout of its halls and aisles, Buddhist statues, and trees and flowers. When taken to the temple, the picture was found to be very accurate. However, for some reason he adamantly refused to go there himself. That was a genuine case of reincarnation.

According to the renowned Song dynasty scholar Zhu Xi, reincarnation is merely a chance occurrence which happens when the remnant of vital energy from a dead person is reborn by a lucky coincidence. Things like that do happen occasionally. In Cui village my family had a tenant named Shang Long, whose son was reborn in a neighboring family right after death. In less than a month the baby started talking. On New Year's Day his parents went out, leaving him in his swaddling clothes. Just then a fellow villager coming to offer New Year greetings knocked on the door. Recognizing the man's voice, the baby called out, "Is this Uncle so-and-so? My parents are out, but the door is not locked. Please come in and sit for a while." The man could not help laughing in astonishment. However, the baby died prematurely soon afterwards. Perhaps Zhu Xi had such cases in mind when he talked about reincarnation. There are an infinite variety of phenomena in the world, and an infinite number of hows and whys concerning them. It is imperative to remember one must not be induced by his own experience to put undue emphasis on a single point.

131. A Hero Is No Match for a Beauty

Li Qiuya, a native of Dezhou, once left for Jinan with some friends to take the provincial examination. One night they were given a very shabby room at an inn. In the adjacent courtyard there were two locked rooms that looked slightly more comfortable. The travellers concluded that the innkeeper was reserving the rooms for wealthier customers. The innkeeper explained that this was not the case. "The rooms there are haunted by a ghost or fox-spirit. They have remained vacant for a long time, that's why they look clean and orderly. It's not that I make any distinction among guests." One of Li's friends forced the innkeeper to unlock one of the rooms and moved in all by himself. Before going to bed he boasted, "If you are a male demon, I will engage you in a test of strength; if you are a female demon, come sleep with me. Don't be too scared to show up!" Then he blew out the candle and went to bed.

Late at night all became quiet, when a voice whispered at the window, "Someone has come to sleep with you!" He was about to get up and take a look when a huge object landed on him without warning. As heavy as a big rock, the demon made it hard for him to breathe. He felt with his hand to find the demon covered in long hair, and he heard it puffing and blowing heavily. A man of unusual strength, he began to fight with the demon, who proved to be a formidable opponent. They grappled in the room, rolling all over the floor. Awakened by the racket, the others came to take a look, but as the door was bolted they could only stand there listening to the fight going on inside. After a while the demon, dealt a blow in its vital part, uttered a loud cry and fled. When the man, opening the door, saw a crowd outside, he embarked on a colorful description of his exploits, look-

163

ing extremely pleased with himself. As it was just after the third watch, the guests returned to sleep in their respective rooms.

The man was about to fall asleep when he heard a whisper outside the window, "Someone has come to sleep with you for real! My brother stopped me from coming just now because he wanted to test your strength. Now that he is too ashamed to show up again, I have come to keep you company." The next thing he knew, a woman was standing by his bed, fondling his face with her hand. She had slender fingers and soft, creamy skin, giving off a fragrance of powder and perfume. Though aware of her ill-intention, he was captivated by her alluring charms and just wanted to sleep with her before deciding what to do next. Pulling her into his arms, he made love to her passionately. In the moment of his utmost pleasure the female demon sucked forcefully with her abdomen. His mind suddenly became confused, then he went into a coma. When he did not answer the door the next morning, his friends entered the room by breaking through the window and woke him up by spraying cold water on his face. He felt weak all over, as if taken down by a serious illness. Sent back home, he took medicine for half a year before he could walk with a stick. He was no longer bold and vigorous in his behavior, his militant pride totally gone. With enough courage to vanquish the powerful enemy, this man had fallen victim to its deceitful wiles. The Song dynasty writer Ouyang Xiu remarked, "A great disaster often results from a slight negligence, and the bold and wise are mostly defeated by their own weakness." What a wise saying!

132. A Courtesan Identifies Her Lover

During my stay in Urumqi a clerk in the army told me the following story. In Gansu there was a rich old man named Du, who lived close to an open country dotted with lairs of foxes and badgers. Disgusted with their howling at night, Du drove them away by smoke. After that the family suddenly found themselves facing over a dozen lookalikes of their master—in the inner room, the hall, and just about every corner of the house. Indistinguishable in voice, appearance, and clothes, they ordered the servants about in the same manner. As chaos broke out in the family, Du's wife and concubine locked themselves up in their rooms for safety.

It occurred to the concubine that an embroidered packet tied to Du's waist belt could be used to tell him from the fakes. But none of the old men had the packet, which must have been stolen. Then someone suggested to the wife and concubine, "At night the old men will come to seek your company. Do not let any of them enter your room. The one who turns to go away should be our master, and those who insist on entering will be fiends." This plan was duly carried out, but all the old men turned to leave after being denied entry. Someone else came up with another idea. "Let them sit in the hall one at a time," he said. "Send a servant to walk by and pretend to break something by accident. If the old man looks distressed over the loss and swears angrily, he must be our master; if he looks totally indifferent, that must be a demon." When this plan was carried out, every old man looked upset over the broken vessel and gave the servant a severe dressing-down. A frantic night went by without any success in identifying the master of the house.

Du had a favorite courtesan whom he went to spend the night with once every three or four days. Informed of what was going on, she visited the family to offer her help. "The demons have underlings to send them secret messages about whatever can be explained in words. Why not bring all of them to my house. As a call girl I have nothing to lose. Make a hefty fellow stand by my bed holding a big axe. After I undress myself, let those old men come to join me in bed one by one. During our hugging and fondling, the turning of the body, bending and stretching of the limbs, and the force and rhythm of every move are things that can be felt but not put into words. The demons will know nothing about them, for even Du himself cannot give a clear description. If the man standing by my bed brings down his axe when I cry 'chop', no demon will be able to get away." Everything was arranged according to her plan. The first old man climbed into bed and lifted the quilt to get in, only to be greeted by the courtesan with a shout, "Chop!" The hefty man, bringing down his axe, broke the head of the old man, whose body transformed back into a fox. The second old man went in and paused a moment, when the courtesan shouted again, "Chop!" Covering his head with both hands, he darted out of the room in terror. When the third old man came in, the courtesan fell on his shoulders and announced in delight, "Here's the real one! Kill off the rest!" Wielding clubs and broadswords, the house servants slew most of the fake old men, who indeed were foxes or badgers. The few who managed to escape never showed up again. The howling of wild animals at night does not really constitute an affront to people. Du was inviting trouble when he drove the beasts away by force. As for those foxes and badgers, who were capable of assuming the human form, why didn't they call on the old man to dissuade him? Instead, they chose to make trouble in his house, a suicidal move that killed most of them. Both the old man and the beasts had less brains than the courtesan.

133. Reincarnated as a Pig

An old monk walking past a butcher's shop burst into tears. Surprised, people asked him what was wrong. "It's a long story," replied the monk. "I can remember two previous lives. I was once a butcher and died in my thirties. My spirit was seized by a few ghost guards, tied up and brought before an official in the underworld, who blamed me for killing too many lives and ordered me to pay for it in my next reincarnation. Then I fell into a daze, feeling unbearably hot. Suddenly I was cool and fresh all over, only to find myself in a pigsty. After being weaned off, I was given pig feed to eat. Though I knew it was filthy, I ate it anyway as my internal organs seemed to be scorched by hunger. Gradually I learned to speak the pigs' tongue and often talked with my companions. Most of them remembered their past lives, but there was no way to tell people about it. Aware that we would die a cruel death, we often moaned in anguish and shed tears of grief. Clumsy as we were, we could hardly bear the heat in sum-

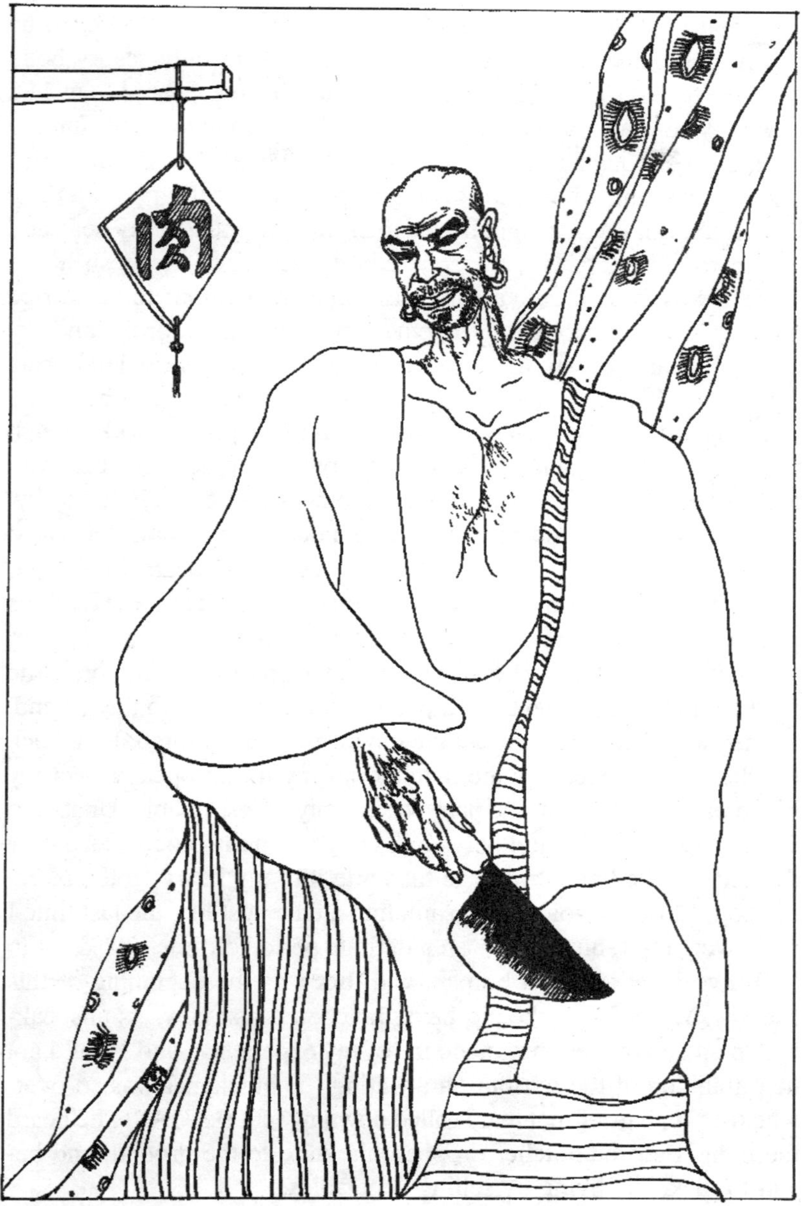
肉

mer, and only felt a bit better if we could find a muddy pool to lie down, but chances like that were very rare. With only scanty body hair, we feared the cold in winter; dogs and sheep appeared to us like heavenly animals for they had such long hair. Finally a man came to tie me up. Though I knew there was no escape from death, I still dodged and jumped around, hoping to prolong my life by a moment or two. At last I was caught by the man, who stepped on my head and bound my feet together, the rope cutting deep into the flesh like a knife. I was thrown onto a cart with some companions to be carried away. As we were piled up together, my ribs almost broke and my stomach nearly burst under the pressure. Then I was carried upside down on a bamboo pole, the pain growing even more unbearable. Arriving at the meat market, I was thrown to the ground with enough force to smash my heart and spleen into pieces. Some of my companions were slaughtered at once, while others had to wait for a few days. I stood and trembled with fear, wondering how painful it would be to have my throat cut. It occurred to me that at death I would be cut up and cooked into dishes, which would be served at some family's dinner table; the very thought filled me with sorrow and despair. When it was my turn to be slaughtered, I nearly fainted in horror the moment the butcher gave me a pull. I sank helplessly to the ground, and my spirit floated right out the top of my head before falling back to where it belonged. As the butcher cut my throat open and let my blood drip into a basin, the pain was simply indescribable. Unable to die a quick death, I could only wail. Only when my blood was nearly drained did the butcher plunge his knife into my heart. In the piercing pain I lost my voice, then sank into a daze just like the last time I underwent my rebirth. After an indefinite period of time I woke up to find myself reborn as a human, and that was the beginning of this lifetime. When I saw the pig being butchered just now, its unspeakable pain and distress reminded me of my experience, and I could not help thinking of the retribution awaiting the butcher. I was so overwhelmed with grief that tears rolled down my cheeks." After he heard the monk out, the butcher dropped his knife to the ground, and began to make his living by selling vegetables.

134. Marking a Ghost

An old Confucian scholar had just found a lodging in the house of a relative when his host's son-in-law, a young rogue, arrived for a visit. Feeling an aversion to each other, the two of them didn't want to share a room, so the old scholar was moved into another one. At this he noticed the young man eyeing him narrowly and chuckling to himself. The new room was complete with books, writing brushes and ink, so he sat down to write a family letter under the lamp. All of a sudden a woman appeared before him. Though not exceptionally pretty, she carried herself with much grace. Though he knew this was a ghost, the old scholar remained fearless. Pointing to the oil-lamp, he said, "Since you are here, don't stand there idling. Trim the lamp for me." But the woman blew out the lamp and stepped closer. Enraged, he dipped one hand in the ink stone and slapped her, smearing the ink all over her face. "By this mark I'll find your body tomorrow and have it chopped up and burned!" With a shriek the ghost fled.

The following day the old scholar told his host about the incident. "A maid died in that room," the host confessed. "Her ghost often comes out to make trouble at night, so the room is only used for receiving guests in the day, with no one staying the night there. Last night there was no other place to put you up, and I reasoned that the ghost would not dare approach a man of your learning and virtue. But she showed up after all." Only then did the old scholar realize why the host's son-in-law had chuckled to himself. The ghost continued to stalk in the courtyard on moonlit nights. When a servant ran into her, she hurried away covering her face. Later it was discovered that her face was messy with ink stains. How can a ghost with no physical body be colored? Perhaps that was a demon evolving from a solid object, who then took on the maid's appearance.

Duan Chengshi of the Tang dynasty told the following story in his *Miscellany of the Youyang Mountains*. One night a man living in the mountain saw a figure with a big, saucer-like face pop up before the lamp without warning. Taking up his brush, he wrote a couplet on the demon's face:

> As soldiers grow old after a lengthy service at the frontier,
> So horses become bony at the end of a drawn-out expedition.

The demon then vanished. Later the man was strolling in the mountain one day when he found these two lines written on a giant white fugus growing on a big tree. This story was somewhat similar to the old scholar's experience described above.

135. The End of a Family of Robbers

Most peasants in Urumqi plant crops near a pool of water and have their house built by the crop field. Therefore families cannot gather in the same area to form a neighborhood. One can often see a few rooms occupied by a family, with no neighbor nearby, to constitute a "single-household village." People there are exempt from conscript labor, and as the land has never been measured they can plant several hundred *mu* and pay tax on only thirty. This is especially true in remote mountainous areas.

A band of troops once entered the mountain in a hunting trip. They saw a house with its gate and windows firmly closed; over a dozen horses complete with saddles and halters were tethered in the courtyard. Convinced that it was a hiding place of bandits, they charged forth uttering battle-cries. Finding themselves outnumbered, the bandits abandoned their tents and cooking vessels to fight their way out of the encirclement. As the soldiers were unwilling to risk their lives fighting the bandits, they did not give chase. On entering the house they found the ground scattered with bones and carcasses, but there was no one in sight. Then they dimly heard a weeping voice. Tracing the sound to its source, they saw a boy about thirteen to fourteen hanging naked on a window bar. They untied him and took him down, and the boy told them of his woes. "The bandits arrived four days ago," he said. "After my father and brother lost the fight, my whole family were tied up. Each day two of us were taken to a mountain stream to be washed. After this they were dragged back and cut up to make grilled meat. In this way the bandits ate eight people of my family. They wanted to set out today. I was washed and about to be cut up and grilled when one of them waved his hand. Though I did not understand his dialect, I could tell by his gestures that he wanted to have me chopped into a few pieces, which they could take along with them on their horses. Fortunately the troops came, and I had a narrow escape." With this the boy began to sob. Taking pity on him, the soldiers took him back to the camp, where he did odd jobs for them. Then the boy admitted that his family had treasures buried in a cellar. At the order of the camp commander, a few soldiers went with the boy to dig up the treasures and returned with a huge quantity of silver, coins, clothes and other valuables.

Closely questioned, the boy confessed that his father and elder brother had both been highwaymen. For each robbery they would lie in ambush where the official thoroughfare came close to a mountainous area. When they spotted a carriage or two on the road, they would make sure there was no one else within ten li of the carriage to come to its rescue before rushing out to attack. They would kill everyone in the carriage and drive it deep into the mountain until it could go no further. Then they would chop the carriage into pieces, which they threw into a stream along with the dead bodies and bedding, and go on traveling on foot, with the valuables being carried on horseback. When even the horses could go no further, they would cast the saddles and halters into a stream, set the horses free, and carry the valuables on their own backs to return home by a roundabout route. At that time they would be several hundred li from the site of the robbery. Back home, they would store their booties in the cellar for a year or two, and then had the loot sold at a distant market. They had committed robberies in this way for many years without leaving a trace until the bandits came to wipe out the entire family. After making his confession, the boy was spared prosecution on account of his young age. Later he died falling down a cliff while herding horses, thereby putting an end to his family name. This case happened to come into my hands when I was working as a military advisor. Come to think of it, these robbers were too secret and slippery in their movements to be caught, but the bandits arrived in time so that they got the punishment they deserved for killing for money. As voracious man-eaters the bandits left the boy alive as if by accident, so that people would know why the family was destroyed. This seems to have been an act of higher justice rather than a coincidence. The boy was known by his pet name Qiu'er, but the names of the robbers have now escaped my memory.

136. Help from One Fox Provokes Ill Will from Another

One day a man walked into a courtyard to find a black fox in a drunken sleep there. His first impulse was to go up and catch it, then it occurred to him that foxes can help one get rich. So he covered the fox with a piece of clothing and sat down to keep watch. Waking up, the fox stretched its limbs and in an instant changed back to human form. Grateful to the man for watching over it, the fox became his friend and brought him presents occasionally. One day the man asked the fox, "If someone hides himself in your house, can you make him invisible?" The fox said it could. "Can you attach your spirit to someone and make him run swiftly?" Again the fox answered in the positive. The man then came out with his request. "My family is so poor that we can't make ends meet even with your gifts. Moreover, I am reluctant to trouble you so often. My fellow villager, A, is a very rich man extremely afraid of getting involved in lawsuits. He is said to be looking for a kitchen maid, and I decide to let my wife try to get the job. A few days afterward she will find a chance to run away and hide herself in your house. Then I will threaten to sue A, as it is in his house that my wife is found missing. My wife is rather good-looking, so I can accuse him of abducting her because of her good looks and force him to pay me a large sum of money. After I get the money, you can attach your spirit to her, make her run into A's cottage, and allow her to be discovered there. If you can do all this for me, I shall be most grateful." With the fox carrying out the plan accordingly, the man succeeded in extorting money from A. Even after the man's wife returned home, A dared not look further into the matter as she had been found in his cottage.

The woman, however, was unable to recover from her demented state. She spent all day putting on make-up, and at night she seemed to be joking and flirting with someone but would not let her husband approach her. The man hurried over to seek help from the fox. Puzzled, the fox went away to take a look. In a short moment it came running back and stamped its feet in distress. "What rotten luck! That is the fox who lives upstairs in A's house. He must have had his eyes on your wife, for the moment my spirit took leave of her body, he seized the chance to attach himself to her. As I am no match for that fox, there's nothing I can do to help you." When the man went on importuning, the fox's face fell. "Suppose so-and-so in your village, who is as fierce as a tiger, has taken someone's wife by force. Would you be able to stand up for that poor man?" The woman's conditions went from bad to worse. In great detail she described to others how her husband had used her to extort money. Doctors and magicians invited to treat her were at a loss as what to do, and she finally died of exhaustion. The villagers all agreed that the man's scheme had appeared to be flawless, for he was as wily as a ghost and had a fox to abet him. Yet the assistance of a friendly fox roused the ill-intention of another, so that the man ended up like the proverbial mantis stalking a cicada, unaware of the oriole behind. It is written in an ancient poem, "As profit has a dagger leaning on it, so a greedy man will inflict harm on himself." How precisely true!

137. The Fateful End of an Evil Taoist

In Xinzhou there was a man forced by dire poverty to sell his wife. She was taken to a house, where a Taoist priest came to lead her into the mountains. Scared as she was, there was nothing she could do as she had already been sold. She closed her eyes as instructed by the Taoist and heard wind rustling past. After a while, told to open her eyes, she found herself standing with him on top of a mountain. From a clean, splendid house over twenty young women came out to greet her. When she asked where it was, they described it as the residence of an immortal where everyone enjoyed a comfortable life. To her question about what they were doing there, they replied, "We just take turns sleeping with the master. Here we have heaps of gold and silver. The master has demons and deities at his beck and call, so he can obtain precious jewelry, rare dishes, and exotic fruits in an instant. We live like lords and princes, and only have to endure a little pain once every month, but that's nothing serious." They showed her the storehouse, the kitchen, their bed chambers, and the master's bed chamber. Then they pointed at two rooms located high above. "That is the place where the master worships the moon and the stars, and that is where he forges silver." They had some servant women, but no other male except the Taoist himself.

After that the woman, like her companions, began to be called into the Taoist's room to sleep with him during the day. He sat in deep meditation at night, when all the young women could return to rest in their respective rooms. The most afflictive experience came right after menstruation, when she was stripped off her clothes and tied to a big tree with a rope made of red floss so that she could not move her limbs. Nor could she utter a sound since her mouth was gaged with a piece of cotton. With a metal tube as thick as a chopstick, the Taoist stabbed into her acupuncture points in her arms and legs to suck her blood. Then he applied powder to her wounds, which instantly relieved her of all pain. Scabs formed quickly and came off the next day, thus the wounds were totally healed. They lived in such a high place that clouds and rain came and went underneath. One day a violent wind arose, as pitch-black clouds gathered over the mountain, accompanied by flashes of lightning and loud peals of thunder. Terrified, the Taoist surrounded himself with over twenty naked young women, who formed a protective screen of flesh. Several times a flash of lightning struck into the room, only to draw back instantly. Then a dragon's paw the size of a dustpan emerged from the clouds and snatched the Taoist out of the crowd. As the mountain shook in a deafening thunderbolt, the woman fainted. She finally woke up to find herself lying on the roadside. A local inhabitant told her she was a few hundred li away from home. She bartered her bracelets for some old clothes to cover herself up, then begged her way back home. With her blood and vital energy drained by the Taoist, she looked haggard on her return and died soon afterwards. Though capable of such magical feats, the Taoist was struck dead by heaven in the end. Yet there are people misled into a vain attempt to seek immortality without learning any true formula. How preposterous they are!

138. A Case of Robbery and Adultery

In this world of ours not a single day goes by without an adultery or robbery being committed somewhere, and it seems this is nothing to raise eyebrows about. In the following story, however, a robbery was committed that could not be called robbery, and an adultery committed that could not be called adultery. They took place at the same time and both were exposed, but due to their entanglement both were immediately resolved. Such a case was truly peculiar. The story began with a man who lost his wife in middle age. Though he had a son already, he bought a married woman to be his concubine, and somehow managed to make her get along in peace with his son. Shortly afterwards he died, and his lifetime savings fell into the woman's hands. On learning this, his son came to demand the money back, but as he could produce no evidence, she denied having it. Later he found out where she hid the money, so he dug a hole in the wall late at night, slipped into the house and opened a chest to take things out. Hearing the noise, the woman shouted "thief." All the house servants were awakened and burst in with clubs. As the son scurried out of the hole in the wall, he suffered a blow in the head and fell to the ground. When the servants entered the room in search of other robbers, they heard someone gasping for breath under the bed. "There's another thief!" They called out. The man was dragged out and tied up. When candles were brought, they found out the man escaping through the hole in the wall was the late master's son, and the man hiding under the bed was the concubine's former husband.

When the son woke up, he and the woman fell into a bitter quarrel. The son declared he was no robber since he was merely trying to take back his father's property, and the concubine denied having committed adultery since she was simply having a tête-à-tête with her former husband. He argued that she could have remarried her former husband rather than meet him in secret, while she contended that he should come to request the return of his father's property rather than dig a hole in the wall to sneak into the house. They reviled and swore at each other, each holding fast to his or her own opinion. The following day the clansmen of the two families met in secret to discuss the matter. To bring the case to court, they argued, would only result in mutual defeats and disgrace their family names. Therefore they persuaded the son and the concubine to reach a compromise. He would get back the household property of his late father, while she was allowed to rejoin her former husband. The contention was thus resolved. By this time, however, many people had heard of the story and got a good laugh out of it.

139. The Slaying of a Picture-Demon

A scholar who had just taken up lodgings in a temple was attracted by a painting on the wall. The beauty in the picture looked very much alive with her vivid features, and the folds of her dress seemed to be rippling in the wind. "Doesn't this painting disturb your mind during meditation?" he asked the monk. "This picture portrays a heavenly maiden scattering blossoms," the monk said. "It has been kept in this temple for over a hundred years, but I have never looked at it closely." One evening the scholar was sitting before a lamp gazing at the picture when he noticed the girl seemed to be protruding from the surface. "This must be a Western painting," he mused to himself. "That's why it gives one a sense of perspective." Just then a voice said in the picture, "Don't be startled, I'll get down right away." A stern and upright man, the scholar shot back harshly, "What demon

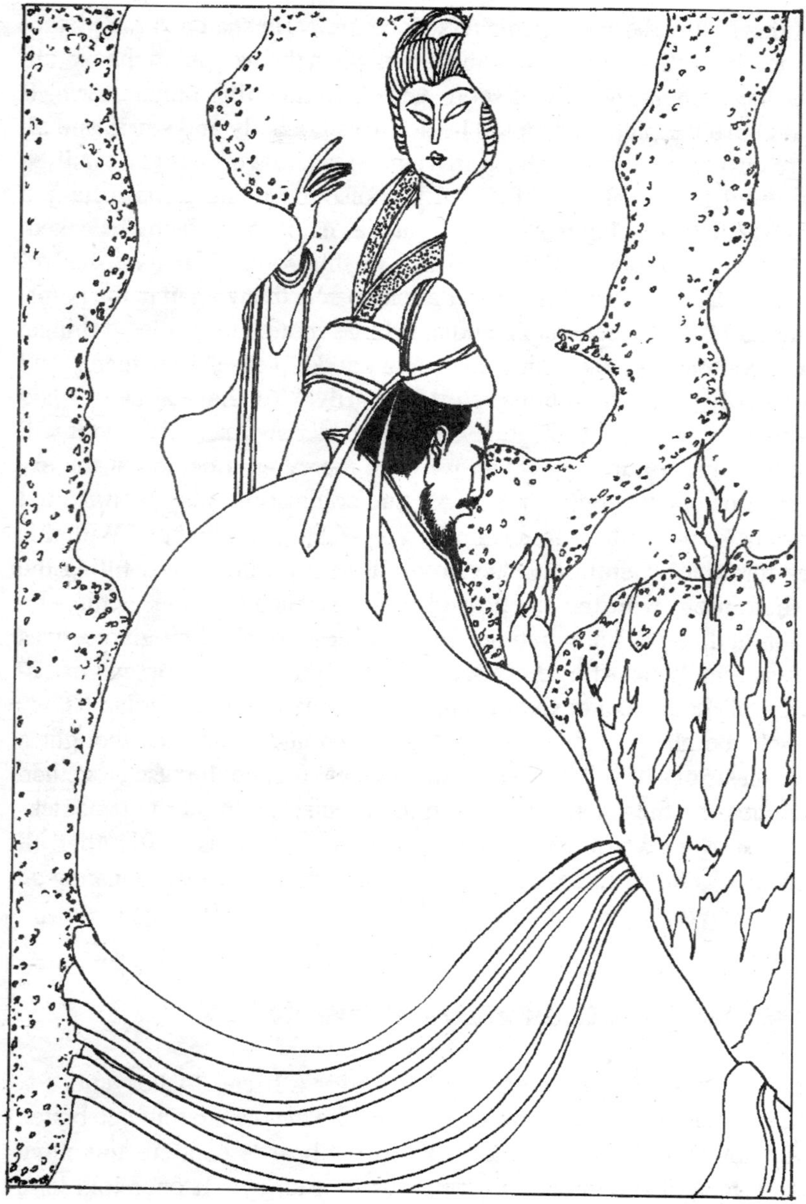

is this? How dare you come to seduce me?" He snatched the picture from the wall to burn it over the lamp, when the woman in the picture pleaded sobbingly, "I will soon succeed in attaining human form. If you burn the picture, I would be destroyed in body and spirit, and all my efforts would have been in vain. Please have mercy; I shall be grateful to you all my life." At the noise the monk came to take a look. After the scholar told him what was happening, the monk asked, "I had a disciple who used to live in this room. Later he died of illness. Did you kill him?" After a long pause the woman in the painting said, "As the realm of Buddha is large enough to enfold all things, and compassion, the principle of monkhood, please show mercy and spare my life!" The scholar retorted angrily, "You have already killed a man. If we let you off today, who knows how many lives you will harm in the future? How can we have mercy on a demon at the expense of many people's lives? As true compassion may be impaired by cheap sympathy, master, I pray you take no pity on her." With this he threw the picture into the stove. It went up in flames, filling the whole room with the smell of blood. It seemed that the picture-demon had killed more than one man. Afterward, a sobbing voice was occasionally heard in that room late at night. "The remnants of energy of the demon have not scattered," remarked the scholar. "They might be able to get together if given enough time." He bought a dozen strings of firecrackers in the market and tied the fuses together. On hearing the weeping sound in the evening he lit all the firecrackers, and the whole room shook in loud explosions. After that all became quiet in the room. That scholar was good at exterminating an evil from the very root.

140. Taught a Lesson by a Heavenly Fox

There was once a man who had a fox for a friend. A heavenly fox with fantastic magical powers, it could take the man to tour celebrated mountains and other scenic spots to his heart's content, travelling thousands of li and back in the twinkle of an eye. It once told him,

"Except for residences of sages and immortals, I can get to any spot on the map at will." One day the man said to the fox, "Since you can take me to any place a thousand li away, how about putting me in the boudoir of someone else's house?" When the fox asked him what was on his mind, he explained, "I am often invited by a friend to feast in his backyard, where we are entertained by song and dance performances. A favorite concubine of his has cast me many amorous glances. Though we have not exchanged a single word, our hearts are already linked together. Unfortunately she remains out of my reach, living in a secluded corner of that big house, and in vain do I yearn for her. If you can take me to her boudoir in the dead of night, I will enjoy a fabulous moment with her."

After hearing the man out, the fox hesitated for a long time. "This is not impossible to arrange," it finally said, "but what if her husband happens to be with her?" To this the man replied, "I'll go only after I have made sure he is staying the night with another concubine." Later he got the news he had been waiting for and asked the fox to take him there. Before he could get dressed properly, the fox picked him up and flew into the air. After a while it put him down, saying, "Here you are," and left. Feeling his way in the dark, the man found himself alone in a room with books everywhere. The fox, he realized, had played a trick by putting him in his friend's library. In his panic he knocked over a desk, the items on the surface crashing to the floor. The watchman cried "thief" on hearing the noise, and a crowd of armed servants came at once with lit candles to search the place. As soon as they heard someone shuddering behind a screen, they rushed over to strike him down and tie him up. Looking closely under the candlelight, they were amazed to recognize their master's friend. This man had the presence of mind to tell a lie, saying he had offended his fox-friend, who therefore had taken him there against his will. Well-acquainted with him, the master of the house dismissed the incident with a smile. "So the mischievous fox wants me to beat you up," he said. "I'll spare you the thrashing this time and just throw you out of my house!" A servant was sent to take the man home.

His anger was not yet appeased when he described his experience to a good friend a few days later. "Foxes are indeed inhuman," he said. "I've known this one for ten years, yet it betrayed me like that!" His friend was outraged. "You've known that friend of yours for more than ten years," he said, "yet you wanted to seduce his woman with the help of a fox. Who deserved to be called inhuman? Though the fox detested you for your faithlessness and punished you with a prank, it acted with such restraint as to allow you an excuse to clear yourself. That was rather tolerant on its part. If it had made you dress up and put you under the man's bed, how would you be able to extricate yourself? From this point of view, the fox is actually human, and you are a fox in nature. Don't you feel no remorse at all?" At this a wave of shame flooded the man's face. The fox never visited him again, and that friend of his gradually ceased to see him.

141. A Folly Repaid by Good Fortune

A petty man's cunning scheme always benefits a gentleman in the end. This seems far-fetched but is actually valid. A roving scholar in Guangdong was given lots of presents by friends and relatives he called on in the area south of the Five Ridges. On his way home his luggage, in addition to clothes and a bedroll, included two huge chests that had to be carried by four men. When he had to change boats one day, the chests were fastened by a thick cord to be carried from one boat to the other. Suddenly the rope broke with a snap, and the chests tumbled to the deck and cracked open. Stamping his feet in dismay, the scholar hastily opened the chests to check the damage. One contained new ink stones manufactured in Duanzhou, and the other, decorational rocks from Yingde together with a packet of silver about sixty to seventy taels, the wrapping paper torn open. Picking up the silver for a close look, he accidentally dropped it into the river. The fishermen hired to salvage the silver only managed to retrieve a small portion. While the scholar was lamenting his ill luck, a boatman who had travelled along with him offered his congratulations, saying, "A band of robbers had trailed you for several days for these two chests.

They did not dare take action because the boat was always moored at populated places. They just found out there was nothing valuable in the chests, so they cursed their ill luck and scattered away. You are truly a lucky man! Have you by any chance done a good deed recently to win the gods' blessing?"

"Rather than a good deed," whispered a passenger to a few others, "he did a very stupid thing recently. When he was staying in Guangdong he asked the innkeeper to purchase a concubine for him at a hundred and twenty taels. The woman, he was told, had been married for a year or so, and agreed to sell herself only because her family was on the point of starvation. When she arrived on the wedding day, her husband and parents-in-law came along to bid her good-bye. They looked thin and feeble like a bunch of beggars. They stopped in front of the house to embrace and weep bitterly. After she parted with her family, the bride ran out again to say a few more words to them, and had to be dragged back into the room by the matchmaker. Then her father-in-law kowtowed to this man and showed him a baby just a few months old. 'This child can no longer feed on its mother's milk, and we don't know if it will survive. Please let its mother milk it one more time to make it live through today. We'll think of something when tomorrow comes.' After he heard this, this good chap leapt to his feet and said, 'I thought the woman had been sent home for an offense. I'm so sad to find you in such terrible conditions. You can take back your daughter-in-law and keep the money.' Then he burned the woman's indenture on the spot. Actually she was the daughter of the innkeeper, who cheated him out of his money in this way by taking advantage of his goodwill. If he should have received her into his house, there would have been another scheme awaiting him. All the guests at the inn knew the secret, and he was the only one kept in the dark to this day. Do you suppose the gods would count this as a good deed?" "It is a good deed," responded one of the listeners. "Though what he did was a foolish thing, he did it out of compassion, and the gods judge a man only by his motivation. So the incident should be the reason why he was able to avoid a calamity today. As for the innkeeper, who knows what punishment the gods have in store for him?"

142. A Fox Painter

One often reads about foxes with a flair for poetry, but fox painters are a rare phenomenon. The following story is told by Li Yanting, a native of Haiyang. Toward the end of the Shunzhi reign and at the beginning of the Kangxi reign a scholar named Zhou Xun made frequent tours in Hunan and Henan. Famous for his painting of pine trees, Zhou was once invited by a scholar to paint the wall of his studio. In the finished work the pine tree had its roots in a corner of the west wall, its trunk sweeping across the north wall and the top branches brushing the east wall by a foot or two. A look at the picture made one feel cool and fresh, as if being bathed in a gentle breeze. The scholar invited some friends to a feast to appreciate the painting together.

The guests were standing before the wall gesticulating and uttering cries of admiration when one of them clapped his hands and burst out laughing. In the next moment the whole room was rocking with laughter. What they saw was a pornographic picture under the pine tree depicting a large wooden bed covered in a long mat. In this bed lay a naked couple in passionate love-making while exchanging amorous glances. Two young maids, also stark naked, stood beside the bed to wait on the couple, one waving a fan to keep off flies and mosquitoes, the other putting her hands on the pillow of her mistress to prevent it from being shaken to the floor by the vigorous movements of the couple. These were none other than the scholar with his wife and concubines. The guests went up to take a close look and found the portraits extremely lifelike; even the servants recognized the characters and covered their mouths to hide their smiles. Furious, the scholar looked up into the air and flung a string of abuses against some evil fox. Suddenly they heard laughter on the eaves. "You are such a rude man," the voice said. "Mr. Zhou's expertise in painting pine trees reached my ears long ago, but it was not until last night that I finally had a chance to feast my eyes on his masterpiece. I sat before the painting unwilling to leave, so I did not avoid you in time, but neither did I throw bricks or tiles at you. Your rude remarks came as a gratuitous insult, so I got my own back by playing this prank on you. If you do not repent and go on giving yourself airs like that, I will draw that little picture on your gate to amuse the passers-by. Think about it carefully." It turned out that the scholar, carrying lit candles, had come to the studio with a servant the night before to get some vessels ready for the feast, when a dark creature jumped up and scurried out of the door. Knowing it must be a fox, the scholar had hurled abuses at it.

With the guests acting as mediators, the fox was invited to join them at the table. A chair was brought for the fox, who remained invisible although people could hear its voice. It downed the wine cup at one gulp whenever it was filled, but did not touch any dish, saying it had abstained from meat for over four hundred years. When the feast was coming to an end, the fox said to the scholar, "You are such a clever man that you tend to be proud and insolent because of your ability. This is harmful to the cultivation of virtue and self-preservation. Take what happened today for instance. It is lucky for you to have met me. If it had been a fox as easily offended as you are, you would have got yourself into an endless string of troubles. Only knowledge can transform a person's disposition, so please strive for improvement in that respect." By this time the fox's painting had vanished without a trace.

The following day there suddenly appeared on the east wall of the studio several sprays of peach blossoms in a backdrop of black moss and green grass. The blossoms were not dense. Some were in full bloom, some still in petals, some scattered on the ground, and some on the point of withering. Especially vivid and enchanting were about eight or nine petals floating in mid-air and dancing in the wind. Two lines by the early Tang poet Yang Shidao were inscribed on the painting:

> *Among fragrant grass untrodden by man,*
> *Petals are falling in the empty hill.*

No signature was found on the painting, which must have been done by the fox in return for the previous day's feast. At the sight of the painting Zhou Xun gasped in admiration. "The use of ink and brush strokes is perfectly natural! In comparison, my works look affected and lacking in sincerity."

143. A Prophetic Poem

A man's fate, being fixed, can be prophesied by ghosts and deities. However, sometimes a prediction can be made even though no portent has yet appeared, no thought has yet been engendered in the mind of the person involved, and the occurrences are trivial things like little games with nothing to do with destiny or retributive justice and therefore impossible to have been predetermined in the underworld. In the thirty-fifth year of the Qianlong reign a scholar of the Hanlin Academy consulted his future official career by calling up spirits in planchette writing. A spirit emerged with an answer in the form of a poem:

> *A joyous laughter puts a stick into his hand.*
> *Peach and plum blossoms dazzle the eyes.*
> *Two butterflies run into each other*
> *After flying over the wall in a quest for fragrance.*

The scholar did not understand a single word of it.

Soon afterward he was appointed a county magistrate after passing a test given by the emperor. Thus the second line of the poem became comprehensible, for it predicted the scholar's appointment to county magistrate away from the capital by quoting a well-known story about Pan Yue of the Jin dynasty, who had planted peach and plum trees right after he took office as magistrate of Heyang County. But the other three lines remained unintelligible. When friends called on the scholar to offer congratulations, his gatekeeper limped out with a walking stick to receive them. It turned out that servants were always overjoyed if their master got a position away from the capital.

When he learned of the scholar's appointment, the gatekeeper had leapt in exultation and shouted, "I've turned an immortal today!" Unluckily he fell down the stairs and broke his shank. Thus the first line of the poem came true.

    A few days later the scholar suddenly drove two servants out of the house for no apparent reason. People then learned from an insider what had taken place. The two servants, both eager to replace the lame man as gatekeeper, secretly told their wives to make up and seduce the master after he retired to his studio for a rest. That evening one woman prepared some cookies while the other poured a cup of tea. Stealthily they felt their way in the dark to the corridor outside the studio, only to bump into each other and drop whatever they were carrying. Shamed into anger, they began swearing at each other. The scholar had no intention to look further into the matter but simply sent the two servants packing. In this way the third and fourth lines of the poem also came true. The poem's author must have been an enlightened ghost, but how he managed to make a prediction like that defies our rational understanding.

144. A Ghost Who Has Read the Wrong Books

Nowadays some illustrious men from ancient times receive sacrifices in their memorial temples, a practice that enables people today to cherish the memory of their lofty deeds and emulate them, thereby contributing to the moral education of the common folks. The spirits of some of the ancients still exist and are capable of manifesting themselves, but there are also ghosts who usurp the names of the ancients to obtain food. A scholar was once put up in a village in Chenliu County. As it was in hot summer, he took a walk in the open field to enjoy the cool. As it got dark at nightfall, a man suddenly emerged and bowed to him. They sat down under an old scholartree to exchange their names. "Don't be startled," the man said, "for I am Court Gentleman Cai of the Han dynasty. Though my grave and memorial hall remain, sacrifices are seldom offered. Moreover, I lived as a scholar and am reluctant, even after death, to seek food from commoners. I have disclosed my true identity because I feel a certain affinity with you. Could you come here to offer a sacrifice to me tomorrow?" The scholar, a large-minded man, did not feel afraid. When he asked about events in the late Han dynasty, the ghost's answer coincided mostly with the novel *Romance of the Three Kingdoms*. Growing suspicious, the scholar went on to ask the ghost about his life experiences, and its answer matched the drama *Story of the Pipa Player* perfectly. With a smile the scholar said, "Since I am financially embarrassed and unable to afford an offering, you'd better try your luck with some wealthy man. But take this advice from me: There are three books you should find and read—*History of the Later Han Dynasty, History of the Three Kingdoms* and *Collected Works of Court Gentleman Cai*. That would give you a better chance of success when you seek food like this in the future." Its face turning crimson, the ghost jumped to its feet and ran away.

1. 老学究遇亡友

一位老学究以教书为生。他有天夜里赶路,碰见一位已经去世的朋友。性情刚直的老学究并不害怕,就问:"你往哪儿去?"鬼答道:"我如今在冥司任职,要去南村拘拿一个人的魂,正好与你同路。"于是他们并肩而行。

经过一所破屋时,鬼说:"这儿住着一位文士。"老学究问他何以得知。鬼解释说:"白天大家为了生计而忙忙碌碌,天生的灵气被掩盖起来了。等睡着以后,因为没有杂念,精神澄澈,平时所读的书,字字都放出光芒,由身体里发射出来,灿烂夺目。如果一个人具有杰出的学问和文采,他的光芒就直冲霄汉,可以和日月争辉。比这次一等的,光芒可达数丈;再差一点的,可达数尺。最差的就象一盏灯,仅能照亮门窗而已。这种光芒凡人看不见,唯有鬼神能够洞察。刚才那间屋子里的光芒有七八尺高,所以我知道那是文士的居处。"

听到此处,老学究问:"我读了一辈子书,不知睡觉时能发出多少光芒?"鬼吞吞吐吐,好半天才说:"昨天经过你的私塾,碰巧你正打瞌睡。我看见你平生所读之经书策略,字字化为黑烟,学生们都在烟雾笼罩下诵读,实在并无一丝光芒。"老学究一听就怒骂起来。鬼纵声大笑,转眼之间不见了踪影。

2. 狐妻

献县周家有个仆人周虎,与一个狐女相好,二十年来象夫妻一样相亲相爱。狐女曾对周虎说:"我已经修炼四百多年,因为上辈子欠了你的情,今生必须偿还,还不清就不能升天。等我们缘份用尽时,我就会离你而去。"有一天,她显得特别高兴,转而又伤心地落泪,对周虎说:"这个月十九号我们的缘份就用尽,到了分别的时候。我已经为你相中了一位女子,可以出钱聘她为妻。"她给周虎一些银子,让他准备彩礼。从这天起,她对周虎格外亲昵,一天到晚形影不离。

到了十五号早晨,狐女突然起身告别。周虎觉得奇怪,问她为什么要提前走。她抽泣着说:"缘份一天都不能增减,或迟或早则有变通余地。我留下三天的缘份,将来就有机会再与你相会。"

数年之后,她果然回来和周虎欢聚了三天。临别时她呜咽着说:"这回是真的永别了!"

有人评论说:"这个狐狸做事留有余地,这样珍惜福份的行为值得效仿。"又有人说:"欢聚三日,终须一别,又何必往后拖延呢!这个狐狸为了升天,修炼了四百多年,还是对尘缘难以舍弃,做事怎么能这样!"我觉得这两位的意见各有各的道理。

3. 道士谈天命

献县的县令明晟是应山人。有一回他想昭雪一桩冤案,又怕上司不准许,犹豫不决。本县儒学有名差役,人称王半仙,认识一个能够预言日常吉凶的狐狸。明晟打发王半仙就这件事情去问问狐狸。狐狸面色郑重地答道:"明先生身为百姓的父母官,只应该考虑这个案子冤不冤,不应该担心上司准不准。难道他不记得制府李卫的话了吗?"

听了王半仙的讲述,明晟不由心头一震。原来,李卫尚未当官时,曾在乘船渡江时遇见一位道士。当时有个乘客跟船夫争吵,道士叹息道:"此人命在须臾,何必还计较几文钱的得失!"不久那人就被船帆扫了一下,跌进江里淹死了。李卫不禁暗暗惊异。到了江心,忽然刮起大风,几乎要把船吹翻。道士在船上转着圈子念咒语,结果风停下来,船安全靠岸。李卫一再拜谢道士的救命之恩。道士说:"刚才那人掉到江里淹死,是命中注定,我救不了他。你是个贵人,逢凶化吉也是命中注定,我不能不救。何必要谢我呢!"李卫听了又施礼道:"我一定牢记您的教诲,终生听天由命。"

道士却说:"道理不完全是这样。一个人是穷困还是显贵,应该安于天命,否则就会四处钻营,排挤倾轧,无所不至。关系到国计民生的大事,则不能听从命运。天地造就才俊之士,朝廷设置百官,都是为了弥补命运的不足。假若手中掌据权柄,却无所事事,一切听从命运的安排,那么天地何必要造就他的才能,朝廷何必要设置这个官位呢?"

李卫恭敬地接受了道士的劝导,并请教他的姓名。道士答道:"说出来怕吓着你。"他下船走了几十步,忽然消失不见了。李卫后来跟人讲过此事,不知那狐狸是从哪儿听说的。

4. 夜话无鬼论

交河的及孺爱和青县的张文甫两位老儒同在献县教书。有一回他们在南村与北村之间散步,离开住处比较远,到了寂静的荒野之中。张文甫有些害怕,想往回走,并说:"墓地间多鬼,不是久留之地!"正在这时,一位拄着拐杖的老人出现在他们面前,作了一个揖说:"这世界哪里有鬼? 难道你们没听说过晋人阮瞻的无鬼论吗?你们两位身为儒者,不应当听信佛/教的妄言。"他坐下来侃侃而谈,用宋代大儒的观点论证世上无鬼。两位老儒大为折服,认为他的论述颇有见地。在攀谈之际,他们都没有想到询问老人的姓名。

恰在这时,几辆大车从远处驶来,牛铃发出铮然的响声。老人急忙站起身来说:"泉下之人,寂寞太久了,不持无鬼论,就不能留下你们二位彻夜长谈。分别时我以实相告,千万别以为我是有意戏弄。"说完,老人在眨眼之间就消失了。那一带很少葬有读书人,只有一位董空如先生葬在附近,那老人莫非就是他的鬼魂?

5. 见怪不怪,其怪自败

有一位姓曹的由歙县去扬州,路过朋友家,被请进宽敞的书房小叙。当晚曹某想在书房留宿,朋友说:"这屋里有怪物,夜里不能呆在这儿。"他不听劝告,坚持住了下来。到了半夜,有东西从门缝往里蠕动,看上去薄得象片纸。进门之后,它慢慢地舒展开,变成女人的形状。曹某丝毫不觉得害怕。那怪物突然披散头发,吐出舌头,变成吊死鬼的样子。曹某笑道:"头发还是头发,不过有点乱;舌头还是舌头,不过有点长——那又有什么可怕呢!"怪物猛然把自己的头摘下来,往桌上一放。曹某又笑道:"你有头的时候我都不怕你,何况没头呢!"怪物无计可施,忽地一下就不见了。

从扬州回来的路上,曹某又在朋友的书房借宿。半夜,又有东西从门缝往里蠕动。他吐了口唾沫道:"又是那个不争气的东西吧!"那怪物就没再往里钻。由此看来,畏惧则心乱,心乱则神志涣散,神志涣散则鬼怪得以乘虚而入。无畏则心定,心定则神志清朗,神志清朗则邪气无机可乘,鬼怪也只得羞惭而退了。

6. 吕道士

吕道士擅长幻术,曾在一位姓田的官员家作客。正值紫藤花盛开,田某摆下酒席,邀来许多客人共同观赏。有一个鄙俗的客人在座中喋喋不休,惹人腻烦。一个少年脾气急躁,很生气地让俗客住嘴,两人差点儿打了起来。一个老儒上来劝解,两人都不加理会,他因此也变得怒形于色。这样一来,所有客人都觉得扫兴。

这时,吕道士要了纸和笔,画了三道符当场焚掉了。那三个人忽然都站了起来,在院中来回转了几圈。俗客走到东南角坐下,喃喃自语,细听之下,原来是在对妻妾谈论家事。他先是左顾右盼,好象在为双方劝解,接着又怡然自得地为自己辩解,然后又作出服罪的样子,先是一膝跪地,继而双膝跪地,最后不停地叩头。那个少年则坐在西南角花栏旁,眼波流动,软语轻声,一会儿嬉笑,一会儿谦让,接着又唱起了小曲,自己用手打着节拍,一派风流放荡的丑态。老儒则端坐在石凳上,好象在对四五个人讲解经文,一会儿摇头回答说不对,一会儿瞪眼斥问怎么还不明白,又不停地咯咯咳嗽。众客人又吃惊,又好笑,但吕道士摇手让他们别出声。

等酒喝得差不多了,吕道士又焚了三道符。那三个人坐着发了会儿呆,渐渐清醒过来,自称不胜酒力,不知不觉地睡了过去,请大家原谅他们的失礼。众客人强忍着笑走散了。吕道士说:"这是小把戏而已,算不得什么。当年叶法善引唐明皇入月宫,用的就是这种符。老百姓误以为他是真仙,而迂腐的儒生们又说根本没这回事,他们都属于井底之蛙。"后来,吕道士在旅店里用符勾摄一个过路贵官爱妾的生魂。那位女子苏醒后,坐上车凭着记忆找到了吕道士的住处,请贵官火速派人捉拿,但吕道士已经逃走了。

7. 两位术士

据说吴三桂叛乱时,有个术士精于算卦,能预卜吉凶,打算去投奔他。走在路上,他遇见一个人,自称也正要去投吴三桂,于是两人搭伴赶路,晚上住在一起。那个人靠着西边的墙躺了下来,术士就对他说:"你最好别在那儿睡,那面墙半夜前要坍塌。"那人却说:"你的推算不够精确,这面墙到时候要往外倒塌,而不是往里。"到了夜里,果然如那人所说。我觉得这个故事不可信。那人既然能预知一面墙会往哪个方向倒塌,怎么却没有预见到吴三桂必然失败呢?

8. 神奇的瓦片

交河县一位姓苏的官员在家里接待过一个游方和尚。这个和尚擅长幻术,自称曾与吕道士同师学艺。有一回,他用泥巴捏成猪,对它念咒,它就慢慢蠕动起来。他接着念下去,那猪开始发出声音,然后就一跃而起。和尚把猪交给厨子屠宰,作成菜给客人们吃,味道却不甚鲜美。吃完之后,客人们都呕吐起来,吐出来的都是泥。

当天晚上,有个客人因雨在苏家留宿,与和尚共住一室。他悄悄对和尚说:"我在书中曾读到过,有术士对着瓦片念咒语,别人拿着它能划开墙壁,潜入女子的闺房之中。不知您是否有这样的本事?"和尚说:"这并不难。"他捡起一片瓦,对它念了一会儿咒语,递给客人说:"你可以拿这个去试一试,但千万别说话,否则就不灵验了。"客人用瓦片一划,墙壁果然开了。他来到一间屋子,见到一位使他心动的女子正在脱衣就寝。他心里记着和尚的告戒,不敢开口,径自把门插好,上床与那女子亲热,那女子也显出欢快惬意的样子。后来他倦意上来,打了会儿盹,醒来睁眼一看,自己原来和妻子一起躺在自家床上。

正在夫妻俩不知所措,相互质疑的时候,和尚登门来数落他说:"吕道士因为一念之差,已经被雷击死了,你又要引我去造孽!我略施小计,捉弄你一回,幸亏对你的德行没有太大损害。以后千万不要再起邪念了。"随即他又叹了口气道:"你邪念一动,掌管你命运的神祇就会把它登录在案,恐怕会影响到你的前程。"这位客人后来果然仕途坎坷,晚年才谋得训导的职位,终生未摆脱贫困。

9. 冥司通行证

我在乌鲁木齐的时候,一个军吏拿来几十张印好的文件请我签字,对我解释说:"凡是外乡籍兵士死在这里,需要把棺柩迁回故土的,照例发给通行证,否则鬼魂入不了关。"据说这种通行证是发给冥司的。我读了一下,文笔粗陋可笑,说什么"某人于某年某月某日在此病故,今其亲属移柩回乡,发给此证,沿路守关鬼卒应放此鬼魂通过,不得阻挡勒索。"我对军吏说:"这显然是胥吏们巧立名目,想从中捞钱。"于是我呈请将军破除了这条规矩。

过了十天,有人说听见城西墓地里鬼哭,因为它们得不到通行证,无法返回故乡。我斥责那是一派胡言。又过了十天,有人报告说鬼哭已经近城,我还是加以斥责。再过了十天,我住处的墙外有呜呜的鬼叫声,我依然认为是胥吏们在捣鬼。又过了几天,那声音传到了窗外。当时月明如昼,我起身亲自查看了一番,确实没有一个人。我的一位同僚说:"你所持的观点是正理,将军无法驳回,然而鬼哭却是大家亲耳听到的。死者假如真的需要通行证,就会因为得不到而怨恨你。不如干脆签发通行证,让奸佞小人没有借口诽谤你。假如鬼哭仍不停止,你就更可以理直气壮了。"我勉强听从了这个建议,当天晚上周围就安寂下来了。真是天下之大,无奇不有,一般儒生却惯于用常理来判断一切事物。

10. 诗僧

范蘅洲渡钱塘江时,有个和尚要求搭船。他径自把坐具放在船上,倚靠着桅杆,也不打招呼。范蘅洲主动搭话,和尚随意答应着,眼睛却望着别处,一副心不在焉的样子。范蘅洲怪和尚太傲慢,不再理会他。当时西风刮得很紧,他偶然作得了两句诗:"白浪簸船头,行人怯石尤。"他反复念了几遍,还是想不出下面两句怎么接。那和尚闭着眼睛,忽然轻声吟道:"如何红袖女,尚倚最高楼?"范蘅洲不知和尚这两句说的是什么意思,再问他话,和尚又闭口不言了。等船靠岸系缆绳时,恰好有位少女站在一座小楼上,衣袖果然是红色的。范蘅洲大吃一惊,再三地请那和尚解释。和尚回答说:"我不过偶然望见罢了。"然而那时烟水渺茫,小楼又被别的屋舍遮挡,从船上根本不可能望见。范蘅洲怀疑那和尚有先知之能,想对他行礼致意,和尚却挂着锡杖径自走掉了。范蘅洲搞不清和尚究竟是什么人,不由得怅惘若失。

11. 醉死鬼

屠夫许方有天晚上挑着两坛酒走路,走累了就在一棵大树下歇脚。当时月明如昼,远处忽然传来呜呜的声音,随即一个长相骇人的鬼从树丛里跳了出来。许方躲到大树后面,手持扁担准备自卫。鬼跑到酒坛前,高兴得手舞足蹈,上去就喝了起来,喝完一坛,又要开第二坛。刚把盖子掀开一半,鬼却已醉倒在地。许方恨得咬牙切齿,又觉得鬼似乎没有太大本事,于是突然抡起扁担打过去,感觉好象打在虚空中。在他接连痛击之下,那个鬼渐渐化为一团浓烟。许方怕它还要变幻,就不停手地打了一百多下。只见那团烟在地上渐渐散开,颜色越来越淡,直至完全消失。

在我看来,鬼既然是人死后剩余的气,便只会渐渐消散,所以古书里记载说新鬼大,旧鬼小。现今有人能见到鬼,但从没见过古代的鬼,因为那些鬼已经消亡了。酒具有散气的功能,所以医生行血发汗之药常用酒泡制。那个鬼本来剩余的气就不多,喝了一坛酒之后,自然就消散不见了。所以说,它是醉死的,而不是被扁担打死的。有位从不喝酒的人评论说:"鬼原本善于变幻,因为喝了酒,只能躺在地下挨揍。鬼原本让人惧怕,因为喝了酒,最终被人消灭。贪酒之人应该引以为戒!"有位爱喝酒的人反驳说:"鬼虽然没有实体,但仍未摆脱喜怒哀乐各种情绪。等醉卧于地,以至化为乌有,那才是获得了真解脱啊!那才是饮酒的真谛啊!这就象佛教所追求的涅槃,整日为生计奔忙的芸芸众生怎么能理解呢?"

12. 糊涂鬼复仇

我的先父曾讲到他在雍正八年参加会考,与雄县汤某分在同一号舍。半夜里,一个披头散发的女鬼突然掀起帘子闯了进来,伸手就去撕汤某的试卷。汤某素来刚毅正直,心里并无畏惧,坐起身来对女鬼说:"上辈子的事情我不知道,这辈子则从没有害过人。你想要干什么?"女鬼愕然退后一步,问:"你不是四十七号吗?"汤某回答说:"我是四十九号。"原来在此之前有两间号舍里面没人,被女鬼漏数了。女鬼对汤某端详许久,施礼道歉后走掉了。过了一会儿,就听见第四十七号舍里面喧嚷说有人中邪。这个鬼真够糊涂,让汤某平空受难。幸亏他问心无愧,仓猝之间敢于和鬼争辩,只被撕坏了一张卷子,否则吃亏就大了。

13. 贪心的塾师

肃宁县有位塾师讲授程朱理学。一天有个游方和尚在学堂外化缘,从早晨到中午不停手地敲打着木鱼。塾师心里厌烦,出门去赶他走,并且说:"你是异端邪教之人,只能够愚弄无知的百姓。这里都是圣贤的弟子,你又何必妄想打动我们呢?"和尚行了个礼说:"身为佛教徒却向人化募衣食,正如身为儒士却追求富贵一样,都迷失了目标,先生又何必跟我为难呢?"塾师生气了,操起棍子来打和尚。和尚一边躲闪,一边说:"这真是太不象话了!"

和尚走了,落下一个布口袋。塾师原以为他会回来取,但天黑了也不见他来。塾师用手一摸,袋里装的都是零散的钱币。学生们想从布袋里拿钱,塾师拦住说:"我们等和尚确实不回来了再说。还有,应该先把钱数清楚,免得你争我抢。"他们刚把袋子打开,一群马蜂飞了出来,把塾师和学生们的脸面都螫肿了。听见呼叫声,附近的居民都赶来询问。这时和尚突然闯进门来说:"圣贤的弟子们难道想贪匿他人钱财不成?"说完提起布袋就走。临出门,他又合掌向塾师说:"异端之人偶然触犯圣贤的弟子,请不要生气。"围观的人都轰然大笑。有人认为和尚使的是幻术。又有人说:"塾师平时喜欢攻击佛教,所以和尚把马蜂藏在布袋里捉弄他。"我的一个远房叔叔当时在场,他说:"如果事先把马蜂藏在袋子里,必能见到它们在里面蠕动,而我并没看见。应该说那和尚使用了幻术。"

14. 土地神显灵

离我们家十八里地有个杜生村,村里有家人贪图钱财,把童养媳卖给一个富人作妾。女孩与未婚夫相处数年,不愿意改嫁别人,但又无力反抗,于是两人相约出逃。公婆发觉后就追了下去。两人夜里逃到我们村的土地庙,无处藏身,便绝望地痛哭起来。忽然庙里有人说:"追赶的人马上就到,你们可以在神案下躲一躲。"他们刚在庙里藏好身,守庙人喝得醉熏熏的,跌跌撞撞地回来了,横躺在庙门口。等女孩的公婆追到,打听两人的踪迹,守庙人说:"你们是找一对年轻男女吗?他们沿那条路走了。"他们走了之后,那对年轻人沿路讨饭,找到了女孩父母家。父母威胁要打官司,这才使女孩免于被卖。当女孩和她的未婚夫进庙藏身时,发现里面空无一人。守庙人事后说:"我并不知道发生了这件事,也不记得说过那些话。"看来果然是土地神显灵。

15. 老儒闹鬼

在献县以东五十五里的淮镇,有一户姓马的人家突然遭到妖怪的骚扰,夜里投掷石块,呜呜作鬼叫,还在没人的地方放火,闹腾了一年多。马家祭典祈祷,又请术士镇治,都毫无效果,只得另买房子搬过去住。他们把旧宅租出,住户依然受到骚扰,不久也搬走了,随后没有人再敢问津。有位老儒偏不信邪,花很低的价钱买下了房子,选了个吉日搬进去住,没有遇见怪异之事。人们都传说老儒德行高尚,妖怪吓得不敢露面了。后来,有强盗上门与老儒争吵,其中的阴谋才败露。原来先前是老儒花钱雇强盗夜里捣鬼,并非真有妖物。我父亲评论说:"妖怪之为妖怪,不过擅长变幻而已。老儒所使手段变幻莫测,把他称作妖怪也不算错。"

16. 厉鬼扮少女

我们家的奴仆魏藻性情轻佻,喜欢窥视妇女。有一天他在村外遇见一位少女,看着有点面熟,但不知其姓名住所。上前与她搭话,少女不答,只若有所动地看了他一眼,就往西去了。魏藻正盯着她看时,少女一回头,似乎招呼他过去。他沿路跟了下去,渐渐与她靠近。少女脸色羞红,小声说:"来往行人太多,恐怕他们见了起疑心。你可以隔着半里地跟着我。等到了家,我在墙外车棚里等你。我们家屋外枣树下系着一头牛,旁边放着一个石磙。"

魏藻跟着少女越走越远,黄昏时分到了李家洼,离家已有三十里地了。头天刚下过雨,路面泥泞,一直埋过小腿,魏藻走得脚趾头都疼了。远远望见少女进了车棚,他心中窃喜,急忙赶过去。少女背对他站着,猛然转过脸,现出厉鬼的模样,牙齿象锯子,手爪象钩子,面色铁青,眼睛象两盏灯一样闪闪发亮。魏藻惊恐万状,回身便逃,厉鬼在后面紧追不舍。他狂奔二十余里,到达相国庄时已是深夜。他认出岳父母家,急忙上前拼命敲门。门刚打开,他就一头冲进去,把一个少女撞倒在地,自己也摔倒了。好几个仆妇都气愤地大叫起来,争相用捣衣棒乱打他的腿。他一时岔了气,说不清话,只能"我、我"地叫着。过了一会儿,一位老妇人从屋里拿着灯出来,才照见原来是主人的女婿,大家不禁又吃惊,又好笑。第二天,用牛车把他送回家。他卧床养了两个月才好。

当魏藻跟踪少女和被厉鬼追赶时,路人只见到他自来自往,并没有见到少女和厉鬼。是不是因为他起了邪心,狐怪乘机戏弄他呢?我的哥哥晴湖说:"魏藻从那以后不敢再干荒唐事,走路遇见女子必定低头不看。所以不妨说他是受到了神明的惩戒。"

17. 短暂轮回

孙峨山先生曾经在高邮县染病,躺在船中休养。睡梦中他好象到岸上散步,心里感觉很爽快。这时有人为他领路,他恍惚之间也不加询

197

问,就跟着走。到了一处人家,门前的道路很洁净,居室也很体面。进入内室,见到一位临产少妇,他正想退避,领路人在他背后猛击一掌,他就昏了过去。等他渐渐醒来,发现自己缩成婴儿,躺在锦缎做的襁褓中。他知道自己已经转生,但也无可奈何。想要张口说话,只觉一股寒气从顶门儿逼下,让他的话根本出不了口。环视屋中,他见到几案床榻、各种古玩器皿和对联字画。

到了第三天,婢女抱着他洗浴,失手把他摔在地下。他又昏了过去,醒来发现自己回到了船上。听家人说,他断气已经三天了,因为四肢柔软,心口尚有余温,所以没有敢装殓。他连忙拿过纸笔,记下自己的见闻,派人送到他梦中去过的那家,并请主人不要责打摔死孩子的婢女。然后他才慢慢地讲了他的经历。当天他的病就好了,于是就去梦中的那家拜访。他一进门,见到仆妇们都很面熟。主人年老无子,听了孙峨山的讲述,只有怅然叹息,觉得不可思议。

儒生们一般不相信轮回,可生活中往往有轮回的事例,追究起前因后果,自有其道理。唯有象孙峨山先生这样三日一次短暂轮回,随即回归本体,不知其中有什么缘故,只有当成一桩疑案了。

18. 山西商人

有个山西商人住在京城的信成客栈里,衣饰华丽,连仆人穿得都很体面,自称打算花钱捐个官做。一天有个穷老头来找他,被仆人拦住不让进。老头站在门口守候,一直等到他出来。山西商人冷淡地接待了他,只请他喝了杯茶,并不嘘寒问暖。老头小心翼翼地说出求助的意思,商人不高兴地说:"我现在捐官的钱都不够,哪有余力帮助你呢?"老头觉得忿忿不平,就对众人说,从前山西商人穷困潦倒,有十多年是靠自己的接济才能过活。后来他又拿着老头借给他的一百两银子去做生意,这才慢慢发了财。如今老头罢了官,生活困难,听说商人来京,欣喜不已,只希望能要回原先借给他的银子,以便还清债务,回归故乡。说完这番话,老头伤心地抽泣起来,可是山西商人却象没有听见,根本不加理睬。

　　同客栈有位江西来的客人,自称姓杨。他对山西商人作了个揖,问道:"这位老先生所说的确有其事吗?"商人面色一红,答道:"是有这么件事,可是想让我帮助他,的确力不从心。"姓杨的说:"你马上要做官了,不愁没有借钱的地方。假如有人肯借给你一百两银子,一年内偿还,而且不要利息,你愿意把它送给老人作为报偿吗?"商人勉强说愿意。姓杨的就说:"那你就写借据吧,银子我这里有。"商人迫于众人的压力,不得已写了借据。姓杨的把借据收好,打开他的破箱子,拿出一百两银子给商人。商人怏怏地把银子递给老头。随后姓杨的出钱,请商人和老头吃酒。席间那老头兴高采烈,商人却闷闷不乐,草草喝了几杯。酒席一散,老头谢过姓杨的就告辞而去。几天后,姓杨的也离开了客栈,没有再露面。后来山西商人发觉自己箱子里少了一百两银子,可是锁并没有被撬过,无从追究。还发觉少了一个狐皮背心,却多出一张当票,面值二千个铜钱,大致相当于姓杨的置办酒席的花费。山西商人这才知道姓杨的原来是位术士,自己被捉弄了。他又羞又恼,马上离开了客栈,不知搬到哪里去了。

19. 假狐仙

有个姓郝的女巫,算得上是村妇中的狡黠者了。我小时候在沧州吕氏姑母家见到过她。她自称狐仙附体,能够预言吉凶。因为她对别人家里的琐事知之甚详,就吸引了很多人相信她。暗地里她派同伙结交村里的仆妇,让她们刺探各家的隐密之事,以此来蒙骗众人。曾经有位孕妇问她自己所怀是男是女,女巫说是男孩,结果却生了女孩。当妇人来质问为何狐仙的话不灵验时,女巫瞪着眼睛说:"你本来应该生男孩,可是在某月某日你娘家给了二十张饼,你拿出六张给公婆,其余十四张自己偷偷吃掉了。冥司为了惩罚你的不孝,让你改生女孩。你怎么还不悔悟呢?"那妇人不知道女

199

巫事先侦得了这件事,惊惶之下表示服罪。女巫就是这样骗过了不少人。

有一天,女巫正在焚香招狐仙,忽然直起身子,朗声说道:"我是真狐仙。我们狐狸虽然与人杂处,但整日忙于修炼,怎么会和一个老妇人合伙,干预各家各户的琐事?这个老妇人诡计多端,多方敛取不义之财,却假冒了我的名义。今天我附在她的身上说话,为的是让大家识破她的阴谋。"然后,狐仙述说了女巫的种种劣迹,并点出了她一帮同伙的姓名。说完这些话,女巫一下清醒了过来,狼狈地逃走了,后来下落不明。

20. 老儒白日遇鬼

肃宁县的老儒王德安是康熙四十五年的进士,我父亲曾拜他为师。有一年夏天他到朋友家,喜爱园中亭子宽敞清爽,要在那里下榻。朋友劝他不要住,因为里面有鬼。于是王德安讲了下面这件事:

江南有位姓岑的书生,曾在沧州张喋庄家借宿。屋里的墙上挂着钟馗像,有真人那么高;前面还放着一架自鸣钟。岑某喝得醉醺醺地入睡,没有看见这些。他半夜酒醒,听见格格的机轮响,正在诧异,又借着窗外射入的月光看见画像,以为是奇鬼,操起桌上的端州石砚往上就砸了过去。听见砰地一声响,仆人们闯进屋来查看,发现岑某满头满脸都是墨汁,画像前面摆的自鸣钟和玉瓶、瓷鼎都被砸碎了。听说这件事的人都笑破了肚皮。

王德安讲完这个故事,总结说:"有些人动不动就说见到了鬼,其实不过是自己心虚罢了。哪儿真的有鬼呢?"话音未落,只听墙角里面出声道:"鬼就在这里,夜里会出来拜访,请不要用砚石砸我才好。"王德安一言不发地离开了亭子。后来他把这件事讲给学生们听,并且说:"鬼怎么可能大白天跟人说话,那一定是狐狸。我的德行恐怕不足以制服妖狐,所以避开它。"也就是说,他依然坚持无鬼论。

21. 毛驴开口惹祸

即墨一位姓于的书生有次骑着毛驴赶赴京城。路经一处高岗,他把毛驴系在树上,自己倚着块石头打盹。忽然见那毛驴昂首四顾,浩然长叹说:"几十年不来这里,青山依旧,村庄却已改换了模样。"于某本来就好奇,一下跳起身来说:"古人宋处宗曾养过会说话的长鸣鸡。如今我有这头毛驴,每天骑着一起聊天,用不着发愁旅途寂寞了。"他向毛驴作了个揖,跟它说话,毛驴却只顾低头吃草。于某反复劝说,保证要和它交朋友,不以异类看待,毛驴却毫无反应。于某怒气上涌,用鞭子痛打毛驴,它却只会蹦跳狂叫,始终说不出一句话。最后于某竟打折了它的一条腿,牵到屠宰场卖掉,自己徒步回家。这件事非常荒唐可笑,莫非于某在睡梦中听错了?也有可能这头毛驴前世得罪过某个妖物,这妖物附在它身上说话,激怒于某杀了它。

22. 鳖宝

我的祖母有位堂弟叫张宝南,在四川任布政使。他的夫人喜欢吃鳖羹。这天,厨子买到一只巨鳖,刚把头切掉,鳖颈中跳出一个四五寸长的小人,绕着鳖奔跑。厨子吓得昏倒在地,那个小人则不知去向。等把鳖剖开,发现小人仍在腹中,已经死掉了。它戴着黄色的帽子,夹衣是蓝色的,腰带是红色的,靴子是黑色的,面目手足都看得十分清楚。家里一位姓岑的教师见了说:"这叫做鳖宝,如果活捉它,就可以切开手臂把它养起来。它专靠吃人血为生。谁手臂中养着鳖宝,就能透过地面看见埋藏的金银珠宝。血被吸尽之后,这人就会死掉,但他的孩子可以剖开手臂继续养鳖宝,这家人就能世世代代富裕下去了。"厨子听了极为懊悔,一想到自己错过的大好机会,就恼恨得直抽自己的耳光。我的外祖母说:"据岑先生所讲,这不过是拼上性命去获得财宝。人如果肯拼上性命去获得财宝,办法多的是,何必定要剖臂喂养鳖宝呢!"可是那厨子不明白其中的道理,最后竟伤心地死掉了。

23. 鬼控告人

乾隆四年,我曾与东光县的李云举、霍养仲在同一学舍里读书。有天晚上,大家偶然争论起世上倒底有没有鬼。李云举认为有鬼,霍养仲认为没有。这时李云举的仆人插话道:"世界有些事确实很古怪,假如不是亲身经历,我也不敢相信。有一次我走过城隍庙前的墓地,失足踏破了一口棺材。当天夜里我梦见被城隍派人捉去,说有人控告我毁了他的房子。我知道是因为踏破棺材的事情,就争辩说:'他的房子不应该挡在路上,并不是我有意侵犯。'那鬼却说:'是路扩展到了我的家门口,并不是我起初就把家建在路上。'城隍笑了笑,看着我说:'那条路大家都走,不能因此而责怪你;可是别人都没有把他的屋子踏破,偏偏你把它踏破了,所以你也推卸不了责任。你应该赔偿他一些冥钱。'随即又说:'鬼不能自行修理棺材,你可以用一块板子把它盖好,上面再堆上土就可以了。'第二天我依照城隍的指示,把棺材盖好,又烧了冥钱,只见一股旋风把钱灰卷走了。后来,有天晚上我再次路过那个地方,有人叫我过去坐一会儿。我听出那个鬼的声音,急忙跑开了。他在我身后一阵大笑,就象猫头鹰的叫声一样,至今想起来我还觉得毛骨悚然。"

霍养仲听了,对李云举说:"你的仆人帮你说话,我一张嘴说不过你们两张嘴。但我仍然不能把别人的见闻当作自己的见闻那样相信。"李云举反驳说:"假如让你审案子,难道你必须事事都亲眼见到才相信吗?还是要从众人的口中获得线索呢?事事都亲眼见到显然是不可能的;如果从众人的口中获得线索,岂不是把别人的见闻当作自己的见闻吗?你那时该怎么办呢?"说到这里,大家相对一笑,不再往下争论了。

24. 异僧之死

郑成功占据台湾时,有个广东和尚渡海来投奔。和尚武艺高强,光着手臂坐着让人用刀砍,感觉就象砍在石头上一样。他还精通兵法，谈论起来很有见地。当时郑成功正在招募四方人才，对和尚礼敬有加。过了一段时间，和尚表现得越来越骄横，让郑成功难以容忍，同时又怀疑他是奸细，便想除掉他，但又怕杀不成。郑成功手下的大将刘国轩说："真想除掉他，把这事交给我来办。"

刘国轩去拜访和尚，先是和言悦色地闲聊了一阵，忽然说："师父道行高深，但不知见到美女是否还会动心？"和尚答道："我对这种事早就不再感兴趣了。"刘国轩用开玩笑的口气说："我想试一试你的道力，也好让众人更信服于你。"于是他叫来十几位美少年和妓女，在旁边铺开褥子垫上枕头，然后宽衣解带，恣意地调情交合，其妖媚之态天下无双。和尚谈笑自若，似乎视而不见。过了许久，他忽然把眼睛闭上了。刘国轩拔剑一挥，和尚的头就掉了下来。刘国轩事后解释说："和尚的本事并非借助于鬼神，不过是练气自强罢了。心静则气聚，心动则气散。起初他心不动，所以敢于睁着眼睛。后来他闭上眼睛不看，我就知道他心动了，在勉强抑制着，这时剑砍下去他无力抵御。"刘国轩论述的道理很精辟。由此看来，他能够在台湾率领叛军纵横十几年，并非偶然。

25. 驱鬼有术

南皮县的许南金先生，胆子特别大。他曾经在庙里读书，和一位朋友同屋而宿。半夜里，北墙忽然亮起两盏灯，仔细一看，原来是一张簸箕般的大脸，那两盏灯其实是它的眼睛。朋友吓得浑身发抖。许南金披上衣服，慢慢地坐起来说："刚才我还想读书，可惜蜡烛烧尽了，你来得正好。"于是他背朝怪物坐着，拿起一本书朗声读了起来。念了几页，那怪物的目光渐渐暗了下去。许南金敲打着墙壁呼叫，它却不出来。

又有一天晚上，许南金上厕所，有一个小童跟在身后，替他拿着灯。那张怪脸突然从地里冒出来，对着他们笑。小童吓得跌倒在地，手里的灯也掉了。许南金把灯捡起来放在怪物头上，说："正愁没有灯台,你来得正是时候。"那怪物仰视着不动。许南金又说:"你想去哪儿便去哪儿,却偏偏在茅房出现,难道是偶然的吗?我不能让你白来一趟。"说着,他拿起脏纸就往怪物嘴上擦。怪物一下子呕吐起来,大吼数声,把灯吹灭,自己也消失了。从此之后,怪物再没露过面。许先生曾对人说:"鬼怪确实存在,偶然也会让我遇上。然而回顾自己这辈子,从没干过亏心事,所以面对鬼怪就无所畏惧。"

26. 鬼隐士

明朝有位姓宋的人选择坟地,来到了歙县的深山里。天色已晚,风雨欲来,他见到一个山洞,就想钻进去躲一躲。只听洞中有人说:"这里有鬼,请别进来。"宋某问:"那你怎么进去了?"对方答道:"我就是鬼。"宋某请求和鬼见面。鬼回答说:"假如我们见面,我的阴气肯定要侵蚀你的阳气,让你觉得浑身发冷。我们还是隔着一段距离谈话为好,你可以在洞口生堆火御寒。"

宋某照鬼说的做了,然后问:"你一定有自己的坟墓,为什么要住在这里呢?"鬼答道:"我在神宗时担任县令,因为厌恶官场中的尔虞我诈,相互排挤,就弃职归田。死后我向阎罗王请求不再转世为人,阎罗王同意了,把我下辈子应享的福禄转到阴间,让我作了冥官。没想到阴间也象阳世一样官场险恶,你争我斗,我只好弃职归墓。可是我坟墓周围还住着许多鬼,他们往来吵闹,使我不胜厌烦,不得已搬进这个山洞。虽然长年风吹雨打,寂寞难奈,但比起宦海风波,仕途陷阱,又不知强了多少倍。我独自住在空山里,不再顾及岁月的流逝。我记不得多少年没见到鬼了,更记不得多少年没见到人了。我心里还挺高兴,自以为摆脱了各种烦恼,可以自在地存活于天地之间,不料这里如今也通了人迹。明天一早我就搬走,你也不用再来探访我了。"鬼至此闭口不再说话,问他姓名也不回答。宋某正好带着笔墨,临走前就在洞口写了"鬼隐"两个大字。

27. 大盗被擒

大盗齐舜庭剽悍绝伦,能用绳子系住刀柄,远距离掷刀伤人。他为了扩建自家的马厩,逼迫邻居张七卖掉所住房屋。他派手下人威胁张七道:"你要是不赶快搬走,倒霉就在眼前。"张七无可奈何,带着妻子和女儿仓皇离家。他不知道该往哪儿去,就到庙里祈祷说:"我不幸被强盗逼迫,无家可归。现在我把这根木棍竖立在神案前,看它倒下指向哪里,我就向哪里去。"结果木棍指向东北,于是他们一家沿路乞讨来到天津。在当地,女儿嫁了个靠煮盐为生的盐丁,帮助他晒盐,一家人勉强能够糊口。

三四年后,齐舜庭因为抢劫军饷,被人告发。官兵来追捕时,他在黑夜乘着风雨逃掉了。他想到有同党在天津商船上做事,打算去投奔,然后从海路逃走。他白天藏起来,晚上赶路,偷瓜果充饥,一直没有被人发觉。这天晚上,他饥渴交加,远远望见一间屋子里亮着灯,就上前敲门。一位少妇盯着他看了许久,突然大叫道:"齐舜庭在此!"原来,官府悬赏捉拿他的公告已经发到天津了。众盐丁闻声齐至,齐舜庭手无寸铁,只得俯首就擒。那位少妇正是张七的女儿。假如当年齐舜庭不逼迫张七背井离乡,他如今改装逃亡时就不会有人认出他。他当时已经到达了离海几里的地方,马上就能够平安地扬帆远去了。

28. 善鬼求食

佣工秦尔严曾经驾车从李家洼去淮镇。走到半路,有人用火铳打鸟,拉车的马都受了惊,狂奔起来。秦尔严在慌乱中摔下车,横卧在车轮前,料想性命不保,谁知那些马突然停住不动了。晚上回到家,他买了酒来庆贺,并向众人讲述了他死里逃生的经历。这时窗外有人说:"你以为是马自己停下了吗?是我们俩把它们的笼头抓住了。"秦尔严急忙开门看,屋外什么人都没有。第二天,他带了酒到他摔下车的地方去祭奠救他的两个鬼。我父亲听说这件事后评论道:"鬼都用这种方式求食,大家就没有理由讨厌鬼了!"

29. 义牛救主

雍正初年,李家洼佃户董某的父亲去世了,留下一头跛脚的老牛,准备把它卖给屠宰场。牛却跑掉了,到董某父亲的坟墓前躺下,无论牵拉还是鞭打都不肯动,只是摇着尾巴长鸣。村里人听说了,就渐渐地聚拢来围观。突然一位姓刘的老人面露怒色,拿手杖敲打着牛说:"他的父亲掉到河里,与你有什么相干?让他随波漂没,葬身鱼腹,岂不美妙?你倒好,没事找事,把他救上来,让他多活了十多年。他活的时候需要供养,病的时候需要医药,死后还留下这个坟,每年都需要打扫、上供,给董家的儿孙们添了无数麻烦。你犯下这么大的罪过,理应被宰掉,在这里哞哞叫个不停又有什么用?"原来,董某的父亲曾掉到河里,快要没顶了,这头牛随后跳了下去,让他抓住牛尾巴爬上了岸。董某一直不知道这件事,此时感觉非常惭愧,马上把牛牵回家去了。几个月后,老牛病死,董某流着泪把它掩埋了。

30. 鬼讲鬼故事

有个书生乘船旅行,夜里泊靠在鄱阳湖边,借着月色上岸散步纳凉。到了一家酒肆,见到好几个人,与他通了姓名,说是同乡,于是坐下喝酒,一同谈笑,讲起鬼故事。各人所说都颇有新意。其中一人道:"你们讲的事都挺奇特,但还是比不上我的经历。从前我在京城,曾在丰台一个花匠家躲避都市的喧闹。偶然遇见一位文士打扮的人,和他攀谈起来。我提到当地花木繁盛,只是坟地间多鬼,让人厌烦。那人说:'鬼也有俗有雅,不能一概厌弃。我从前游西山时碰见一个人和我论诗,见解精妙。他吟诵了一些自己的诗句,比如说:深山迟见日,古寺早生秋。又如:钟声散墟落,灯火见人家。我正想打听此人的居所,远处传来车队的铃声,他一下子就不见了。这个鬼难道让人讨厌吗?'我喜欢这位文士谈吐洒脱,就请他留下来一起喝酒。那人却说:'不惹你厌烦,已经非常荣幸了,怎么敢叨扰你的酒食呢?'说完一笑就不见了。我这才知道跟我谈论鬼的原来也是鬼。"

书生听到这儿,开玩笑地说:"这样的奇事真是闻所未闻。不过话说回来,有时奇事中还藏着奇事。谁敢肯定现在谈论鬼的不会也是鬼呢?"此话一出口,同坐的几个人脸色大变。一阵微风过后,灯光突然黯淡下来,那几个人都化作薄雾轻烟,很快向四周散开飘走了。

31. 种瓜得瓜

丰宜门内玉皇庙街有几间破屋,很长时间锁着没人住,据说里面有狐狸。恰好江西一位举人和几个朋友科举落第,准备留在京城复习,等待下次再考,发现这个地方比较幽静,就在旁边租了房子住下。有一天,举人看到房檐下站着一位妩媚的少妇,虽然知道是狐女,却因少年气盛,心中毫不惧怕。黄昏后他到破屋门外行礼,说了一番挑逗的话。当天夜里,他暗中听见床前有动静,知道是狐女来了,就伸手把她拉上床。那狐女纵身扑入他的怀中,两人尽情狂欢,直至他精疲力竭。等月亮升起,从窗口照进来,举人发现怀中抱着一个白发老妪,长得又黑又丑。他惊问道:"你是谁?"老妪毫无愧色地说:"我原来是城楼上的老狐,主妇嫌我好吃懒做,把我赶到这儿的破屋里居住,已经有好多年寂寞冷清,无人过问了。幸而得到你的爱怜,这才不避羞耻,献身于你。"举人大怒,伸手猛抽她的耳光,打算把她绑捆起来拷打。两人搏斗的声响惊动了同舍其他人,都赶来帮忙。老狐从举人手中挣脱出去,破窗而逃。

第二天晚上,老妪又坐在屋檐下,柔声呼唤。举人张口斥骂,突然被一块飞来的瓦片击中。又有一天晚上,举人揭开床帐想睡觉,发现老妪赤身裸体躺在床上,笑着向他招手。举人拔出佩剑直刺过去,老妪这才哭着悻悻而去。举人害怕老狐狸再来纠缠,就赶紧另找了住处。他登车正要离开,忽然发现前几天见过的妩媚少妇从里面走出来。举人连忙派一个仆人去打听,原来少妇是房东的外甥女,前几天偶然出门到街上去买过花粉。

32. 李代桃僵

一位候补官员住在京城的会馆里等待任命。在会馆后墙缺口处,他见到一位颇有姿色的少妇,衣服虽然破旧,却相当整洁,不由起了爱慕之意。会馆主人的母亲五十多岁,以前在大户人家当婢女,举止颇为得体,经常代替儿子应酬客人。候补官估计她能帮上忙,就塞给她一些钱,请她安排他与少妇幽会。老妇人说:"以前我没见过她,大概是新搬来的。我先去探探消息,你也别抱太大希望。"过了十几天,老妇人回报说:"已经替你安排好了。她本是良家女子,因为家里太穷才忍羞答应下来。不过她怕被人察觉,等夜深月黑时才能来。请你别点蜡烛,别跟她说笑,别让仆人和其它客人听见动静。晨钟一响,就让她离开,每夜送她二两银子就可以了。"候补官按照这种约定,与那少妇暗中来往了将近一个月。

有天晚上,邻家不慎失火。候补官惊慌地起身,仆人们都冲进房里抢搬箱子。忙乱之中,有人伸手猛拉床垫,只听砰地一声,一个赤身裸体的妇人摔在床下,却是会馆主人的老母,大家又吃惊,又好笑。原来,京城的媒人最为狡猾,遇见候补官员纳妾时,常以美女让其过目,等娶亲时却变成相貌平庸之辈。有时新郎发现及时,就到官府控告这种诈骗行为。有时新娘蒙着头进门,背对着灯,用扇子挡着脸,直到度过一夜之欢,新郎才发觉受骗,只得将错就错。没想到那位老妇人居然沿袭了这种风气,以身相代。然而候补官后来向四邻打听,附近并没有住着他先前所见的秀丽少妇。有人说:"那肯定是妖怪。"又有人说:"那是老妇人花钱雇的妓女,用来诱他上钩的。"

33. 扫帚精

青县有户农家,除夕日听见一个卖通草花的在外敲门大叫:"我等了半天,怎么还不给买花钱?"主人把家里人问了个遍,谁也没买过花。可卖花人坚持说,有一个女童拿了几朵花进门去了。双方正在争执,一个老妇人忽然叫道:"真是怪事!茅房里的旧扫帚上居然插着几朵花呢!"把扫帚拿来给卖花人验看,果然是刚才被女童取走的那些花。于是把扫帚扔在火中焚烧。扫帚发出呦呦的呻吟声,还冒出一缕鲜血。这个妖怪既然学会了变形,就应该潜心修炼,何必要无事生非,自取灭亡呢?天下常有这样的人:尚未练成本事,就先向人炫耀;刚得到一点收获,却不懂得检点收敛。他们就象这扫帚精一样愚蠢啊!

34. 跳出轮回的鬼

道士王昆霞一次到嘉禾县游玩。时值初秋,天气爽朗。他散步于湖滨,走到一处荒废的花园,里面树木茂密,寂无人踪。他漫步其间,感到困倦,不知不觉地睡着了。梦中,一个穿戴着古代衣冠的人向他作揖道:"荒寂的丛林里很少得遇嘉宾,见到你真是太高兴了。请不要因为我是异类而躲避。"道士知道对方是鬼,就问他从哪里来。鬼说:"我姓张,是耒阳人,元朝末年流落到这里,死后被就地安葬。因为喜爱这儿的风土,不想回归故乡。花园先后换了十几位主人,我却一直留在这里。"

　　道士问:"一般人都贪生怕死,为什么你却宁愿长期作鬼?"鬼答道:"死生虽然状态不同,但人的心灵却没有改变,这个世界也没有改变。山川风月人看得见,鬼也看得见。登高赋诗,人可以做,鬼也可以做。鬼为什么就不如人呢?此外,有些幽深险阻的地方,人不能去,鬼却能去;有些清绝寂寥的景致,人没有机会见到,鬼却能在深夜尽情观赏。所以说,在某些方面人还不如鬼。再说,人之所以贪生怕死,无非是舍弃不了日常的嗜欲,眷恋妻子孩子;一旦

209

进入冥界,就好象高官解职归田一般,觉得寂寞难耐。但也有那么一些人,原本就住在山林之中,耕田挖井,恬然自得,并不为此感到悲戚。"

道士又问:"轮回是世间常理,你怎么能够不受约束呢?"鬼说:"鬼求生,就象人求官一样,都是出于自己的意愿。鬼不求生,就象人避官不就一样,也是行得通的,神并不会加以勉强。"道士说:"你既然喜欢游历山水,想必作了不少诗吧。"鬼答道:"兴之所至,有时吟上一两句,大多联不成完整的诗篇。而且境过即忘,也不去追想。现在能够记起,可以拿来向你请教的,不过三五篇罢了。"说着,鬼曼声吟道:"残照下空山,暝色苍然合。"道士不由发出赞叹。此时突然一阵吆喝声,把他惊醒,原来是湖中渔人相互打招呼。道士重新闭上眼睛,倚靠着树静坐,却无法返回原先的梦境了。

35. 奇门遁甲

关于奇门遁甲的书有不少,但都不是真传。真传不过是几句口诀,并不能在书里找到。德州的宋清远先生曾经去拜访一位朋友,当晚在那里借宿。朋友对他说:"在这个美妙的月明之夜,请你看一出戏怎么样?"他取来十几个凳子,交错着摆放在院子里,然后和宋清远在堂上点着蜡烛喝酒。二更后,只见一个人翻墙进来,在台阶前面兜圈子,每遇一个凳子都停下来,费很大力气才跨过去。他就这样在凳子堆中来回穿行,最后疲惫不堪,倒在地下。这时天已经快亮了。

朋友把那人带到堂上,问他从何而来。那人叩头说:"我是个贼,跳进院子之后,发现到处都是矮墙,跨过一堵又是一堵,无穷无尽。我想退回去,又遇见一堵一堵的矮墙,越走越看不到头。最后我累得不行了,只有束手就擒,听任处置。"朋友笑了笑把他打发走了,然后对宋清远说:"昨天占卦,知道小偷要来,所以用这小法术捉弄他一下。"宋清远问:"这是什么法术?"朋友答道:"是奇门之法。一般人学了恐怕会招来祸患。你为人正直谨慎,假如想学我一定教给你。"宋清远谢绝了。朋友长叹一声说:"愿意学的不能教,能教的又不愿意学,难道这门法术最终要失传吗?"

36. 姜三莽捉鬼

景城有个叫姜三莽的人,楞头楞脑,胆子很大。他听人讲了从前南阳人宋定伯卖鬼的故事,兴奋不已地说:"我如今才知道捉鬼也可以卖钱!如果每天晚上捉一个鬼,让它变成一只羊,第二天早上牵到屠宰场卖掉,一天的酒肉钱就到手了!"于是他每天夜里都扛着棍子,带着绳子,悄悄行走在坟地里,就象准备打兔子的猎人一样,但从来没有遇见鬼。即使在据说多鬼的地方,他假装醉酒,到那里一躺,想诱鬼上钩,还是什么动静都没有。一天晚上,他隔着树林看见数点鬼火,高兴得马上冲了过去。可是还没等他赶到,那些鬼火就四散逃走了。他只好恨恨地空手回家。就这样过了一个多月,姜三莽一无所获,只得放弃。想来鬼欺侮人是利用了人的畏惧心理。姜三莽确信自己可以捉鬼,心里对鬼自然十分藐视,其气势就足以战胜鬼怪,所以鬼反而躲避他。

37. 求仙遇妖

申铁蟾是阳曲县人,乾隆二十五年中举,被任命为知县。乾隆五十五年秋,他在陕西任职试用,忽然寄给我一封诀别信,词语迷离恍惚,抑郁忧伤,看不明白具体要说什么。他并非郁郁不得志的人,所以我想不出其中缘故。过了不久,传来他的死讯。后来我才听说,申铁蟾在西安时曾病了几个月。病愈之后他到山里打猎,回来觉得眼前有两个圆东西象风轮一般旋转,即使闭上眼睛也能看见。就这样持续几天后,圆球忽然爆裂,两个婢女从中跳出,声称仙女请他去。申铁蟾不由自主地跟着她们,来到一处琼楼贝阙,那里有位绝色佳人对他以身相许。他借口住不惯那样的房子,坚决地谢绝了。女子面露怒色,挥手让他离开,他猛地醒了过来。过了一个多月,眼前又出现两个圆球,它们再次爆裂,从中跳出那两个婢女。他跟随她们,来到新建造的一处住宅,幽深恬静,十分可爱。先前那位女子再次向他求婚,他不能自持,与她定情欢好。从此他不断梦游到那里与她相会。时间一长,那女子白天也出现,并且不让申铁蟾与朋友来往。他渐渐病弱,后来吃了方士李某的红色药丸,呕吐而死。他给我写信时正在病中。

申铁蟾聪明绝顶,擅长诗歌书法,风流倜傥,广交朋友,名声远扬。中年他忽然羡慕神仙,于是遇见这件怪事,稀里糊涂地死掉了。妖怪因人而兴,幻象由心而造。象他这样才能出众,志向远大,却因追慕神仙而丧生,真是可惜之极。

38. 鬼为媒

有位姓孟的老妇人清明节去上坟,在回家的路上感到口渴,便到附近人家去要口水喝。她看见一位少女站在树下,体态优美,仪容端方。少女取水让老妇人喝,又请她坐下歇息,态度很热情。老妇人问起她父母兄弟的情况,少女的应答十分有条理。老妇人开玩笑地说:"你订亲了吗?要是还没有婆家,让我给你作媒吧。"少女羞红了脸,跑回屋里,怎么叫她也不肯出来。当时天色已晚,老妇人没有告别就离开了。

半年后,有人来给老妇人的儿子提亲,一问之下,知道就是上次遇见过的少女。老妇人大喜过望,极力促成这门亲事。等少女嫁来之后,老妇人抚着她的肩膀说:"几个月不见,你又长高了一些。"少女愕然,不知该怎么回答。细问之下,才知道少女十岁丧母,随后六年托养在外祖父家,订亲之后家里才把她接回来。当老妇人清明节上坟时,少女还没有回到自己家中呢。少女来自小户人家,生活清苦,要不是老妇人亲身了解到她的聪明贤惠,不见得会结成这门亲事。不知道哪里来的鬼魅,假扮成少女来促成这件婚事,也不知道它为什么要成人之美。天下事有些不能以常理推断,这就是其中一例。

39. 破镜重圆

雍正四、五年间,有一家人流浪乞讨经过崔庄,夫妇都染上重病。临死前,他们在市场上举着一纸文书向行人哀告,说愿意将幼女卖为婢女,用这笔钱买两个棺材。我的祖母出钱安葬了那对夫妇,收留了他们的女儿,起名叫连贵。从文书上得知她父亲叫张立,母亲姓黄,但没有写明籍贯。等询问的时候,他们已经说不出话来了。连贵只知家在山东,住处邻近官道,常有贵官的车马往来;从家到这儿,他们走了一个多月。至于家乡属于什么县的辖界,她却说不出。连贵还提到前一年曾与对门的胡家订亲。后来胡家外出乞讨,不知去了什么地方。

过了十多年,一直没有亲戚从连贵的家乡来访,就让她嫁给了马倌刘登。听刘登说,他原本姓胡,家乡是山东新泰县。后来父母双亡,他被刘家收养,改从刘姓。小时候听说父母为他订了亲,但他不清楚对方的姓名。刘登本来姓胡,新泰又是官道所经之地,而且从那里沿路乞讨而来,估算起来正好有一个多月的路程。由于这些情况与连贵所说都相符合,大家猜想这是个破镜重圆的故事,只可惜没有明确的证据。有人评论说:"这件事稍加渲染,完全可以编成一部传奇。可惜女主角蠢得象头猪,只知道吃饱了睡,想要渲染却无从下笔。"另外一人反驳道:"即使史书上的记载,也有夸大不实之处,何况传奇故事?《西楼记》把穆素晖写得貌若天仙,可我有一个朋友的祖父幼年时曾见过她,身材丰满但矮小,不过是位寻常女子。由此看来,传奇中的所谓绝色佳人,多半出于虚构。这个婢女虽然粗笨,但若有好事者为她写诗作曲,何愁舞台上的她不能变得千娇百媚呢?按你那么说,未免太迷信书了。"

40. 骄者必败

记得我七八岁的时候,家里的仆人赵平自负胆大。老仆人施祥对他摆手道:"你不要光凭自己胆子大,就任意妄为,我曾经为此吃过亏。从前我年轻气盛,听说某家有间凶宅没人敢住,就独自去那儿过夜。夜将过半时,只听一声脆响,顶棚从中间断裂,掉下一条手臂,在地上跳来跳去。过一会儿,又掉下一条手臂,接着又掉下两条腿,然后是身子,最后人头才下来。这些东西满屋乱蹦乱跳,象猿猴一样敏捷。我惊愕之下,不知所措。没多久,这些东西聚拢起来,合成了一个人。他浑身都是刀砍棒打的伤痕,鲜血淋漓,伸手就来掐我的脖子。幸好当时是夏天,窗子开着,我急忙从窗口跳出,狂奔着逃走了。我因为那件事受了惊吓,至今仍然不敢一个人睡觉。你要是总这样自负胆大,难免有一天象我那样遇见对头。"赵平听了,不以为然地说:"本来就是你自己失策嘛。当时你为什么不抓住其中的一截,让它们不能合并成一人?"后来,有天夜里,赵平喝醉了酒回家,被一群鬼挡住去路,扔进粪坑中,差点儿淹死。

41. 船怪

这是发生在我外祖父家的事。家里人晚上常见到一个东西在楼前手舞足蹈,有人靠近就赶紧逃走。借着月光,从屋里透过窗缝向外看,发现它穿着绿色衣衫,形状蠢笨得象只巨鳖,只有手足,不见脑袋,不知是什么怪物。一天晚上,家里派了几个健壮的仆人,拿着刀杖绳索隐伏在门口。怪物刚一露面,他们就冲上去捕捉。那怪物踉踉跄跄地逃到楼梯下,停在那儿不动了。点起灯来一看,原来靠墙放着一个绿锦缎包裹着的银船,左右共有四个轮子。这原来是家道兴盛时孩子们的玩具。众人这才知道怪物穿的绿衣衫就是这块绿锦缎,它的四肢就是这四只轮子。于是把船熔化了,得到三十多两银子。一位老仆妇说:"我年青的时候,这件东西有一天突然不见了,同辈的仆人都受到了责打。不知被谁偷走放到这儿,天长日久就变成了妖怪。"

42. 堕胎是非

有个医生处事十分谨慎。一天晚上,有个老妇人拿着一对金手镯来买堕胎药。医生吓了一跳,严辞拒绝了。第二天晚上,老妇人又添了两枝珠花来买药。医生更为惊骇,声色俱厉地把她赶走了。过了半年多,医生忽然在梦中被冥吏拘拿,说有人控告他杀害人命。到了冥司,见到一个女子披头散发,脖子上勒着红头巾,哭诉医生拒绝卖堕胎药,致使她命归黄泉的情形。医生争辩说:"药是用来救人的,我怎么敢用来杀人谋利呢!何况你因为通奸而死,跟我有什么关系!"女子说:"我派人向你买药时,胎儿尚未成形,如果堕了胎,不过是去掉了一个无知无觉的血块,但却救了我的性命。后来买不到药,只好把孩子生下。结果儿子被掐死,白白受了罪,我也被逼上吊。你原想救一条命,却害死了两条命。你要是没罪,谁又有罪呢?"

冥官听了,叹息着对女子说:"据你所说,是强调当时的具体情况,而医生所持的乃是正理。自宋朝以来,执着于正理而不考虑具体情况的,又何止他一个人呢?我看这件事还是算了吧。"冥官说着,在桌上猛地一拍,医生一下子从梦中惊醒了。

43. 濒死经历

翰林院的笔帖式伊实随军出征伊犁时,血战突围,身中七矛而死。过了两天两夜,他苏醒过来,疾驰一昼夜,终于赶上了大军。我和博晰斋同在翰林院任职时,见到伊实身上的伤痕,问起原委,这才了解到他的奇特经历。他身受重伤时并不觉得疼,只好象沉入梦乡。

过了一阵,他开始有知觉,发现自己的灵魂已经离开了身体。四周望去,到处是风沙弥漫,不辨方向。他突然想到家中贫困,儿子年幼,不由悲从中来,刹那间感到自己就象一片落叶,飘飘荡荡,似乎就要被风吹跑了。而后他又觉得就这样死掉很不甘心,发誓要变为厉鬼,继续杀敌。这个念头一动,他马上感到自己象铁柱一般坚实,风根本吹不动他分毫。他徘徊一阵,正想冲上山巅去了望敌军的去向,猛然间象从梦中醒来,自己又回到了受伤的躯体,躺在血泊之中。博晰斋听罢叹息道:"听你这么一说,我觉得战死沙场真没什么可怕。要当忠臣烈士,其实很容易,为何大家不都那么做呢!"

44. 老儒的积蓄

山西有个老儒路过一处古墓,听同行者说那里住着狐狸,张口就痛骂了几句。当时并没有发生不寻常的事情。老儒善于积蓄,冬天不穿皮,夏天不穿麻,平时不吃肉,不喝茶,妻子孩子常饿肚子。他就这样日积月累,省下来四十两银子,熔化成四锭,偷偷收藏起来,对别人总说自己穷得快断粮了。自从骂过狐狸之后,那四锭银子有时突然出现在房顶或者树梢上,需要爬梯子才能取回。有时突然出现在淤泥当中,需要蹚着泥水过去捡起来。有时突然被扔进茅坑,需要捞出来清洗一番。有时突然被挪了地方,需要搜寻半天才能找到。有时几天不见踪影,又突然从空中落下。有一次,老儒正坐着与客人交谈,银子突然出现在他的帽檐上。又有一次,老儒正躬身对人作揖,银子突然从他衣袖中掉了出来。如此千变万化,让人不可思议。有一天,四锭银子突然跳到空中,象蝴蝶一样飞翔,越来越高,眼看就要飞走了。老儒被逼无奈,焚香下拜,向狐狸求情,银子这才落回他的怀中。从此那四锭银子再也没有消失过,老儒则再也不敢义正辞严地对人讲大道理了。有人评论道:"据我听说,战胜妖魅要靠道德修养,不能靠辱骂。那老儒受捉弄是他自找的。"另有一人说:"假如真正的儒学大师咒骂狐狸,它肯定不敢兴妖作怪。可惜那老儒道貌岸然,修养却远远不够。"又有一人说:"真正的儒学大师不会轻易出口咒骂。那老儒正因为内心修养不够,所以才表现得气势汹汹。"这话真是说到了点子上。

45. 老妪劫女案

人到了危急关头,有时能想出奇谋;有些事情看似不合情理,背后却一定另有缘故。处理这类事情需要随机应变,不能墨守成规。我的家乡有一位老妪,无故带领几十个妇人闯入邻村一户人家,把那家的女儿抢走了。要说是寻衅闹事,两家却素无往来;要说是抢婚,老妪却没有儿子。周围人都惊讶不已,想不出是怎么回事。女家去报了官,可是等官府派人捉拿时,老妪已带着抢来的姑娘逃走,不知去向,连帮她抢人的妇人们也四散逃亡。

为了这件官司,有许多人被拘去盘问,终于有人说出了其中的底细。老妪原来有个儿子。他生病将死时,老妪伤心欲绝,抚着他哭泣道:"你要死了,也许是命中注定,只可惜没给我留下个孙子,让你父亲九泉之下无人祭典,成为饿鬼。"儿子呻吟着说:"孙子不一定有,但仍有希望。我和邻村一位姑娘私下相好,她如今已有八个月的身孕了。我只担心孩子生下来会被她家里人杀掉。"儿子死后,老妇人一连十多天总是自言自语,然后突然率人劫走了姑娘。推想起来,她是要借此保住那胎儿。

听了这个情况,县官说:"既然如此,用不着发通辑了,过两三个月她自己会回来。"到时候,老妪果然抱着孙子回乡,向官府自首了。县官判定她的行为算不上重罪,只应受杖责,而且可以交钱免刑。这件事来得十分突然,老妪的行动可谓迅雷不及掩耳。她劫走姑娘时,用另外三辆车载着其它那些妇人,大家分四路逃亡,使人无法判断她的去向。她不走大道,只拣偏僻的小路走,使人无从探寻她的踪迹。她清晨起身赶路,晚上住宿,从不在同一地方停留一天以上,一直到姑娘分娩才租房暂住,因而无法查知她的停留之所。由此可见她思虑多么周密。姑娘回乡后,被她的父母厌弃,于是就跟着老妪过,抚养儿子长大,一辈子再也没有嫁人。因为她和老妪的儿子属于偷情,并非明媒正娶,所以她并没有因为守节得到官府的表彰。

46. 恶少装鬼

有位农家少妇和她的小姑长得都很漂亮。她们俩有次月夜乘凉,睡在屋檐下。突然有个红发青面鬼从牛栏后跳出来,手舞足蹈,作出要吃人的样子。当时家里的男人们全都在外看守田地和园子,两位女子吓得不敢出声,那鬼就上来把她们轮番强奸了。鬼纵身跃上院子的矮墙,刚要离开,突然哇地一声惊叫,仰面跌回院子里。姑嫂俩见鬼倒在地上好久不动,这才敢大声呼救。等邻居们赶来察看,发现墙内的鬼原来是当地的一个恶少装扮的,已经昏迷不醒了。墙外也站着一个鬼,却是土地庙里的泥偶。人们都议论说土地神显灵,准备天亮去祭祀一番。

这时,人群中有位少年笑道:"张三每天一大早挑粪从此路过,是我把土地庙里的小鬼搬来搁在路边,想要吓他一大跳,给大家逗个乐。没想到让这个装鬼的坏小子撞上,以为遇见真鬼,吓得摔下去起不来了。怎么能说是土地神显灵呢?"有个老翁反驳说:"张三每天都挑粪路过此地,你为什么别的时候想不到戏弄他,偏巧今天想到呢?要戏弄他,办法多的是,你为什么偏巧把这泥偶抱来呢?泥偶可以放在沿路任何地方,你为什么偏巧放在这家人院外呢?其中必定有神明的指点,尽管你自己并不知道。"大家都觉得老翁的话有道理,就凑了钱去土地庙上供。那个恶少被他父母抬回家,昏睡了几天,竟然再也没有苏醒。

47. 滴血验亲

有个山西商人把家产托付给弟弟,自己出门做生意,在外娶妻,生了个儿子。十几年后,妻子病故,他带着儿子回到故乡。弟弟怕他讨还家产,就诬称他的儿子并非亲生,而是抱养的,不能继承父业。兄弟间由此引发一场纠纷,一直闹到官府。不料碰上个糊涂县官,不去询问调查实情,却使用古代的滴血法来验证父子关系。幸亏父子俩血滴相合。商人的弟弟挨了一顿板子,被赶出衙门。

商人的弟弟不相信滴血法,就用自己和儿子的血来试验,果然不相合。他以此为理由,说县令的判决不公正。村民们都厌恶他贪婪而没有人性,就联名向官府作证,说他的妻子与别人私通,那孩子并不是他亲生,自然血滴不合。众口一辞,证据确凿。把奸夫拘来审问,他俯首招供。商人的弟弟颜面扫地,竟然休掉妻子,赶走了儿子,离家出走,财产反而全都归了哥哥。听说这件事的人无不拍手称快。

滴血检验血缘关系,这种方法自汉朝就有了。不过我曾听一位老吏说:"骨肉至亲的血滴相合,那只是就一般情况而言。如果冬天把验血的器皿放在冰雪上冻得极冷,或者夏天用盐和醋擦试器皿,这时滴血进去马上就凝结,就是骨肉至亲的血也不会聚合。所以滴血法不足以定案。"然而,假若县令不用滴血法,商人的弟弟就不会上诉,他妻子的奸情就不会被揭露。这背后或许有神秘力量的指引,不能完全怪罪县令拘泥古法。

48. 申先生遇狐

景州人申谦居先生和我父亲同在康熙五十二年中举。他为人平和,从不动怒,而且性情孤高,是个耿直君子。平时他穿的是粗麻袍子,吃的是粗茶淡饭。偶然有门生送肉给他,他就拿到市场上换豆腐吃,说:"我并不想标榜自己与众不同,实在是吃不惯这个。"他从前到河间参加岁试,回来骑着驴子,由一个童子牵着。他见童子走累了,就让他骑上驴,自己牵着。傍晚遇雨,他们在一座破庙投宿。庙只有一间屋,里面空空荡荡,地下脏得无法落脚。于是他摘下一扇门板,横躺在庙门前面。半夜醒来,听见庙中有人小声说:"我想出庙回避您,被您挡着门,出不去。"他说:"你在屋内,我在门外,互不相扰,何必回避?"过了一会儿,庙里又小声说:"男女有别,您还是放我出去为好。"他说:"一个在里一个在外,正好显出男女有别,让你出来反而不便。"说完,他翻了个身,接着酣睡。第二天早上，有个村民见到他，吃惊地说："这庙里住着狐狸，曾出来勾引少年，一进去就挨了一通砖头瓦片。您怎么能平安在此过夜呢？"后来，申先生与我父亲谈起这次经历，仰面笑道："居然有狐狸想引诱申谦居，真是莫大怪事！"我父亲开玩笑地说："狐狸就是把天下人引诱遍了，也轮不到你。你这副奇形怪状的尊容，狐狸一见之下，不知是什么怪物，早吓得落荒而逃了。"由这件事也可以想见申先生的为人。

49. 喝酒趁年华

孙端人先生文笔含蓄典雅，特别爱喝酒，醉了依然能写文章，与平时并无两样。大家觉得他象唐代大诗人李白一样，纵情豪饮就才思泉涌。他在云南任督学时，曾于月夜独自坐在竹林旁饮酒，恍惚看到一人注视着酒壶酒杯，似乎露出渴望的神情。孙端人知道那是个鬼，心里倒也不怕，只是用手遮住酒杯说："今天酒不多了，不能请你喝。"那鬼缩回身子，消失掉了。孙端人酒醒后，不由后悔起来，说道："能来找酒喝，必定不是俗鬼。能向我借酒喝，说明他很看得起我。可惜我竟让他失望而去了！"于是他买了三大碗好酒，晚上用一张小桌子摆在竹林间。第二天去一看，酒并没有动过。他叹了口气说："看来这鬼不但风雅，而且高傲。稍微慢待他一回，干脆一滴酒都不肯尝了。"有个幕客对他说："鬼和神都只能闻闻酒气罢了，岂能真的喝下去呢！"孙端人感慨道："既然如此，就趁活的时候赶紧多喝酒，不要等到成了鬼，只有闻酒气的份儿。"

50. 狐女事二夫

一个猎人在少华山脚下，见到两个男子无精打采地躺在一棵树下面。他上前打招呼，那两人勉强能够起身。猎人就问："你们怎么会流落到这里？"其中一人说："我们两个都是受了狐女的诱惑。我有天晚上迷了路，到山里一户人家借宿。那家有位少女长得十分俊俏，伺机向我调情。我不能自持，就与她偷情。不料被她父母发觉，严厉地责骂我。我跪下来求饶，才免于拷打。随即听见她父母絮絮叨叨地谈论，好象在商量什么事情。到了第二天，他们竟说愿意认我作女婿，只是提出一条约定，说女儿需要给山上的一家人打工，每次去五天，然后回家住五天。我觉得这么安排并无不妥，就欣然接受。半年后，我开始感到体力不支。有天夜里，我因为咳嗽睡不着，走到林子里散步，忽然听见有男女调笑的声音，就走过去看个究竟。我见到一处房屋，门前有个人把我妻子抱在怀里，坐在石头上赏月。我怒不可遏，冲上去和他动手。那人也怒气冲冲地对我大嚷：'你是哪里来的鼠辈，竟敢打我夫人的主意！'说着，他也向我冲来。幸亏他也病病歪歪的，我们两个互相拉扯着，一起摔倒在地。那女子一直安坐在石头嬉笑，这时开口道：'你们两个别打了，我跟你们把事情挑明吧。其实我一直轮流和你们住，都以打工为借口，让你们各自有五天的休息时间，以便养精蓄锐，供我采补。如今事情已经败露，你们也已经精疲力尽，对我不再有用。咱们就此分手吧。'说完，她忽然不见了。我们两人想寻路出去，却迷失了方向，又饿又累，倒在此处，幸亏遇见你救了我们。"另外一个人所说也大致相同。

　　猎人听完他们的讲述，把随身所带干粮拿出来给他们吃。他们稍稍恢复了体力，带猎人去狐女的住处察看。到了那儿，两人都惊诧不已地说："原先这里墙是土的，梁柱是木头的，门窗都可以开关，都是实实在在的东西，而不是幻影。怎么如今变成一个土洞了？原先院子里地面平整洁净，怎么如今土洞以外的地面变得崎岖不平了？况且这土洞如此狭小，只能装下狐狸自己，怎么能装下我们两个人呢？难道我们当时也化成了幻影不成？"其中一人见到对面山崖上散落的碎瓷片，就说："那是我爬楼梯时失手摔碎的。如今那里只有峭壁，无路可走，当时我是怎么上上下下的？"两人四顾徘徊，感觉象在梦中。他们越想越痛恨狐女，请求猎人入山捕杀。猎人说："邂逅相遇，就配成佳偶，天下本来没有这样的便宜事。事情太便宜了，其中必有不便宜的地方。正象鱼因为贪食诱饵而上钩,你们应该自己反省一下才对,何必对狐狸怀恨呢?"两人听了无言以对,只得作罢。

51. 鬼的智谋

有个人不怕鬼,听说哪间屋子闹鬼,就要搬进去住。有人告诉他,西山某座寺庙后面的阁楼里常有鬼怪出现。他当年正好要参加乡试,就租下那处房子读书。每天夜里,果然有许多奇形怪状的黑影围绕在床前,他都处之泰然。一天晚上,月光明朗,他推窗四望,见一位美女站立在树下,就笑道:"你不能把我吓跑,就想来引诱我吗?你是什么妖怪,不妨近前说话。"那女子也笑道:"你自然不认识我,我是你的姑奶奶啊,死后就葬在这山里。我听说你每天在这里和众鬼争斗。你读书十多年,是想赢得一个不怕鬼的名声呢,还是想发奋走上仕途,光宗耀祖呢?如今你夜里和鬼较量,白天睡大觉;考试的日期越来越近,你的学业却被荒废。这难道是你父母让你带着钱粮进山的本意吗?我虽然在九泉之下,亲情却不能不顾,所以来劝告你。你好好想想吧。"说完,那女鬼就消失了。他觉得鬼的话颇为有理,就打点行装,离寺回家。等回来向父母打听,才知道自己并没有这么一位姑奶奶。他非常悔恨,跺着脚说:"我让那狡猾的鬼给要了!"忿忿然地又要回寺庙。有位朋友劝他说:"鬼不敢和你斗力,却变了形来好言相劝,说明它已经怕你了。你何必去追打已经认输的敌人呢?"他听从了朋友的意见。这位朋友确实善于解决纠纷,然而那鬼的话却是正理。正理不能说服此人,朋友的权变之言却说服了,由此可以悟出销熔强悍之气的方法。

52. 打虎老翁

我的远房哥哥纪中涵任旌德县知县时,城区附近有猛虎接连伤了好几个猎人。百姓请求说:"必须到徽州聘请唐家人,否则除不了虎患。"原来,明朝的时候唐家有个人新婚不久就被虎咬死了。他妻子后来生下一个儿子,祷告说:"你要是不能杀虎,就不是我的儿子。后世子孙要是不能杀虎,就不是我的后世子孙。"从此唐家世世代代都是捕虎能手。纪中涵答应了百姓的请求,派人带着礼物去请唐家人。使者回来报告说,唐家答应选派技艺最精的两人,随后就到。等唐家人来了,却是一个白发老翁,时不时咳嗽,还有一个十六七岁的少年。纪中涵很失望,勉强下令准备酒食招待他们。那老翁看出知县的不满,就行礼说:"听说那只虎出没之地离城不过五里,我们先去捕杀它,然后再吃饭不迟。"于是县里派了一名衙役给两人带路。到了山谷口,那衙役不敢再往里走。老翁笑道:"有我在,你有什么可怕的?"进入山谷将近一半,老翁回身对少年说:"那畜牲好象在睡觉,你把它叫醒吧。"于是少年发出虎啸声。那猛虎果然闻声从林中跑出,直奔老翁而来。老翁手里拿着一把锋利的短柄斧头,把手臂高高举起。虎往上一扑,老翁侧身让开,虎从他头顶一跃而过,随即跌落地下,流血不止。仔细一看,那虎从颔下到尾巴,全被斧头劈裂。纪中涵厚赏了唐家人。据老翁说,他花了十年时间炼臂力,又花了十年时间炼目力。他的眼睛用扫帚去扫也不会眨,他的手臂伸出,让壮汉全身压上去都不能撼动。

53. 少年半日变老翁

京城从黄村到丰宜门有四十里,要是下起雨来,这一带的路就泥泞难走。有个叫李秀的人,驾着空车从固安县回城,见到一个十五六岁的少年,面貌娟丽得象少女,艰难地走在泥泞的路上。当时太阳快要西下。少年见到李秀驾车经过,露出想搭车的神情,却又羞怯地不敢开口。李秀生性轻薄,起了挑逗之心,就邀少年上车。少年扭捏着上了车。沿路买零食给少年吃,他也不太拒绝。李秀柔声细语和他谈话,时而调笑一句,那少年只是脸红微笑,并不回答。往前走了几里,李秀发觉少年的面容好象变老了一些,起初还不太在意。又走了十几里,暮色昏黄,少年的面容好象又变了一些。等接近南苑的西门,那人已经变成宽脑门、高颧骨、满脸胡子的壮年人。最后到达客店时,那人已是须发皆白的老翁了。他和李秀握手告别说:"承蒙爱慕,不胜感激。可惜年老貌衰,今晚不能与您同榻,辜负您的期望了。"老翁说完,笑了笑就走掉了,最终也不知他是什么怪物。李秀的表弟在我们家厨房干活,曾听李秀讲起这桩事情。李秀为此自悔少年轻狂,以致受到狐鬼的戏弄。

54. 子债父还

有个少年,父亲长年在外经商。他没有了管束,被庄家骗去赌博,输了数百两银子。庄家提出由他出钱代付赌债,却逼少年写了卖房的字据,少年无可奈何地照办了。他觉得无脸去见妻子和母亲,晚上没有回家,却跑到林子里去上吊。他刚把绳子扣系好,就听见隆隆马蹄声,回头一看,原来是自己的父亲。父亲吃惊地问:"你怎么会落到这步田地?"少年知道无法隐瞒,就如实相告。父亲并不生气,对他说:"这不过是小事一桩,哪里至于如此呢!我这次出门赚的钱大致可以抵偿你的赌债。你先回家,我到庄家付钱,把卖房字据要回来就是了。"当时庄家聚众赌博还没收摊,少年的父亲破门而入。那些人原本都是他的相识,就逐一点出他们的名字,先是责备他们把少年引入歧途,而后又责备他们催逼赌债。众人惊愕之下,无言以对。少年的父亲又对庄家说:"既然我那不肖的儿子写了卖房字据,我也难以去控告你们。现在我把赌债还给你,你明天分给大家,现在就把字据还我如何?"庄家自知理亏,同意照办。少年的父亲解开腰袋,把钱如数取出,付给庄家。他拿到卖房字据,当时就在灯上烧掉,然后怂然出门而去。

少年回到家中,准备了饭菜,直等到第二天清晨,父亲还是没有回来。找庄家去问,说他把字据烧掉后就走了。少年知道其中必有缘故。等天亮庄家开箱,发现头天晚上收的银子居然全是纸做的。然而当时在众目睽睽之下收了钱,实在解释不清,只得自掏腰包替少年还了赌债。他疑心自己遇见了鬼。果然,十多天后消息传来,少年的父亲在几个月前就客死他乡了。

55. 狐女还债

朱某家有一个婢女,原本生得很粗笨。长大后,她渐渐变得聪慧,眉目也清秀起来,朱某便娶她为妾。她颇有心计,家里事无巨细,都了然于心,仆人们偶然作弊则必定败露,于是再也不敢耍滑头。她还善于经营,凡是她主张购入的货品,来年必然价高。朱某因此慢慢富裕起来,对她更为宠爱。

忽然有一天爱妾对朱某说:"你知道我是谁?"朱某笑道:"你疯了吗?"说着就叫她的小名。她却答道:"你错了,我并不是那个婢女。她早就逃走了,如今嫁了人,儿子也有七八岁了。我原本是狐女。九世前你是个富商,我为你管帐。你待我很好,我却贪污了你三千多两银子。在冥司我受到责罚,轮回成为狐狸。我修炼了几百年,终于成功,但因为欠你的夙债,不能成仙。所以我借着婢女逃跑的机会,变化成她的模样来服侍你。这十多年来,我为你赚到的钱足以抵偿我所欠数目。如今我要舍弃肉身,离你而去了。我离开之后,躯体必然现出狐狸的原形。你可以让某某仆人去埋我,而他肯定会把我剥皮裂尸,但你不要为此责备他。他四世前饿死在路边,当时我修炼未成,把他的尸体吃掉了。现在把我的遗蜕让他处置,正好抵销这段冤仇。"说完,她倒在地上,变成一个狐狸,同时有一位身长数寸的美丽女子从狐狸头上冒出来,慢慢地飞走了。这个女子的相貌和朱某的爱妾并不相同。朱某不忍心照她的话做,自己把狐狸的尸首掩埋了。不料那个仆人去偷偷挖了出来,把狐狸皮剥下卖掉了。朱某意识到这是前世欠下的债,不得不偿还,只能长叹而已。

56. 狐狸救老儒

霸州有位老儒,是个正人君子,颇孚众望。突然有一天,他家里开始有狐狸作祟。当老儒在家的时候,就平安无事;一旦他出门,那狐狸就摇撼门窗、砸毁器物、投掷破烂,无所不至。这样一来,老儒就不敢外出了,整天在家读书养性。恰在此时,霸州一群书生为了治河工程的事联名投诉州官,在学宫里聚会,准备推举老儒当他们的首领。老儒因为家中狐狸作怪,不能参加聚会,他们就另推了一位王某。后来,王某以聚众抗官的罪名被处死,老儒则幸免于难。此案一发,老儒家就不再闹狐狸了,这才知道它是有意拖住老儒,不让他牵连进去。所以说,小人不会遇见吉事,若有吉事,必定是上天让他加重自己的罪恶。君子不会遇见妖怪,若有妖怪,必定是上天帮助他逃避灾难。

57. 神奇卦术

康熙末年有位李鹭汀,以买卖古玩为生。他擅长占卦,每天早上起床便为自己占一卦,却从不肯为别人算命,曾解释说:"经常泄露未来的事情,会引起神的厌恶。"有人把他比作宋朝的易学大师邵康节,他谦虚说:"我只学到了他的六七分本领罢了。我曾经占得某日将有仙人持竹杖来,饮酒题诗而去。届时我就焚香等候。结果有个人拿着一幅竹雕的仙人吕洞宾像求售,旁边有个装酒的葫芦,上面刻着一首诗。邵康节占卦会错成这样吗?"

李鹭汀五十多岁了,没有孩子,只有一个小妾。这天,一位老朋友来看他,听见他的妾边哭边埋怨:"怎么说这样的话来戏弄人,难道是想试探我吗?"李鹭汀分辩说:"我不是跟你开玩笑,占卦的结果确实如此。"朋友就问是怎么回事。李鹭汀说:"这件事真是奇怪。今天早起占卦,算出将有两位客人来买古玩,其中一位上辈子是她的丈夫,今生和她还有一夕的缘份,另一位是她未来的丈夫,将在半年之内结合。我把占卦的结果讲给她听,她却恼怒起来。

人的命运是天注定的,无法更改。我不因此哭泣,她倒哭了起来;我不因此忌讳,她倒忌讳起来,真是个痴女子啊!"过了半年,李鹭汀果然去世了。他的小妾卖给一位翰林,因正妻不能相容,住了一夜就被赶走。后来又转卖给另一位官员作妾,这才相安无事。

58. 和尚遭暗算

汉朝的费长房能辖制各种鬼怪,后来丢了符策,被鬼杀害。唐朝的明崇俨被利刃刺入胸膛而死,据说是鬼下的手,因为他役使它们太苦了。仰仗法术的人最终因法术而遇难,这是常有的事。有个和尚善于念禁咒。有一回他被诱骗到旷野,成百上千的狐狸嗥叫着向他扑来。他挥动铁棍,击倒了一个幻化成人形的老狐狸,这才突围而出。后来,他在路上遇到那老狐狸。老狐狸趴在地上叩头说:"上次蒙你饶命,我已诚心悔过。如今我愿意皈依佛祖,受戒为僧。"和尚把手伸出,刚要为老狐狸摩顶受戒,他却突然扔出一件东西蒙在和尚脸上,随后隐形逃走了。那东西不是布也不是皮,颜色象琥珀,象油漆一样粘得十分牢固。和尚憋闷得无法忍受,让人用力把那东西揭掉,结果脸上的皮肤都被撕扯下来,痛得他晕了过去。等他脸上结痂脱落,已经没有个人样了。

还有一个游方和尚,在门上贴着"驱狐"的告示。曾有狐狸来诱骗他,被他认出原形,摇铃念起佛咒,狐狸慌忙逃窜。过了十来天,有个老妇来敲门,说她住在坟地边,天天受狐狸的侵扰,请和尚去禁治。和尚取出照妖镜一看,老妇的确是个人,就跟着她走了。老妇把他领到水堤边,忽然抢过他的书袋扔到河里,袋里的符策和法器都顺流而下,她则跑到高粱地里藏了起来。和尚正在懊丧,瓦片砖头猛地向他飞来,砸得他鼻青脸肿。他连忙念起佛咒,狐狸不敢靠近,这才狼狈逃回。第二天他就羞愧地悄悄离开了那里。后来才知道那老妇是当地人。狐狸和她女儿相好,塞给她一些钱,让她去偷走和尚的符策。上面两个和尚的法术都足以战胜狐狸,却

227

都吃了狐狸的亏,这是因为狐狸暗施诡计,和尚却无防备,狐狸有同党,和尚却孤立无援。而那些法术并不高明,却轻率地与妖怪较量的人,更不会有好结果了。

59. 算卦肇祸

献县留福庄有个木匠,去向算卦的问婚姻大事。算卦的捉弄他说:"离这儿西南百里,某地的某甲今天要死,他的妻子命中注定要嫁给你。你赶紧去那儿,事情就能办成。"木匠信以为真,就赶到那个地方,在客店里住下。他见到一位当地人,就打听说:"某甲住在哪儿?"那人反问道:"你找他有什么事?"木匠如实相告。碰巧那人正是某甲,听了之后气得要命,拔出佩刀就要砍。木匠逃回客店,然后翻墙跑掉了。某甲认为店主把木匠藏了起来,硬要进去搜,店主不让。结果两人动起手,某甲把店主杀了,自己也被逮捕,最后依法给店主偿了命。至于木匠的姓名住处,当时谁都没有想到去问,也无从追究。

一年多以后,有个老妪带着一男一女来到献县,据说是小叔和寡嫂。老妪突然得病死了,那男的就想让嫂子出嫁,用所得彩礼来料理母亲的后事。妇人无可奈何地答应下来。当时木匠正好未娶,于是在大家的撮合下,成就了一段姻缘。后来问起那妇人的前夫,原来正是某甲。这件事真是够奇怪的。假若占卦的人不开玩笑,木匠就不会去找某甲,某甲也不会和店主斗殴,店主也不会被杀,某甲也不会抵命,他妻子也不会最终嫁给木匠。这其中的前因后果,一环扣着一环,似乎真是命中注定。

还有一桩事与此类似。在京城西四牌楼,有个人每天在街上摆摊算命。这天他突然算出自己过两天要死于横祸。他实在想不出祸事会从何而来,但卦象显示的结果却十分明白。于是到了那一天,他闭门不出,想看看自己会怎么死。不料发生了地震,房子倒塌,把他砸死了。假如事先不占这一卦,他当天肯定要去街上摆摊,就不会死于地震了。这件事似乎也是命中注定,他的占卦本反而把他引向了死路。

60. 糊涂案

我父亲任刑部江苏司郎中时,西城呈上一个少年强奸幼女案。那少年十六岁,女孩只有十四岁。那日他游玩回家,见女孩正在园子里摘菜,就上前胁迫,试图奸污她。巡逻兵士听见女孩的呼救声赶来,当场把少年抓获。正在审讯之时,两家的父母却到衙门投了状子,说女孩是少年的未婚妻,他因为不认识她而冒犯。按照法律,男方对未婚妻不存在强奸罪。正在讨论如何处置,女孩突然也改了口供,说少年只是调戏了她。于是把少年申斥了一顿就放走了。有人说:"女方的父母受了大笔贿赂,女孩也喜欢少年的风度,所以编出瞎话来平息这场纠纷。"我父亲说:"是有这种可能。不过这件事只牵涉到婚姻,不象有些案子事关人命,若因贿赂而平息,就会使死者含冤地下。少年属强奸未遂,无从验明;说女家受贿,并无证据,也难以质问。女孩认可了,她父母也认可了,媒人、保人提出了证词,四邻也没有异议,双方的说法也没有矛盾的地方。遇见这种情况,君子只能自甘受蒙骗,总不能穷追不舍,把一个少年发配到远方去吧。"

61. 钟怪

据文水县李华廷说,离他家百里有一座废弃的寺庙,传说里面有怪物,没有人敢去住。一次,十多个羊贩子行路遇雨,在庙中住下。夜里听见呜呜的声音,随即在暗中见到一个怪物,蹒跚而来。它身材臃肿,面目模糊不清。那些羊贩子原本是些无赖少年,不但不害怕,还一起拾起破砖打过去。每次击中怪物,就听到金属撞击声。那怪物徘徊着想退走,羊贩子们觉出它没什么本事,就喊叫着在后面追打。赶到庙门口一堵坏墙旁边,那怪物停住不动了。近前一看,原来是一只破钟,里面有许多碎骨头,大概是它吞吃的食物。第二天,他们把这事告诉当地人,于是把破钟熔化,用以铸造其它器具。从此怪物就绝迹了。这个怪物本身蠢笨迟钝,却敢出来骚扰人,真是自取灭亡。大概它见到别的善于变化的怪物,能够与人作对,于是就想学学样子吧。我们家有个婢女,是沧州山果庄人。据她说,那个村子有不少人当了强盗。有个人没什么能耐,见别人当强盗发了财,就去投奔他们。后来,强盗们受到官兵的围捕,别人都奋力格斗,突围逃跑了,只有这个人被抓住处死。此人所作所为正和那个破钟类似。

62. 礼不可缺

有位候补官员在京城虎坊桥租了一处房宅。有人告诉他说:"这里面有狐狸,入住之时祭拜一下就不会有事。"他生性吝啬,不肯照办。搬进去之后,并没有发生怪异之事。随即他娶了一个妾。娶进家那天,她独坐在屋里,只听窗外有几十个人交头接耳地评论她的长相,羞得她不敢抬头。晚上吹灭烛火,两人上床就寝,却听见满屋都是吃吃的笑声。候补官每有所动作,都被高声描述。就这样一连几夜,他实在忍受不了,就去求道士驱狐。道士听了答道:"怪物害了人,才能奏请天神捉拿惩处。假如怪物只是嬉笑,并没有造成多大伤害,神明就没有必要管束;这就象人和人之间开玩笑,并未酿成事端,官府也不会禁止。你怎么能拿这样的琐事去亵渎神明呢!"候补官无可奈何,只好摆下酒肉祭拜狐狸,当天晚上屋里就安静下来了。他不由叹息道:"如今我才知道应酬的礼数不可缺啊!"

63. 自己戏弄自己

董秋原说,东昌府有位书生,夜里在郊外赶路,忽然见到一座宏大的宅院。他心想,这儿应是某家的墓地,怎么会有这座宅院,难道是狐狸变化出来的?他想起读过的那些书生邂逅狐女,配成佳偶的记载,就踯躅不前,希望能有奇遇。没多久,一队车马从西而来,众人服饰华丽。一位中年妇人揭开帘子,指着书生说:"这位少年不错,可以请他进来。"书生偷眼一看,车后面坐着一位美若天仙的妙龄少女,不禁大喜过望。车马进门之后,随即两位婢女出来邀请书生。既然认定对方是狐狸,书生也不问主人的姓氏,跟着进屋。主人并没有马上露面,但摆上了丰盛的酒席。书生心醉神迷,等待和狐女入洞房。到了晚上,锣鼓喧天,管箫齐奏,一位老翁掀帘进屋,向书生作揖道:"新郎已经到了。您是读书人,对婚礼的仪式一定熟悉。有您作为傧相,我们家真是面上有光啊。"书生听了大失所望。然而原本并没有人和他谈到婚姻之事,又已吃了对方的酒席,无法推托,只得草草主持了婚礼,扫兴而归。家里人因为书生彻夜不回,正在到处寻找他呢。书生忿忿地讲述了他的遭遇,听的人都拍掌大笑。有人说:"这不能算狐狸戏弄你,是你自己戏弄自己啊!"

听完这个故事,我也说了一件事。有个叫李二混的,穷得日子过不下去,动身到京城去谋生。他在路上遇见一位骑驴的少妇,就上前搭话,略微露出挑逗的意思。少妇既不搭理他,也没显得生气。第二天,他们又在路上相遇。少妇扔给李二混一个手绢包,回头对他说:"我今晚住在固安县。"他打开手绢包,里面有几件首饰。正好他路费用完了,就拿着首饰去了附近的当铺,没想到这些首饰恰好是当铺刚刚丢失的。李二混被捆起来拷打,只得承认自己是窃贼。我认为象李二混这样才是真正遭到了狐狸的戏弄。董秋原听了却道:"他不去调戏少妇,何至于落得如此下场?还是他自己戏弄了自己。"

64. 渎神的报应

苏州人朱生焕于乾隆二十七年考中顺天乡试第二名举人,是经我阅卷后录取的。有一天,我们几个人聚集在阅微草堂,酒席上讲起了奇闻异事。朱生焕说,他有次坐船,见一个舵工额头上总贴着膏药。他自称长了疮,需要避风。航行了几天,有个篙工悄悄对乘客们说:"那可是件怪事,说长疮是假的。他曾是船工行会的头儿,祭祀水神时应该由他捧着香火祷告。有天晚上他没守斋戒,干了不洁之事,结果就在他跪着祝祷时,突然一阵风把香灰吹到他脸上。他被吓坏了,差点儿没完成仪式。等下来拂去炉灰,他额头上出现一幅水墨秘戏图,画中人维妙维肖,正是他们夫妇俩。那画用水洗不掉,反而越洗越清楚,所以他用膏药来遮挡。"大家都不大相信,但既然听篙工那么说,出来进去时就难免往舵工额头上多看几眼。舵工察觉了,说:"那小子又在多嘴!"随后深深地叹气。看来确有其事,可惜不能揭开膏药瞧上一眼。

我也想起乳母李婆婆讲她从前登泰山时遇上的一件事。有个妓女和她的相好不约而同到庙里进香,在旅店相遇,就找机会亲了个嘴,不料他们的嘴唇竟粘在一起分不开了,稍一使劲就痛得不行。众人为他们在佛前忏悔,这才分开。当时就有人说:"这是守庙人贿赂妓女假装的,为的是让大家相信那座庙有多么灵验。"是否如此,不得而知。

65. 假冒的狐女

某个士人在广陵娶了一妾。她颇通文墨,两人情投意和,常在闺房吟诗作对。一天他在外饮酒,很晚才回家,仆人婢女都已睡下,屋里黑着灯。他进屋一看,爱妾不见了,桌子上留着一张纸,上面写道:"我本是狐女,住在山林深处。因为前世欠你的情,所以跟随你半年,作为今世的补偿。如今缘份已尽,不敢再停留。原想当面对你说明,又怕承受不了那凄惨的别离场面,所以我忍痛不辞而别。

临行前我柔肠寸断,难以抑制心中的酸楚。也许就因为这份思念,又种下了来世的缘份,那也未可知。只希望你多加珍重,不要因为我的离去而过于伤心,那样对我也是一种安慰啊。"

士人看到这封诀别书,心中悲感交集。朋友们看了此信,也都赞叹惋惜不已。因为这种事情古书中多有记载,并没有人产生怀疑。过了一个多月,那女子和她的相好坐船北上时财物被盗。他们去官府报了案,等待捉拿盗贼后,返还财物,不料一等就是好几个月,由此行踪暴露。原来,女子的母亲已把她转卖,她假冒狐女以便脱身。有人评论说:"这女子是真狐狸,何假之有?各类志怪书所记载的那些邂逅仙女,后来对方不辞而别的故事,其中大概不乏此类情况吧!"

66. 女鬼为夫谋职

有个候补官员晚上在酒肆喝完酒,趁着月色回家,一个童子提着灯笼走在前面。走到半道,灯笼突然灭了。他看到路旁一间屋子里还点着灯,就进去借火。有位少妇来开门,邀请他进去喝茶。他猜想少妇必是妓女,就打算借此消遣一下。可是进屋之后,发现少妇含羞低头,神色惨然。候补官起身告辞,少妇却拉着他的衣襟挽留。他近前去挑逗,少妇曲意顺从,两人携手上床,成就了一段露水姻缘。

候补官正好身边带着几两银子,就拿出来相赠。少妇不要,却对他说:"如果你顾念到今宵的情意,我有一事相求。有个人住在某处,妻子去世,子女尚幼,很长时间无人雇用,一家人饥寒交迫。你赴任时如果能雇他当随从,我会永远记住你的大恩大德。"候补官开玩笑地说:"你也跟着去吗?"少妇含泪答道:"我不是人,就是那人死去的妻子。因为他无力养活子女,我只好忍辱含羞,向你求助。"候补官听了,不由心惊胆战,连忙告辞。出门后回头一望,那屋子已变成一座新坟。后来,他得到任命时,想起那少妇的请求,终于雇了那人,带着他及其子女一起赴任。为了让丈夫得到官员

233

随从这个美差,女鬼不惜含羞自荐,随从所能得到的好处可想而知。随从的好处从何而来?还不是靠欺瞒官员、敲榨百姓。

67. 瓷片精

蒙阴县刘某曾有一阵在亲戚家借宿,偶然听说那儿有怪物不时出现,但没人知道它平时潜伏在何处。如果在黑暗中相遇,就会被它撞倒,好象撞在坚硬的石头上一样。刘某喜欢打猎,随身总带着鸟枪,就说:"既然如此,我就用这杆枪来自卫吧。"

家里有三间书斋,刘某住在东间。这天晚上他独自坐在灯下,见到西间里有一怪物,五官四肢都象人,但眼睛与眉毛距离很远,嘴巴与鼻子几乎贴到了一起。刘某刚举枪瞄准,怪物就缩身躲避。随即它手扶着一扇门,露出半边脸往外看,似乎要跑出来。刘某把枪一举,怪物又躲回去了,好象害怕出门后刘某从后面攻击它。刘某也怕怪物有什么厉害招数,不敢出门去追打。那怪物露了几次面,突然一下子把整个脸都伸出来,向刘某摇首吐舌。刘某急忙扣动扳机,铅弹打在门上,那怪物却乘机逃跑了。兵法说两军相持,先动者败,就是这个道理吧!假使刘某忍住不开枪,拖到天亮,怪物既然不能破窗而出,必然要走门,定会被枪打中。要是它不出门,则定会现出原形。但通过这件事,刘某知道那怪物怕枪。后来有天夜里,他潜伏在窗后,终于等到怪物出现,开枪命中。怪物中弹倒地,发出的声音就象瓦片掉到地上摔裂一样。近前一瞧,原来是破瓮一片,被小孩在瓮口无釉处画了张人脸,笔法幼稚,五官离位,正如刘某那晚所见。

68. 占小便宜吃大亏

我的先师陈文勤说,他有位同乡,平生并没有犯过大错,只是遇事总要把好处留给自己,把坏处推给他人。这一年他和几个朋友进京赶考,途中在旅店投宿。外面下起大雨,屋里漏得很厉害,只有靠北的墙壁有一处是干的。那人忽然说自己受了寒气,需要蒙上被子出汗来治病,就自行占据了那块地方。别人知道他是装病,但找不到理由把他赶开。雨越下越大,屋里漏得也越来越厉害,众人简直象身处旷野一般,只有此人蒙头酣睡。就在这时,北墙轰然倒塌。大家都没有睡下,急忙躲到屋外去,只有此人被压在墙下,头破血流,一条手臂和一只脚骨折,最后只得雇人把他抬回家。这件事可以让那些惯于挖空心思占便宜的人引以为戒。

此事让我联想起我原先的仆人于禄。他天性狡猾,我到乌鲁木齐赴任时他跟随前往。一天早起出发赶路,天上布满乌云,好象马上要下雨。他就悄悄把自己的衣服装进箱子,而把我的衣服盖在上面。谁知走了十多里地,天气转晴,车却陷到水沟里,水从下面灌进箱子,把他的衣服全弄湿了。看来上天似乎也不大喜欢玩弄心计的人。

69.點鬼骗食

有位姓廖的太学生因为爱妾去世,悲伤不已,整日郁郁寡欢。夏天他到别墅避暑,从所住屋子的窗口俯视,可见一道清澈的溪水。晚上他习惯开着窗,让月光洒到屋里。这天晚上,他听见小溪对面的山崖上有拷打和哀求的声音,放眼望去,有位女子正趴在地上受杖刑。正在凝视之时,那女子叫道:"您原来在这里,怎忍心不伸手救我一把呢?"他仔细一看,正是已故爱妾,不禁又吃惊又心疼,但隔着深溪陡崖,无路可过。他就问:"你葬在别处,怎么会到了这里?"女子抽泣道:"生前我仗着您的宠爱,干了不少坏事,死后被发配到这里,就象人间被判流放一样。土地神心狠手毒,动不动就责打我。希望您能请和尚做法事,为此地的众鬼施食,否则我就无法逃离苦难。"说完,女子就被一群穷凶极恶的鬼拖走了。廖某对爱妾一往情深,无法回绝她的请求,便出钱请和尚为众鬼施食,希望借此帮助爱妾摆脱困境。

谁知才过了一个多月,他又听到了拷打声。从窗口往对面山崖一看,那女子赤身裸体,双臂反绑,被一大群鬼围着拷打,比从前更加楚楚可怜。她见到廖某就哀告说:"上一次法事不够完备,上神不肯开释我,土地神因此变本加厉地虐待我。如今必须做七天七夜的大法事,才能让我解脱。"廖某听到这儿,心里一动,突然产生了怀疑。假如土地神不在场,谁来监刑呢?假如土地神在场,她怎么敢当面指责呢?这会不会是狡猾的鬼骗食的花招呢?正在疑虑之间,那女子说:"我确实是您的亡妾,请别太多疑了。"廖某至此心里完全明白了,就质问说:"你身上有颗红痣,你能说出它长在哪里,我就相信你。"那女子回答不出。过了一会儿,那群鬼渐渐散去,从此再也没有出现。从这件事可以看出,世情狡诈,不仅人间如此,冥界也不例外。廖某后来对人说,家里有个婢女死后葬在那座山下,推想是她知道主人对爱妾的思念,就串通众鬼演出了那场骗局。

70. 家猫复仇

我的舅爷爷陈德音家养着一只猫。有个婢女特别痛恨猫偷食,有机会就打它。猫只要听见婢女轻轻咳嗽一声,就赶紧逃窜。有一天主人出门,让婢女看家。她闲着无事,就关了门睡觉,醒来发现盘子里的梨少了几个。周围没有别人,而猫又从不吃梨。婢女无法向主人证明自己清白,挨了一顿打。到了晚上,忽然在炉灶里找到了那几个梨,大家都惊讶不已。仔细一检查,每个梨上面都有猫爪印儿,这才知道是猫有意陷害婢女。婢女气愤之下,想去把猫痛打一顿。我的舅奶奶拦住她说:"我当然不会让你把猫打死。何况猫死了,定要报复,不知又会闹出什么事儿来。"那婢女听从了,从此不再打猫,猫见了她也就不再逃避了。

71. 今生好友，来世夫妻

一位书生游览嵩山，搜集抄录古代碑文，不觉天色已晚。当时正值盛夏，他就挨着一棵松树露宿在草地上。半夜他被冻醒，衣袖已被露水打湿。他一时睡不着，就躺着观赏月景。忽然远处几个人沿着小路走来，到山顶铺好席子，坐下喝酒。书生知道对方不是人，心中惊惧，不敢出声，静听他们说些什么。其中一人对上坐的两人说："你们二位在冥界的期限已满，即将重入轮回，再见天日。你们知不知道要在哪儿投生？"那两人说："还不知道呢。"

正在这时，那些人同时站起身说："土地公来了。"不一会儿，一位老人拄着拐杖走来，对那两人拱手道："刚刚得到冥司的公文，来向你们报喜：你们两位前生是好朋友，来生是恩爱夫妻。"他指着右边那人说："你是丈夫。"又对左边那人说："你是他夫人。"右边那人笑了起来。看到左边那人沉默不语，土地神就对他说："你为何闷闷不乐呢？难道阎罗王会误判吗？你的朋友生性刚直，不知体察人情，顺应时势，一生虽有相当建树，也有不少过失，所以在冥界沉沦二百年才得解脱。毕竟他的过失是君子之过，所以来世仍能当达官。至于你，遇事明哲保身，不肯用自己的行为来影响别人的祸福。然而有些祸端若不及时防治，最终将遗害无穷。所以你也在冥界作鬼二百年，来世被贬为女子。但你为人深沉而不阴险，和气而不谄媚，所以还能享受富贵。又因为他在交往中经常得罪人，而你却自始至终和他友好相处，这样就种下了你们来世的姻缘。神的判决是公正英明的，你何必这样闷闷不乐呢！"众鬼都哗然笑道："他不是不开心，是头一回当新娘子，未免害羞吧！这里有酒有肉，就请土地公作主，提前让他们拜堂成亲吧！"随即喧嚷声响成一片，再也听不清众鬼说的话。等晨鸡报晓时，那些鬼匆匆散去。书生最终也不知道那两位前世究竟是什么人。

72. 失望的猎艳者

桐城人姚别峰,擅长写诗和书法。一次他被人邀请到家写字,安排住宿在宅院西侧的小花园里。一个月光清朗的夜晚,他看见窗外有女子的身影,连忙走出去查看,外面却没有人。他四处张望,似乎看到穿着绿裙红衫的女子隐约从树石花竹间露出身影。他刚走上前,女子就躲到园子另一边;等他追寻而去,女子又躲开了。就这样折腾了半夜,他还是没能一睹那女子的月容花貌,只好回到屋中休息。这时窗外传来女子的声音:"您若肯费心为我抄写一部《金刚经》,我必定前来拜谢。此经不过七千余字,您是否答应呢?"姚别峰急忙追问:"你是谁?"窗外却没有回答。当时他手边正好有一册宣纸,于是从次日起,他把别的事情暂时放开,一心一意抄写《金刚经》。写成之后,把它供在桌上,还点上一炷香,等候那女子来取。过了一夜,那本经不见了。次日他苦等到夜幕降临,果然见到一位女子轻盈地从花丛中走出来,向他一拜到地。他刚想伸手相搀,女子猛地站起身,抬起脸,双眼上翻,胸前鲜血淋漓,原来是个自杀鬼。姚别峰吓得大叫一声,跌倒在地。等仆人手持蜡烛寻声赶来,那鬼已经离开了。姚别峰跳脚大骂,恨自己被鬼欺骗了。主人听说了这件事,就对他说:"鬼答应拜谢你,最后确实拜谢了。鬼并没有欺骗你,是你自己有了非份之想,这怎么能怨鬼呢?"

73. 梦与真

我在西域时,曾陪同一位姓巴的办事大臣视察军台。他先回去了,我还有事要办,就和一位梁副将暂时在军台留宿。当天夜里送来一封紧急公文,可是台兵都派出去了,我就把梁副将从梦中叫醒,让他骑马赶送,并嘱咐他说,假若在路上遇见台兵,可以把公文转交他们传送。梁副将驱马疾驰十余里,遇上了台兵,自己回来接着睡觉。第二天起来,他对我说:"昨天梦见您派我送紧急公文,我怕耽误时间,策马狂奔。今天早上起来,大腿却觉得酸痛,真是一件大怪事！"仆从们听他把真事当成做梦，都忍不住笑起来。我曾为此事赋诗一首。与上面的事情相反，还有以梦为真的例子。我的一位远房哥哥说，静海县有个人，有天晚上他先睡了，妻子还在另一间屋里织布。他睡着后，梦见妻子被几个人劫走，等惊醒过来，不知刚才自己是做梦，操起一条棒子就出门追赶。跑了十多里，果然见到旷野里几个人挟持着一个少妇，正要强行无礼，少妇大声呼救。此人怒火万丈，奋勇上前，拼死搭救，那几个人都被他打伤，四散逃跑了。他近前一看，认出被劫持的是邻村的一位妇人，原先也相互认识，就把她护送回家。等到他茫然地回到自己家里，发现妻子还在灯下织布呢。他也许做的不是普通的梦，而是接受了神的指点吧。

74. 仙女的礼物

有个士人住在武夷山脚下，听采茶人说，山中某块岩石处，每到月明之夜都有吹笛歌唱之声，远远望去好象是一群仙女。士人生性轻狂，就到山里一户人家借宿，晚上月亮一出来就到岩石边等着，可是接连几夜一无所见。听那家人说，确实有仙女奏乐的事，但一年听不到几回，而且都是在月圆之夜。于是士人耐住性子等待了十多天。这晚他隐隐听到声音，连忙悄悄赶去，躲在树丛间窥视，果然见到几位绝色少女。其中一位拿着笛子放到唇边正要吹，一眼瞥见树丛中的人影，就用笛子一指。士人身上一麻，就动弹不得，但心里依然清醒。少女吹起笛子，乐声摄人心魄，响遏行云。士人不由赞叹道："虽然身体被定住，但仙女的妙音媚态，已让我尽情欣赏了。"语音未落，突然一条手帕飞来，盖住了他的脸，这一下他既听不见，也看不着，脑子昏昏沉沉，似睡似醒。

不知过了多久，士人慢慢清醒过来。那些少女让几个婢女把士人从树丛里拖出来，呵斥道："无礼的狂徒，竟敢窥视天上的花朵吗？"婢女们折下竹枝，准备责打士人。他连忙苦苦哀求，自称酷爱音乐，来此只希望偷听仙曲，一饱耳福，绝对没有非份之想。一位少女微笑道:"难得你如此心诚。我们有个婢女也会吹笛,就把她赏给你吧。"士人连忙跪下,叩头致谢。等他站起身来,那些仙女都不见了。回头看那留下的婢女,宽脑门,大眼睛,短头发,粗腰身,嘴里呼呼地喘着粗气。他又惊又恼,掉头就要走。那婢女冲上来拉住他,硬要与他亲热。士人被纠缠不过,气急之下,举手将她打倒在地。婢女立刻变成一只猪,嗥叫着跑掉了。那处山岩下的乐声从此绝迹。从婢女变猪这件事来判断,那些少女可能是妖怪,而不是天仙。也有人推断那些仙女事先把一只猪变成婢女,用来戏弄士人。

75. 以彼之矛,攻彼之盾

一位儒生平日道貌岸然,处事谨慎,对别人却过份苛求,不近人情。一位朋友五月脱去丧服,七月打算娶妾,他就写信说:"丧满不到三个月就要纳妾,可知蓄志已久,从内心讲就有违礼法。朋友之间应该相互规劝,我不敢不提醒你。你对此有何见教?"这样的做法在儒生已习以为常。

有一次,儒生的妻子回娘家,约好某日返回。到了约定日子的前一天,妻子就回来了。儒生感到奇怪,问是怎么回事。妻子回答说:"我把日子算错了。"儒生信以为真。等到第二天,又一位妻子回家来了。儒生大吃一惊,再找前一位妇人,已经不见了。从那天起,儒生渐渐羸弱下去,竟发展成痨病。原来是狐女假扮了他妻子的模样,来摄取他的精气;那一夜他纵欲过度,伤了元气。前面那位娶妾的朋友听说了这件事,就写信给儒生说:"夫妻房中之事,原本是人伦之常。狐狸扮人,也不是可以预料的。然而一夜之间大损元气,若非过份纵情则不至如此。难道夫妻欢好,可以不加节制吗?何况妖物不敢侵犯有德之人,古往今来,大贤大德之人从未遇到过妖魅。可是狐狸却公然对您无礼,莫非您的德行尚有不足吗?朋友之间应该相互规劝,我不敢不提醒您。不知您对此有何见教?"儒生接到这封信,竭力否认狐女之事,说那只是村里人造谣而已。那个朋友真可谓以彼之矛,攻彼之盾。

76. 捕狐道士

有位书生和一个狐女相好。起初相识时,狐女把一个小葫芦送给书生,让他系在衣带上,自己钻进去。每当书生想见她,只要把葫芦塞打开,狐女就出来和他亲热,随后再钻进去,让书生重新塞好。有一天,书生走在市场上,不慎让人把葫芦偷走了,狐女就此绝迹。为此书生很长时间闷闷不乐。

这天他到郊外散心,听树丛中有人叫他的名字,正是狐女的声音。他赶紧过去问候,狐女却不肯露面,对他说:"我已经变回狐形,不能与你相见了。"书生问是怎么回事。狐女哽咽着说:"狐狸修炼时,通常从人身上采取精气。近来不知从哪儿来了个道士,搜捕狐狸供他采补。他每抓到一个狐女,就念起咒语,使她变得象木偶一样动弹不得,只能任其所为。偶然有功力较高的狐女,竭力不让他把精气采走,道士就把她蒸熟作肉脯。我原先在葫芦里藏身,就是想躲避道士的追捕,没想到最终还是落到他手里。我害怕被扔到锅里,主动把内丹献出,总算保住一命。然而失去内丹,我就恢复成兽形,需要再修炼二三百年,才能重新变化成人。天长地久,我们再次相会的日子却遥遥无期。因为感念你深挚的情意,所以我特意在此等候,与你诀别。希望你多加珍重,不用再挂念我了。"

书生听了她的话,很气愤地问:"你为什么不向天神控告道士呢?"狐女答道:"很多狐女都去控告过了。神认为狐狸的精气原是采补而来,然后又被道士采走,是自作自受。如今我才知道,用不正当的手段得到的东西,只能给自己带来祸害。往后我要专心吐纳,绝不重操旧术了。"过了几年,有一个道人被雷击死,有人推测就是那个迫害狐女的道士终于恶贯满盈,受到天诛。螳螂捕蝉,黄雀在后,又有人手持弹弓,瞄准黄雀,这正是上面这件事的写照啊。

77. 因势出奇谋

奸邪小人诡计多端,抓住机会就要施展。我小时候听说,一户村民夜里听见院子里有脚步声,以为来了盗贼,就点起火把四处搜捕,结果一无所获。他们知道是鬼魅作怪,就不再理会。后来一个小偷听说此事,就在深夜溜进这家。家里人听见响动,以为还是闹鬼,就接着安心睡觉。小偷乘机大肆盗窃,收获颇丰。

还有一位县令,尊儒斥佛,对和尚极端厌恶。有一次,当地一座寺庙失窃,主持的和尚来县里报案。县令斥责他说:"假如佛不灵验,又何必享受供养?假如佛灵验,怎么不让小偷得到报应,反而来烦扰官府?"他就这样把和尚打发走了,并且得意地声称:"假如天下的官员都采用我这种办法,和尚们不用驱赶就自行散掉了。"不料那个和尚非常狡黠,表面上和徒弟们在佛前忏悔祷告,暗地里收买了一个乞丐,让他手捧着一些衣物满脸痴呆地跪在庙门外。这样一来,人们都传说庙里的佛显灵,让小偷自首了,施舍变得比从前更多。靠这个办法,和尚把一件原本不利的事情转而为他所用。世间的机巧如此之多,象那位县令那样拘泥于一己之见,与这样的狡黠之徒较量,怎么会占到上风呢?

78. 鬼扯谎,露马脚

献县城外有一些土丘,民间传说那里埋葬着汉朝人。有个农人耕田时不慎犁过了一座坟,回家就病倒了,身子忽冷忽热,而且有鬼附体,责备农人弄坏了它的坟。当时正好一位读书人在旁,就问:"你是什么人?"鬼答道:"汉朝人。"又问:"汉朝什么地方的人?"鬼说:"我就是汉朝献县人,所以坟墓在此,你何必多此一问?"读书人又问:"这个地方汉朝就叫献县吗?"鬼说:"不错。"读书人说:"这就奇怪了。汉朝这儿属河间国管辖,县名叫乐成。金朝这儿改名叫献州,明朝才改称献县。汉朝怎么会用献县这个地名呢?"鬼无言以对。再追问下去,那个农人苏醒过来,当时病就好了。看来大家都传说那儿是汉墓,鬼也知道这个说法,于是就假冒汉朝鬼,附在农人身体上,想借机求点祭典,没想到谎话被读书人当场戳穿。

79. 乡下鬼传错信

有位姓韩的书生,夏天住在山里读书。窗外是悬崖,崖下是深涧。山涧十分陡峭,对岸虽近,却是可望不可及。月明之夜,书生常能见到对岸有人影,知道那是鬼,但因为它不能跨过山涧,所以也就不太害怕。久而久之,他见惯了,就试着打招呼。那鬼和他搭上了话,自称是堕涧摔死的,正在等待转世轮回。书生半开玩笑地把喝剩的酒从窗口洒入涧内,那鬼就下去喝,显出感激的样子。从此他们就成了朋友。书生在苦读之余,与鬼谈天,颇解寂寞。

有一次书生问:"据说鬼能预知未来。我今年要参加科举考试,你看我能不能考中?"鬼回答说:"神如果不查看典籍,尚且不能预知,更何况是鬼呢!鬼可以从一个人身上阳气的盛衰,推知他的寿命,从他身上光芒的明亮程度,判断他正直还是邪恶。至于一个人应享的福禄,冥界办事的鬼隶也许能窃听到消息,城市里的鬼也许能相互通风报信,而乡下鬼就无从得知了。即使是城市里的鬼,也有机灵和迟钝之分,笨鬼是打听不到消息的。好比你跑到山里读书,官府的事情尚且不知,何况朝廷的机密大事呢?"几天后的一个晚上,那鬼隔着山涧叫道:"向你贺喜了!刚才城隍巡山,我听见他和土地神说话,好象今年乡试头一名正是你。"书生听了暗暗高兴。等到考试结果出来,第一名却是另一个姓韩的考生。书生叹息道:"看来向乡下人打听官府的事,果然靠不住啊!"

80. 仙人报恩

一个姓崔的人触犯了刑律被流放到广东。他怕带着家属发生意外,就告别了妻妾,只身来到异乡。在广东,他穷愁抑郁,无以自慰,想到妻妾也在饱受相思之苦,更添愁怅。他偶然结识了一位姓董的老翁,两人谈得很投机。老翁对崔某的遭遇表示同情,聘他教自己的儿子读书。一天晚上,老翁请他在楼上喝酒。皎洁的月色勾起崔某的心事,他手持酒杯倚靠着栏杆,全然忘了身在何处。老翁笑道:"你是在思念家眷吧?这件事我早就牵挂于心,代你操办了;但不知能否把你的妻妾接来,所以没有事先告诉你。慢慢会有消息的。"

半年后,老翁忽然让家仆婢女们另外打扫布置房间,象是非常急迫。随即三乘小轿抬到,崔某的妻妾和一个婢女从里面走出来。崔某又惊又喜,忙问是怎么回事。妻妾回答说:"前些日子接到你的信要我们来,嘱托我们跟随某个官员的家属搭伴儿赶路。我们匆匆收拾一下就来了。家中之事已托付给一位兄长代为办理,约定每年收到租米就卖了钱寄来。"崔某又问:"婢女是哪里来的?"妻子答道:"就是那个官员的小妾,因为正妻不能相容,所以我出贱价把她买下了。"崔生感激涕零,连忙拜谢老翁。从此他家庭团聚,不再思念故乡了。几个月后,老翁对崔某说:"那个婢女和你的家眷在路上邂逅,也算是一种缘份。你似乎应当把她也收到房中,不要让她独自寂寞。"崔某照办了。

又过了几年,皇帝大赦天下,崔某获准返回故乡。听到消息,他高兴得夜里睡不着觉。然而妻妾和婢女都露出惨然的神情。崔某安慰说:"你们是怀恋老人的恩德吗?只要我不死,准有一天会报答他。"她们都不回答,只是开始为他收拾行装。临行时,老翁摆酒相送,把三个女子叫过来,对崔某说:"今天必须把事情向你说明了。我是地仙,上辈子曾和你一道作官。我死后,你不遗余力地照顾资助我的妻儿,此恩让我铭记在心。几年前你告别家人,远离故土,我理当为你一家团聚出力。然而山高路远,两位弱女子实在不能前来。于是我就派三位花妖先到你家里住了半年,窥视到你家眷的面貌和言语习惯,并探听到家中旧事,使你不至于疑心。她们本是三姐妹,所以多了一个婢女。她们的形象都是幻化而成,你也不必多加思念。等回到家中,与家眷团聚,和在这里不会有什么两样。"

崔某心中不舍,请求带三位花妖回家。老翁说:"鬼神各有自己的地界,在异地只能暂住,不能久留。"三位女子和他洒泪相别,转眼就不见了。崔某登舟时,远远望见她们站在岸上眺望。他回到家里,听妻子说家境日渐败落,幸亏他年年寄钱,才能维持生活。这想来也是老翁所为了。假若世间离别的人都能遇见这位老翁,那就能免于相思之苦了。讲这个故事的是翰林院编修王史亭。他说:"既然广东有地仙,其它地方也一定有地仙。假若姓董的老翁有这种法术,别的地仙也一定有这种法术。之所以别人没有崔某的际遇,是上辈子并没有神仙受过其恩惠,自然不会竭尽全力相帮了。"

81. 狐鬼嫖妓

有个客商在泊镇宿妓,付钱时,妓女把银子拿在手里反复察看,又放在灯上烧,微笑道:"这不会是纸做的吧?"客商觉得她问得奇怪。妓女解释说,几天前有运粮船演戏祭神,她跑去看,夜深才回来,路上遇见一个少年给她银子,两人就在河边草棚里野合。回到家里,她从怀中掏出银子,觉得太轻,仔细一看却是纸做的,原来是遇见鬼了。她还说,附近有个妓女,接到一个客人,送给她许多衣服首饰。等他走后,妓女才发现那些衣服首饰都是自己箱子里的,而箱子一直锁着没打开过,所以疑心被狐狸耍了。客商听了,开玩笑地说:"一报还一报!"

还有一件事,是盲人刘君端讲的。青县有人和一个狐狸交了朋友,经常一起喝酒,十分亲热。忽然他有很长时间见不到狐狸。这天他走过一片荒地,听见草丛中有呻吟声,过去一看,正是自己的狐友,就问:"你怎么弄得这样狼狈?"狐狸满脸沮丧惭愧,好半天才说:"前些日子我见到一个小妓女颇为健壮,就化成人形去嫖宿,希望能采她的精气。不料她已经染上恶疾,我采得了她的精气,病毒也随之进入我的身体,和平生采到的精气混在一块儿,就象把油掺到面里,再也分不开了。那毒气慢慢扩散,传到脸上,使我羞于见人,所以长时间没和朋友们往来了。"

82. 婢女离魂

有位富人,喜欢一个婢女,对她宠爱倍至。婢女也对主人十分倾心,发誓非他不嫁。富人的正妻醋意大发,却也无可奈何。恰巧富人有事外出,他妻子趁机偷偷找来个女侩,让他把婢女卖掉,打算等富人回来,就说婢女自行逃走了。一个家人知道主人一旦回来,此事必定会有变故,就从女侩手里把婢女买回来,藏在尼姑庵里。婢女自从到了女侩家,就眼睛发直,闭口不语,拉她站就站,扶她走就走,按她躺下就躺下。如果不去管她,就象木偶一样,整天一动不动。给她饭她就吃,递她水她就喝;不给,她也不主动要。到了尼姑庵,情况照旧。请来的医生认为她气愤过度而痰迷心窍,照此开方吃药,却毫无效果。她就这样半死不活地在尼姑庵住下了。

过了一个多月,富人回家,发现心上人被妻子卖掉,怒不可遏,甚至拔刀要和她拼命。那个家人知道这件事不可隐瞒,就说出了实情。富人急忙到尼姑庵接回了婢女,但她还是如痴如梦。富人贴着她的耳朵叫她的名字,她才忽然象是从梦中惊醒。她自述刚到女侩家时,想到卖她是主母的意思,主人肯定不会抛弃她,就自行跑回家。她怕被主母看见,一直藏在隐蔽处,等待主人的归来。今天听见主人呼唤自己的名字,心里一高兴,马上就跑出来了。她回忆起某日见到某人做某事,讲得一清二楚,丝毫不差。由此知道在那段日子里,她身体虽在尼姑庵,魂却回到了家中。

83. 鬼怕横人

有个雇工叫田不满,一天夜里走岔了路,误入坟地,踩在了一个骷髅上面。那骷髅张口说道:"别踏坏我的脸!小心我收拾你!"田不满又愣又横,呵斥道:"谁让你挡我的路!"骷髅说:"不是我有意挡路,是别人把我挪到这儿来的。"田不满又骂道:"那你为什么不去收拾那个人?"骷髅说:"那个人运气旺,我奈何他不得。"田不满又好气又好笑,说:"难道我走霉运吗?你这样畏强凌弱,是何道理?"骷髅哭着说:"你运气也旺,所以我不敢报复,只好说大话吓唬你。畏强凌弱,是人之常情,你何必为此责备鬼呢?希望你可怜可怜我,把我移到土坑里,那我就感恩不尽了。"田不满不加理睬,大步走过去,只听背后骷髅呜呜的哭声。后来他并未因此遇上怪事。我觉得田不满缺乏仁爱之心。不过那个鬼遇到卤莽之人,却说大话激怒对方,这是很不足取的。

84. 君子不施鬼计

我的先师陈白崖先生说,他的启蒙老师(我记得好象姓周)笃信程朱理学,却不追求道学家的名声,所以一辈子不得志,少为人知。然而他修养深厚,是个真正的君子。他曾经租了几间空屋住下。一天晚上,只听窗外有人说:"我有事奉告,又怕吓着您,怎么办?"先生说:"进来无妨。"那人走进屋,只见他双手扶着脑袋,没带头巾,身上的长衫有一半已被鲜血浸透。先生拱手请他落座,那人也谦逊地还礼。先生问:"你有什么话要讲?"那人答道:"我在明朝末年不幸被强盗杀害,魂灵滞留在这个屋子里。原来这里也住过人,虽然我不愿意作怪,但人的阳气和鬼的阴气相互冲撞,人受到惊吓,我也不得安宁。如今我有个办法:邻居家有处住宅,可以容下您一家人。我到那里作怪闹事,住户必然搬走。再有来住的,我仍然去骚扰,最后那宅子必然荒废。那时您花低价把宅子买下,搬过去住,我就可以在此安居了。这不是一举两得吗?"

先生说:"我平生从不搞阴谋诡计,况且是帮鬼去害人。我决不会这么做的。我来这屋里读书,只是图个清静。既然你在这里,我把这屋改放杂物,平时上锁,你看怎么样?"那鬼惭愧地道歉说:

"我见您桌上放着关于人性道德的书籍,所以敢提出这样的计策。不料您真是位正人君子,恕我失言了。既然您肯容纳我,那我寄住在这里就行了。"先生在那里住了四年,再也没发生怪异之事。大概因为他一身正气,把鬼完全镇慑住了。

85. 前世冤仇一笔销

姜挺以贩布为生,身边总带着一条花狗。这天他独自走在路上,被一个老翁叫住。姜挺问:"素不相识,叫我有什么事?"老翁跪下叩头说:"我是个狐狸,曾在前世害了你的命,三天后你会放花狗咬断我的喉咙。这件事冥司注定,难以逃避。可是我私下想,我害死你是一百多年前的事情。现在我已堕落为狐,你却转世为人;你追杀一个狐狸,也没什么好处。况且你早已记不起前世被杀的事情,偶然杀个狐狸,也不会觉得痛快。我愿意把女儿送给你,以赎回我的性命,你看可以吗?"

姜挺回答说:"我可不敢引狐入室,也不愿意乘机强占别人的女儿。我倒是愿意饶你,但谁能保证我的狗以后也不再咬你呢?"老翁说:"你只要写个条子,说明某某所欠夙债,你自愿销除不计就行了。我拿条子去给神看,花狗就不会再咬我了。只要当事人肯捐释前怨,神是不会反对的。"姜挺正好带着记帐的纸笔,当下就写了条子。老翁接到手里,兴高采烈地走了。

七八年后,姜挺在外贩布,渡大江时突然遇上暴风。在这紧要关头,帆却落不下来,船马上要被刮翻了。此时只见一个人迅速爬上桅杆,拉断了绳子,骑着帆布一起落下来。姜挺远远望去,好象是先前遇见的那个老翁,但转眼之间就不见了踪影。听说此事的人都赞叹说,那个狐狸懂得报恩,对此我不敢苟同。那狐狸的本事不足以自救,哪里能够到千里之外救人呢?这必定是神因为姜挺有好生之德,延长了他的寿命,所以派那狐狸去搭救他。

86. 占物术

甘肃驻军有个参将叫李璇,精于观物占事之术,颇为灵验。在一次平定西域的战役中,他随军出征,跟从温大学士。当时有个士兵不慎失火,把辕门前的枯草烧掉一片。温请李璇占一下它预示什么。李璇答道:"没有别的事,就是您几天后将发出一份秘密奏折。火遇枯草烧得极快,说明是急递。烟气上行,说明是往上送交。这样就推断是密奏。"温说:"我并没有事情要写密奏。"李璇说:"失火也出于无心,并非预定的。"过了几天,果然被他说中。

李璇给人占前途,就让对方随手拿起一件东西。有时两人拿了同一件东西,李璇给出的断语却不一样。一次他来到京城,一位翰林拿起一个铜烟筒请他占卜。他说:"烟筒贮火,而且有烟流通于内,说明你不是冷官,但位置也不算显贵,因为需要人来吹嘘。"又问:"能作几年官?"李璇答道:"恕我直言。火本来不算大,一旦灭掉就只剩下灰烬,说明其热力不会持续太久。"又问:"寿命能有多少?"李璇回答:"铜器原本经久耐用,但也没听说过哪个烟筒能用一百年。"那翰林听了悻悻而去。后来他的经历印证了李璇的预言。当时有位郎官也在座,他又把烟筒拿起,看李璇怎样断。李璇说:"烟筒里的火已经熄灭,你必定是个冷官。它刚才放在床上,说明你曾被罢官。现在又拿在手上,说明你又受到别人提携而复出。将来尚有发热的时候,但那以后的断语同前面那位就相同了。"后来证明李璇说的不错。

87. 狐狸打抱不平

程某是村里的老夫子,有个颇为俊秀的女儿。有一次她到门前买脂粉,受到邻里少年的调戏,回家向父母哭诉。程某忿忿不平,但因那少年素来横行乡里,不敢上门去理论,为此郁闷不乐。他和一个狐狸是朋友,常请对方喝酒。一天,狐狸看出老人神情沮丧,问是怎么回事,程某就以实相告。狐狸听完,什么都没说就告辞走了。

后来,那恶少又到程家门前,见姑娘倚门对着他笑。两人渐渐搭上话,当下就在菜园的空屋里成就好事。临别时,姑娘含着眼泪,恋恋不舍,约他一同私奔。少年当夜又来到程家门外,把姑娘领回了自己家。他怕程老头追访到女儿行踪,拿刀对着自己妻子威胁说:"你敢泄露出去,就杀了你!"过了几天,并未听到什么动静。少年认为程老头定是把女儿私奔视为门户之辱,不敢声张,就愈发得意,与姑娘狎昵无度。

　　过了一些日子,姑娘逐渐露出诡异的行迹,少年这才知道她是狐魅,但已经被她迷惑,不愿赶她走。再过一年多,少年纵欲过度,身体垮掉了,只剩下一口气,狐女这才离他而去。为了求医用药,少年花光了家产,总算保住了性命。夫妻露宿街头,少年羸弱不能干活,只能靠妻子卖淫赚到的钱来填肚子,从前的暴戾之气一扫而光。程某不知其中的前因后果,有次向狐狸提起这件事。狐狸说:"那是我打发了一个狡黠的婢女去戏弄他的。最先变化成你女儿的模样,是为了诱少年上钩。后来让他明白是狐魅,是为了维护你女儿的名声。等他奄奄一息就离去,是因为他并无死罪。现在他已经受到了足够的惩罚,你也用不着郁闷不乐了。"这个狐狸勇于为人济危解难,又懂得把握分寸,实在是难能可贵。

88. 生死恋

　　董家庄佃户丁锦有个儿子叫二牛,有个女儿招赘了曹宁为夫婿,在家帮工。二牛生了儿子,取名三宝;曹宁得了女儿,因为大家住在一起,就取名四宝。两个孩子同年同月生,只相差几天而已。姑嫂间相互抱携,相互哺乳。三宝四宝相亲相爱,稍稍长大些就寸步不离。小户人家不知避嫌,大人常在两个孩子玩耍时,指点着说:"这是你的丈夫,这是你的夫人。"两个孩子当时不知什么叫做夫妻,但已经听惯了这种叫法。他们长到七八岁,稍微懂了点事儿,但仍与丁锦的妻子同起同睡,不相回避。

后来,连着几年收成不好,丁锦夫妇都病故了。曹宁先流落到京城,贫困得难以自立,就把四宝卖到陈家作婢。随后二牛也到了京城,正好陈家需要一个童仆,就把三宝也卖到他家,告诫他不要提与四宝约为夫妇的事。陈家规矩特别严,常常责打仆人。每当四宝被打,三宝定要暗暗哭泣;每当三宝被打,四宝也要默默垂泪。陈某生了疑心,就把四宝转卖给郑家,把三宝赶出门去。三宝另外找了一家当童仆。过了一段日子,他打听到四宝的所在,就投奔到郑家。两人相见,抱头痛哭,当时他们都已十三四岁了。郑某觉得奇怪,追问其中的缘故,他们假称是兄妹。郑某因为他们名字相连,也就信以为真。因为内外宅被隔开,两人只能在出入时眉目传情而已。

后来,家乡收成好了,二牛和曹宁同时又来到京城赎回子女,辗转寻找到郑家。郑某这才知道三宝和四宝原来早已订亲,不由心生怜悯,想帮助他们成婚,然后让他们继续留下服役。然而家中馆师严某是个讲学先生,振振有辞地说:"中表结亲不合礼仪,也违反法律,这么做会受上天惩罚的。主人虽然出于好意,但象我这样的读书人,当以维持风化为己任;假若见到乱伦的事情不管,就是成人之恶,不是正人君子所为。"郑某生性懦弱,二牛和曹宁都是没读过书的乡下人,听严某说让三宝四宝成婚竟是重罪,就不敢再提这件事了。后来,四宝被卖给一个候补官员作妾,几个月后就病死了。三宝发狂离家出走,不知所终。有知情者说:"四宝虽然被迫嫁人,却自毁容貌,整日以泪洗面,实际并未与丈夫同过房。"果真如此的话,这段情缘决不会就此了结;两人天上人间,终有重新聚首的时候。严某做出这种罪孽,不知是何居心。然而天理昭昭,他必定得不到善报。又有人说:"严某并非食古不化,也不是想沽名钓誉。他只是看上了四宝的姿色,想伺机据为己有罢了。"要真是这样,那么地狱正是为这种人预备的。

89. 巧断鬼案

有两个人到甘州张掖县令处告状。甲说乙造谣污蔑,乙说确有其事。讯问之下,得知这两人是表兄弟。甲带着妻子出塞,乙随之同行。到了甘州东几十里处,夜里走迷了路。这时遇见一人,打扮得象富贵人家的奴仆,对他们说他主人住处离此不远,可以到那儿投宿,次日再指点他们回到大路上。他们跟随那人走了三四里,果然见到一个小城堡。那人进去,过了好久才出来,招手说:"主人让你们进来。"走过好几道门,只见一人坐在堂上,询问了他们的姓名和籍贯,然后说:"夜深了,不能招待你们吃饭,只能让你们留宿。门旁的小屋可以住两个人。这位女眷就和仆妇们同睡吧。"两人就寝后,似乎隐隐听见妇人的叫声。暗中摸索着起身,却找不到门。这时叫声又停止了,两人以为先前是误听,就重新睡下。

第二天醒来,他们发现自己躺在旷野中。急忙去找甲的妻子,她却在半里外的树下,双臂反绑,赤身裸体,头发散乱,衣裳高挂在树枝上。她说头天晚上有婢女拿着灯带她到这儿,有好几间华美的屋子,还有另外几个婢女仆妇。过了一会儿,主人进来,让她坐到他身边去。她不肯,那几个婢女仆妇就上来抓住她,剥掉衣衫,绑在床上。她大声呼救,却没有人来,于是被主人强奸。天快亮的时候,主人把两块东西放在她脖子旁边,然后房子突然消失,她发现自己已经躺在地上了。看她脖子旁边,放着两个银元宝,每个重五十两,上面镌刻着明朝崇祯年间铸造。银子久置土中,已经发黑了,看来真是百年前的旧物。甲让乙别把这件事说出去,约好把银子给他一半儿。后来甲反悔了,乙气得吵闹起来,这件事才传开。受到县令审讯时,甲夫妇坚决否认此事。问银子是怎么来的,说是拾到的;问妇人身上捆绑的伤痕,说是抓破的。回答支支吾吾,想来乙的陈述不见得是瞎编。县令笑着对甲说:"按照法律,拾得的财物要交官。姑且念你家贫,就让你拿走吧。"又瞪着眼对乙说:"要是你说了假话,那么银子就是拾来的,该如数交官,你什么也得不到。要是你说了真话,那么银子就是那个鬼酬谢甲妇的,更没有你的份儿。你再敢多嘴,就给你一顿板子。"就这样把两人打发走。县令用不合常理的办法判了这个不合常理的案子,的确善于变通。

90. 狐婢巧脱身

我的乳母李婆婆是沧州人。她的儿子柱儿从前在海边放牧时听到这么一件事。有个煮盐人夜里刚上床,听见屋中有细微的响动。借着窗外投入的月光查看,并没有人进来,以为是老鼠。过了一会儿,听见外面人声嘈杂,由远而近。有男子叫道:"窜入这间屋子了。"煮盐人正在疑虑,那人敲着窗问道:"你在里面吗?"屋内答道:"在。"窗外又问:"主人留下你了吗?"屋内答道:"留了。"又问:"你和他同床,还是分屋而睡?"回答说:"不同床,谁又肯收留呢!"窗外人跺脚大叫:"糟了,糟了!"忽然外面又有个妇人大笑道:"我料想她去投奔别家,主人定不会白白收留她,你还不信。如今怎样?你还有脸把她带回家吗?"随后就是一些人走动的声音。过了片刻,那妇人又大笑道:"这点事情还犹豫不决,你算是什么男人!"随即她敲着窗对里面说:"我们家逃婢投奔了你,既然已经留宿,没有再领回的道理。你并未引诱胁迫,那老东西没有借口找你报复。就算他怀恨在心,有我在,他也不能怎么样。你们只管接着睡觉,我们走了。"

煮盐人从窗户的缝隙窥探,外面已经空无一人。回身再看,身边躺着位美女。他又惊又喜,问她从哪里来。女子回答说:"我是狐女,被刚才那个狐狸买作妾。主妇好妒,每天寻衅责打我。我实在住不下去,就逃走求生。之所以不事先告诉你,是担心你害怕,不愿收留,我就会被他们抓回去。我躲在床角,等他们追来,这才谎称已经失身于你,希望借此能摆脱他们。如今幸而脱身,情愿生死相伴。"煮盐人怕突然得到艳妻,引起别人的怀疑和妒忌,招来祸患。女子说:"我会隐身,不让人看见。你忘了我刚才缩着身子躲在床边吗?"于是她留了下来,勤谨耐劳地操持家务,日子渐渐富裕起来。柱儿和那煮盐人是远亲,所以对此事知道得很详细。那婢女遭遇不幸,不惜说谎言自

253

污,可谓铤而走险。然而正是借口失身,才使丈夫无法把她接回家,使主母有理由把她赶走。这虽然冒险,但正是决胜之策。婢女这一招果然高明。至于她的前夫,起初娶她不考虑后果,发生纠纷又无力解决,最终把她逼得走投无路,只有离家出逃。他要是稍微有些自知之明,又何至于弄到这一步呢!

91. 死囚的报复

据说孔夫子做事从不过头,这并不仅仅是防止矫枉过正;圣人也是在为未来考虑。老子说:"民不畏死,奈何以死惧之!"其实百姓并非不怕死,而是自知必死之后才不再害怕。而人一旦真不怕死,那就什么事情都干得出来。我小时候听说有一大户人家被抢,悬赏捉拿盗贼。过了半年多,强盗全都落网,对罪行也供认不讳。可是那大户的主人对强盗切齿痛恨,又花了大笔钱贿赂狱卒,让强盗受尽折磨。结果那些强盗站也站不住,躺也躺不下,绑着不让上厕所,裤子里蛆虫蠕动。但还供给他们饮食,让他们活受罪。强盗们对大户恨之入骨,暗地商议说:抢财物,不论主犯从犯一律斩首;强奸妇女,也是一样。假如两罪同犯,按刑律还是斩首,绝不会加重成碎尸示众。于是在审讯时,他们供称把大户家的妇女全部奸污了。虽然官员没有把这录入口供,但强盗们众口一辞,大家听得清清楚楚,事情也就传开了。平日跟大户不和的人又趁机附和说,那些强盗抢了财物,已经要依法抵罪,而大户却不惜重金,千方百计折磨他们,正是因为怀着家眷被污的仇恨。这种说法盛传一时,无从分辨真伪。大户家族的名声受到玷污,不禁后悔不已。

强盗被判死罪,怨不得大户;被关入囚牢,拷打审讯,也怨不得大户。至于在刑律之外,又受到百般折磨,他们自然不会甘心。以石击石,用力过猛,必会反弹而害及自身。只贪图一时之快,使家族受到百世之辱,岂不是做事过头的后果吗?

92. 借尸还魂

有个候补官员张某,带着妻子和婢女来到京城,在海丰寺街租房住下。一年后,他妻子得病去世。又过一年多,婢女也暴病而亡。正准备入殓时,忽然听见她又有了气儿。再过一会儿,只见她眼珠转动,醒了过来。她拉着丈夫的手,哽咽着说:"分别一年多,没想到还能再见到你!"候补官吃惊地看着她,不知她是什么意思。复活的婢女说:"别以为我在说胡话。我就是你的妻子,借婢女的尸身还魂了。这个婢女虽然得以进房侍奉你,却不甘心居我之下。她和一个妖尼暗地商量,用法术害我。我病死后,魂灵被收入瓶中,贴上符咒,埋在尼姑庵的墙角下。瓶里狭小昏暗,使我苦不堪言。后来那堵墙倒塌了,掘地重建时,有人刨土打破了瓶子,我才脱身出来。当时我四顾茫然,不知该去哪儿,幸亏遇上伽蓝神,指点我向城隍申诉。谁知会妖法的人都有邪神作后台,因此告状不准。最后我直接向东岳神君投诉,这才把妖尼拘来,讯得实情,把婢女逮捕下了地狱。我的阳寿未尽,而尸身已经腐坏,所以让我借婢女的尸身再生。"

听完她的话,家里人都很欢喜,把她当作女主人对待。而她所说的会妖法的尼姑却声称,候补官想立婢女为正妻,所以让她诈死片刻,来掩人耳目。她还威胁要到官府,控告他造谣中伤。候补官并没有亡妻复活的实证,怕被官府视为妖言惑众,所以闭口不再提这件事。然而据家里仆人们讲,主妇再生后,提起往事丝毫无差,其言语举止,也和从前无异。另外,婢女拙于女红,而主妇善于刺绣,先前曾有一只鞋没绣完。复活后她接着把那只鞋绣完,宛然出自同一手工。这样看来,主妇复活是确有其事了。这件事发生在雍正末年。

93. 患难夫妻

下面的故事讲的是一对夫妻起初分离,后来经常相见,却咫尺天涯,真不知是何因缘。中州有位姓李的书生,娶妻才过了十余日,母亲就病倒了。随后七八个月,夫妻俩轮流侍候,衣不解带。母亲病故后,他们遵从古礼,三年未曾同房。后来,因生活贫困,难以维持,就投奔到外祖父家。外祖父家也仅够温饱,房子不多,打扫出一间给他们夫妻住。没住上一个月,李某岳母的弟弟出远门就职,把母亲托给姐姐照料。因为没有空房了,就让李某妻子和她母亲同住,李某则在书斋里搭了张床睡,夫妻从此只是吃饭时才见面。过了两年,李某独自到京城谋职,他岳父也带着全家到江西去任幕僚。后来捎来消息,说李某的妻子去世了。李某听了伤心不已,更无意进取,就南下去投靠岳父。谁知到了江西,岳父已另找了主人,不知搬到哪儿去了。

李某没有办法,只得在街上卖字糊口。这天,一个彪形大汉看了他写的字,对他说:"你的书法非常好,肯不肯给人当书记,每年挣三四十两银钱?"李某喜出望外,跟着大汉上了船。船在烟水渺茫的江上行驶,看不出是往哪里去。到了主人家中,李某受到款待。等他看到来往信件,才发现主人是个绿林豪客。李某无可奈何,只得留了下来,但为了避免后患,谎报了姓名和家乡。主人性情豪侈,养着许多歌女,每次宴乐都召李某就座。一次,李某偶然看到主人的一个妾,长得酷似自己的亡妻,不禁怀疑她是鬼。她也不时朝李某看,好象认识他,然而两人不敢搭话。原来,李某的岳父渡江时,正好被这大盗抢了。大盗看到李妻有姿色,就顺势掳走了。岳父视之为家族的耻辱,对外声称李妻已死,急忙买了个薄皮棺材,运回家草草下葬。李妻在大盗胁迫下,作了他的妾。如今夫妻相见,李某相信妻子已死,他妻子又不知道他已经更改姓名,怀疑是相貌神似的另一个人,所以彼此都不敢相认。此后每过几天他们都要见上一面,天长日久也习惯了,不再相互注视。就这样过了六七年。

这天大盗把李某找去,对他说:"我马上要祸事临头了。你是个读书人,不必受牵连。这儿有五十两黄金,你把它收好,躲到芦苇丛里去。等官兵退走之后,你马上搭渔船离开。这儿的人都认识你,会送你出去的。"说完,挥手让他赶紧藏起来。片刻之后,就听见哄然格斗的声音。后来听见有人喊道:"强盗都乘船逃走了。我们把他们留下的财物妇人清点一下。"当时天色已晚,借着火光,李某窥见那些歌女个个披头散发,衣不遮体,手臂反绑,被鞭打驱赶着往前走;那个妾也在其中,吓得浑身发抖,那情景令人惨不忍睹。每二天,岛上空无一人,李某正呆呆地站在水边,忽然有人划着小船,叫他说:"是先生您吗?我们大王安然无恙,派我来接您离开这里。"小船走了一天一夜才靠岸。李某怕被当地人认出,急忙带着金子北归。

他到了家,发现岳父已经先回来了。李某卖了金子,生活变得丰裕起来。他想到夫妻相爱,结婚多年,同床共枕却不足一个月。如今日子稍为宽裕,不忍心妻子的遗体埋在薄皮棺材里。他准备买个上等棺木重葬,而且想看一眼妻子的遗骨,缅怀往昔之情。岳父竭力劝说无效,这才讲出实情。李某听后连忙兼程南下,期望能和妻子团聚。然而官军所俘的歌女姬妾早已分赏完毕,不知流落到哪里去了。李某每当想起过去六七年间,与妻子咫尺天涯,就怅惘若失。又想到她和那些歌女被俘时受到捆绑鞭打的惨状,不知她后来又要遭受多少苦楚,不由得肝肠寸断。他一直没再娶妻,后来竟出家当了和尚。

94. 邪术

某人客居他乡,应邀游湖,登上一只画舫,有箫鼓助兴,还有位红裙女子给客人们陪酒。仔细一看,却是自己的妻子。此地离家两千里,他纳闷妻子怎么会流落到这儿,又怕引起旁人耻笑,不敢上前相认。那妇人似乎不认识他,既不害怕,也不惭愧,一会儿奏乐,一会儿敬酒,恬然自若。他注意到她声音也不象他妻子。再有,他妻子笑的时候爱用手捂着嘴,这妇人却不然。可他又发现妇人象他妻子一样,右手腕上长了颗红痣。他心里疑惑不定,无心吃酒,宴会一散就离开,收拾行装打算回家。恰在这时来了封家书,说他妻子半年前病故。他觉得在船上是遇见鬼了。同伴们见他神态异常,追问不休,他这才说出其中的缘故。他们都认为那少妇只是碰巧相貌与他妻子神似而已。

后来,听说有个人经常往来于吴越间,却从不和别人交往,也不做买卖,只是带着一群姬妾闭门独居。有时,他会找来中间人,卖掉一两个妇人。别人以为他是专门贩卖妇女的,因为事不关己,也不去过问。有一天,这人慌慌张张地买船去天目山,临行前到寺庙请高僧作道场,说道:"我的本事原是佛传,应当求佛保佑。"再要细问,他支支吾吾,含糊其辞。高僧怀疑其中另有隐情,就把布施还给他,把他打发走了。他走到半道,遭雷击而死。后来,他的一个随从透露了其中的秘密,说他曾从一个红衣番僧那里学会异术,能用咒语摄取刚下葬女子的尸身,然后又摄取妖狐淫鬼的魂附尸而生,让其侍候自己。再有新人来,就把旧的转卖,获利丰厚。后来他梦见神警告他恶贯满盈,将受天诛,所以赶忙去佛寺忏悔,希望能得到宽恕,但最终还是在劫难逃。这件事传开后,人们这才想到,原先那人妻子的尸身可能就是被这样摄取了。

95. 虎伥

我的门生葛正华是吉州人。他说家乡曾有几个商人赶着骡子在山里行走,见一位穿青袍戴棕笠的道士站在砍柴人上山走的小径上,向他们当中的一个人招手说:"你叫什么名字?"那人答过,道士又问了他的籍贯,然后说:"我要找的就是你。你是被贬下凡的天仙,如今期限已满,可以回归天庭了。我原是你的师父,特意来为你引路。你跟我走吧。"那人心想,自己生来蠢笨,而且一个大字不识,不应该是天仙转世;再说,父母年事已高,没有理由抛下他们不管,自己去作神仙,于是执意回绝了道士。道士长叹一声,转而对众人说:"他既然自甘堕落,需要另一个人来顶替。你们在这里见到我,也算有缘。有没有愿跟我走的?不要错过这千载难逢的机会。"大家既惊异,又有些疑心,没有人响应。道士很生气地走了。众人来到客店,把这事讲给别人听,结果有的说是仙人引路,不去可惜;有的说道士是妖怪,还是不去为妙。第二天,有几个好事之徒找到那条小径,一直爬上山岭,在草丛里发现了新近被老虎吃掉的人的残骸,吓得连忙跑回来。那道士难道就是传说中的虎伥吗?无缘无故降临的好运气让贪心冒失的人欣喜,却让明智的人心惊。那个不肯跟道士走的人自以为蠢笨,实际却很聪明。

96. 半梦半真

至今也弄不清楚梦究竟是怎么回事。史书记载楚怀王梦游高唐,与神女幽会,传为佳话。我的哥哥晴湖曾写诗提出质疑,认为做梦乃是一个人的事情,楚怀王做梦与神女并不相干。不过,的确有人见过别人的梦境。仆人李星月夜在村外乘凉,远远望见邻居家的少妇在枣树林中,以为她在守园防盗,怕有公婆或丈夫相伴,不便和她打招呼。随后见她沿着田畦往西走了半里,进入高粱丛中。李星怀疑她要去幽会,更不敢靠近,只是从远处张望。不一会儿,见她从高粱地走出来,被水沟挡住路,呆呆站了片刻,沿着沟往北走了百余步,前方道路泥泞,又回身折向东北,进入豆田,艰难地走了一段,两次绊倒在地。李星看出她迷了路,就冲她喊:"你大晚上到哪儿去?再往北没路可走,要掉到泥潭里去了!"妇人回头见到是他,就说:"我走不出去了,请你把我带回家。"李星急忙赶过去,妇人却倏然不见了。他知道遇见了鬼,不由毛骨悚然,拼命跑回家,却看见那个妇人和她母亲坐在房外墙下。那妇人说,刚才纺线累了,沉睡过去,梦中到了林子里,迷路走不出来,听见李星在后面叫她,这才猛然惊醒。她讲述的经历和李星刚才所见完全相符。看来妇人因过于疲累,魂灵暂时离开了躯体;这不同于人死之后魂与身体完全分离,所以有时会被人看见。

97. 石兽的下落

沧州南边有一座临河的寺庙,山门在一次洪水中被冲垮,门前的两个石兽也沉到河里。过了十多年,僧人们募到了钱,准备重修寺庙,到河里找那两个石兽,却没有找到。他们认为石兽定是顺流而下了,就乘了几只小船,拿着铁钯子去搜寻,走出十多里地,还是没有找到。有个儒生在庙里设帐授徒,他听说了此事,笑道:"你们这些人不懂得探究事物的本性。石兽不同于木头,岂能被河水冲走?石头的本性是坚实沉重的,沙子的本性是松动飘浮的;石头处于沙上,必然越陷越深。你们却以为它会顺流而下,真是不明事理啊!"

众人听了儒生的议论,都十分佩服,只有一位护河老兵不以为然。他对大家说:"凡是在河中寻找石器,必须求之于上游。石头的本性是坚实沉重的,沙子的本性是松动飘浮的;河水冲不动石头,被反激回来,渐渐就把石头下面的沙子冲走。一旦石下铺垫的沙子有一多半被冲掉,石头必然翻倒下来。随后水流又冲击石下沙层,石头又翻倒,如此下去,它就一步一步逆流而上了。在下游找石兽固然不对,在沙下找石兽就更不对了。"众人按照他的指点,果然在河上游数里外的地方找到了石兽。由此可见,天下之事很容易只知其一,不知其二,绝不能凭简单的推理匆忙下结论。

98. 阴差阳错

天津有个少年元宵节出门观灯,晚上回家时见到一位秀丽的少妇在路口徘徊,象在等人。少年起初猜想她是出来看灯,和同伴们走散了,就上前搭话,少妇却默不出声。询问姓氏住处,她也不回答。少年便怀疑她正等着与情人幽会,不妨以此要挟,就上前邀请她到自己家中小憩。少妇坚决不肯。少年不顾她的反对,强行拉扯着她回到家中。当时家里酒席还未撤,少年就让少妇坐在妻子和妹妹当中,同桌而食。

少妇起初腼腆拘谨,渐渐开始说笑,与少年的妻子、妹妹相互劝酒、调笑,媚态横生。少年不由大喜,试探着提议要她当晚留宿。少妇微笑道:"承蒙不弃,借你家的地方卸一下妆。恐怕同伴们等着心焦,恕我不能久留了。"说完,她把外衣解下,卷起来包好,向少年深深一揖,往外就走。原来,这是位在秧歌队里扮女角的男子。少年十分气恼,一直追到门外,要跟那人动手,引得邻里街坊都聚过来询问。其中有人曾见到少年把那人强行带回家,因而不能给他扣上夜闯民宅的罪名。也有人曾见到那人在秧歌队中表演,因而也不能指控他有意改妆,调戏少年的妻子和妹妹。结果少年只有眼睁睁看着那人扬长而去,众人也随即一哄而散。这位少年真是自取其辱啊。

99. 敌友不分

京城海淀有个人靠为贵家守墓为生。有一次,几只狗追赶着一只狐狸从他门前跑过。见那狐狸身上已被咬得血迹斑斑,他不由生出恻隐之心,就挥起木棍驱散狗群,把狐狸抱到屋里。过了好一会儿,狐狸才缓过来,他便把它带到旷野放走了。几天后的一个晚上,他的屋门忽然被推开,走进一位美艳绝伦的少女。守墓人惊问她是谁,从哪里来。少女向他行礼道:"我是个狐女。那次我大难临头,幸亏你救了我的性命。如今我特来为你侍候枕席。"守墓人料想她不会有恶意,就让她留了下来。此后两个月,两人聚在一起,狎昵无度,他身体也日渐瘦弱,但因宠爱狐女,对她并未产生疑心。有一天,两人正在同床共眠,忽听窗外有人喊道:"阿六,你这个贱人!我伤还没养好,来不及报恩,你怎么竟敢假冒我的名义,把郎君害成这样?他万一有个好歹,族人们指责我忘恩负义,我该如何分辩?就算最后能够证明是你在捣鬼,我又怎么可以坐视自己的救命恩人被你害死?今天我带着姐妹们来除掉你!"狐女惊惶之下,起身想要逃走,几个女子却已破门而人,一起下手,把她当场打死。守墓人与那狐女日久生情,不由悲愤交加,斥责后来那几位女子害死了他的爱侣。那女子反复向他解释其中缘由,守墓人根本听不进去,最后竟拔刀相向,要为死去的狐女报仇。那女子这才痛哭着翻墙走掉了。守墓人后来给别人讲述这件事时,仍然愤愤不平,余怒未消。

100. 道学先生现原形

有个儒士性情乖僻,喜欢以苛刻的礼节管教学生。学生们都感到难以忍受,但此人平日行为端方,让人无从指摘。学塾后面有个小花园。一天晚上,儒士散步月下,瞥见花丛间隐约有个人影。当时久雨初晴,花园的土墙有的地方被冲坏,儒士怀疑邻人乘机来园子里偷菜。他走上前去责问,却见一位丽人躲在树后。她跪下施礼说:"我是个狐女。因为你是正人君子,我不敢冒犯,所以乘着夜色来摘花,不料还是被发觉,希望你别见怪。"她言词柔婉,顾盼之间娇媚无限。儒士被迷住了,试探着与她调情,女子竟顺从地投入他的怀抱。她说自己能够隐形,往来毫无踪迹,旁人根本看不见,不至于被学生们发觉。于是两人携手入帐,享受一夕之欢。

次日早上,天色朦胧之时,儒士催促狐女赶紧离开。她却说:"外面已有人声了。过一会儿我能从窗缝钻出去,你不用担心。"等到天光大亮,学生们都来到学塾,那女子却依然躺在帐中不肯起来。儒士心里忐忑不安,希望别人确实看不见她。忽然外面有个老妇来接人。女子这才披上衣裳,从容走出去,坐在儒士讲学的座位上,用手大致理了理头发,然后说:"我没带梳妆用具,只好回去打扮了,以后有空再来讨取昨晚的酬金。"原来,她是附近新来的妓女,被几个学生出钱雇来捉弄儒士。儒士大为狼狈。学生们听完课,回家吃早饭,儒士趁机打点行装,悄悄溜走了。外有余则中不足,这话确实不差啊!

101. 官员变仆妇

乾隆初年,户部员外郎长泰家中有个仆人的妻子突然中风昏迷,奄奄一息,当晚就断了气,年仅二十多岁。第二天,正准备把她装敛,她的手脚却动弹起来,渐渐能够屈伸。过了一会儿,她坐起身问:"这是哪儿?"众人以为她在说胡话。后来她环视屋中,好象有所醒悟,叹息了几声,并不说话,病却完全好了。但从此她举止言谈都象男子,不会自己梳妆,见了丈夫也似乎不认识。大家发现事情不对,追问之下,她说出了其中的缘由。她原来是个男子,几天前去世,灵魂被带到冥司。主管官员查出他阳寿未尽,但应贬为女身,命令他借用这个妇人的躯体复活。他当时只觉得睡了过去,然后一下惊醒,已经躺在这里了。问她原来的姓名住处,则坚决不肯吐露,声称事已至此,何必要说出来,给祖宗蒙上羞辱。起初她不肯和那个仆人同床共寝,后来实在没有理由拒绝,才勉强顺从了。然而每一次同房后,她都要哭泣到天明。有人曾听她自言自语地说:"读书二十年,作官三十多年,最后却要受奴仆的欺辱吗?"那仆人还听见她说梦话:"攒下那么多钱财,最后却供儿孙享用,真是何苦!"把她叫醒询问,她却不承认。长泰向来不喜欢谈论神怪的事情,责令家人们不要传扬此事,所以知道的人不多。过了三年多,那妇人郁郁而死,最终也不知她本来是谁。

102. 狐鬼的戏侮

有位姓郭的书生刚直好胜。一次中秋聚会,他和朋友们谈论起鬼神,声称自己不怕鬼。大家怂恿他到某处闹鬼的房子去证明一下,他慨然应允,仗剑而往。那处房子有几十间屋,长久无人居住,院里杂草丛生,有股阴森之气。郭某关上门,独自坐下,周围静悄悄的。到了四更天,一个人忽然出现在门口。郭某拔剑刚想起身,那人挥袖一拂,他觉得身子一僵,嘴也说不出话来,只有心中依然清醒。那人向他施礼说:"你算是位豪杰,被人激将来到这里。好胜乃是人之常情,也不该过份责怪你。既然承蒙光顾,本应稍稍尽些地主之谊。但今晚恰逢中秋佳节,家中的女眷都出来赏月。男女有别,实在不想让你看见。而如此夜深,你又无处可去。现在我想出一个办法,请君入瓮,希望不要见怪。里面有酒有菜,也希望不要嫌弃。"

这时又来了几个人,把郭某抬起放入一个大缸,上面盖上方桌,再压上巨石。过了一会儿,只听外面欢声笑语,约摸有几十个男女,劝酒上菜,热闹非凡。郭某忽然闻到酒香,这时手足也能活动了,就暗中摸索,发现缸里有一壶酒、一只杯子,四小碟菜肴,还有双象牙筷子。他正在饥渴之际,也顾不得许多,马上吃喝起来。随后听见几个童子绕缸唱起情歌,又有人敲着缸向里面说:"这是主人吩咐娱乐客人的。"那歌声倒也宛转入耳。过了许久,又有人敲着缸说:"郭先生请别见怪,大家都喝醉了,搬不动巨石。你暂且忍耐一会儿,你的朋友们马上就要来了。"说完,周围突然安静下来。第二天早晨,朋友们来找他,见大门紧闭,怀疑出了事,急忙翻墙而入。郭某听见人声,在缸里大叫起来。众人费尽力气才把巨石移开,让郭某爬出来。听完他叙述前天晚上的经历,大家不禁拍掌大笑。郭某回视缸中的用具,似乎是自己家的。等回家一问,前一天晚上家里正准备吃宴席,突然酒菜都不见了,如今正在一边怒骂,一边到处搜寻呢。那些鬼魅真够狡猾的,但这种恶作剧令人发笑而不使人愤怒。当郭某被人从缸里救出时,连他自己都禁不住笑起来。

还有一件事就不仅是开玩笑了。有位少年跟着老师在山中寺庙里读书。他听别人说寺庙小楼里住着狐女,常出来勾引人。他心想,狐女肯定姿色艳丽,便每天晚上到小楼下默默许愿,希望能有艳遇。一天夜里,他在树下徘徊,见到一个小丫鬟向他招手。他知道是狐女相招,欣然迎上前去。小丫鬟悄声说:"你是明白人,不需要我多说。我家娘子很喜欢你,可是这种事情怎么能公开祈求呢?主人很生气,但因为你是贵人,不敢加害,只能对娘子严加管束。今夜主人碰巧外出,娘子让我悄悄来找你。你跟我来。"少年跟着她,曲曲折折走了很久,都不是寺庙原有的路。到了一间屋前,门虚掩着,虽然里面没点灯,却能隐隐约约看见床帐。小丫鬟说:"娘子初次与你相会,有些怕羞,已在帐内躺下了。你只管把衣服脱了,悄悄上床去,别出声说话,免得让别的婢女听见。"说完她就转身离去。少年喜不自禁,上前一把掀开被子,抱住里面的人就亲嘴,那人却大叫起来。少年愕然倒退几步,定睛一看,周围房子都消失了,原来却是老师在屋檐下乘凉。老师惊怒之下,严厉地责打了少年。少年不得已吐露了真情,结果被老师赶走了。这才是真正的恶作剧。我的先师裘文达说:"郭某只是争强好胜,所以仅被鬼魅戏弄;这个少年则心怀邪念,所以被妖狐陷害。这两个人都是咎由自取,并不是妖怪有善恶之分。"

103. 狐女逃婚

有个候补官员在钓鱼台游览时,正赶上附近办庙会,街上有许多妇女。到了黄昏,车马渐稀,却见一位女子左手抱着婴孩,右手拿着拨浪鼓,娉娉袅袅地走来。她看见候补官,把手中小鼓摇了摇。他们相视一笑。候补官心很细,暗想:这位女子从装束看是富贵人家,却象村妇般抱着孩子独自走路,行为如此诡异,多半是狐魅。他便凑上前去攀谈。女子说到她丈夫过世了,儿子尚幼。候补官笑道:"你不用多说,我知道你是什么人,也不怕你。不过我比较穷,听说象你这样的人生财有道,要是能养活我,就跟你去。"女子听了笑道:"那就一起回家吧!"到了家,房子不算太宽敞,却也洁净华美。家里还有父母婆婆姐妹等人。在饭桌上,彼此心照不宣,也不相互询问姓氏和家族情况。酒足饭饱之后,候补官与女子同人鸳帐,共度良宵。

　　第二天他回了趟城,带来一个童仆和自己的被褥,从此就在女子家住下了。那女子淫荡无度,让他应接不暇,渐渐疲惫。而且她开始颐指气使,命他铺床叠被,侍候梳洗,整理衣裳,甚至端茶递

265

烟。过了一阵,她的婆婆姐妹也开始随便支使他,要他干这干那,象对待仆人那样。候补官贪财好色,只得默默忍受。终于有一天,女子让他打扫厕所,被他拒绝了。女子生气地说:"平时事事都依你,难道这点小事都不肯听我的吗?"其他几个女人也在旁帮腔,指责嘲笑他。从此两人的关系越来越紧张。随即那女子常常夜出不归,声称是亲戚留宿。又常常有客人来,都说是亲戚,却和她喝酒嬉笑,打情骂俏,而且不许他靠前。候补官表示愤怒,那女子也发怒了,转而笑道:"不这样,钱财从哪里来?让我不接客人容易,你来养活我一家三十多口就行了。你能做到吗?"候补官知道住不下去了,就带着童仆回城租了一处房子。等次日再回来,那所房子连同里面的一切衣服用具都消失了,只剩一片杂草丛生的荒地。候补官进京时虽带了几百两银子,但生性节俭,穿得颇为褴褛。后来忽然衣着鲜亮起来,让周围人觉得奇怪。等他解释说被招入赘,大家并未疑心。不料如今他又变得衣衫褴褛,而且不肯告诉别人是怎么回事。后来还是那个童仆泄露了其中的秘密。有人评论说:"那个狐女携带衣物逃走,按人世间的常理还说得过去。我见过有些人的所作所为远比这要过份。"

104. 狐狸抓差

郑州修筑水堤时,有个少妇抱着包袱在堤上走,好象很吃力,就坐到一棵柳树下歇脚。当时有几十个做工的也散坐在树下休息。那少妇自称从娘家回来,弟弟牵着驴相送,不料半道驴受了惊,把她摔到地下。弟弟进高梁地追驴,从早上追到中午还没回来。她家在西北面,离这儿有四五里远。她提出,如果有人能抱着包袱送她回家,就用一百个铜钱答谢。有个少年暗想,可以趁机在她身上占点儿便宜,即使不成,也能得到赏钱,于是就跟着她走了。

一路之上,少年不断用话调戏少妇,她既不答理,也不斥责。走了三四里,突然有七八个人拦住去路,其中一个叫道:"哪里来的狂徒,竟敢打我家女人的主意?"他们一拥而上,把少年绑起来一顿痛打,都说:"与其押送官府,不如把他就地活埋了吧!"少妇又诉说少年一路如何调戏,他无可辩解,只得再三乞求饶命。有个人说:"姑且饶了你,不过要罚你挖开这个田埂,把里面的水都排出去。"他们给少年一把铁锹,坐在旁边催促他挖泥。少年一直干到半夜,终于疏通了积水,那些人也都不见了。他环顾四周,芦苇丛生,附近并无村庄。有人怀疑是狐狸洞被水淹了,诱使少年来疏通。

105. 夫妻偷情案

郎中顾德懋,属于那种活着的时候就在冥司任职的人。他自称曾平反一桩冤案,颇为得意。当事人的姓名他不敢泄露,只说是有个妇人,被婆婆赶出家门。其实她并没有过错,而是被小姑说了坏话。婆婆很顽固,一时半会儿不可能回心转意。妇人娘家已经没有人了,实在走投无路,就出家当了尼姑。她丈夫时常来探望她,两人难免动情。尼姑庵旁边有个废弃的园子,她就让丈夫晚上到那儿的破屋里,她从院墙的缺口翻过去与他相会。就这样来往了一年多,终于被她师父发觉。她师父严守戒律,认为这种行为玷污了佛门圣地,不许她丈夫再来,否则就赶她走。从此她丈夫不再露面,她终日郁郁寡欢,不久竟死掉了。

到了阴间,冥官认为她既然遁入空门,就应遵守佛法,然而她却沉溺于情欲,违反戒律,应象任何犯淫戒的和尚尼姑一样被押入地狱。顾德懋反对道:"尼姑犯淫戒,自然有明确的处罚规定。然而当事人必须是起初自愿皈依佛门,中途违背誓约而受罚,这样她才无话可说。而这位妇人无辜被逐出家门,心里还期待着与丈夫重聚,只是因为孤苦无助才寄身尼庵。她剃发为尼,只可称之为毁容,不可称之为皈依佛法;她进入尼庵,只可称之为借宿,不可称之为安心参禅。至于她与丈夫情丝不断,翻墙幽会,虽说行为近于淫荡,但两人原本是同床共寝的夫妻,这和失节是两回事。人世间的法律对于未婚私通者只处以杖刑,还允许交钱免刑;这两人违背礼法的程度相比之下还要轻一些。更何况她已因此郁郁而死,就算有小过错,也足以抵销了。所以应该判她无罪,让她直接转世投生。这样于情于理似乎都说得过去。"他的意见报上去后,得到了阎罗王的批准。这件事的真假无从得知,但顾德懋的议论则是很公平的。后来,顾德懋临死之时对人说,他因为泄露冥司的事情太多,被贬为土地神了。

106. 黠盗自投罗网

李印是个台军,曾跟随一位官员在山中赶路,看见悬崖上有棵老松树,上面钉着一支箭,不知是怎么回事。晚上在驿站住宿,李印才对官员说,他上次经过那个地方时看见远处一骑飞驰而来。他怀疑是土匪,就埋伏在草丛中。等渐渐靠近,才看清是个似人非人的东西骑在马上,那马也是无鞍的野马。他意识到那是妖怪,就向它射了一箭,射中了,发出嗡然的钟声,那怪物化成黑烟逃走了。这回在老松树上见到那支箭,他才知道那原来是个树精。官员问:"当时你怎么不说?"李印答道:"我射中它时,它并没看见我。它既然成了精,我怕它听见我的话,追来报复。"由此可见李印行事之机警。

然而李印也有失手之时。一次他受命押送犯人满答尔。满答尔双手戴着铁手铐,两脚用铁链从马腹下面锁在一起。他当时病得奄奄一息,饭都难以咽下,骑在马上摇摇欲坠,幸亏双脚锁住才不至于跌下。李印只担心他死掉,而不担心他会逃跑。到了戈壁滩上,两马并行,眼看满答尔好象又要跌下马去,李印就伸手去扶他。不料他突然举起双手,用手铐把李印击下马,然后掉转马头逃跑了。原来满答尔一直在装病。后来,李印因此受到严厉的处分。但没过多久,满答尔又被抓到了,这次却是他自己送上门来的。原来,凡是前来自首的土匪都能得到丰厚赏赐,满答尔因为贪图钱财而自投罗网。问他为什么敢来,他说:"我身负重罪,应该没人想到我会来;我混在众人当中,应该不会被认出。"这话倒也有理,可他没想到额上的箭伤被人认出来了。以李印之心思细密,而不免被迷惑;以满答尔之老奸巨猾,而不免落入自设的陷阱。看来智者千虑,终有一失,惯于运用奇谋诡计的人终究会遇见克星。

107. 鬼打赌

有位老儒在一个寺庙里教学生。庙外有一片荒废的坟地,每当夜幕降临,常能看见鬼影儿,听见鬼说话。老儒胆子大,并不畏惧,连他的仆人们也习以为常了。一天晚上,他听见墙外有人说:"与您为邻这么久,知道您不避讳我们。曾听见您吟咏温庭筠的诗,想必手边有他的集子。请您把他的《达摩支曲》抄一份烧了。"然后,鬼又压低声音说:"最后一句'邺城风雨连天草',请把'连'改写成'粘',我将不胜感激。刚才为了争这个字,和别人打赌请客,希望您能帮我一把。"老儒恰好有温庭筠的诗集,就拿起来扔到窗外。大约过了一顿饭的工夫,外面忽然刮起一阵旋风,吹得树叶乱飞,泥沙象雨点一样洒落在窗子上。老儒笑骂道:"你们用不着如此胡闹,我这样做自有道理。双方打赌,必然有一方要输,输者必然心里怨恨。如果我改字招埋怨,我就理亏;如果我给出原诗招埋怨,我就有理,不管你们怎么闹,反正我问心无愧。"他的话音刚落,外面风就停了。有人评论说:"毕竟是读书鬼,尽管想作弊求胜,但还是能服之以理。不过老儒若不扔那本诗集,不就完全免掉纷争了吗?"另一人说:"你所说的是处世常理。可那老儒要是懂得处世常理,那他还是老儒吗?"

108. 农妇救狐

一户农家养着两条狗。有天晚上,狗突然叫得特别凶。农妇出门查看,外面并没来人。这时屋顶上一个声音说:"你家的狗太凶,我不敢下去。有个私逃的婢女藏在你家的炉灶里,麻烦你用烟把她熏出来。"农妇吓了一跳,连忙回屋查看,果然听到灶内有嘤嘤的哭泣声。农妇问里面是谁,为什么到此。灶内小声回答说:"我叫绿云,是刚才那个狐狸家的婢女。我忍受不了鞭打,逃到这里来,想多活几天,请可怜可怜我吧。"农妇向来吃斋礼佛,对狐女产生了恻隐之心,便走出去向着屋上说:"她害怕,不肯出来,我也不忍心用烟熏她。假如她没有太大的罪过,请你高抬贵手吧。"屋上回答说:"我花了两千钱刚买的,哪能白白放她走?"农妇说:"我用两千钱赎她可以吗?"过了一会儿,屋上才答道:"这倒可以。"农妇取来钱,扔到屋顶上,然后进屋敲着灶壁说:"绿云,你出来吧,我已经用钱把你从主人那里赎出来了。"灶内说:"多谢救命之恩,从今之后我就供您使唤吧。"农妇说:"人怎么能用狐狸作婢女,你还是走吧。注意别露出形迹,免得吓着家里的孩子。"果然有个黑东西从灶中窜出,一晃就不见了。以后每到新年,农妇就听到窗外叫道:"绿云给您叩头。"

109. 婢女遭狐戏

在张铉耳家,有天晚上一个婢女失踪,大家以为她逃走了,第二天却发现她醉卧在房后一间堆放柴草的屋子里。那个屋子平时上锁,不知她是怎么进去的。到中午她才醒过来,讲述了她的经历。头天晚上,她听见柴草屋里有嬉笑声,因为向来知道那儿住着狐狸,也不觉得害怕,就从门缝往里张望,只见桌上摆着酒肉,几个少年正在大吃大喝呢。他们发觉了她,跳起身来把她拉进屋。她只觉脑子突然木了,象做梦一般,话也说不出,任由他们拉去坐下,慢慢被灌醉,不知自己什么时候睡着,也不知那些少年什么时候离开的。

张铉耳性格刚直,亲自到那间屋子去斥责说:"相处多年,除了每天取柴草外,并没有冒犯。为什么突然干出这样无礼的事,强迫良家婢女陪酒?少年行为如此轻狂,长辈为何不加管教?难道不感到惭愧吗?"到了半夜,他听见窗外有人说:"儿辈行为放荡,我已责打过他们了。不过其中有个缘故要说明白。是那婢女先向屋里伸手要肉吃,并不是被强拉进去的。另外,她在花前月下,交了不止一个相好,早就不是贞洁的处女,所以儿辈们才敢和她调笑。要不然,你家还有几位姿色出众的婢女,他们怎么不敢对之无礼呢?管教不严的责任,你我似乎应该各担一半儿。"张铉耳说:"你既然责打了你的儿辈,我也会痛责那个婢女的。"窗外老狐笑道:"过了婚配的年纪,却不为她找人家,以至她干出伤风败俗之事,难道过错都在于她吗?"张铉耳听了默不作声。第二天,他就找来媒婆,把年纪较大的几个婢女都嫁了出去。

110. 两个捕狐人

王某张某两人都以捕狐为业,两家相距十余里。有一天,他们发现一处坟墓有狐狸的行踪,准备一起去捕捉,约定日落后在某处碰头。张某到达约定地点时,王某已先到了。两人来到坟墓旁,发现墓穴宽敞,可以容下人。王某让张某藏在穴中,自己则隐蔽在旁边树丛里,打算等狐狸归穴时,王某从外面断其后路,张某则在里面擒拿。张某一直等到夜里,却毫无动静。他想出去和王某商量一下该怎么办,却发现出口已被两块墓碑压住,只留出一点缝隙。墓碑很沉,他根本无力搬开。第二天,他听见外面有赶牛的声音,连忙大声呼救。牧牛人到他家中传信,这才请人搬开墓碑。张某怀疑王某想谋害自己,便带着家里人去找他,打算告官。

他们走到半道,看见王某被剥光衣服,反绑在柳树上,一群人围着他唾骂鞭打。原来,王某赴约时,在路上遇见个送饭的农妇向他调情,两人携手走进高粱地,开始宽衣解带。王某刚把衣服脱下,农妇跳起来抱着衣服就跑,不知去向。幸好周围无人,王某只得狼狈地往家赶。不料路上遇见一群人,举着火把,带着器械,见到他就大叫:"找到流氓了!"原来,王某邻居家有三四个少妇晚上睡在院中,忽然王某跑来,脱光衣服就在她们身边躺下。听见少妇们的惊叫,家里人起来查看,王某丢下衣服跳墙逃走了。王某被众人抓住辱骂殴打,无力辨白,只能呼天唤地而已。等见到张某,相互讲述各自经历,这才明白两人都被狐狸捉弄了。不过仔细想想,他们去墓穴伏击,原是想捕杀狐狸,而狐狸仅仅戏弄他们一场作为报复。张某被关在墓穴里一整夜,但给他留出了缝隙,使他不至于被闷死;王某被剥光衣服,挨了一顿痛打,不能为自己辨白,但那狐狸并未真正奸淫少妇,所以众人并不会把王某致于死地。狐狸的所作所为都是留有余地的。

111. 假如山川会说话

有位官员晚上走进书房,看见桌上放着一个人头,不禁大惊失色,视之为不祥之兆。正好附近有个道士擅长写符念咒,人家有丧葬事常请他。官员急忙把他请到家,让他占了一卦。道士脸色大变道:"卦象大凶!不过可以设法避开。只需花一百多两银子设坛祈祷就行了。"正在商议之时,听见窗外有人说:"我不幸被依法处决,身首异处。灵魂无首,就不能转生,所以我随身提着它,真是累赘得很。刚才看见您的桌子很干净,就偶然放在上面。您突然走来,我惊慌躲避,忘了把它拿走,以致使您受惊。这是我的失礼,与您的祸福并不相干。道士的胡言乱语请不要轻信。"道士听了这话,垂头丧气地走掉了。

还有一位官员家里闹狐狸。请了位术士来驱狐,他的法术不灵验,反而被狐狸捉弄了一番。他回去找师父,求来一道符,又要登坛招神将,只听楼上搬运声、招呼声响成一片,那些狐狸闹哄哄地都走掉了。术士环顾众人,满脸得意之色,官员全家也心怀感激。这时忽见墙壁上有一张帖子,墨迹未干,上面写道:"您衰运将至,因而我们敢于滋扰。昨天您捐了九百两银子修建育婴堂,感动了神明,也增加了您的福泽,我们只好搬走。术士作法恰逢其时,便把这算成他的功劳,自鸣得意。您招待他吃点儿东西,把他打发走,也就可以了;若要给他酬谢,未免太便宜无能小人了。"术士看了满面羞惭,一声不敢吭。民间有两句谚语说:假如山川会说话,风水先生就要丢饭碗;假如脏腑会说话,医生就要没钱赚。从上面两个故事看,鬼魅要是开口说话,术士还是小心为妙。

112. 京城骗术

人情狡诈,无过于京城。我曾买过十六块明代名家罗小华制作的墨锭,它们装在一个褪了色的漆匣里,看上去年代久远。回家一试,才发现是些染成黑色的泥条。又曾买过蜡烛,却点不着,原来是泥做的,外面抹上羊脂。又有人晚上在灯下卖烤鸭,我的堂哥买了一只。拿回家一看,鸭肉已被吃空,骨架里面填满泥巴,外面糊上纸,染上烤鸭的颜色,再涂上油,只有鸭掌和鸭头不是假做的。我们家的仆人赵平有一次花两千钱就买了双皮靴,觉得很划算。一天突然下雨,他换上靴子出门,却光着脚回来了。原来靴面是用油纸揉成皱纹,靴底则是用布包起的一堆破绵花。

上面那些例子还只算小骗术。曾有位候补官员见到对门的少妇姿色甚美,向邻人打听,说她丈夫在外地当幕僚,她和母亲住在一起。过了几个月,对面忽然白纸糊门,合家号哭,原来收到了她丈夫去世的消息。家中设了灵位祭奠,还请了和尚来做法事,追荐亡灵,颇有些人前来吊唁。渐渐地,那家就开始出卖衣服,据说吃不饱饭了,而且托媒人让少妇再嫁。这正中候补官下怀,他就入赘到她家中。又过了几个月,她丈夫突然回来了,这才知道原先的凶信是误传。她丈夫怒不可遏,定要告官。在母女苦苦劝解下,这才让候补官留下所有财物,把他赶出家门。过了半年,候补官在巡城御史那里见到少妇受审。原来,先归者是她的相好,两人合谋骗取候补官的钱财;等她丈夫回来,事情才败露。

西城一处宅院,有四五十间屋,每月租金二十多两银子。有个房客一连住了半年多,每月都提前付租金,所以房主也不去过问。一天,房客突然不告而别。房主赶去查看,那里已被拆成一片废墟,仅有两间街面房幸存。原来这所住宅前后都有门。房客在后门开店卖木材,却拆了里面的房子,把木料夹在里面卖掉。房主在前街住,所以不曾发觉。就这样把几十间屋子不知不觉都拆尽卖光,也算神乎其神了。不过从上面几件事看,被骗者或者贪便宜,或者图省事,不能完全归咎于人。钱文敏先生说:"和京城人打交道,时时要小心,不上当就算幸运了。要是遇上便宜事,其中必然有骗局。世上有那么多贪婪奸诈之徒,怎么会有便宜落到我们身上?"这话真是有道理。

113. 以贼攻贼

在沧州城南,强盗夜里抢劫了一家大户,把主人夫妇都抓住当人质,全家谁都不敢妄动。主人有个妾住在东厢房,换了身衣服悄悄跑到厨房里,对烧火的婢女说:"主人被强盗抓住,所以大家都不敢动手。他们在屋顶上也派人看守,以防有人救应,但他们看不到屋檐下。你跳出后窗,沿着屋檐出去,告诉仆人们赶紧带上器械,骑快马到三五里外埋伏起来。强盗四更后必然离开,否则天亮前就赶不回老巢。他们走的时候肯定押着主人当人质,但走了一二里地必定会放了他,否则就会暴露他们的去向。等主人被释放,赶紧把他背回家,其余众人跟在强盗后面,相距半里。强盗假如回身而战,你们就往回跑;等他们接着赶路,你们就继续跟踪。假如强盗再回身而战,你们就再往回跑。就这样一直跟到他们的老巢。强盗既不能战,又不能逃,等拖到天亮,一个都跑不掉。"烧火的婢女冒着生命危险溜出屋子,依样吩咐了家仆们。大家认为有理,就依计而行,果然把强盗全数抓获。那个烧火的婢女因此得到重赏。正妻原来与妾不和,经过此事也捐弃前嫌,两相和睦了。后来,她问妾怎么能想出那种办法,她流泪答道:"我的先父就是强盗头儿,他曾说过打劫时最怕对方用这种办法,却没人采用。这次危急关头,试用此法,竟然奏效。"所以说,用兵者务必要了解敌人。又说要以贼攻贼。

114. 求人帮忙,得不偿失

有户人家的一间空屋里住着狐狸,时常与主人谈天。他们互赠礼物,互借用具,相安无事,象邻居一般。有一天狐狸对主人说:"你别院的空屋里有个吊死鬼,许多年来一直住在那里。最近你把那屋子拆了,鬼无处栖身,竟跑来要强占我这间屋子。他经常露出凶相吓唬孩子们。这还不算,他还兴妖作怪,让孩子们患上寒热病,真让我不能忍受。附近道观里有个道士能治鬼,你能不能去求他来除掉这一害?"那人果然去求道士,带回来一道符,就在院子里烧了。没多久,暴风骤起,响起轰轰的声音,象打雷一样。主人正在惊愕之时,只听屋顶瓦片格格乱响,似乎有几十个人在上面奔跑。狐狸在屋上叫道:"我真是失策,如今后悔也来不及了!刚才神兵下临,鬼被绑走了,我也被驱逐。这就和你告别了!"有些人一时忍不下愤怒,只想痛快地报复一番,结果往往是两败俱伤。他们所犯的错误跟这个狐狸类似。

还有一个人,家里受到狐狸的骚扰,就请术士来镇治。狐狸被赶跑了,术士却贪得无厌,不断派些木头人、纸老虎到他家捣乱。送给术士一些钱财,才能获得暂时的安宁。过了十来天,术士又想出花招来勒索,闹得比狐狸还凶。那人没办法,带着全家搬到京城去住,这才摆脱了纠缠。有些人急于求胜,不惜向小人求助,最终总要吃小人的亏。上面这件事就是一个明证。

115. 侠妓

有个富人从不存金银,却积聚谷物,认为这样能防盗。康熙、雍正年间,当地连年歉收,米价昂贵。富人关闭粮仓不卖,想等价格再涨。

众人都很气愤,但也无可奈何。有个外号叫玉面狐的妓女说:"这件事好办,你们只管把买米钱准备好就是了。"她去拜访富人,对他说:"我是鸨母的摇钱树,却常常受到她的虐待。昨天和她吵了起来,她让我用一千两银子赎身。我也早就厌倦风尘,愿找一位忠厚之人托付终身。想来想去,没有人能比得上您。如果您肯出一千两银子,我情愿终生伺候您。听说您不喜欢存金银,折合成两千贯也可以。昨天有个木材商人听说此事,已回天津取钱去了,估计半月后能赶回来。我心里很不愿意嫁给那个庸俗的家伙。您如果在十天之内先付钱把事定下来,我会感恩不尽。"富人原来就迷恋这个妓女,听她这么一说,真是喜出望外。为了得到两千贯钱,他急忙开仓降价售谷。粮仓一开,买者从四面八方赶来,挡也挡不住,只好把平素积聚的谷子全都卖出。谷子卖完那天,妓女打发人去向富人道歉说:"鸨母抚养我多年,那天一时生气,要我赎身,如今悔过挽留,我不能拒绝。我们的约定就以后再说吧。"富人原先只和她口头约定,没有媒人,没有立字据,也没有付聘金,所以对她的反悔无可奈何。这位妓女当时只有十六七岁,竟能有如此义举,不愧为女侠。

116. 农妇的智谋

交河县有个农民被强盗诬陷为同谋,被捕入狱。他不知怎样为自己辨白,就请人去贿赂一个县吏,求他帮忙。县吏听说强盗之所以诬告,是因为他调戏过农人的妻子,被农人揍了一顿,就猜想那农妇一定美貌。于是他不肯收钱,对来人说:"这种机密的事情,必须让他妻子悄悄来找我一趟,我才能帮上忙。"听了中间人的回报,农人因怕死而丧失了志气,就请人把岳母找到狱中说明了缘故。老人回家跟女儿一说,就被她生气地拒绝了。

  过了几天,有人晚上到县吏家敲门。他开门一看,是个丐妇,用布包着头,穿着破衣烂衫,问话也不答。她径自闯进来,一边往里走,一边解开头巾,脱掉破衣,露出里面华美的装束。在县吏惊问之下,少妇脸泛红晕,低头不语,从袖中掏出一张纸。县吏拿到灯下一看,上面写着某某妻三个字。县吏大喜,把少妇带入内室,故意问她的来意。少妇擦着泪说:"我要是不明白你的意思,何必夜里来?既然来了,不必多问,只希望你别失信才好。"县吏听了赌咒发誓。于是两人当晚同睡。少妇留宿了数日,县吏神魂颠倒,惟恐不如她的意。少妇向他暂时告别,说自己在村里总受人欺侮,如果他能在县城中另外租处房子,让她搬过去,就能长相往来了。县吏更是喜出望外,于是尽全力为农人洗清了罪名。农人出狱后,见到县吏,神情冷漠。县吏以为他是因被迫献出妻子而心中羞愧。后来因事到村里,去农人家拜访,竟吃了闭门羹,这才知道农人与他绝交了,不由心中生怨。

这时发生了一件案子,有人用妓女诱人赌博被告发,判决妓女受杖后押解回原籍。县吏仔细一看,那妓女就是农人的妻子,就上前和她说话。少妇告诉他,自己被丈夫严加看管,无法与他相会,深感愧咎。现在有幸相逢,她希望县吏看在他们的数夜之情的份儿上,帮她免受杖刑和押解。县吏听了,不由心生一计,就去跟县官说:"妓女原先供出的是她父母家,她现在是某农人之妻,应该追究她丈夫的责任。"原来,他想让县官以官府名义将少妇拍卖,他可以趁机买下。可等县官把农人拘来,他却带着一个妇人,且说是他妻子。找同村人一问,都说不假。这时那妓女才说出真相。先前,县吏想逼奸农人的妻子。听了母亲的讲述,农妇左右为难,既不肯失身,又不能坐视丈夫屈死狱中。恰好附近新来一个妓女,农妇就脱下自己的衣饰送给妓女,请她冒名前往。如今妓女正要受刑时与县吏重逢,就依然假冒农妇,想借此免于杖刑。没想到县吏另有图谋,结果两人都败露了。县官重新审查了农人被控为盗一事,发现他果然冤枉。于是把农人夫妻放走,而严惩了县吏。世上奸猾之徒莫过于衙吏,而这个县吏却被一位村妇玩于股掌之上。一般地说,愚者斗不过智者;然而物极必反,所谓智者,也难免弄巧成拙,为人所败。天之道,损有余以补不足。假若智者始终不败,那么天地间就只剩下智者,没有愚者了,那怎么可能呢!

117. 吃人鬼

鬼有时害人至死,不知出于什么用意。有种解释说,鬼需要吃活人的魂。鬼是人的余气,难免渐渐减少,以至于消失;假如它能吸食活人的元气来补充自己,就能延长寿命。所以女鬼经常要勾引男子以摄取精气。至于男鬼,只能杀人吸食其生气。这两者都和狐狸媚人采补是同一个道理。

记得刘挺生说过,康熙五十九年,有五位举子一同赶路,晚上遇雨,在一所破庙里栖身。四人都已睡着,只有一人醒着。他忽然感到阴风森森,有几个黑影从窗口飘进来,先向那四个人吹气。随后又向自己吹气。刚开始他心里还清醒着,渐渐就觉得昏昏沉沉,身子好象被拖着走。等稍稍明白一些,他发现自己连同那四人都被捆住。他想叫,却出不了声。那几个鬼把其中一人抓住,大吃起来,不一会儿就吃掉了,然后又吃了两人。正要吃第四人时,从外面闯进一个老翁,厉声喝道:"你们这群野鬼,不许放肆!这两人将来有官运,你们怎么敢冒犯?"那几个鬼吓得赶紧跑掉了。剩下的两人都猛然清醒过来,讲起刚才梦中所见,完全相同。后来,他们一个当了教谕官,一个做了训导官。鲍敬亭先生听了这个故事,笑道:"我向来瞧不起这种官职,没想到鬼神还挺看重!"

118. 代鬼传信

书生朱立园于乾隆六年北上参加顺天乡试,晚上到达羊留店北边时,原想绕道避开泥泞之处,结果走迷了路,周围找不到旅店。他远远望见林子外面有人家,打算到那儿借宿。走到近前,见有六七间土墙瓦房。一个童子应声出来,朱立园说明自己想投宿。随即走出一位衣冠朴素而雅致的老翁,请他进去,把他安顿在厢房里,并叫人拿灯来。那灯显得黯然无光。老翁说:"收成不好,油质也很差,让人心烦,但也没有办法。夜深了,来不及准备饭菜,就请喝点薄酒,千万不要嫌弃。"他表现得非常殷勤。朱生园问他家里还有什么人。老翁答道:"我孤苦伶仃,只有老伴和仆人婢女陪我住。"当他听说朱立园要北上进京时,就说:"有封信和一点东西,想送到京城,苦于此地太偏僻,邮路不通。今天能遇见你真是太幸运了。"朱立园问:"你一家住在这里,四处没有邻居,不觉得害怕吗?"老翁说:"这里有几亩薄田,让仆人们耕作,我也就住在这儿了。反正家里没什么值钱东西,也不怕盗贼。"朱立园说:"听人说旷野里鬼比较多。"老翁说:"我倒是没见过鬼。不过既然你害怕,我就陪你坐到天亮吧。"他借了朱立园的纸笔,回到内室去写信,然后封在信封里,用旧布包上,外面密密地缝好。他把包裹交给朱立园,嘱咐道:"地址已经写在信封上,到京城你拆开一看就知道了。"第二天黎明,朱立园起身告别,老翁又嘱咐说千万别把信弄丢了,这才依依分手。

朱立园到了京城,把布包拆开,见到金簪和银镯各一副,信封上写着朱立园先生启。信中写道:"我年老无子,误听妻子的话,把女婿当后嗣。到了外孙那一辈,还偶然祭祀我一回,后来就不再把我当先人。纸钱、麦饭早就无人上供了,这座孤坟也快要倒塌。我在九泉之下真是痛苦万分,追悔莫及。我拿出区区的殉葬物,请求你把它们卖掉,在回来的路上用卖得的钱修一下坟,并稍微疏通南边的水道,以免坟让水淹了。如果你能够照我的请求去做,来世我定会报答大恩。我知道你怕鬼,就在暗中向你行礼,不再现形,请不要有什么疑虑。"信后署名是"亡人杨宁"。朱立园这才知道遇见了鬼,吓得浑身直冒冷汗。因为信中提到"回来的路上",他推测自己这回要落榜,后来果然如此。回程路过羊留店,他打发仆人用卖簪镯得来的钱去修整老翁的坟墓,自己没敢再到那儿去。

119. 道士驯悍妻

有个人到了四十多岁还没有儿子,家有悍妻,坚决不让他纳妾。为此他总是闷闷不乐。有一回,他来到附近一所道观,有个道士对他说:"瞧你面色凝重,好象有什么心事。道家向来以助人济世为己任,你何不说出你的烦恼,也许我能帮你呢!"那人觉得道士的话很奇怪,就如实相告。道士说:"这事我其实早已听说,只是想向你证实一下。如果你能请人制作十多套鬼卒的衣装,我就能为你出力。要不然找戏子借一下也可以。"那人愈发惊异。他觉得道士不大可能骗人,因为把那些衣装骗去也没什么用,于是答应照办。当晚,他妻子开始做恶梦,叫也叫不醒,而且梦中不断呻吟惨叫。第二天,发现她两腿发青。问她,她不答,只是叹气。同样的事情三天后又发生了。此后每隔三天,她就做一回恶梦。半个月后,妻子忽然命令仆人出去找媒婆,要为丈夫买妾。众人都不信,她丈夫也迟疑不定,怕她出尔反尔。随后,她接连几天昏昏沉沉,醒来更为着急地催着买妾。她把仆人们招来,桌上摆着所需银两,对他们说:三天之内买不到妾就要重责,买到妾而姿色不佳也要重责。瞧她那样子,不象假装。于是买来了两个女子,都被妻子留下了。她当晚就把新房布置好,催促丈夫进去。大家都很吃惊,她丈夫也惘惘然,仿佛身在梦中。

后来,他又见到那位道士,这才知道他有摄魂的法术。晚上他让道众换上鬼装,自己打扮成冥官的模样,把那妇人的魂招来,告诉她,她丈夫的先人在冥司控告她使丈夫绝后,然后打了她一百桃杖,限期让她为丈夫纳妾。妇人起初以为是偶然做恶梦,但以后每隔三天就重复一次。有几天她一直昏昏沉沉,就是被道士摄去,吊了起来,往鼻子里灌醋,并警告她说:三天之内找不到漂亮女子,就把她打入地狱。按说勾摄灵魂算不得正法。但归根结底,法术并无邪正之分,关键看如何运用。象那位悍妇,既不能晓之以理,又不能绳之以法,道士却能用法术制她,这就是所谓一物降一物。

120. 老狐仗义执言

一次,刘拟山家里丢了金镯子。小女仆在拷问之下,承认偷走卖给收旧货的了。问她收旧货人的长相打扮,去找却没有找到,就继续拷打。正在这时,顶棚上传来一声轻轻的咳嗽,说:"我在你们家住了四十年,从来不露丝毫形迹,所以你们从未察觉。今天我却实在忍不住要说话了。那金镯子难道不是夫人检点杂物时误放在漆盒里了吗?"赶紧去找,果然不错。然而这时小女仆已被打得体无完肤了。刘拟山为此终生愧悔,常告诫自己说:"时时难免犯这种错,怎能处处有这样的狐狸?"后来他为官二十多年,审案子时从来不动刑。

121. 救人遭鬼怨

仆人王发一天夜里打猎归来,在月光下看见一人被另外两人各抓住一条手臂,东拉西扯,却听不到声音。王发以为那两人是趁着夜黑抢人衣物,就对天上放了一枪,那两人慌忙奔散,中间那人却往村中跑去,三人都在瞬间消失。王发这才意识到那几个都是鬼。到了村口,看到一家点着灯,人声嘈杂,说是新娘子上了吊,刚被救醒。那位少妇:"婆婆让我做饼当晚饭,不料被狗叼走了两三张。婆婆以为我偷吃了,使劲儿抽我的耳光。我有冤无处讲,呆呆站在树下。这时有个妇人来劝我说:'受这样的委屈,还不如死了的好。'我正在犹豫不决,又有一个妇人,也来劝我自杀。我迷迷糊糊,不由自主就解带上吊了,那两个妇人还上前帮我。起初闷塞不堪,说不出地难受,后来恍惚觉得睡了过去,身子飘出门外。一个妇人说:'我先劝她的,她应该代替我。'另一个妇人说:'要不是我来劝,她不会最后下决心,她应该代替我才是。'两人正在争吵,忽然一声响雷,火光四照,两个妇人都吓跑了,我这才回来。"

　　后来,王发在晚上回家的路上,时常听见远远有妇人哭骂的声音,说他坏了她们的事,发誓要取他的性命,但他并不害怕。这天晚上,他又听见哭骂声,就呵斥道:"你杀人,我救人,就算告到神那里,我照样理直气壮。你敢杀就杀,何必拿大话吓唬人!"从此他就听不到那声音了。看来,救人性命,也能招来凶手的怨恨,难怪遇事袖手旁观者居多。这个仆人也算难得了。

122. 调戏狐妻的后果

有个商人和一个狐狸关系不错。狐狸常请他到家中作客,房舍和普通人家没什么两样,只是出门回头再看,房子就不见了。一天晚上,他在狐狸家喝酒,狐妻出来斟酒。她容貌十分俏丽。商人有几分醉,不由心旌荡漾,伸手捏了捏她的手腕。狐妻看了丈夫一眼,他只微微一笑,并不动怒,依旧谈笑风生。

商人回到住处后,有天早上一个家奴忽然牵着驴把他妻子驮来,说得到急信,说他中风了,所以借了条驴连夜赶来。商人吃了一惊,猜想是同伴的恶作剧。旅店没有多余的地方让妻子住,他就想让家奴把她送回去,但家奴已经走掉了。当地距家不到一天的路程,他只好自己牵着驴子送妻子回去。走到半路,一位少年从旁经过,用手摸了妇人的脚。妇人怒声喝骂,少年笑嘻嘻地道歉,又说些挑逗的话。商人忍无可忍,和少年打了起来。驴受了惊吓,跑上岔道,很快消失在高粱丛中。商人放过少年,急忙追赶妻子,沿路赶了一会儿,发现驴陷在泥淖中,妻子却不见了。他四处搜寻,折腾了一整夜。第二天拂晓,他骑着驴子往家走,打算到家再想法寻找妻子。没走几里地,听见路边有人大叫:"贼在这儿呢!"原来附近村子前一天有条驴被偷,正四处搜寻呢。众人把商人抓住,捆绑起来拷打。幸亏遇上认识的人,多方求情,才放了他。他垂头丧气回到家中,发现妻子正在纺线。问起昨晚的事,她茫然不知。商人这才意识到那妇人、家奴和少年都是狐狸变的,只有驴是真的。狐狸的报复确实厉害,但商人也是咎由自取。

123. 祈祷招妖

沧州前锋营有个人的女儿叫平姐,十八九岁尚未订亲。有一天她出门买脂粉,受到一个少年的调戏。她怒骂了几句,转身回家。父母连忙出去瞧,路上却没有人,邻居们也说没见到那个少年。到了晚上,平姐插上门准备睡觉,少年忽然出现在灯前。平姐知道他是妖怪,既不惊呼,也不搭话,却拿着一把锋利的剪刀假装睡觉。那少年不敢靠近,只是站在床边,花言巧语地引诱,平姐却毫不理睬。少年突然离开,过了片刻又回来,把几十件金银首饰放在床上,平姐连看都不看。少年把东西留下,径自走掉了。天快亮的时候,少年又出现了,对平姐说:"我盯了你一整夜,你竟然没有过去看一眼。人如果不为利所动,那么他不想干的事情,神也无法勉强,何况象我这样的妖魅呢?我误会了你私下的祝祷词,以为你只是拿父母作借口,所以我才会来找你。请你不要见怪。"说完,少年拿起东西就走了。原来,平姐家中贫困,母亲年老多病,父亲的俸禄不够养家,所以她有一回在佛前暗暗祈祷,希望早日找到个夫婿,以赡养父母,不料被那妖怪偷听去了。由此看来,说一句话,起一个念头,冥冥之间都会被察觉,在人前摆出一副假面孔又有什么用呢?

124. 鬼卒偷食

孙虚船尚未及第时,曾在一户人家教私塾。正值主人的母亲病危,小童给他送来晚饭。他因为手上有些事情,就让先放在旁边屋子里。忽然他瞥见一个白衣人闪身走进那间屋。正在他疑惑之时,又有一个穿黑衣的小个子也转进那间屋。他走过去一瞧,见那两人正坐在桌前大吃,就厉声呵斥。白衣人赶紧逃掉了,这时孙虚船已经堵在门口,黑衣人来不及出去,就跑到墙角躲起来。孙虚船拉了把椅子坐下,看他下一步会做什么。这时,主人慌慌张张跑过来对他说:"刚才有鬼附在我母亲身上讲话,说是冥司派了两个鬼卒来拘人,其中一位被先生您挡住门,出不来。假若误了期限,死者在冥司会被治罪的。我不知是真是假,就过

283

来看一看。"孙虚船听了,往后退了几步,看见那黑衣人狼狈地跑了出去,随即内室响起哭声,主人的母亲咽气了。尽管冥司法律森严,冥官洞察秋毫,勾魂鬼卒还是敢在垂死病人家偷吃酒食。人间的官吏衙役就更需要严加督察了!

125. 真假仙人

要说世上没神仙,有人却遇见过。可要说有神仙,却很少有人能碰上。自汉代以来,记载神仙之事的书不下百部,其中提到的神仙不下千人。古人提过的神仙,却与后人无缘。后人所见的神仙,总是另有其人。莫非那些所谓神仙仅仅保存了精气,得以延年,最终还是难逃一死?还有,神仙好清静,方士喜幻术,原本不属同类。那些书却不加区分地把一切会幻术的都称为神仙。有位姓王的老妪是房山人,家住深山。她曾经给我母亲讲了这么一件事。山中有个道人,大约六七十岁,住在一座小庵里,捡山果为食,渴了就喝泉水,整日整夜敲着木鱼念经,从来不与人来往。有人到庵中与他攀谈,他不太答话,送东西也不要。老妪有个侄子在外给人帮工。一天晚上,他回家看望母亲,路过小庵。道人见了他大惊道:"深夜老虎已经出来了,你这时候赶路多危险啊!我得送你一程。"于是他就敲着木鱼在前面带路。走了不到半里,果然跳出一只老虎。道人挺身而出,挡住少年,那老虎见了掉头就跑开了。道人话也没说,转身走了。后来,道人突然不见去向。他或许是个神仙吧?

我的堂叔张梅庵说,他曾见人让一个童子登上三层楼,然后伸手一招,童子从楼上翩然而下,毫发无损。这人还能把铜盂沉入溪水,然后张嘴一喊,那铜盂就缓缓浮出水面。然而这些都是方士的法术,不是神仙所为。舅舅张健亭说,有一农人正在野外牧牛,突然那几头牛都倒地而死。恰好有位道士路过,对农人说:"这些牛不是真死,而是灵魂被妖怪勾走了。先把我这药灌进去,保住脏腑不坏,我再设法为它们招魂。"道士被农人请回家,绕着圈子施法术。过了一会儿,那些牛果然都活了过来。农人留道士吃饭,道士不理,径自走了。有知情人说:"那个道士先把毒草放在草地里,然后用解药把牛救活。他不要酬谢,是假装不图财,以便将来能骗更多的钱。我在外地见过这个道士行骗。"这话一传出,那道人就没再出现。看来方士中间,也有不会法术的骗子,怎么能把这些人一概称作神仙呢!

126. 假狐女媚死人

京城有个富贵人家的少年,身材蠢笨,步履蹒跚,总是不修边幅,满面污垢。尽管如此,他却喜欢出入青楼,路遇女子必要驻足凝视。有一天他独自走着,见到一位楚楚动人的少妇。当时刚下过雨,路上泥泞难行,他便上前挑逗说:"路这么滑,要不要我扶你一把?"少妇正色道:"你不要胡来。我是狐女,平生只是拜月修炼,从不媚人采补。你瞧瞧自己那模样,竟敢这样对我无礼,小心惹祸上身!"说完,她抓起一把沙子朝他脸上扔去。少年吓得倒退几步,失足掉到沟里。等他费力爬出来时,少妇早已不见踪影了。他心里惴惴不安,担心狐女报复,但这并没有发生。

几天后,一位朋友请他吃饭。宴席上有个妓女出来斟酒。他凝神一看,正是先前在路上遇见的少妇,便立刻不安起来,终于忍不住问道:"某日雨后,你是不是去过东村?"那妓女不经意地答道:"那天我姐姐去东村走亲戚。我们姐妹俩长得挺象,你见到的是不是她?"少年听她含糊其辞,搞不清她究竟是人还是狐,就找了个借口离席而去。等他走后,妓女讲述了那次遭遇,说:"当时实在讨厌他那副丑样子,怕他上来强行无礼,所以就编个谎话以便脱身。幸好他自己跌了一跤,我趁机躲在一堆柴草后面。不料他竟然把我的话当真了。"众人听了无不捧腹大笑。一个客人说:"既然你已干上这一行,怎么能对客人挑三拣四?他可是个能千金买笑的富家子弟,你干嘛不去和他认识一下?"于是带着妓女到那少年家,说出她丈夫是谁,公婆是谁,把事情讲明。妓女又甜言蜜语一番,说从小就认识少年,那日承蒙他上前搭话,一时高兴,开了个玩笑,不料反致冒犯,真是万万过意不去。今天特来与他同床共枕,以赎罪过。她谈吐娴雅,妙态横生。

少年听了,不禁心花怒放,留下妓女连住了好几夜,随后把她丈夫找来,商量好把她包下,按月付钱。就这样,少年和妓女狎昵无度,竟然染上了消渴症,过了一年多就死掉了。我哥哥晴湖评论说:"狐具人形,少年就害怕,担心丢掉性命。人具狐性,少年就不怕,甚至连性命都不顾,尽管那少妇警告过他别惹祸上身。所以他虽然狎妓身亡,但说他死于狐魅也未尝不可。"

127. 妻作妾

沧州上河涯有两户小康人家。甲家的女儿许给了乙家的儿子,婚期定在一两年内。有位算卦的行路遇雨,在甲家借宿,甲就让他给女儿测测命。算卦的沉思良久,最后说:"我的卦书没有带在身边,不好推算。"甲察觉其中有异,就追问下去。算卦的终于说:"据她的生辰八字来看,命里注定要给人作妾,可按照你们家的情形,似乎不该如此。况且听说婚期已经定下,她又没有夫死再嫁的命,所以愈发难以判断。"

有个狡猾的家伙听说此事,想从中牟利,就跑来对甲说:"你们家本来就不富裕,又要给女儿准备一大笔嫁妆,那日子就更不好过了。既然女儿命中注定要作妾,不如对外谎称她病了,再说她死了,买个空棺材埋起来。然后你夜里离家,把女儿带到京城,更改名姓,卖给富贵人家作妾,这样就能得到一大笔钱。"甲认为这主意不错。正好这时有位高官要嫁女儿,征求美女作为姬妾陪伴小姐。甲趁势把女儿卖了二百两银子。过了一个多月,高官带着女儿坐船南下。不料走到天妃闸,船失事沉没,高官全家葬身鱼腹,只有甲的女儿获救。因为是个未婚少女,当地无人敢收养,就报告了官府。询问起她家里情况,因为她到高官家没多久,只知其姓氏,不知其职位和原籍,于是说出了自己父母的姓名住处。官府移文到沧州,甲家女儿诈死的骗局就此败露。

当时,乙家儿子已经和表妹结婚,不可能再退亲。乙听说甲把女儿卖了许多银子,气愤地要去告官。甲在窘迫之下,表示愿意同乙家恢复婚约。这一来,表妹家又不干了,也要告官。眼看事情就要闹大,甲乙两家的亲戚朋友们出面调解,让甲出钱把女儿接回来,嫁给乙的儿子为妾。甲的女儿回到家中,乙的儿子就来迎亲了。乙用牛车把甲的女儿接到家。她见到婆婆苦苦辨白,说诈死之事并非出于自己本意。婆婆说:"既然你不情愿,当初卖你时,你为什么不明说自己已经有丈夫了?"姑娘无言以对。让她拜正妻时,她稍一迟疑,婆婆就说:"你卖身为妾时,难道就不拜正室了吗?"姑娘又无言以对,只得接照规矩拜了下去。婆婆终生把她象奴婢一样对待。这是雍正末年的事。我的祖母对这件事知道得很详细,曾对婢女们说:"那女孩的父亲不过是想多得些银子,她也不过是想过上富贵日子,所以才想出那么个计策。谁知弄巧成拙,把原属于自己的福分也失掉了!你们要是明白其中道理,就不再会痴心妄想了。"

128. 杨横虎

殷赞庵是个外科医生,一次到深州给人看完病,主人派个姓杨的仆人送他回家。杨某性情暴戾,外号"横虎"。一路之上他不停地寻衅找事,没有一天不跟别人发生争执。这天傍晚,他们来到一个村子,旅店全部客满,只好去庙里投宿。和尚对他们说:"佛殿后面空着三间屋子,但实不相瞒,那里常有妖怪作祟。"杨某一听,怒道:"什么妖怪敢冒犯我杨横虎!我正想找它呢!"他让和尚把其中一间屋子打扫干净,和殷赞庵一起住了进去。殷赞庵胆子小,靠墙睡在床里边;杨某则睡在外侧,点着蜡烛等待怪物出现。夜深人静之时,果然有呜呜的声音由远而近,随即一位美丽的少妇飘然而至。

她刚到床前,杨某一跃而起,一把将她搂住,开始轻薄起来。少妇突然变成吊死鬼的骇人模样。殷赞庵见了,吓得浑身发抖,牙齿打战。杨某却不慌不忙,笑道:"你虽然面目可憎,下身想来跟常人没什么两样,先让我乐一回再说!"说着,他左手搂住少妇的背,伸右手扯下她的裤子,要把她按到床上。那鬼大叫一声,往外就跑。杨某追在后面喊她,那鬼却再也没敢露面。于是两人安睡到天明。临走时,杨某对和尚说:"这间屋真是不错。我过几天回来,还要住这儿,请不要留别的客人。"殷赞庵跟朋友讲起此事,说:"世上竟然有人要强奸吊死鬼!横虎这个外号确实不是浪得虚名。"

129. 鬼报夺妻之仇

诡计多端,机巧百出的人也有败露的时候;财大气粗,仗势横行的人也有倒霉的一天。但有的人既诡计多端,又财大气粗,并不惜花费钱财来实施诡计,那就难以追究了。景州人李露园讲了下面这件事。在河北和山东交界处有个富人死了妻子,见到本乡有个新出嫁的少妇,暗中喜欢上了。他派一个老妇人在少妇家旁边租了房子住下,千方百计去游说,并用重金贿赂少妇的公婆,让他们以不孝的罪名休了儿媳,却把真相瞒着儿子。然后他又另派一个素来与少妇家相识的老妇人,用重金贿赂其父母,让他们假意把少妇送回婆家。公婆也假装回心转意,留他们吃饭,并允许少妇回来。随即双方话不投机,吵了起来,少妇重被赶回娘家。这一切安排,少妇也都毫不知情。就这样,两家关系破裂,同谋休少妇之事就被掩盖得无迹可寻。然后就有两个老妇人出面,给少妇和富人做媒。富人表示不愿意,说担心少妇不孝;女家也表示不愿意,说觉得两家贫富悬殊。这样一来,富人谋娶少妇的计策更加不露痕迹。又过了一些日子,再有亲友从中撮合,亲事终于定了下来。

少妇的前夫虽然贫穷,却出身士族。在父母逼迫之下,他把无辜的妻子休掉,因而忧郁成疾,但还期待着破镜重圆。当他听说原妻再嫁日期已定,竟然悲愤而死,鬼魂到富人家里作祟。新婚之夜,他在灯前现形扰乱,不让双方同床共枕。连续数日都是如此。富人要与少妇在白天同房,她听了非常生气,流着泪拒绝了。富人没有办法,请了个术士来驱鬼。术士登坛烧了符,指挥叱咤之间,好象看见了什么,马上起身告辞说:"我能驱妖邪,不能逐冤魂。"富人又请了和尚作法事,超度亡灵,也不灵验。富人忽然想到此人是个孝子,所以当初妻子被逐时不敢违抗,于是再次贿赂了他父母,让他们赶他走。父母虽然心疼儿子,但更贪图钱财,就一起来骂他。鬼哭道:"被父母驱赶,我自然不敢再住下去。我要到冥司去告状。"从此冤鬼不再显形。过了不到半年,富人竟死掉了。或许那鬼在冥司告赢了官司吧!富人使用的手段,就算包公复生也不能洞察。而且他仗着钱多,居然能成功地驱鬼,心计算得上巧妙了。然而他最终逃不了冥司的审判。听说他前后花了数千两银子,只换得一时的快活,却把命搭上了。这与其说是巧妙,不如说是蠢笨之极。

130. 能说会道的婴儿

轮回之说,确有其事。恒兰台的叔父才几岁的时候,就自称前世是城西万寿寺的和尚。他从未到过那里,但能用笔大略画下它的殿廊门径,佛像陈设,以及花草树木的布局。别人去那里对照着一看,完全符合。但不知为什么,他从不肯去万寿寺。这是真正的转世轮回。

朱熹认为,轮回是偶然现象,是人死之后,生气未尽,遇上机缘就再次转生。这种情况也是有的。我们家在崔庄有个佃户叫商龙,他的儿子刚死就转生在邻居家。那个婴儿未满月就能说话。新年那天,父母偶然外出,把他留在襁褓中。这时有同村人敲门来贺岁。婴儿听出了对方的声音,就在屋里答道:"是某某大叔吗?我父母出去了,房门没锁,请进来坐一会儿吧。"外面的人听了,又是吃惊又是好笑。然而过了不久那婴儿就夭折了。朱熹所说的轮回,大概就指这类情形吧。天下的事情千变万化,天下的道理也无穷无尽,不能依照自己的所见所闻,只强调某一点。

131. 英雄难过美人关

德州人李秋崖曾与几个朋友一起赴济南参加乡试。这天晚上到旅舍投宿,安排给他们的屋子相当破旧。旁边的院子有两间屋,看上去比较整洁,但门锁着。他们责怪主人不让他们住到那里,怀疑他想留给有钱的客人。主人解释说:"那房子里有妖魅,不知道是鬼是狐,好久没人住了,所以显得整洁一些。并不是我把客人分成三六九等。"李秋崖的一个朋友强迫主人开了锁,独自住了进去。临睡前,他夸口说:"你要是男妖,我就和你较量力气;你要是女妖,就来陪我睡觉。千万别吓得不敢出来!"他说完就吹灭蜡烛上床睡觉。

等到夜深人静之时,窗外有人小声说:"陪你睡觉的人来了!"他刚想起身查看,猛然间一个巨物压到他身上,重若盘石,让他几乎喘不过气来。他伸手一摸,那东西浑身长着长毛,还呼呼喘着粗气。此人天生力气大,就与怪物搏斗起来。怪物力气也很大,两人相互抱持着在屋里滚来滚去。别人听见响动都来探视,但因为门插着,进不去,只能听着里面的打斗声。过了一阵,怪物被击中要害,嗷地叫了一声逃走了。这人把门打开,见大家围在外面,就眉飞色舞地讲述刚才的情形,颇为自得。当时刚打过三更鼓,大家便各自回去睡觉。

这人正要朦胧睡去,又听窗外小声说:"陪你睡觉的人真的来了!刚才想来找你,被哥哥拦住,硬要和你较量力气。如今他羞愧难当,不敢再露面,我这就来陪你了。"话音未落,那女子已到了床前,伸手摸这人的脸。他感到她手指纤纤,肌肤细腻,脂粉香气迎面扑来。尽管知道对方不怀好意,他却喜欢她的柔媚之态,打算先和她共寝,再见机行事。于是把她拉入怀中,尽情缠绵。正当他极度欢畅之时,那女妖腹中突然往里一吸,他立刻觉得心神恍惚,昏然不醒人事。第二天早上,别人敲不开他的屋门,就破窗而入,往他脸上喷凉水,这才将他弄醒。他此时浑身无力,象生了场大病。把他送回家,吃了半年药,才能拄着拐杖走路。从此他豪气顿消,再也不象从前那样斗志昂扬了。他的勇力足以战胜强暴,却最终败于妖媚。欧阳修说过:"祸患常生于忽微,智勇多困于所溺。"确实如此啊!

132. 妓女巧认情郎

我在乌鲁木齐时,听军吏巴哈布讲了这么件事。甘肃有个姓杜的老翁,日子很富裕。他居住的地方临近旷野,周围有许多狐狸和獾的巢穴。这些兽类常在夜里嗥叫,老翁很厌恶,就用烟把它们都熏跑了。随后家里人看见里屋、厅堂,凡是行走坐卧之处,都有一个老翁,加起来共有十多个。他们的声音、相貌、服饰完全一样,而且同样使唤仆人。全家陷入一片混乱,妻妾都插上门自保。

这时,妾想起杜老翁腰间系有绣囊,可以据此辨别真伪。不料那些老翁都没有绣囊,看来是预先被偷走了。有人向妻妾出主意说:"到了晚上老翁一定要来睡觉,你们都别让他进屋。如果他转身回去,就是真的;如果他硬往里闯,就是妖怪。"依计而行,那些老翁被拒之门外后都转身离去。又有人出主意说:"让他们轮流坐在厅房里,派个仆人从旁边走过,假装失手打破一件东西,看他有什么反应。如果他非常痛惜,厉声责骂,就是真的;如果他漠然无动于衷,就是妖怪。"依计而行,那些老翁见到打碎东西都显得很痛惜,厉声责骂肇事的仆人。就这样闹腾了一昼夜,还是没辨出真假。

杜老翁宠爱一个妓女,隔三岔五在她那里留宿。她听说了发生的事情,就来拜访说:"妖怪有党羽,凡是可以言传的,它们都能相互报信。不如让他们都来我家。反正我是青楼女子,无所顾惜。

让一名壮士手执巨斧站在床前,我脱衣上床,再让那些老翁依次与我交合。在抚摸偎倚之间,动作的辗转屈伸,轻重缓急,有些是只能意会,不可言传,连杜翁自己都说不清,妖怪就更不会知道了。我一叫'砍',壮士手起斧落,妖怪肯定逃不了。"众人按照她的建议做了安排。一位老翁上得床来,刚掀开被子进去,妓女就大叫:"砍!"壮士斧头落下,老翁脑瓜破裂,果然现出狐狸的原形。又进来一位老翁,稍一迟疑,妓女又叫:"砍!"吓得他抱头鼠窜而去。轮到第三位老翁,妓女抱住他高兴地说:"真人在此,其余的一概杀掉!"家人们刀杖并举,把那些假老翁杀死大半,都是狐和獾变的。那少数逃走的再也没敢露面。野兽夜里嚎叫,算不上对人的侵犯,杜老翁却硬要驱逐它们,实在是自取其扰。那些狐獾既然能够变化成人,为什么不面见杜老翁,劝说他手下留情?却非要到杜家兴妖作怪,最后大多被杀,也是自取其死。无论杜老翁还是狐獾,心智都比不上那位妓女啊!

133. 转世为猪

有位老和尚路过屠市,忽然泪流满面。有人见了奇怪,问他是怎么回事。老和尚答道:"说来话长。我能记起两辈子的事情。我曾是个屠夫,三十多岁死去,魂被几个鬼卒绑起来带走了。冥官责备我杀业太重,判我来世受恶报。随即我就觉得恍惚迷离,酷热难耐。猛然全身一阵清凉,发现自己在猪圈里。断奶后,见到猪食,明明知道不干不净,却因为饥火难忍,五脏好象要被烤焦一般,只好去吃。后来渐渐学会了猪语,经常与同类交谈,它们当中很多都还记得自己上辈子的事,只是无法对人讲。大家差不多都知道最终要被屠宰,经常愁苦地呻吟,因悲伤而眼中含泪。躯体笨重,夏天怕热,躺在泥水里才稍微好受些,但很少有那样的机会。因为体毛稀疏,冬天怕冷,看到狗和羊长着长毛,觉得它们简直是仙兽。受捆绑时,自知难免一死,却仍要跳跃逃避,只希望能多活片刻。被人追到,一脚踩在头上,四蹄被绳索捆住,深深勒到肉里,好象刀割一般疼痛。然后被装车运走,与同伴重叠相压,肋骨几乎折断,肚子差点挤破。有时又被人倒挂在竿子上扛着,那就更加痛苦难忍了。到了屠市,被重重扔在地上,摔得心脾欲碎。同伴们有的立即就被屠宰,有的还要等上几天。那时见到刀俎在左,汤锅在右,不知被杀之时,会有怎样的痛苦,浑身不停地发抖。有时想到自己死后任人切割,变成不知谁家的碗中食,心里不禁凄惨欲绝。等到受戮之时,屠夫刚一牵拉,就差点吓昏过去,全身瘫软,魂好象从头顶飞出,随即又落了下来。屠夫先用刀割开喉咙,往盆中放血,那种痛苦难以言表。求死不得,唯有长嚎。直到血快被放光,屠夫才把刀刺入心脏,只感到一阵剧痛,随即不能出声,又象当初转生时那样恍惚迷离。过了不知多久,才清醒过来,发现自己已转世为人,这就是现在的我。刚才看见那头猪被宰,它那痛苦万分的样子让我想起自己的经历,又想到现在的操刀人将来会受到的报应,不由得悲从中来,泪流满面。"屠夫听了和尚的话,当时就把刀扔在地上,从此改行卖菜去了。

134. 给鬼作记号

有位老儒在亲戚家借宿,恰好主人的女婿也来了。他是个无赖少年,与老儒格格不入,两人谁都不愿和对方同住,于是老儒被安排到另外一间屋子。老儒发现那少年不时斜眼看着自己,偷偷地乐。到了那间屋,笔砚书籍一应俱全。老儒正在灯下写家信,忽然一位女子出现在面前。她的姿容算不上特别秀丽,但风度颇为优雅。老儒知道她是鬼,并不惧怕,指着油灯说:"既然来了,就别闲站在那里,可以帮我剪灯花。"那女子却猛地把灯弄灭,向老儒逼近。老儒大怒,用手蘸了蘸砚台里的剩墨,打了女子一记耳光,顺势把墨水涂了她满脸,说道:"以此为记号,明天找到你尸体,剁碎了烧掉!"那鬼惊叫一声逃走了。

第二天,老儒把这件事讲给主人听。主人说:"原先有个婢女死在这间屋里,夜间常出来骚扰人。所以这屋子只在白天招待客人,晚上却没有人住。昨晚没有地方安置你,料想以你的学问德行,那鬼必不敢露面。谁知她还是出来了。"老儒这才明白为什么主人的女婿窃笑。那女鬼经常在月夜来往于院中,后来有一次被家人遇见,她掩面而逃。再后来,家人仔细窥视,发现女鬼脸上乱糟糟地涂着墨。鬼有形状而无实体,怎么能染上颜色呢?那大概是有实体的怪物,日久天长成了精,变化成那婢女的模样。

唐朝段成式的《酉阳杂俎》里记载,有人住在山中,夜里忽见一个人出现在灯前,脸象盘子那么大。他提笔在怪物脸上题了两句诗:"久成人偏老,长征马不肥。"那怪物就消失了。后来此人在山中散步,见一棵大树上长着一只巨大的白木耳,他先前所题诗句就在上面。这跟上面那件事有相似之处。

135. 土匪杀强盗

乌鲁木齐的农人大多在近水处种田,在田地旁建屋,所以不能比邻而居。常能见到一家人住着几间屋,四周并无邻舍,构成所谓"一家村"。那里的人不用服徭役,土地没有经过丈量,耕种几百亩地,只需纳三十亩的税,这种情况在深山穷谷尤为多见。曾有一队军士进山打猎,望见一户人家门窗紧闭,院子里系着十几匹马,鞍辔齐备。他们料定那里藏着土匪,就呐喊着包抄上去。土匪见官军人多势众,扔下炊具帐篷突围而去。军士们不愿和土匪拼命,并不追赶。进到房内,只见尸骨狼藉,空无一人,却隐隐有哭声。寻声而去,见一位十三四岁的男童裸体吊在窗棂上,就把他解下询问。男童说:"土匪是四天前来的。父亲和哥哥打不过他们,全家人都被绑了起来。土匪每天牵着两个人到山溪里冲洗,再拖回来割肉烤了吃,就这样把一家七八口人都吃光了。今天他们准备动身,把我洗干净了,正要烤着吃,有个人摇手制止。我虽然听不懂他们的话,但看他比画的意思,是想把我砍成几块,带在马上当粮食。幸亏官兵赶到,我才捡回了一条命。"他说完就抽泣起来。军士们可怜他,把他带回营地,让他干些杂活。他又说家里有财物埋在地窖里。营官让他领着人去挖,果然得到许多银子、钱币和衣物。

细问之下,男童才说出他父亲和哥哥都是拦路抢劫的强盗。行劫之时,他们总是埋伏在驿路近山的地方,看见一两辆车独行,前后十里并无救应,这才突然冲出。他们把车中人杀死,驾车继续赶路,进入深山。到了车路不通的地方,他们用大斧把车砍碎,连着尸体和铺盖一起扔到山涧中,再用马驮着财物往前赶。到了马也走不通的地方,把马的鞍辔扔入绝涧,把马放了,然后背着财物,经由人迹不通之处绕道回家。那时距离行劫处已有好几百里地了。回家之后,把劫得的财物在地窖里存放一两年,再让人到远方的市场上去卖掉。他们就这样行劫多年,从没有暴露形迹,不料遇上土匪,遭到灭门之灾。男童讲出这些事情后,因为年幼而没有受到追究。后来,他放马时坠崖而死,他们一家就此绝后。我在军幕中正好经手这件事。如今想来,这家强盗行踪诡秘,很难缉拿,却招来了土匪,使他们谋财害命的罪过得到惩处。土匪吃人无餍,却留下一个小孩,让人明白他们全家灭门的缘由。这其中似乎有神理,并非偶然。强盗的姓名我早就忘了,只记得那个男童小名叫秋儿。

136. 以狐召狐

有人见到一只黑狐醉卧在场院的屋子里。他正要上前捉拿,转念一想,狐狸能给人带来财物,就用衣服盖住它,坐在旁边守着。狐狸醒来,又伸臂又蹬腿,转眼变成人形。它感激那人的守护之恩,和他作了朋友,有时还带给他一些礼物。有一天他问狐狸:"假如有人藏在你家,你能使他不露形迹吗?"狐狸说能。他又问:"你能附在人身上飞跑吗?"狐狸又说能。这人就恳求说:"我家里特别穷,靠你的馈赠不足以维持;并且总这样麻烦你,我心中有愧。如今村里的某甲,家里非常有钱,又特别害怕打官司。我听说他想雇个厨娘,打算让我妻子去应聘。几天后让她伺机逃出,藏在你家,而我借口妻子在他家失踪,扬言要告官。我妻子略有几分姿色,我就诬赖他见色起意,逼他给我一大笔钱。等钱到手之后,你附在她身上,跑到某甲的别墅里,然后叫人在那里发现她。你要是肯这么做,我将非常感激。"狐狸依计而行,果然使此人敲诈到一笔钱。等他把妻子找回来,某甲因为她是在自己别墅被发现的,也不敢往下追究。

然而从此那妇人竟得了癫狂病,治不好了。她白天没完没了地梳妆打扮,晚上好象跟人一同嬉笑,却不让丈夫靠前。他急忙跑去问狐狸。狐狸说没这个道理,就亲自去察看。不一会儿它就跑回来,跺着脚说:"坏事了!那是某甲楼上的狐狸,看上了你夫人的姿色,乘我离开那一刹那附到她身体上。我不是那狐狸的对手,帮不上你了。"这人还是不停地恳求。狐狸板起脸说:"你们村里的某某,凶暴如虎,假若他霸占人妻,你能出面替人讨回公道吗?"后来那妇人病得越来越重,而且把丈夫的诡计都揭露出来。请医生和术士来救治,全都无效,最后她竟死于痨病。村里人都说,此人狡猾如鬼,又借用狐狸的幻术,应该是万无一失了。不料却以狐召狐,正好比螳螂捕蝉,黄雀在后。古诗说:"利旁有倚刀,贪人还自贼。"一点儿不差啊!

137. 邪道士受天诛

忻州有个人贫不聊生,把妻子卖了。她被带到一处人家,随后来了个道士,把她领入山中。她心里颇为疑惧,但身已被卖,无可奈何。道士让她把眼闭上,只听耳旁呼呼风响。过了片刻,道士让她睁开眼,两人已站在山顶,这里有一处华美整洁的房子。二十多位少妇前来问候她。她问这是哪里,她们回答说是仙人的府宅,这里日子过得很舒服。她问大家在这儿干什么,她们答道:"轮流陪主人睡觉罢了。这里金银堆积如山,主人能驱使鬼神,珠翠锦绣、山珍海味、珍奇果品之类一呼即来。我们的吃穿日用不亚于王侯,只是每月要忍受一次小痛苦,但并无大的妨害。"她们还指给她看,哪儿是仓库,哪儿是厨房,哪儿是她们的寝室,哪儿是主人的寝室。又指着最高处的两间屋子说:"那是主人拜月亮星斗的地方,那是主人炼银子的地方。"山上还有些仆妇,但没有其它男子。

自此之后,她就和其它少妇一样,白天被叫到道士房中陪他睡觉。到了夜里,道士要打坐炼功,少妇们才回寝室休息。最痛苦的是每次月经后,她就被剥掉衣裳,用红绒线制成的粗索绑在大树上,手脚丝毫动弹不得,嘴里还塞上棉花团,叫不出声。这时道士手拿一根象筷子粗细的金属管,刺入她两臂两腿的穴位里吸血。吸过之处用药末敷上,她马上就不痛了。伤口随即结痂,第二天痂落,恢复如初。她们住的地方非常高,积云下雨都在下面。忽然有一天刮起狂风,黑云如墨,直压山顶,雷电下击,令人惊骇。道士惊惶万状,让二十多位少妇赤身裸体环绕在他四周,象肉屏风一般。闪电几次进入屋内,都是一触即返。随即只见一只象簸箕那么大的龙瓜从云中伸出,在人丛中一把将道士抓走了。只听霹雳一声,山谷震动,她也昏了过去。稍微清醒过来,她发现自己躺在路旁。找到附近居民一问,此地距家有数百里地。于是她用手镯换了身破旧衣服遮体,沿路乞讨回家。她这时面容枯槁,因为她的精血已被道士吸尽,不久就病死了。尽管那个道士法术十分精妙,最终仍不免受到天诛。而有些人不得真传,受人蛊惑就妄想修炼成仙,不是太愚蠢了吗!

138. 奸盗奇案

天下之大,奸淫偷盗之事各地都有,每天都在发生,算不上奇怪。在下面的故事中,说是偷盗又算不得偷盗,说是奸淫又算不得奸淫,两者凑到一块儿,全都暴露,又因为两者相互牵连,即刻就平息,这才称得上奇怪。有个人中年丧妻,虽然有个儿子,却又买了个有夫之妇作妾。不知他用了什么法子,能让儿子和妾相安无事。不久他死了,平日家中积蓄都落在妇人之手。儿子听说了,就来向她索要,却拿不出证据,她也不肯承认。后来他探听出她藏财物的地方,深夜在墙上挖了个洞,溜进屋子,打开箱子往外拿。不料被妇人发觉,大叫有贼。家人们都被惊醒,拿着棍棒闯了进来。儿子仓皇从墙洞往外钻,遭到迎头痛击,被打翻在地。众人进屋搜寻其它贼人,听见床下有喘息声,大叫还有贼,就把那人拖出来绑了。等拿过灯来一照,发现钻墙洞的是儿子,藏在床下的却是那妇人的前夫。

等儿子苏醒过来,与妇人各执一辞。儿子说他取用父亲的财物,不算偷盗,妇人说她与前夫重聚,不算奸淫。他说她可以与前夫正式复婚,但不应私会,她说他可以索要父亲的财物,但不应挖墙。两人攻击诟骂,互不相让。第二天,族人秘密聚会,商量这件事,认为要是打起官司来,只会两败俱伤,白白玷污门风。于是给双方暗中调停,把财物归还给儿子,让妇人重新回到前夫那里,终于平息了这场风波。然而此事还是不免传开,被外人引为笑谈。

139. 诛灭画妖

有个士人在寺庙租屋住下,发现墙上挂着一幅画,图中美人眉目如生,衣褶似乎在飘动。士人对和尚说:"大师难道不怕这幅画扰乱参禅的心境吗?"和尚说:"这是天女散花图,保存在寺中有一百多年了,我倒还没仔细看过。"有天晚上,士人在灯下注目细瞧,见画中人似乎微微往外凸起,就自言自语地说:"这应该是幅西洋画,所以才有这种立体感。"画中忽然传出声音:"请不要惊讶,我马上就下来。"士人生性刚直,厉声喝道:"什么鬼怪敢来媚我!"他一把抓下画,就要在灯上烧掉。只听画中人哭道:"我就要炼形成功,一旦被烧就会形消神散,前功尽弃。万望手下留情,我将终生感恩不尽。"和尚听见响动,也过来看个究竟。听了士人的讲述,和尚说:"我有个弟子曾住在此屋,后来病死了,是不是你害的?"画中人沉默不答,过了一阵才说:"佛门广大,无所不容。和尚以慈悲为怀,应该手下超生。"士人怒道:"你已经杀了一人,今天要是放过你,不知又要害死多少人。不能因饶恕一妖,而害死无数人命。施行小慈悲就会妨害大慈悲,请大师不要怜惜。"说着,就把整幅画扔到炉子里。火焰一起,满屋都充满了血腥气,看来被画妖害死的恐怕不止一人。后来,晚上那屋子附近有时会听见嘤嘤的哭泣声。士人说:"妖怪余气未散,日久天长恐怕会重新聚结起来。"他去市场上买了十多串爆竹,把药信结在一起。晚上一听见哭声,他就把爆竹点燃,劈啪作响,门窗都被震动。从此那屋就安静无事了。这位士人作到了除恶务尽。

140. 天狐的惩诫

有人和一个狐狸交上了朋友。这是个天狐,有神奇的法术,能把此人带到千万里之外的名山胜境,让他尽情游览,来去都在弹指之间。狐狸曾告诉他:"除了圣贤的居处,真仙的府第我不敢去,其余只要地图上有的地方,我都可以随意往来。"有一天,此人对狐狸说:"你既然能把我带到千里之外,能不能把我放到人家的闺房里?"狐狸问他想做什么。他答道:"我经常拜访一个朋友,参加在后院举行的歌舞宴会。他的爱妾对我暗送秋波,虽然未能说上一句话,但已两心相印。可惜那里庭院幽深,我只能怅然相思。你若能在夜深人静时把我带到她的闺房中,必会成就我的好事。"狐狸沉思良久,才说:"这并非不能办到。但要是主人在那儿怎么办?"那人说:"我探听到主人在别的姬妾处留宿时再去。"后来他果然探听到实信,就请狐狸把他送过去。狐狸不等他穿戴齐整,就带着他飞行。到了一个地方,狐狸把他放下说:"就是这儿了。"说完就走了。那人暗中摸索,听不见人声,手里摸到的都是书卷,知道上了狐狸的当,自己在朋友的藏书楼里。他心里一慌,碰倒了一张桌子,上面的器物摔到地上,砰然作响。守楼人听见动静,大叫有贼,马上来了一大群仆人,点着烛火,带着器械进房搜查。他们见到有人哆哆索索地躲在屏风后面,就冲上去把他打翻在地,捆绑起来。在灯下一照,认出是主人的朋友,不禁都大吃一惊。此人生性狡猾,马上撒谎说因故得罪了狐狸,被它强行带到这里。主人跟他很熟,并不追究,只是笑道:"狐狸恶作剧,想借我的手痛打你一顿。暂且饶你一回,赶出门去!"说完就打发仆人把他送回家。

　　过了几天,此人与一个好友讲起这段遭遇,忿忿骂道:"狐狸果然不是人,与我相交十年,居然这样出卖我。"他的好友怒道:"你和那位朋友交往不止十年,却想借狐狸的法术去奸淫他的女眷,究竟谁不是人?狐狸虽然恨你不讲义气,用恶作剧来加以惩戒,却给你留下了余地,让你能为自己开脱,心地够忠厚的了。假若他让你打扮齐整,把你放在主人床下,你怎么找借口脱身? 由此看来,那狐狸是人,你却是狐狸。难道你还不知悔悟吗?"一番话说得此人满面羞惭。狐狸以后再也没出现,而那位好友也渐渐和他中断了往来。

141. 做蠢事,得好报

小人的阴谋,总是为君子造福,这种说法看似迂腐,其实不错。广东有个游学的士子,到岭南去拜访亲友,得到不少礼物,归途上除了带着被褥衣裳,还有两只大箱子,要四个人才能抬动。这一天他到某处换船,让人用粗绳绑住箱子,扛到另一只船上,不料绳子突然象刀割一样齐刷刷地断开,两只箱子轰然掉到甲板上,都摔裂了。那人跺着脚惋惜不已,急忙开箱察看,一箱装着新端砚,另一箱装着英德石。装石头的箱子里还有一封银子,大约六七十两,包的纸也破了。他拿起银子查看,不料失手落入水中,连忙请渔民下河打捞,只找回一小半。正在他懊恼之际,同行的船夫向他祝贺道:"强盗盯上这两只箱子,已经跟了你好几天了,只因停靠时岸上总有人家,所以迟迟没敢下手。如今一看里面没有财物,他们只好自认倒霉,都散去了。你真是有福之人啊!也许你最近积了什么德,所以受到神的保佑吧?"

　　同船的一个客人悄悄说:"他哪里积过什么德,最近倒是干了件蠢事。他在广东曾花一百二十两银子托旅店主人买妾,据说那妇人出嫁一年多,因为家里穷得揭不开锅,才卖身求条活路。娶进门那天,她的公婆和丈夫都来送别,看上去都羸弱不堪,象乞丐一样。临进屋,他们相互抱头痛哭。新妇已经与家人分了手,又追出去絮说,被媒婆硬拉了回来。她的公公又抱着几个月大的婴儿对他叩头说:'这个孩子从此吃不到奶,不知能不能活下去。恳求您允许他妈再喂他一次,让他活过今日,明天再想明天的办法。'这位老兄听了,忽然跳起身来说:'我原以为这女子是被休掉的。如今看你们这种情形,让我心里凄然。你把媳妇领回去,钱也不必还我了。'说完,他竟当众焚烧了卖身契。他哪里知道是旅店主人看出他心地忠厚,就让自己的女儿假扮民妇来骗他的钱。假若他真把她娶进门,还有别的计谋在等着他呢。同旅店的人都明白其中秘密,只有他至今蒙在鼓里。难道神会把这事当成他的一件功德吗?"这时船上另一位客人说:"这确实是件功德。他虽然办了件蠢事,却是出于恻隐之心。神判定人凭据的就是其真心。今天他免了大祸,可以说就是因为那件事。至于旅店主人,还不知有什么报应等着他呢。"

142. 狐狸画家

能写诗的狐狸在书中多有记载,擅长绘画的则较为少见。据海阳人李砚亭说,在顺治、康熙年间,处士周玗游历于湖南河南一带。周玗以画松闻名,有位士人请他在自己书房的墙壁上作画。画成的松树根部起于西边墙角,枝干横贯北墙,树梢扫到东墙一二尺,一眼望去,顿觉满座阴凉,清风欲来。士人于是摆下酒席请朋友们一同观赏。

大家正站在墙前,指点赞叹,忽然一人拍掌大笑,随即众人也哄然大笑。原来松树下面还有一幅春画,一张大木床上铺着长席子,有一对男女裸体交合,眉目传情,媚态横生。旁边还站着两个服侍的婢女,也都一丝不挂,一个挥着扇子驱赶蚊蝇,一个用双手扶着女子的枕头,以防因床上人动作过猛被弄掉。这正是士人与妻妾的画像。大家凑上前去细瞧,画中人形象逼真,连仆人们都能辨认出来,无不掩口而笑。士人气愤之极,仰头望天,大骂妖狐。忽听屋檐上大笑道:"你这人太不文雅。先前我听说周先生擅长画松,可惜未得一见。昨天晚上终于见到他的妙笔,坐在画前不忍离去,以致没及时避开你,但并未向你抛砖掷瓦。你却口出恶言,难以让我心服。这回只是开个小玩笑。你要是不反省,还是那样盛气凌人,我就要把这幅小像画在你家大门上,让过往行人看着取乐。你好好想一想吧。"原来,前一天晚上士人带着仆人秉烛到书房,准备请客用的器具,突见一个黑乎乎的东西窜到门外。士人知道是狐狸,当下就骂了一通。

众人连忙为双方调解,并请狐狸入座,在桌前加了一把椅子,只闻其声,不见其形。给狐狸满上酒,马上就一饮而尽,菜肴则丝毫不动。狐狸自称它已四百多年没有吃荤了。快散席时,狐狸对士人说:"你太聪明了,所以容易恃才傲物。这对于涵养道德、保全自身都没有好处。今天这件事,你幸亏遇见了我。要是换个象你这样爱赌气的狐狸,你就会招来无穷祸患了。只有学问能够改变人的气质,请你多下功夫。"这时再看狐狸的那幅作品,已经消失得不留一点痕迹。

第二天,书房东墙上忽然出现几枝鲜艳的桃花,背景衬以青苔碧草。花朵不算密,有的已经盛开,有的含苞待放,有的已经落地,有的即将凋零。还有八九片花瓣在空中随风起舞,尤其生动传神。画上题着初唐杨师道的两句诗:"芳草无行径,空山正落花。"画上未署姓名,料想是狐狸用来答谢前一天的酒席的。后来周圬见到这幅画,不禁叹道:"真是毫无笔墨痕迹!相比之下,我的画则是有意作态,生硬造作了。"

143. 预言诗

命运都有定数,所以鬼神能够预知。然而有些事尚未出现征兆,当事人尚未产生念头,并且无关吉凶祸福、因果报应,属于游戏之类的琐事,殊不足道,不可能是冥司预定的,却依然能够被预知。乾隆三十五年,有个翰林偶然占乩,问乩仙自己的官运如何。乩仙的回答是一首诗:"春风一笑手扶筇,桃李花开泼眼浓。好是寻香双蛱蝶,粉墙才过巧相逢。"他一点也看不懂其中的含义。

  过了不久,翰林经过皇上考核,被任命为知县。众人这才明白,诗中第二句沿用了晋人潘岳任河阳县令时种植桃李的典故,预示翰林将出外当县官。至于其它三句,依然难以理解。等朋友们来向他祝贺时,发现他的看门人拄着拐杖出来接待。原来,京官的奴仆向来把主人外调视为莫大喜事。看门人听说翰林外调的消息,当时就兴奋得跳起来大叫:"我今天成仙了!"不料失足跌下台阶,把小腿摔断了。就这样,诗的第一句也应验了。

  几天后,又听说翰林不知何故在一日之内赶走了两个仆人。随即有知情者泄露出其中缘由。原来,那两个仆人都想代替那个瘸子,得到看门人的职位,就私下让自己的妻子打扮一番,等主人休息后去引诱他。到了晚上,那两个妇人一个偷偷准备了点心,一个偷偷泡好了茶,暗中摸到书房的廊下,不料撞了个满怀,把带的东西都打翻了。两人恼羞成怒,对骂起来。主人不肯深究,只是把两个仆人都打发走了。就这样,诗的三四句也得到应验。那个乩仙看来是个灵鬼,但他如何能预知这样的事情,其中的道理让人难以推断。

144. 笨鬼读错书

一些古代贤人在祠堂里受到祭祀，使后人能够缅怀他们的风范，进而学习效法，由此起到教化民众的作用。不少古人的精魂确实存在，能够显灵，但偶而也有鬼假托古人的名义来骗取食物。曾有个士人在陈留县的一个村子里借宿。正值炎夏，他走到野外散步纳凉。日渐黄昏，冥色苍茫，忽然有一人向他作揖。两人靠着一颗老槐树坐下，互相询问名姓。那人说："请别惊讶，我就是汉朝的蔡中郎。虽然我的祠堂坟墓还在，却难得有人祭祀；况且我生前是个士人，死后也不太愿意向世俗之辈求食。因为感觉和你气味相投，所以向你表明身份。明天你能不能到这儿祭我一次？"士人气量宽宏，也不害怕，就问起汉朝末年的一些事情。鬼的回答多是小说《三国演义》里的内容，士人难免起了疑心。再问他的生平，鬼的回答与传奇剧《琵琶记》完全相符。士人于是笑道："我手头不大宽裕，没有余力祭奠你，你还是去找有钱人吧。不过我要提醒你一句：从此应该把《后汉书》、《三国志》和蔡中郎的文集找来看一看，这样求食就更有可能成功了。"那鬼一下子面红耳赤，跳起身来跑掉了。

(京)新登字 136 号

图书在版编目(CIP)数据

纪晓岚志怪故事选：汉英对照 /孙海晨编．
－北京：新世界出版社，1998.2
ISBN 7-80005-357-1

Ⅰ．纪… Ⅱ．孙… Ⅲ．笔记小说-中国-清代-汉、英
Ⅳ．I242.1

责任编辑：王健英
版面设计：倪真如

纪晓岚志怪故事选

孙海晨 编

*

新世界出版社出版
(北京百万庄路24号)
邮政编码 100037
北京外文印刷厂印刷
中国国际图书贸易总公司发行
(中国北京车公庄西路35号)
北京邮政信箱第399号 邮政编码100044
新华书店北京发行所国内发行
1998年(汉英)第一版 1998年北京第一次印刷
850×1168 毫米 1 /32 开本
ISBN 7-80005-357-1 /G·098
02400
10-CE-3228P